Understanding Anger Disorders

Understanding Anger Disorders

Raymond DiGiuseppe
and
Raymond Chip Tafrate

OXFORD
UNIVERSITY PRESS

2007

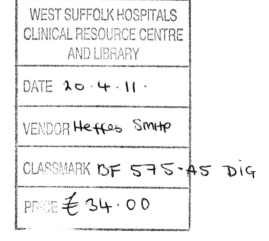

OXFORD
UNIVERSITY PRESS

Oxford University Press, Inc., publishes works that further
Oxford University's objective of excellence
in research, scholarship, and education.

Oxford New York
Auckland Cape Town Dar es Salaam Hong Kong Karachi
Kuala Lumpur Madrid Melbourne Mexico City Nairobi
New Delhi Shanghai Taipei Toronto

With offices in
Argentina Austria Brazil Chile Czech Republic France Greece
Guatemala Hungary Italy Japan Poland Portugal Singapore
South Korea Switzerland Thailand Turkey Ukraine Vietnam

Published by Oxford University Press, Inc.
198 Madison Avenue, New York, New York 10016

www.oup.com

Oxford is a registered trademark of Oxford University Press

Library of Congress Cataloging-in-Publication Data
DiGiuseppe, Raymond.
Understanding anger disorders / Raymond DiGiuseppe and Raymond Chip Tafrate.
p. cm.
Includes bibliographical references and index.
ISBN-13 978-0-19-517079-5

1. Anger. 2. Anger—Treatment. I. Tafrate, Raymond Chip. II. Title.
RC569.5.A53D54 2006
616.85′81—dc22   2006002297

Printed in the United States of America
on acid-free paper

To

Roseanne, Anna, Thomas, Dan, and Matt
—RD

Lauren, Jacob, and Samantha
—RCT

Acknowledgments

Over the 10 years we have worked on this project we have discussed the topic of anger with almost everyone we know. We would like to take this opportunity to acknowledge those who have been most helpful to us. First we want to thank Joan Bossert, our editor at Oxford University Press. When most other publishers wanted a quick and speedy "how-to-do-it" manual, she encouraged us to answer the more difficult questions about anger and take the time to write thoughtfully about them. Joan shared our vision for this book and without her it would have remained a treatment manual rather than a more interesting and extensive volume. Joan also secured two reviewers to whom we remain indebted for their feedback on an earlier version of this project. They managed to strike a balance between positive reinforcement and meaningful suggestions for change. Their recommendations are echoed throughout the final work. We thank Mallory Jensen and Stephanie Attia at Oxford University Press for their detailed, quick, and helpful work in the final, production phase of this project.

We are also grateful for the support we have received from our respective universities. St. John's University and its Department of Psychology have provided us with research assistants, library resources, and financial support for research without which we could not have completed this project. Central Connecticut State University and its Department of Criminology and Criminal Justice have provided release time for research, funding for anger-related projects, and a sabbatical leave, all of which contributed to the completion of this work.

We would also like to acknowledge our common mentors. Albert Ellis has always been a dedicated mentor and his inspiration helped us in many ways.

Watching him practice psychotherapy provided the insight for our focus on developing the therapeutic alliance with angry clients. We also came to see that his REBT model, the place we both started clinically, may be among the most valuable interventions for assisting those with problematic anger reactions.

Howard Kassinove mentored both our doctoral dissertations, although some years apart. He has always been a model for good science and good clinical practice based on science. Whenever we wrote something, we considered how Howie would challenge us to prove it and make it clearer and more parsimonious. He remained with us throughout the project.

Several peers have joined us at symposia over the years and we have benefited from their insights and piercing questions. First we want to thank Chris Eckhardt, who helped launch our interest in this investigation and has made major strides on his own in the understanding of anger and intimate-partner violence. Of course Jerry Deffenbacher has been extremely gracious and helpful throughout the years. He single-handedly created an anger-outcome literature. Jerry has always been an honest, straightforward, accepting colleague by whom one could float any bad idea; he would always respond with candor and kindness. A. G. Ahmed, from the University of Ottawa, started an anger disorders clinic at our urging, thereby helping us by putting our ideas into practice. A. G.'s feedback has provided our work with numerous clinical insights. We would also like to thank the division of Independent Practice of the American Psychological Association. Almost every year over the past decade we have submitted proposals to present symposia at the association's annual convention. These presentations allowed us to share ideas with practitioners and get their feedback and insights.

In addition we would like to thank our graduate assistants who have worked on anger projects with us over the years: Sharon Leis, Jeffrey Froh, Carol Cannella, Jill Kelter, Danielle Rannazzi, and Andrea Camilli at St. John's University. We want to thank Ryan Fuller, who served as Ray's postdoctoral fellow and read and critiqued earlier drafts of the manuscript. We would like to acknowledge Louis Dundin and Mark Ludwig, both from Central Connecticut State University, whose creativity and courage in working with offender samples was always valued.

We would like to acknowledge Jennifer Jablonski, who conducted the literature review on anger in personality disorders and prepared a first draft of chapter 11. Jennifer was a doctoral student at St. John's University when she took up this task. And we thank Faith Unger, who worked as Ray's postdoctoral fellow and who made several revisions to chapter 11 and helped out with many other tasks; and Bernard Gorman, who contributed valuable technical assistance in the cluster analysis that led to the anger subtypes that are presented in chapter 15.

Finally, we would like to thank our clients. We have often sought their opinions about how anger operated in their lives and have tried out new assessment and intervention strategies with them. We have learned the most from them.

Contents

Introduction

Our interest in anger as a clinical problem started in the 1990–1991 academic year. Ray was supervising Chip Tafrate and Chris Eckhardt who were in training at the Albert Ellis Institute. At that time the institute had engaged in a project to develop training programs for professionals who treated victims of violent crime and domestic violence. The agencies working with us then also asked if we would treat the perpetrators. While most of the institute staff felt reluctant to treat such clients, Ray, Chip, and Chris volunteered their services. After a brief time treating these angry, aggressive clients, most of whom were male, a small administrative crisis emerged. A diagnosis was needed in order to file with the clients' health insurance companies. The majority of these patients failed to fit any diagnostic category, despite intense and disruptive anger experiences. At the time, Ray suggested Intermittent Explosive Disorder. One of the interns responded that these particular clients failed to qualify for this diagnosis because they behaved aggressively regularly. Also, anger, the primary emotional problem, was not mentioned in any part of the description. Clearly no diagnostic category existed for patients whose emotional excess was anger and whose behaviors were chronically aggressive. We did what other practitioners do in this situation: found some other aspects of the patient's dysfunction to use as a diagnosis.

Finding an accurate diagnosis was only the beginning of our problems, since the typical clinical intake assessment instruments failed to provide useful anger-related information to develop case conceptualizations and plan treatment. We found that few instruments existed that could adequately assess anger as a clinical problem. Some tests, like the often used

Cook–Medley scale, were old and failed to sample many key characteristics of anger. Spielberger's (1988) State–Trait Anger Expression Inventory had excellent psychometric properties but assessed anger as a normal trait and failed to include items that reflected dysfunction.

The notion of empirically supported treatments was just becoming popular, so we searched the literature to identify proven strategies for treating anger. Although some interventions, such as those of Novaco (1975) and J. L. Deffenbacher and McKay (2000), had been published, they treated all angry clients the same way and often used college students who scored high on trait anger as participants. While Novaco's interventions focused on developing impulse control, we noted that many of our angry clients had serious rumination problems. Of course we attempted to use the work of our mentor Albert Ellis in treating anger. Quickly it was discovered that most of the writings of Ellis, and other prominent cognitive theorists, were, by and large, targeted at the areas of depression and anxiety.

Since we continued to work with clients who had problematic anger reactions, we initially explored some strategies for treating anger, which resulted in our first publication in the area (DiGiuseppe, Tafrate, & Eckhardt, 1994). Chip and Chris went on to do separate dissertations on the topic under the mentorship of Howard Kassinove. Over time Chris relocated to a different part of the country, and Chip and Ray continued to collaborate on projects exploring anger. Initially we decided to write a book on the treatment of anger based on our clinical experiences. As our work began, we hit roadblocks. The first was defining anger. Most scholars failed to differentiate anger from aggression and hostility. Many manuscripts used the three terms interchangeably. This resulted in a significant detour— exploring how to define anger and how it differed from other emotions as well as from aggression, hostility, and irritability. This material forms the basis of chapters 2–6.

Since we were treating anger, we had to acknowledge that anger was conceptualized as a possible form of psychopathology in its own right and not just a symptom of other disorders. This led to discussions on the nature of functional and dysfunctional anger. More time was spent reviewing the literature on how one defines psychopathology and what constituted a new disorder. It quickly became clear that if too much overlap existed between a proposed disorder and an existing disorder, the new disorder would not be needed. This led us to explore, in addition to the nature of functional and dysfunctional anger, the comorbidity of anger symptoms in other forms of psychopathology. These activities are reflected in chapters 9–14. In the course of consulting with colleagues across a variety of treatment settings, we noticed that practitioners from diverse environments provided different descriptions of the typical angry client. Perhaps subtypes of angry clients existed and these subtypes might differ according to their setting. This led to our investigation of anger subtypes and the information in chapter 15.

The next area examined was the issue of how to assess angry clients. As mentioned above, we were dissatisfied with existing anger instruments and noted that anger scales rarely appeared in the larger omnibus psychological tests like the 16 Personality Factor Questionnaire (Cattell, Cattell, & Cattell, 1994) or the Millon Clinical Multiaxial Inventory (MCMI–III; Millon, Davis, & Millon, 1997). Anger did appear in the (MMPI), but as a supplementary test, not as one of the ten primary scales. Thus, we embarked on developing a broader and more clinically relevant scale that measured anger as a disorder—the Anger Disorders Scale (ADS; DiGiuseppe & Tafrate, 2004). It took several years to develop the scale, and research with this instrument challenges much of the long-held accumulated wisdom about anger.

Since we were still trying to write a treatment manual, a comprehensive quantitative review of the clinical-outcome research on anger was needed. Basic questions remained unanswered, such as what worked and how much and for whom? This endeavor led to a meta-analytic review of anger treatments (DiGiuseppe & Tafrate, 2003) and the material in chapters 16 and 19. Along the way, it was recognized that existing studies had assumed that people wanted to change. This clashed with our clinical experiences, as well as our consulting work with criminal justice agencies. Angry clients in many settings resisted change and blamed others for their problems. Thus issues related to developing the therapeutic alliance, increasing awareness, and building motivation for change are covered in chapters 17 and 18.

By now we realized that we had seriously strayed from our original intention of writing a treatment manual. Much was still to be learned about anger as an emotion and as a disorder. At some point we decided to try to write a more comprehensive book than we had originally envisioned. But what model would we follow? Early in the history of cognitive behavior therapy (CBT), Don Meichenbaum commented that he feared that the field would develop a few major theories and that these theories would be superimposed on the treatment of various disorders. He suggested that a potentially more successful strategy would be to explore the nature of a particular disorder from the perspective of behavioral, cognitive, systemic, and other theoretical approaches. The results of these investigations should then guide treatment development. Clearly the major CBT models had focused very little on anger. Nonetheless, we chose to follow Don's strategy. We looked around for books that would serve as models for such an endeavor. The best model seemed to be Tim Beck's 1967 book *Depression: Causes and Treatment*, written before either of us had reached college. In this classic work, Beck reviewed the known theory and research about depression, and synthesized research to produce a model that defined depression. From these insights he developed the Beck Depression Inventory to assess depression and later developed cognitive therapy for depression. We believe that the same type of analysis and exploration will form the foundation for innovations in the treatment of anger.

Thus our efforts shifted away from a solely treatment-oriented volume to a broad-based review and discussion of the theory and research that defines anger, its functional and dysfunctional aspects, and its presentation as a clinical problem. Few publishers wanted such a book. Luckily we connected with Joan Bossert at Oxford University Press. She had faith in our efforts, was patient with our sporadic progress, and has provided many helpful suggestions along the way. We believe that this work and other volumes that will follow may help provide the stepping stones for the understanding of dysfunctional anger that the Roman philosopher Seneca, in his *Moral essays*, wrote "not only vents its fury on a man here or there but rends in pieces whole nations" (Basore, 1958, p. 305).

This book was written for readers interested in understanding anger and either applying these understandings to future research and theoretical investigations or developing clinical interventions based on these discussions. We expect that the conclusions we have drawn concerning anger will be subject to change as new research and new theories evolve and replace what is written here. Our best hope is that this book serves as a compilation of issues related to our understanding about anger, its function, its dysfunction, and the clinical problems of assessment and treatment. If we have offered only a series of testable hypotheses that spark investigation, we have done our job.

The goal of creating an evidence-based treatment manual for practitioners was eventually accomplished by Chip and Howard Kassinove (Kassinove & Tafrate, 2002). Although significant parts of this book address treatment issues, we focus more on a review of the research literature and on what works in treating anger, discuss the problem of engaging clients with anger problems in treatment, and propose a comprehensive model. We have not included a chapter on the assessment of clinical anger because of space constraints. Our views on this topic appear in the manual of the Anger Disorders Scale.

Part I

Theory and Research

1

Anger

The Forgotten Emotion

My purpose is to picture the cruelty of anger which not only vents its fury on a man here and there but rends in pieces whole nations.
—Seneca

Anger is the forgotten emotion. There seems to be agreement among mental health professionals that violence is prevalent in the United States, and many researchers, clinicians, and political leaders focus on the problem of violent behavior. However, little is heard about the emotion that frequently precedes such behavior—anger. This book discusses that emotion.

People of all ages, backgrounds, and cultures experience anger. Because anger is both frequent and universal, most of us have some personal experience of this emotion. Like so many topics in the behavioral sciences, even those that are presumed to be common and understood by everyone, when viewed critically, this topic is characterized by complex causes, manifestations, and consequences. This chapter highlights historical influences on our current understanding of anger in abnormal psychology. The current research status of anger in the areas of assessment, diagnosis, and treatment is highlighted, as are potential reasons that anger has received less attention as a topic of scientific inquiry.

Enduring and Recent Problematic Associations

Throughout the history of philosophy and psychology, scholars and practitioners have recognized the negative physical, interpersonal, and social consequences associated with intense and frequent anger experiences. The

Roman philosopher Seneca was one of the first scholars to recognize the destructive nature of anger. His essay *On Anger* begins as follows:

> We are here to encounter the most outrageous, brutal, dangerous, and intractable of all passions; the most loathsome and unmannerly; nay, the most ridiculous too; and the subduing of this monster will do a great deal toward the establishment of human peace. (Basore, 345/1958)

Seneca chronicled the negative effects of anger on both the social and individual level. He encouraged abstaining from anger, fervently believing that anger clouded a person's judgment, impaired interpersonal effectiveness, and could collectively imbalance an entire society. To Seneca, a truly wise individual would form the correct opinions about events so that anger would not follow under any circumstance. Focusing on "forming the correct opinions" about events to avoid anger, Seneca's prescription preceded many of the developments in cognitive behavior therapies and recognized the importance of cognitive factors such as interpretations and evaluations as keys to controlling anger.

Seneca's warnings about anger apply as much today as they did 2,000 years ago. As discussed in the next chapter, the relationship between anger, as an internal emotional experience, and outward aggressive behaviors is not well documented or understood. Nonetheless, one does not have to look beyond the evening news to find examples of anger's potential to play a motivating role in acts of aggressive behavior or larger-scale atrocities. We certainly recognize that the causes of many modern-day regional conflicts are complicated and cannot be reduced to a single variable. However, the role of anger in such conflicts is hardly ever noted. Perhaps anger's motivating role in violence is of even more concern today because of advancements in weapons technologies. A handful of highly angry individuals can inflict mass harm on those they view as enemies (Friedman, 2000). The attacks on the World Trade Center and the Pentagon on September 11, 2001, exemplify this point.

In addition to links with aggression and violence, chronic and intense anger has been associated with other negative behavioral and medical problems. Some examples include: aversive verbal responding (Tafrate, Kassinove, & Dundin, 2002), disruption of interpersonal and workplace relationships (Tafrate & Kassinove, 2002), poor decision making and increased risk taking (Kassinove, Roth, Owens, & Fuller, 2002), substance use (Awalt & Reilly, 1997), and long-term health problems such as cardiovascular heart disease (Williams, Paton, Siegler, Eigenbrodt, Nieto, et al., 2000), stroke (Everson, Kaplan, Goldberg, Lakka, & Sivenius, 1999), and cancer (Butow, Hiller, Price, Thackway, Kricker, et al., 2000).

Despite Seneca's forewarning about the destructive nature of anger, there has been little progress in defining, understanding, diagnosing, and treating dysfunctional anger. Rothenberg (1971) noted more than 30 years ago that, almost invariably, anger has not been considered an independent topic worthy of investigation . . . [which] has not only deprived anger of its rightful importance in the understanding of human behavior, but has also led to a morass of confused definitions, misconceptions, and simplistic theories. (p. 86)

Unfortunately, we believe this state of affairs remains, as suggested by a more recent conclusion by Berkowitz (1993):

Any really close and thorough examination of the psychological re-search into the origins of anger and emotional aggression must leave the thoughtful reader somewhat dissatisfied. The literature presents us with occasional inconsistencies and unexpected findings that most of the investigators seem not to have noticed. (p. 35)

A more pessimistic view of our species' ability to understand the scourge of anger comes from Kemp and Strongman (1995). They reviewed the conceptualization of anger by ancient and medieval philosophers and compared it with the conceptualization of modern theorists. Their con-clusion: "Finally, it should be said that perhaps it is not surprising that our knowledge of anger and its control has developed little in two millennia" (p. 407).

Historical Perspectives

Most philosophical, psychological, or biological discussions of human emotions, from Aristotle's *Nicomachean Ethics* (355/1943) and *Rhetoric* (345/1963) to Darwin's *The Expression of Emotions in Man and Animals* (1872/1965), discuss anger as both a primary human emotion and potential human problem (see Averill, 1982; Kennedy, 1992, for reviews).

The works of Aristotle, Seneca, and Plutarch (O'Neil, 2000) in the second century set the stage for our understanding of anger, its control, and the major debates that remain (Schimmel, 1979). These three early writers all defined anger as a strong emotion or passion provoked when people suffer or perceive that they suffer a pain, slight, or injury that motivates the desire for vengeance or direct actions to punish or gain restitution from the offender.

Seneca may have been the first to identify anger as a disorder. He considered it the "canker of human nature." Plutarch concurred. He commented, "The only music heard from the house of an angry man is wailing" (Plutarch, 45/2004, p. 159). The Roman physician Galen (180/1963) also wrote of the pathology of anger. Seneca and Plutarch believed anger is never useful and should be avoided even in war and athletic competition because of its capacity to distract the person from developing and following strategies to succeed. This Roman idea can be summed up in a quote from the more contemporary Don Corleone's advice to his son in *The Godfather:* "Never hate your enemies. It clouds your judgment." Aristotle differs in this regard. While he acknowledged the possible destructive nature of anger, he believed that when it was controlled and not too strong, it could result in energy and commitment to help one overcome obstacles. While Seneca and Plutarch advised people to avoid anger at all costs, Aristotle may have been the first to suggest anger management. In chapter 13 we will discuss this distinction made by Aristotle.

Many of the ideas and techniques of cognitive behavioral therapies were first suggested by this ancient trio. In fact, Seneca's *On Anger* and Plutarch's *On the Control of Anger* appear as self-help books or therapy manuals, written with the clear intention of helping those troubled by anger. They instruct one to attend to the negative consequences of anger and to remind oneself of these before acting. This resembles the present problem-solving approach popular among therapists today (Chang, D'Zurilla, & Sanna, 2004; D'Zurilla & Nezu, 1999). Like many psychological theories and treatments today, classical philosophy held that inappropriately appraising a threat aroused anger (A. T. Beck, 1999; R. S. Lazarus, 1991). They identified the role of external blame or hostile attributions (Dodge, 1985) in causing anger. As for treatment, the early philosophers recommended keeping an anger diary (J. Deffenbacher, 1999), challenging one's thoughts about potential threats (A. T. Beck, 1999), recognizing the trivial nature of the things that trigger anger and recognizing that some circumstances in life cannot be changed (Ellis, 1977), substituting alternative behaviors for angry responses—as in assertiveness training (Alberti & Emmons, 2001), and using stimulus-control techniques to avoid anger-provoking situations.

Most philosophers in the first millennium refer to the classical philosophers' writings. The medieval philosophers St. Thomas Aquinas and Roger Bacon base their conceptualizations of anger on the ancient Greco-Roman views (Kemp & Strongman, 1995). Many of the early Christian thinkers such as Augustine and Peter Abelard stressed the dysfunctional nature of anger and the importance of learning self-control based on the Christian teaching of free will.

From the sixteenth through the nineteenth centuries anger was primarily the domain of medicine and the new specialty of psychiatry. Psychiatry at its inception focused primarily on diagnosing lunacy and treating insanity and melancholia. Bright (1586) and Burton (1621), two early physicians who wrote about anger, proposed that anger was a subcondition of melancholia or what we now consider mood disorders (Hunter & Macalpine, 1963). They mentioned anger merely in passing—to differentiate it from melancholia. Despite the attention paid to anger by emotion theorists in philosophy and social psychology, their conclusions are not the same as those that have developed in clinical psychology and psychiatry. Anger was still considered part of melancholia at the beginning of the twentieth century by both Kraeplin and S. Freud, as we will discuss below. One of the first people to identify anger as a form of psychopathology was John Nowname. His 1609 *Treatise on Anger* has a more thorough description of the emotion and the nature of its dysfunction and offers advice on avoiding and controlling it (Hunter & Macalpine, 1963). It is noteworthy that medicine then, as now, focused on the physical treatment of mental diseases. Psychotherapy as we know it was called *spiritual physcke* and was primarily the task of clergy (Hunter & Macalpine, 1963).

Darwin's (1872/1965) evolutionary theory of emotions also offered an explanation of anger and remains the basis of much work in the area today. He believed that emotions were instinctive and that we could develop an understanding of human emotions by studying their counterparts in our ancestral mammalian species. Darwin proposed the principle of "serviceable associated habits" in emotions. This idea suggested that there was a biological relationship between affective experiences, states of arousal, and expressive behaviors. These expressive behaviors were part of an animal's repertoire of communication skills. Communications among members of a species have survival value, and the ability to display emotions and recognize them became inherited. The aggressive snarling and furrowed eyebrows were biologically determined behaviors that served to communicate that the animal was angry. Darwin linked the emotion of anger to these expressive behaviors, and these behaviors were labeled aggressive. Since one of the greatest minds in Western science made the connection between anger and aggression, most assumed that the two constructs were always linked, and this conclusion was readily accepted.

After Darwin, the next major influential theorist to alter the perception of anger was S. Freud (1920). His suppositions about anger are represented by ethologists such as Eibl-Eibesfeldt (1970) and Lorenz (1966). Freud expanded on the presupposed biological relationship between anger and aggression and proposed that anger was a weak expression of the aggressive drive and aggressive behaviors. To furrow one's eyebrows or snarl and show one's teeth were minor aggressive acts along the continuum of aggression that leads to attacking one's victim. Freud supplemented this idea with the notion that all humans possessed an aggression instinct or drive. Accordingly, one needs to display anger, lest the aggressive drive build up. Periodically displaying one's anger rids one of excessive aggressive energy. The message of this theory was that aggression and its "relatives" (anger, hostility, rage, etc.) are natural drives that resist autonomous control (R. S. Lazarus, 1991).

With the rise of behaviorism in psychology during most of the twentieth century, scientists were again hindered from understanding the complexity of anger. Anger is a feeling that can best be comprehended by self-report, but to the radical behaviorists, self-reports of feelings or thoughts are verbal behaviors that follow the same rules as overt behaviors. "Thoughts can be viewed as behaviors in diminished magnitude" (Salzinger, 1995, p. 79). Behaviorists failed to distinguish between anger and aggression and considered the former a covert, diminished response of the latter. Anger was not regarded as a viable, independent, clinical emotional construct and has been subsumed under the general rubric of "aggression" (Rothenberg, 1971). Perhaps the linkage of anger and aggression in previous theories prevented researchers from conceptualizing anger as an emotional experience that can interfere with functioning.

As a strictly clinical concept, anger appears to have been excluded in psychiatry and abnormal and clinical psychology in the twentieth century. Despite Bright's and Burton's early attempts to differentiate anger from melancholia, many mental health professionals today believe that anger is a secondary emotion and part of depression (Hunter & Macalpine, 1963). This idea appears to have emerged early in the twentieth century from the work of Emil Kraeplin and Sigmund Freud. They defined hostility as part of melancholia and depression (see S. W. Jackson, 1986, for a discussion of the history of depression). Melancholia had been identified as a disorder since Hippocrates. However, Kraeplin believed hostility and irritability belonged as part of manic states. He was the first to propose a bipolar or manic-depression disorder. He saw anger then as part of the manic end of mood disturbance. Freud proposed that depressed individuals experienced anger at significant others and feared reprisals for its expression. To resolve this conflict they turned their anger inward, which caused depression. Kraeplin's and Freud's views were interpreted by most clinicians as relegating anger to the status of a secondary emotion, part of depression.

Some truth exists in both these positions. The relationship between anger as mania and depression, first proposed by Kraeplin, has been more fully explained by evolutionary approaches to human behavior. According to this view, both emotional states are part of the dominance–submission display system in humans. When humans wish to express dominance, they experience anger and its corresponding behaviors. When humans would benefit more from the expression of submission, they experience depression and display its corresponding behaviors (Stevens & Price, 1996). While this theory demonstrates a dynamic relationship between anger and depression, in the evolutionary model neither emotion is secondary to the other. They are opposite sides of a crucial system that regulates interpersonal relations. Anger, according to this view, is distinct from depression. A disorder in the dominance–submission system within an individual could result in either a depression or anger disorder.

Freud's notion that some people fear retaliation if they express their anger, which may result in hopelessness and lead to depression, has received some research support (see chapter 10) and explains some but not all of the relationship between anger and depression. The possibility also exists that anger and depression are linked serially. People may become angry at themselves for getting depressed, or become depressed that they have become angry. In this model the experience of one emotion becomes a trigger for another (Barlow, 1991). Our experience suggests this may account for the relationship between anger and depression. Similar sequential triggering of emotions by anger has also been demonstrated. Many socially anxious people refrain from assertive behaviors for fear of failure and rejection and then feel resentful toward those to whom they have not been assertive (Erwin, Heimberg, Schneier, & Liebowitz, 2003). The present understandings of these dynamics would suggest that the emotions do not have to be unconscious and that both emotions are important. Neither is secondary to the other.

At the beginning of the twentieth century, not everyone accepted Kraeplin and Freud's position that anger was secondary to depression. The German psychiatrist Specht argued in 1901 that anger presented as a separate disorder. In 1908 he revised his position to assert that anger was a disorder in the middle of a continuum delimited by depression and mania at either pole (see Kennedy, 1992). Kraeplin and Freud were the two major figures in abnormal psychology at the time, whereas few people had ever heard of Specht. So the idea that anger was part of depression won out and is still the case today. The clinical literature has identified anger within the topic of depression, although all historical and contemporary emotion theorists have identified anger as a basic human emotion. No one has yet successfully challenged Kraeplin and Freud's notion and brought abnormal psychology's conceptualization of anger up-to-date with the long-standing acceptance of anger as a basic emotion.

Because of the legacy of these theories, anger receives very little attention in its own right. Although the clinical sciences have ignored anger and considered it a secondary emotion, modern emotion theorists such as Ekman (1984), Izard (1977), Johnson-Laird and Oats (1989), Kemper (1987), and Tomkins (1962) clearly consider anger a basic emotion universal to all humans. These contemporary authors identify anger as one of the primary human emotions, just as the classical philosophers had. A more detailed examination of the scientific focus that anger has received compared to other emotions is discussed below. In addition, there is little agreement on definitions of the constructs of anger, aggression, and hostility. As addressed in the next chapter, this lack of definitional clarity is a significant factor thwarting research on anger.

Overlooking Anger: Current Research Status

Although research discussed in the following chapters affirms the negative influences of anger on one's health, work effectiveness, interpersonal relationships, and propensity to aggression, anger is rarely regarded as a debilitating emotion to the same extent as anxiety and depression. Of the negative emotions, anxiety and depression have received the most attention in the research literature. In clinical practice, anxiety and depression have received much greater attention in psychopathology texts, diagnostic categories of mental illness, and psychological and pharmacological treatments.

Diagnosis

The lack of consideration given to anger is most evident by the absence of a diagnostic category for an anger disorder in the *Diagnostic and Statistical Manual of Mental Disorders–Fourth Edition–Text Revision* (*DSM–IV–TR*) (American Psychiatric Association, 2000). Presently, the *DSM–IV–TR* contains 10 mood disorders and 12 categories of anxiety disorders. No diagnostic categories exist for anger or irritability disorders (the term irritability is sometimes used in the *DSM* and is discussed in more detail below). Five categories for diagnosing people displaying aberrant aggressive behavior are included in the *DSM*. Anger (or irritability) is specifically mentioned in three Axis I disorders (i.e., manic episodes in Bipolar Disorder, Generalized Anxiety Disorder, and Posttraumatic Stress Disorder) and in three personality disorders (i.e., Borderline, Antisocial, and Paranoid). In each of these disorders, the presence of inappropriate or excessive anger (or irritability) is a criterion for the disorder. However, anger is neither necessary nor sufficient on its own to support the diagnosis in any of these categories. A patient could easily meet the criteria for each of these disorders without experiencing or displaying anger.

Perhaps the best indication that the *DSM* avoids anger is that it is not a diagnosis within the substance-induced disorders included in both mood and anxiety disorders categories. Most psychoactive substances can lead to either a mood (depression) or an anxiety disorder. Caffeine can contribute to an anxiety disorder but not a mood disorder. Opiates can induce a mood disorder but not an anxiety disorder. However, it seems strange that alcohol, amphetamines, caffeine, cannabis, cocaine, hallucinogens, inhalants, opioids, sedatives, and even unknown substances can induce an anxiety and/or mood disorder, but none of them can induce an anger disorder. Our personal and clinical experience with alcohol and drug abusers suggests that anger is frequently an emotional excess that occurs when a person abuses a psychoactive substance. It seems logical that a substance-induced anger experience or disorder be included in the *DSM*, just as substance-induced anxiety and mood disorders are.

As noted above, some disorders in the *DSM–IV* include "irritability" as a possible symptom. *Irritability* is the "quality or state of being irritable; testiness or petulance" (Born & Steiner, 1999). Many see anger and irritability as separate concepts, but patients with these disorders experience an emotion in the anger family. However, the words *irritable, testiness,* and *petulance* denote mild forms of anger when they are used by the general population. The authors of the *DSM–IV* carefully chose the word *irritability* and probably did not intend for anger to be included in the criteria for these disorders. We suspect that many mental health professionals are unclear how the terms *anger* and *irritability* differ. We will attempt to clarify the technical differences in the next chapter.

Although several researchers (J. Deffenbacher, 1993; Novaco, 1985; Tavris, 1989) have called for the inclusion of one or more anger-disorder categories, it seems unlikely that future editions of the *DSM* will include new diagnostic categories for anger. Appendix B of the *DSM–IV–TR* provides diagnostic categories for further study. This list represents disorders currently under empirical investigation and for which sufficient empirical support does not yet exist. If sufficient empirical evidence supports them as reliable and valid constructs with treatment utility, they could be included in a future version of the *DSM*. Few of these proposed categories even mention anger. A review of these proposed categories shows they clearly focus on depression and anxiety and continue to inadequately address anger.

In chapter 14 of the present volume, and elsewhere, we (DiGiuseppe, Eckhardt, Tafrate, & Robin, 1994) and others (Eckhardt & Deffenbacher, 1995) have proposed criteria for an anger disorder and a research agenda that could establish its validity. Blashfield, Sprock, and Fuller (1990) recommend that at least 50 empirical articles support a new category before its inclusion in the *DSM*. While several investigators are busy conducting research to meet these criteria, anger disorders are unlikely to be included in the next several versions of the *DSM*.

Classification, categorization, or nosology forms the basis of most sciences (Gould, 1987, 1995). The development of anger diagnoses would help mental health professionals communicate more effectively, learn to differentiate types of angry clients, develop a more expansive understanding of disturbed anger, better predict dangerous behaviors and the development of illness, and aid in the development of more effective interventions. The absence of an anger diagnostic category ultimately hampers scientific growth in this area. Unfortunately, the current number of discussions in the scientific literature related to anger diagnosis and conceptualization is quite limited. A search of scientific references over the past 35 years comparing depression, anxiety, and anger diagnoses is presented in Figure 1.1. A search of *PsycInfo* was conducted using the following parameters: (a) advanced search option was selected, (b) references were limited to journal articles,

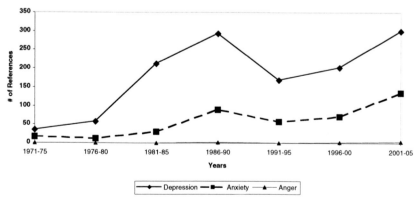

Figure 1.1. *PsycInfo* References for Diagnosis

(c) the terms *diagnosis* and *anger* had to appear in the title or be listed as a key concept or keyword, and (d) the number of references were identified for five-year increments starting with 1971. The above rules were also applied to a search of the terms *diagnosis* and *depression* and *diagnosis* and *anxiety*. Limiting the appearance of the terms to the title or key concept or keyword resulted in a more stringent search, and fewer articles were found than reported in previous estimates (Kassinove & Sukhodolsky, 1995). It is hoped that the more stringent search criteria eliminated many articles that were not directly relevant. It is most likely that some articles that covered the areas of interest were not identified and that other articles identified were only tangentially related. A more exact investigation would require an expansion of search parameters and a visual scan of individual abstracts. Thus, the resulting information presented in the figures that follow is considered an estimate or a snapshot of the scientific attention in each area.

From 1971 to 2005 a total of 1,267 articles were identified to cover the topic of diagnosis and depression, 410 in the area of anxiety, and only 7 related to anger. The top line represents the scientific attention paid to depression, while the middle line represents that for anxiety. It appears that research on the diagnosis of depression and anxiety peaked in the period 1986–1990 and has increased again in the last five years. The attention focused on anger and diagnosis is so limited that it is barely visible on the graph. Two scientific articles were found for the period 1986–1990, two for 1996–2000, and three for 2001–2005. Given the lack of any anger-related diagnostic category, it is certainly not surprising to find far fewer articles devoted to anger. However, the almost complete lack of discussion in the scientific literature indicates that psychology has not considered anger to be an emotional problem worthy of clinical conceptualization and attention.

Despite the scientific advances in reliability and validity in the *DSM*, the system from the beginning has ignored anger and aggression. We suspect this is because most mental health professionals continue to follow Kraeplin and Freud in assuming that anger is part of depression. Given the inability to define clinical or problematic anger reactions, researchers have defined anger as pathological if a person scores significantly higher, usually two standard deviations above the mean, than most individuals on a standardized measure of anger. This reliance on a statistical definition occurs by default because no other criteria for disturbed anger exists. Such a practice may overestimate the number of people who have disturbed anger, because the base rate or number of people who have truly dysfunctional anger may be less than the percentile used as a cutoff score (often 75th percentile). Alternatively, the base rate of persons with dysfunctional anger may be larger than the percentile of people identified by a cutoff score. At present, we just do not know. Practitioners, who may be less likely to use standardized assessment instruments in practice, must rely on their own individual judgments about how to define and conceptualize their clients' disruptive anger reactions.

Assessment

The scientific and professional communities' avoidance of the study of anger is also evident in the paucity of assessment devices used to measure the construct. Few assessment instruments for anger are available. The more "mainstream" emotions such as depression and anxiety have experienced substantial advancements in assessment, whereas similar efforts have been missing in the anger literature. *The Twelfth Mental Measurements Year Book* (Conoley, Impara, & Murphy, 1995) reviews all the psychological-assessment devices published. Periodically new editions are published that review new tests and significant revisions of others. The book has a scale index that allows one to search for subscales that measure the construct in the index. The scale index of the 12th edition has 3 measures of anger–hostility, 10 scales for aggression, 18 scales measuring anxiety or fear, and 13 scales assessing depression or sadness. Clearly, fewer new measures exist to assess anger than anxiety and depression. All major psychological tests such as the Minnesota Multiphasic Personality Inventory–2 (Graham, 1993), the Millon Clinical Multiaxial Inventory–III (Millon, Davis, & Millon, 1997), and the 16 Personality Factor Questionnaire (Cattell, 1975; Cattell, Cattell, & Cattell, 1994) include means to assess anxiety and depression. However, these frequently used omnibus psychological tests do not include subscales to assess anger.

Some scales measure one construct. Here, too, anger has received less attention. Nonetheless, a variety of self-report anger-assessment devices have appeared in the last few decades. These include Spielberger's (1988) State–Trait Anger Expression Inventory (STAXI) and its recent revision, the STAXI–2 (Spielberger, 1999); the revised Buss–Durkee Hostility Inventory (BDHI), resulting in the Aggression Questionnaire (AQ; A. H. Buss & Perry, 1992); Siegel's (1986) Multidimensional Anger Inventory (MAI); the Novaco Anger Scale (NAS; Novaco, 1994), the Clinical Anger Scale (CAS; Snell, Gum, Shuck, Mosley, & Hite, 1995); and the Anger Disorders Scale (ADS) and the Anger Disorders Scale–Screening Version (ADS–S; DiGiuseppe & Tafrate, 2004). Unfortunately, many of the existing anger instruments show only limited evidence of validity and appear to have questionable research and clinical utility. Although most existing anger measures consider anger a multidimensional construct and have subscales that represent several aspects of anger, various instruments use different scales and, thus, assess different dimensions of anger. In the absence of clear diagnostic guidelines, assessment instruments have been developed that measure different aspects of the anger experience. A detailed review of anger instruments is provided in DiGiuseppe and Tafrate (2004).

The scientific attention paid to anger assessment in comparison to assessments for anxiety and depression is depicted in Figure 1.2. The method of identifying relevant scientific articles is the same as outlined above. From 1971 through 2005 there were 1,081 articles related to assessment and depression, 744 for anxiety, and 74 for anger. The top line represents the scientific attention

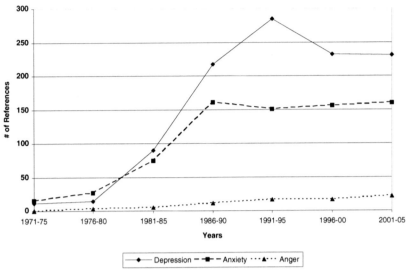

Figure 1.2. *PsyInfo* References for Assessment

paid to depression, the middle line indicates that paid to anxiety, and the bottom line represents that paid to anger. It appears that research on the topic of assessment and depression peaked in the period 1991–1995. Studies of anxiety remained steady from 1986 through 2005. Attention to the anger area, while significantly less, appears to be increasing.

Treatment

The insufficient attention given to anger is also evident by the paucity of treatment studies on anger. A thorough review of the treatment-outcome research is provided in chapter 16 and can also be found in a recent meta-analytic review (DiGiuseppe & Tafrate, 2003). The number of studies related to treatment is provided in Figure 1.3.

The total number of studies mentioning treatment and depression, anxiety, and anger for the years 1971–2005 was 6,356 for depression; 2,516 for anxiety; and 185 for anger. As with the previous graphs, the top line represents the scientific attention paid to depression, the middle line that paid to anxiety, and the bottom line the attention paid to anger. Although research on anger treatment appears to be increasing, the current scientific foundation is not even at the levels seen in the 1970s for depression and anxiety. Thus, as a field, the development of treatment interventions for clients with dysfunctional anger can be viewed as still in its infancy.

Most of the articles uncovered were not solely empirical investigations of the treatment of anger; rather they were theoretical and clinical articles and case studies. Clinicians have fewer studies to guide their choices of

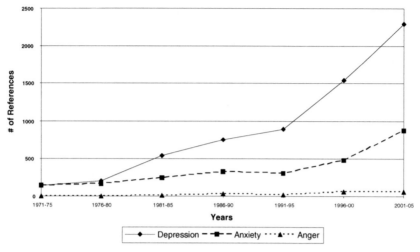

Figure 1.3. *PsyInfo* References for Treatment

empirically supported interventions for anger. The National Institutes of Health has funded large-scale anxiety and depression treatment-outcome projects (e.g., Barlow, Rapee, & Brown, 1992; Elkin, Shea, Watkins, Imber, Sotsky, & Collins, 1989). No such comprehensive, well-controlled research with clinical populations exists for anger. Few scholars are leading programmatic research teams to investigate the treatment of anger. Several notable exceptions are the work of J. L. Deffenbacher, and Kassinove.

Related to treatment issues, another indication of the lack of attention paid to anger is revealed in the coverage of anger in behavioral sciences textbooks. Most behavioral therapy texts devote substantial space and cite many references concerning the treatment of aggression but give little attention and provide fewer references to the treatment of anger (e.g., Masters, Burish, Hollon, & Rimm, 1987; Thorpe & Olsen, 1990). The situation is similar in texts on psychopathology. A recent review of introductory and abnormal psychology textbooks found that a fourth to a third of all texts did not reference anger at all (J. L. Deffenbacher & Deffenbacher, 2003). Our experiences consulting with practitioners in a variety of treatment settings indicates that most clinicians are less confident regarding their skills to assist angry clients.

Reasons for Avoiding Anger

Why have researchers avoided the study of anger? Why do mental health professionals fail to include the emotion of anger in diagnostic manuals, assessment instruments, and treatments? Possibly anger is a more unpleasant emotion to confront than anxiety or depression. It often leads to intimidating behaviors and evokes fear in others. Perhaps mental health professionals avoid the study of anger because, as a profession, we generally dislike working with angry clients and prefer more docile clients, such as those with anxiety and depression.

Another reason may be the narrow scope of mental health services historically offered. It is possible that less attention is paid to anger because it is considered outside the parameters of the mental health profession. Most psychotherapy pioneers worked with self-referred anxious or depressed clients or hospitalized psychotic patients. Therefore, the people who shaped the mental health field did not typically treat angry and aggressive clients. Aggressive behavior was defined as criminal behavior and left to law enforcement and correctional institutions. For practitioners who work in criminal justice settings anger is a major target of intervention. Today psychotherapy and mental health treatments are more accepted, and society expects psychologists and psychiatrists to deal with a range of problems, including anger. As a result, matters that used to be considered "social problems," such as domestic violence, receive more attention, and society expects mental health professionals to provide solutions.

Anger is an emotion that most people do not wish to change in themselves. Perhaps angry people are less inclined to seek mental health services and to stay in treatment. This explanation is plausible. However, our lectures and workshops in recent years have been inundated with practitioners who have few models for treating angry clients. Therefore, we do not concede that clients with anger problems fail to seek treatment services. Angry clients often fail, however, to identify themselves as the problem and fail to seek individual therapy. They come as members of families and seek help for marital, family, or parent–child conflicts. Thus, professionals may have attended to family dysfunctions but not the emotion of anger that drives it. When angry clients arrive for treatment in a family, they usually want to change the targets of their anger rather than themselves. Clinicians may perceive angry clients as more resistant to treatment and therefore experience less empathy and interest in helping them.

A final reason for the lack of clinical research on anger involves the failure of our language to discriminate between functional and dysfunctional anger. The word *anger* refers to an emotional state, a trait, and a mood. An *emotional state* refers to one's present, transient emotional experience. The state of anger sometimes leads to functional behavior; always refraining from anger would interfere with signals to engage in conflict resolution. This is a common reason professionals argue against classifying anger as a disorder. The scarcity of work on anger may have resulted from the lack of a consensus on a definition of anger as an emotion versus anger as a clinical entity (see Tavris, 1989). Although a state of anger may occasionally lead to adaptive behavior, frequently experiencing anger states indicates trait anger, which can be more dysfunctional (J. L. Deffenbacher,

Oetting, Lynch, & Morris, 1996). English has clear words to distinguish between states and excessive traits for other emotions. We distinguish between the state of fear and the trait of anxiety, and between the state of sadness and the trait or mood of depression. No such distinction appears in our language for anger. The word *anger* can describe both a state and a trait.

Intense and frequent anger experiences are associated with a number of serious costs for individuals. The science and practice of psychology has been mostly focused on anxiety and depression. As a result, fewer instruments exist to assess dysfunctional anger, no diagnostic categories exist where anger is the primary focus, and there are only a handful of treatment studies to guide clinical practice. In addition, a lack of consensus regarding terminology for anger and related problems has contributed to conceptual confusion and is the focus of the next chapter.

2

Ubiquitous and Intangible

The Problem of Defining Anger

The first step in the study of clinical constructs is establishing acceptable definitions of those constructs. Without accepted definitions, the ability to measure the construct under investigation is hampered, as is the ability to prove the construct validity of assessment instruments. The primary problem with the study of anger as a clinical phenomenon or as a disorder is definitional confusion. The words *anger, aggression, hostility, irritability,* and *hate* are used interchangeably in our field. This impedes efforts to integrate clinical and research findings into a viable theory (Chesney, 1985). Several authors, such as Averill (1982), Kennedy (1992), Tavris (1989), Spielberger and colleagues (Spielberger, 1988; Spielberger, Jacobs, Russell, & Crane, 1983; Spielberger, Johnson, Russell, Crane, Jacobs, & Worden, 1985), and Born and Steiner (1999), have provided definitions to distinguish among anger, aggression, hostility, and irritability. However, they concluded that providing adequate definitions for these constructs remained elusive. Chesney (1985) believes that confusion about the anger construct, its unique characteristics, and its relationships with other variables continues to hinder efforts to assess, treat, and prevent anger disorders. In this chapter we offer working definitions for *anger, aggression, hostility, irritability,* and *hate,* which serve as the foundation for our research. These definitions are, if nothing else, empirical questions. They are to be regarded as hypotheses open for empirical scrutiny.

Anger

Originally, we (DiGiuseppe, Eckhardt, Tafrate, & Robin, 1994) defined anger as "an internal, mental, subjective feeling–state with associated cognitions and physiological arousal patterns." This definition applies to all emotions. Many mental health professionals, we included, have focused on differentiating anger from aggression and hostility. Broad definitions fail, however, to differentiate anger from other emotions. Thus, in this section, the focus is on how anger differs from the behaviors of aggression, the personality trait of hostility, and the concepts of irritability and hate. In the next chapter we discuss how anger differs from other emotions.

For generations the leaders in the behavioral sciences, such as Darwin, Freud, Lorenz, and the behaviorists, failed to distinguish between the emotion of anger and the behavior of aggression. Many assume that the emotion and its most salient behavioral consequence are the same. Is it reasonable that science has linked the emotion of anger and the behavior of aggression? The field has not used the same distinction in defining the other major emotions or emotional disorders. We (as a profession) do not think that anxiety is the same as and indistinguishable from avoidance or escape, although these are the major and most frequent behaviors resulting from anxiety. Also, we do not assume that depression is the same as and indistinguishable from diminished activity or withdrawal, although these are the major and most frequent behaviors resulting from depression. Anger is the only emotion viewed as synonymous with a behavior that sometimes follows. Thus, for consistency alone, the field needs to acknowledge the difference between anger and aggression, or change the definitions of anxiety and depression.

Earliest attempts to define *anger* focused on physiological indices, such as Ax's (1953) classic study that defined anger as an epinephrine-norepinephrine interaction. His study reflected the logical positivist influence within scientific psychology that eschewed internal cognitive or affective constructs. Unfortunately, analyses such as Ax's fail to clarify how definitions limited only to observable physiological measures are unique to anger and separate from autonomically similar emotions such as fear. Our phenomenological position clearly defines anger as a covert phenomenon that is assessed by observer inferences from behavioral reactions, measures of physiological reactivity, and most important, subjective self-report. Several other authors defined anger less parsimoniously. They define it almost entirely as cognition (e.g., Ellis, 1977; A. Lazarus, 1991), do not emphasize cognition enough (Novaco, 1975), or overemphasize anger's link to aggression (Rubin, 1986).

Our previous definition of *anger* is closely aligned to the definition offered by Spielberger and colleagues (Spielberger, 1988; Spielberger et al., 1983, 1985), who also viewed anger as a phenomenological construct: "The concept of anger usually refers to an emotional state that comprises feelings that vary in intensity from mild annoyance and aggravation to fury and rage, and that is accompanied by arousal of the autonomic nervous system" (Spielberger, 1988, p. 6). Since it is a subjective construct, it is thus amenable only to self-report methods of assessment.

More current definitions regard anger as a multidimensional construct consisting of physiological (general sympathetic arousal, 5–HT suppression), cognitive (irrational beliefs, automatic thoughts, negative automatic thoughts, causal attributions, inflammatory imagery), phenomenological (subjective awareness of angry feelings), and behavioral (facial expressions, verbal or behavioral anger-expression strategies) variables (for reviews see Averill, 1982, 1983; Berkowitz, 1990, 1993; J. Deffenbacher, 1994; Eckhardt & Deffenbacher, 1995; Kassinove & Sukhodolsky, 1995; Tafrate, Kassinove, & Dundin, 2002). Kassinove and Sukhodolsky's (1995) definition characterized the multidimensional approach:

> Anger refers to a label given to a constellation of specific uncomfortable subjective experiences and associated cognitions (e.g., thoughts, beliefs, images) that have variously associated verbal, facial, bodily, and autonomic reactions. It is a transient state, in that it eventually passes, and it is a social role, in that our culture or subculture allows for the display of certain kinds of behaviors associated with the internal experience but punishes others. Thus, anger is felt in people's conscious awareness and is communicated through verbalizations and bodily reactions. (p. 11)

Spielberger's (1988), Kassinove and Sukhodolsky's (1995), and our (DiGiuseppe, Tafrate, & Eckhardt, 1994) previous definitions differentiate *anger* from *aggression* and *hostility*. Unfortunately, all these definitions could describe any emotion. As noted earlier, their characteristics are not unique to anger and thus fail to distinguish anger from other emotions. Spielberger's definition relies mostly on synonyms for anger (e.g., rage and aggravation).

Kennedy defined *anger* as follows:

> Anger is an affective state experienced as the motivation to act in ways that warn, intimidate, or attack those who are perceived as challenging or threatening. Anger is coupled to and is inseparable from a sensitivity to the perception of challenges or a heightened awareness of threats (irritability). This affective motivation and sensitivity can be experienced even if no external action occurs. (1992, p. 150)

Kennedy points out that this definition closely resembles a description of fear. For fear, the sensitivity to a threat would be similar. However, the action tendency for fear would be escape or avoidance rather than harm, intimidation, or attack. Kennedy's definition relies on the motivational aspect of emotions. This idea is consistent with Darwin's notion that emotions motivate adaptation to problems. Emotions differ because of the different motives they elicit.

Novaco defined *anger* as "a negatively toned emotion, subjectively experienced as an aroused state of antagonism toward someone or something perceived to be a source of an aversive event" (1994, p. 330).

Novaco's definition uniquely focuses on the "state of antagonism" that implies an ongoing tension, conflict, struggle, or fight.

These definitions evoke the image of the proverbial three blind men, each of whom feels a different part of the elephant and makes a different, yet accurate, description of the animal. Each of these definitions reveals some aspect of anger. Based on an integration of these definitions we offer the following definition:

> Anger is a subjectively experienced emotional state with high sympathetic autonomic arousal. It is initially elicited by a perception of
> a threat (to one's physical well-being, property, present or future
> resources, self-image, social status or projected image to one's group,
> maintenance of social rules that regulate daily life, or comfort),
> although it may persist even after the threat has passed. Anger is associated with attributional, informational, and evaluative cognitions
> that emphasize the misdeeds of others and motivate a response of antagonism to thwart, drive off, retaliate against, or attack the source of
> the perceived threat. Anger is communicated through facial or postural gestures or vocal inflections, aversive verbalizations, and aggressive
> behavior. One's choice of strategies to communicate anger varies
> with social roles, learning history, and environmental contingencies.

Obviously, the previous definitions (DiGiuseppe, Tafrate, Eckhardt, 1994; Kassinove & Sukhodolsky, 1995; Kennedy, 1992; Novaco, 1994; Spielberger, 1988), including our most recent, have focused on the state of anger. Spielberger's (1972a) distinction between emotional states and traits has become one of the most important ideas in the psychology of emotions. *States* are individual episodes of an emotion, whereas *trait* refers to the tendency to experience that emotion frequently and intensely. Spielberger (1988) applied this distinction to anger and developed a measure that assesses anger as both state and trait. His theory predicts that people who score high on trait anger will (a) experience the state of anger both more frequently and more intensely, (b) experience anger at a wider range of provoking stimuli, (c) express anger more negatively and cope poorly with anger, and (d) experience more dysfunction and negative consequences of anger in their lives. Spielberger suggests that trait anger measures will relate more to other anger measures than measures of other emotional constructs. Recently, J. Deffenbacher and his colleagues (J. Deffenbacher, Oetting, Thwaites, Lynch, Baker, et al., 1996) did eight studies confirming each of the above hypotheses made by Spielberger's state–trait theory of anger. We would therefore define *trait anger* as the propensity to experience intense states of anger (as defined above) frequently. The state of anger is elicited by many stimuli and may lead to poor coping and negative consequences.

Although an agreed-upon definition of *anger* has been hard to pin down, definitional clarity has important implications for assessment and treatment. As will be discussed in the remainder of this chapter, several other emotions and behaviors frequently coexist with anger. The referral of individuals for anger treatment and programming depends largely on the definition of what is and is not considered anger.

Aggression

Dollard, Doob, Miller, Mowrer, and Sears (1939) believed that *aggression* was the affectively driven attack on another with the intent to do harm. Their famous frustration–aggression hypothesis proposed that frustration, or the blocking of a goal, led to the emotion of anger. Anger, then, motivated a desire to harm the person who thwarted one's goal and prompted aggressive behavior.

Buss (1961) added to the definition of *aggression* by emphasizing two points. First, not all aggression is motivated by anger. He identified *instrumental aggression* as violence that is not emotional but is motivated by the conquest or acquisition of the vanquished person's possessions. Feshbach (1964) also distinguished between "hostile" aggression, where aggressive behavior is elicited by anger, and "instrumental" aggression, where the purpose is to obtain some object or goal and there is no harmful intent, but harm results nonetheless.

Second, Buss (1961) disagreed with Dollard et al.'s (1939) definition of aggression to include the intent to do harm. Buss maintained that intent was unnecessary. He proposed that aggression described only overt behavior and that psychology should focus on only the contingencies that reinforce aggressive behavior. However, if a person intends to do harm, the reinforcer for his or her behavior will be the harm inflicted and the suffering of the victim. No other material reward need result. Avoiding the intention would make it difficult to distinguish between aggression and clumsiness and would fail to provide important information on some possible reinforcers.

After reviewing the literature on aggression, Geen (2001) offered a tridimensional definition of *aggression*. The first component included the widely accepted part of Buss's (1961, p. 1) definition: *aggression* is "a response that delivers *noxious stimuli* to another organism." Second, he returned to Dollard et al.'s (1939) focus on intentionality. The noxious stimuli are delivered with the intent to harm the victim. Geen added that, third, the aggressor expects that the noxious stimuli will have their desired effects. This definition considers the distinction originally made by Buss (1961) and Feshbach (1964) between affective and instrumental aggression. The second and third components are similar to Dollard et al.'s (1939) intentionality.

This definition has been accepted by other notable scholars of aggression such as C. Anderson and Bushman (2002).

We define *aggression* as overt motor behavior enacted with the intent to do harm or injury to a person or object, with the expectation that harm will occur. This definition of aggression emphasizes the observable, behavioral aspect of the construct. It also includes a motivational component ("intent") to distinguish harmful accidents (e.g., running into someone while turning a corner) from more deliberate attacks (e.g., approaching, confronting, and knocking down an enemy).

The social–psychological research on aggression indicates that the relationship between anger and aggression remains unclear. People have long assumed that the two constructs are inextricably linked (for a review, see Tavris, 1989). One way to reduce this confusion is to be explicit about the definitional overlap between *anger* and *aggression*. Also, it has been popular since Buss (1963) to split aggression into two types—one form resulting from anger, and one independent from anger. Table 2.1 portrays a simple representation of how anger and aggression can exist independently and interdependently.

The *anger and aggression* cell represents patients who arrive in treatment for hitting their spouses or children because they "lost it" or "could not take it anymore." They frequently become angry with other people and occasionally their anger erupts into aggressive behavior. A substance abuser who harms a victim during a mugging to obtain money for his addiction may do so without anger at the victim. Likewise, an offender who hurts an innocent bystander while evading police may have little anger for the bystander. These are examples of *instrumental aggression*. The individual who steams with resentment over a past transgression and never confronts the transgressor but holds in his or her anger exhibits *anger and no aggression*.

The distinction between instrumental aggression and affective–angry aggression has been used for decades. However, Bushman and Anderson (2001) challenged the usefulness of this distinction. They proposed that many incidences of instrumental aggression do involve emotional arousal and that the emotion of anger leads to behavior that is instrumental and rewarded. We explore this issue in detail in chapter 4. Many people with affective aggression have temper outbursts or are verbally abusive. These outbursts coerce others to comply with the angry person's demands and

Table 2.1
The Proposed Relationship Between Anger and Aggression

Aggression	Anger	
	Present	Absent
Present	Anger and aggression	Instrumental aggression
Absent	Anger and no aggression	No anger or aggression

thus are instrumental and rewarded. Thus, affective aggression sometimes serves a purpose. Also, we find it possible that some perpetrators of aggressive acts do so with no malicious intent or emotional arousal toward their victim. Although this may be less common, wars of conquest may be the most obvious form of instrumental aggression. One nation covets a neighboring nation's land or resources. So they attack, and take what they want. But conquerors experience the emotion of envy, which we will later argue falls within the anger family of emotions. Conquerors also often feel contempt for those they conquer. They justify their acts by demeaning the humanity of the conquered people. Think of the Nazis' view that they were the superior race. Taking the land of the Slavs, French, and other "inferior" races was justified by German "superiority." Consider the conquest of the Native Americans or Aboriginal Australians. European settlers envied their land and resources and felt contempt for these natives. Can we describe these conquests as instrumental aggression, truly being without emotion? We think not, and agree with Bushman and Anderson (2001) that, although anger and aggression are different, the distinction between instrumental and reactive aggression is not so clear.

Another definitional problem centers around the distinctions between behavioral aggression and verbal aggression. Behavioral aggression refers to observable, overt actions designed to harm someone or something. The term *verbal aggression* is not as easily defined in one straightforward statement. The complexities of verbal aggression are more easily understood through an example. One of us recently treated an upper-level manager who believed his behavior with his CEO was assertive. The man's descriptions of his paralinguistic vocal behaviors, verbal responses, and gestures sounded like an assertion. However, the CEO reported that she felt emotionally abused by this manager and referred him for treatment. Many assertive responses have the potential to be perceived as attacks. The attack may be in the mind of the receiver and is not aggressive simply because someone perceives it as such. The effects of verbal behaviors on others are more variable than the effects of physical actions. A linear relationship between the sender's verbal "aggression" and the receiver's emotional consequences does not exist. People may respond in the same situation with apathy, disgust, or an even more heated verbal volley. Also, obnoxious statements may be perceived as aggressive, although the motivation is not harmful intent. Obnoxious statements may instead merely reflect poor social skills.

The problem of recognizing verbal aggression occurs frequently in family therapy when a statement intended to be nonevaluative, supportive, or neutral by the speaker is construed as aggressive by the receiver. Without assigning intent or defining the statement, *any* comment has the potential to be labeled as aggressive if the listener deems it so. Taking into account "perceived aggression" limits precision and adds unnecessary confusion. Because of this possibility, we regard the perception of the response or the social consequences of the statement as irrelevant for defining *verbal aggression.*

Because of such difficulties, Kassinove and Tafrate (2002) abandoned the term *verbal aggression* and labeled verbal expressions of anger that could have malevolent intent, such as yelling, screaming, and cursing, as *aversive verbalizations*. They restrict the term *aggression* to motor behavior. We have found it critical for both practitioners and clients to make a distinction between verbal expressiveness and aggressive motor behaviors. Different reaction patterns by clients (verbal versus physical) may call for different levels of practitioner concern and intervention. Thus, we recommend caution in using the term *verbal aggression* and favor more precisely labeling physical behaviors and verbal behaviors.

Hostility

The term *hostility* is usually used in the cardiologic or behavior-medicine literature. The first definition emphasized a personality trait. People can be viewed as having a generally hostile disposition. In this view *hostility* refers to:

(a) a personality trait evidenced by cross-situational patterns of anger in combination with aversive verbalizations or behavioral aggression, and (b) an attitude of resentment, suspiciousness, and bitterness coupled with the desire to get revenge or to have destructive goals for one's anger. (Endler & Hunt, 1968)

Another view is that *hostility* refers to a more situationally defined phenomenon. For example, Kassinove and Tafrate (2002) defined hostility as "a set of attitudes or semi-permanent thoughts about a person, institution, or group." Thus, it is possible to be hostile toward a class of specific stimuli (e.g., Christians, Northerners, short people) and not show hostility in other life areas.

Complicating the picture even further is that the term *hostility* is often used interchangeably with *aggression* or *anger* or is never explicitly defined. Although different researchers have varying views on *hostility,* the first definition focuses on the pervasive, chronic experience of anger and a display of aggressive behaviors (Endler & Hunt, 1968). The first definition is also similar to Spielberger's (1988) notion of *trait anger,* defined as "the disposition to perceive a wide range of situations as annoying or frustrating, and the tendency to respond to such situations with more frequent elevations in state anger" (p. 1). The concept of *hostility* also refers to some action besides the angry affect. Therefore, behavioral or verbal expressions of anger are required.

The first definition also reflects the cognitive aspect of the personality trait. Research has not yet confirmed whether the personality trait of hostility correlates with the attitudinal qualities of suspiciousness, bitterness, and the desire for revenge. Research by Buss and Perry (1992) shows that items reflecting these attitudes cluster together as one factor. Mikulincer

(1998) demonstrated that adaptive anger fails to include the aspect of hostility. Most likely, anger including these elements is more apt to be dysfunctional. Research is needed to differentiate *trait hostility* from *trait anger* (as proposed here) so that effective assessment techniques can be identified and beneficial treatments offered.

The vagueness of the term *hostility* (general versus situational), and its association with other phenomena (e.g., anger, aggression, disgust, cynicism, Type A behavior), has led researchers down many definitional paths. Spielberger (1988) emphasized the multifarious nature of *hostility*, defining it as a "complex set of feelings and attitudes that motivate[s] aggressive and often vindictive behavior" (p. 6). Spielberger's definition separates hostility into cognitive, affective, and motivational (intent) components. A similar definition provided by Barefoot (1992) organized the facets of hostility into cognitive (negative attributions about others' actions), affective (sympathetic activation), and behavioral (physical aggression) components. Although these definitions differ about the specificity, both highlight theoretical developments and research data showing the complex multivariate nature of hostility. Research is needed to decide which aspects of the construct lead to predictions of health status.

Research investigating the relationship between hostility and health typically assesses hostility using a structured interview (SI). An example of this assessment method is the Interpersonal Hostility Assessment Technique (IHAT; Barefoot, 1992). The IHAT assesses stylistic variables associated with Type A behavior. This research strategy assesses hostility only in the clinical interview. This method assumes that a hostile individual is just as likely to be hostile in the interview as in other domains of life. If one considers hostility from the perspective of the second definition, this assessment strategy is inadequate. Thus, the IHAT measures subject response styles such as hostile withhold–evade (answering the interviewer's questions uncooperatively or evasively), direct challenge (openly confronting and contradicting the interviewer), indirect challenge (answering a question while suggesting it is trivial or pointless), and irritation (vocally evidencing arousal). The total score of the IHAT is significantly correlated with the severity of heart disease, with indirect challenge having the highest correlation (Barefoot, 1992). Again, the results imply that hostility consists of more than angry affect or a discrete aggressive episode. It is multivariate, including affective, attitudinal, and behavioral dimensions. In concurrence with Spielberger, we include the variable of intent since it is also part of our definition of aggression.

Irritability

The term *irritability* has suffered from the same definitional confusion as *anger*. In psychiatric diagnosis and abnormal psychology the term has sometimes served as a substitute for anger or aggression but at other times refers to a low threshold for these to occur. Born and Steiner (1999) reviewed the historical, scientific, and psychometric literature on irritability and noted that irritability was commonly used in philosophy and medicine to describe a persistent problematic human frailty. Plato described irritability as one of three aspects of the human soul, along with reason and appetite. The first medical reference to irritability appeared in the second century and was made by the Roman physician Lucius Apuleius and translated as a proneness to anger (Glare, 1982). The Greek physician Galen, of the same era, described the term *choleric temperament* as associated with yellow bile; many consider Galen's writing an important historical source for the description of irritability. However, it is unclear whether the choleric temperament distinguished between irritability and anger. The term *irritability* received great attention in early-twentieth-century psychiatry, most notably from Kraeplin's use of the word *irritability* as subsumed under bipolar disorder.

Although the term *irritability* has been widely used to describe psychopathology, it was not recognized as a subject heading within the *Index Medicus* until 1985. Presently *irritability* is the most frequently used term in the *DSM–IV* to represent any of the constructs of anger, hostility, or aggression. It occurs as a related symptom for some Axis I disorders including substance abuse, Major Depressive Disorder, Generalized Anxiety Disorder, Posttraumatic Stress Disorder, Schizophrenia, Conduct Disorder, eating disorders, and insomnia. It is a possible symptom of several neurological conditions such as delirium, dementia, epilepsy, head trauma, and Huntington's chorea. Irritability is also associated with several Axis II disorders, such as Antisocial and Borderline personality disorders, as a symptom separate from the symptom of anger. For all these diagnoses, irritability is neither necessary nor sufficient on its own to meet the criteria for the disorder. Clearly irritability, like anger, is seen by contemporary psychiatry as a symptom of many diverse disorders. Born and Steiner pointed out that this view contrasts with the medical literature of previous centuries, which held that irritability was a condition in its own right.

The last half of the twentieth century saw a renewed interest in the concept of irritability. However, researchers in the area have failed to differentiate irritability from aggression, anger, and hostility (e.g., Buss, 1961). For example, in the Present State Examination (Wing, Cooper, & Sartorius, 1974), a structured mental-status interview, irritation was identified as present in patients undergoing a psychiatric evaluation if they displayed verbal or physical aggression. Also, the *Schedule of Affective Disorders and Schizophrenia* (Spitzer & Endicott, 1979) defined the word *anger* as a subjective experience, and *irritability* as an overt behavior.

Moyer recognized that *irritability* was highly related to *aggression,* and offered the following definition:

> In its pure form irritable aggression involves attack without attempts to escape from the object being attacked. The most extreme form of

irritable aggression is exemplified by destructive, uncontrollable rage directed against either animate or inanimate objects. In less extreme forms, it may involve only annoyance, threat, or half-hearted attack. The stimulus situation that evokes irritable aggression is the presence of any attackable organism or object. The range of stimuli that may elicit is extremely broad. (1976, p. 79)

Moyer's definition provided a category of aggressive behavior that is neither predatory, defensive, induced by threat or fear, involved in mating, or related to the protection of offspring. Clearly irritability seems to be on a continuum of a trait involved with anger and aggression.

Most attempts to measure irritability have included items assessing negative emotional arousal and impulsive and aggressive behavior (Buss & Durkee, 1957; Caprara, Cinanni, D'Impario, Passerini, Renzi, et al., 1985; Coccaro, Harvey, Kupsaw-Lawrence, Herbert, & Bernstein, 1991; Snaith, Constantopoulos, Jardine, & McGuffin, 1978). This raises the issue of whether irritability represents an emotion, a subset of aggression that is impulsive, or a combination of the two.

Snaith and Taylor (1985) defined *irritability* similarly to Moyer:

a feeling state characterized by reduced control over temper[,] which usually results in irascible verbal or behavioral outbursts. Although the mood may be present without observed manifestation, it may be experienced as brief episodes, in particular circumstances, or it may be prolonged and generalized. The experience of irritability is always unpleasant for the individual[,] and overt manifestations lack the cathartic effect of justified outbursts of anger. (1985, p. 128)

Born and Steiner (1999) provided a compelling synthesis of this confusing literature. They purposed that *irritability* refers to both a state and trait of physiological arousal, or lowered thresholds to, or increased sensitivity to provoking stimuli. Animals and people experience it as body tension and a lowered threshold to respond with anger or aggression. The aggressive behavior is impulsive and not premeditated. They note that irritability differs from anger in that it lacks a cognitive component.

Born and Steiner (1999, p. 164) characterized irritability by:

(1) a heightened or excessive sensitivity to external stimuli,
(2) a negative affective state,
(3) a state of physical and psychological tension that may suddenly and rapidly escalate,
(4) reduced control over temper; proneness to anger, annoyance, or impatience, and
(5) irascible verbal behavior outbursts, or even explosive behavior.

Considerable evidence supports the possible physiological nature of an irritation–impulsive aggression construct. Animal research has shown that irritable aggression is a destructive uncontrollable reaction of physiologic origin (Moyer, 1976). This reaction is in sharp contrast to how one experiences anger. Support for this hypothesis comes from research in humans that shows that it is easier to arouse fear than anger by electric stimulation. Gloor, Olivier, and Quesney (1982) found that fear could be easily evoked by stimulation of specific limbic-system areas in humans. However, they found that it was more difficult to arouse anger by electric stimulation of limbic-system areas. They believe this fact suggests that anger may be more related to cognitive appraisals. This line of research is consistent with the idea that anger differs from irritability. Anger is easily aroused by thoughts and not as easily aroused by direct electrical stimulation. Irritability seems to be a noncognitive, physiological state of tension that prepares one to respond or lowers the threshold to respond with anger or aggression. This presents the possibility that while some anger and aggression may be more cognitively mediated, another subset of the anger and aggression responses may have a more physiological, impulsive etiology because they are aroused through an irritable state. As we will discuss in chapter 14, Coccaro et al. (1991) have research to support an impulsive anger–aggressive disorder that appears to fit the model of irritability purposed by Born and Steiner.

The term *irritability* as used by Moyer (1976), Snaith and Taylor (1985), and Born and Steiner (1999) represents a complex hypothetical construct. They all believe that irritability is a phenomenological experience, and possibly a trait, and different from anger. Irritability has definite behavioral manifestations that range from angry stares to violent outbursts. The experience includes a reduced threshold to anger. It appears not to be mediated by the perception that anger or aggression is justified by transgressions and is more physiologically or neurologically mediated. However, the exact biological link is not yet known.

Based on this evidence we purpose that *irritability* is a complex construct that involves increased sensitivity to environmental stimulation that causes physiological arousal and tension, without cognitive mediation, and that results in a lowered threshold to experience anger, and/or impulsive, but not premeditated, aggression.

Research on irritability needs to test the notions that this experience can be reliably differentiated from anger and the personality trait of hostility. Considerable definitional overlap exists among *anger, hostility,* and *irritability.* Our reading of scales purporting to measure irritability suggests to us that such scales are very similar to those measuring anger. Research on irritability should focus on developing test items that clearly assess irritability and not anger or aggression. Such irritability items would clearly state that the person experiences variable thresholds of anger or aggression, rather than just different rates of frequency in their experiences of anger or acts of aggression. Such variable threshold items should include factors other than anger and aggression, if irritability is indeed different from anger and aggression. Also, identifying human biological correlates of irritability will help clarify this construct.

Hate

Hate is a word used frequently to describe the sustained negative emotion that one has toward an enemy or transgressor. Although hate is commonly used in conversation, there has been little discussion to identify how this emotion differs from others within the anger family. In fact, there is an almost total absence of studies describing the hate experience, which makes defining the construct awkward (Bartlett, 2005). Recently, Sternberg (2005) has conceptualized hate as having three components. The first involves distancing oneself from the hated object. Hating something entails the perception that the target is unworthy of closeness, understanding, or intimacy. Second is the experience of some type of passion that may include anger or fear. The third component is commitment to the belief system of devaluing the hated individual or group. This may take the form of encouraging others to adopt the hater's view through the use of propaganda. The three proposed components of hate may exist either separately or in combination. The various combinations produce a taxonomy of seven potential types of hate. For example, *cool hate* involves just the distancing component, *cold hate* integrates both the distancing and the decision–commitment components, and *burning hate* combines all three elements. Future research may help identify characteristics of different hate experiences.

In trying to differentiate hate from anger, G. S. Hall (1899) described hate as more enduring than anger. Anger can be an emotional state, or a trait. Hate lasts longer. Also, hate is retrospective, whereas anger is generally current or prospective. One hates someone for what they have done in the past for which they have not been forgiven, and one is angry at someone for what they are doing now that will thwart a future goal.

We think hate differs from anger in a few additional areas. People who hate have thoughts about the disdained person that center on the denigration and condemnation of that person. Also, the past transgressions or faults of the hated person continue to fill the mind of the hateful person. Hate may differ quantitatively in the degree of rumination about past transgression. Hate can be cold and does not necessarily involve high physiological arousal. We are struck by the coldness and lack of arousal that occurs in people who express long-term hatred toward others.

Thus, we would propose that hate involves a long-lasting predisposition to dwell on the faults or transgressions committed by another person who is held in general disdain and condemned for their past transgressions or traits. Although irritability represents the physiological arousal of anger without the cognitions, hate represents an experience of the cognitive aspects of anger without the physiological ones. An analogous model exists for a subtype of depression, Depressive Personality Disorder, a diagnostic category that appears in Appendix B of the *DSM–IV–TR* (American Psychiatric Association, 2000). Appendix B includes disorders that have been suggested but do not yet have sufficient empirical support to appear in the *DSM*. McDermut, Zimmerman, and Cheiminski (2003) found that patients who meet the criteria for Depressive Personality can be described to have the cognitive characteristics that typically occur with depression but not display the physiological symptoms. Hatred appears to be a similar construct as Depressive Personality Disorder within the domain of anger. Hate would differ in one aspect. Although people who hate usually experience the cognitive aspect of anger without experiencing the accompanying physiological arousal associated with anger, when the hateful person comes in contact with the person whom they hate, they can experience a state of anger, and have the physiological arousal typically associated with anger. Hate is an emotion that one has at a distance. Since it does not involve high physiological arousal, the arousal does not interfere with one's cognitive processes or lead to impulsive acts. Hate is the emotion of the terrorist, the saboteur, the vengeful killer, and the stalker. The distance and low arousal allows for the planning of aggressive acts to continue with cold precision.

Anger, aggression, hostility, irritability, and hate are complex mental health issues. These constructs have many implications in today's society. Anger disorders, health conditions, domestic violence, regional conflicts, and hate crimes are a few matters of concern. Questions remain, including what the criteria are for anger, aggression, hostility, irritability, hate, or any combination thereof to be considered clinically significant. Based on the previous review, we will use the following definitions:

Anger refers to a subjectively experienced emotional state that is elicited by a perception of threat. It is associated with cognitions focused on others' misdeeds and is communicated by a variety of behaviors influenced by social roles, learning history, and environmental contingencies.

Aggression refers to motor behavior enacted with the intent to do harm and the expectation that harm will occur.

Hostility refers to a semipermanent set of attitudes that can be either general or situational in nature. Such attitudes are related to both affective and behavioral characteristics.

Irritability is a physiological state characterized by a lowered threshold for responding with anger or aggression to stimuli. It is a partially aroused physiological state without the thoughts that usually occur with anger.

Hate refers to an enduring negative affect of antagonism with a strong desire to effect revenge or hurt an opponent, without the physiological arousal normally associated with anger. Hate can turn to anger when the person actually confronts the object of his or her hate.

By explicitly defining these constructs and their variations, we hope to provide a guideline for future clinical research in this long-neglected area.

3

How Anger Differs From Other Emotions

Our early definition of *anger* (DiGiuseppe, Tafrate, & Eckhardt, 1994; Di-Giuseppe, Tafrate, Eckhardt, & Robin, 1994; Kassinove & Tafrate, 2002), as well as those of Averill (1982), Kassinove and Sukhodolsky (1995), Novaco (1975), Sharkin (1988), Spielberger (1988), and Tavris (1989) suggested how anger differs from aggression and hostility. These definitions failed, however, to specify how anger differs from other emotions. Perhaps the reason definitions of *anger* (and other emotions) provide so little information about the experiences of the emotion is that we take the meaning for granted. We use words for emotions in private conversations. When we use them in a professional context, we rely on our personal use and fail to consider these emotions as technical words. We assume (often correctly) the reader or listener knows what *anger* means. Perhaps all English speakers have an implicit prototype or schema for anger. Although differentiating between anger and anxiety and depression sounds simple, it is more difficult than it first appears.

Before reading any further, try to think about how you would define your own feelings of anger as opposed to depression without using synonyms for the words "anger" or "depression." Rely only on a verbal description of the phenomenological characteristics and physiological sensations of these emotions. This exercise may provide you with some idea about why research and theory of emotions, and specifically anger, has been so difficult.

We are committed to the idea that the best clinical practice emerges from basic scientific knowledge. In reviewing the clinical literature on anger, we were unable to find references to basic research related to the psychology of emotions. Most clinical articles assumed that readers shared the same definition or prototype for anger and went on to discuss some clinical aspect of anger or its relationship to other emotional disorders. Perhaps the controversies concerning the emotion of anger and the confusion facing practitioners about diagnosis and treatment could be resolved by reviewing basic scientific research from the psychology of emotions. Much disagreement exists in the psychology of emotions (see Ekman & Davidson, 1994, for debates on these issues), and three major controversies are reviewed in the present chapter. Examination of these controversies will prove helpful in defining and distinguishing anger from other emotions. The first issue involves the actual experiential differences of emotions. Maybe the words we use to describe emotions all have a great overlap in meaning and we only feel positive or negative emotions. Second, how do we, as psychologists in an English-speaking culture, define emotions generally and anger in particular? Third, how do we define emotions (specifically anger) across cultures, and are emotional experiences (including anger) felt similarly across cultures? The answers to these matters are related, but we will try to answer them separately to organize the theoretical arguments and research findings. Although a full review of these areas is beyond the scope of this book, the answers to these questions have important implications and treatment utility for practitioners. Understanding how anger differs from other emotions will help determine what intrinsic characteristics separate an "anger disorder" from an "anxiety disorder" or a "mood disorder." Examining the universality of emotions, including anger, will tell us what we can expect to be consistent among clients with anger disorders, and how a client's culture of origin influences their experience or expression of anger.

Anger and Negative Affectivity

Much of the clinical literature on anger involves discussions of anger as part of depression or anxiety. Many theorists, researchers, and therapists view anger as part of these emotions or as secondary to these emotions and not as a separate emotion. For example, the classical psychoanalytic view states that depression is anger turned inward. As our colleague Jerry Deffenbacher likes to point out, if this were true then anger is clearly the primary emotion and depression is secondary. The relationship between anger and depression is discussed in detail in chapter 10. Regarding anxiety, both anger and anxiety are responses to a threat. Psychotherapists often suggest that when a patient is angry, the anger is secondary to anxiety. Among angry clients, one often finds a threat and high physiological arousal, but not necessarily anxiety. People believe that anger occurs with depression and anxiety. In addition, anger may coexist with anxiety or depression because anxiety and depression occur together more often than not.

High correlations between measures of depression and anxiety are often reported in the research literature. Watson and Clark (1984) reviewed the factor-analytic research on the experience of emotions and concluded that most research supports two broad factors of emotional experience: positive affectivity and negative affectivity. They found overwhelming support for the concept of negative affectivity, that is, that measures of anxiety, anger, depression, dissatisfaction, shame, guilt, concern, and apprehension highly correlate with each other. However, Watson and Clark's review fails to uncover a single study that used a measure of anger. Thus, the conclusion that anger is part of general negativity is widely accepted but rests on theory rather than firm research support.

Subsequent research by Watson and Clark (Watson, Clark, & Tellegen, 1988; Watson & Clark, 1992) identified a hostility scale that loaded onto a higher order negative affectivity factor with measures of fear, sadness, and guilt. They interpreted this finding to support the view that anger-related constructs could also be conceptualized as part of general negativity. However, as we pointed out in the previous chapter, hostility represents some attitudes of suspiciousness and resentment associated with anger and most likely with anger held in. Watson and Clark (1992) also investigated whether their concept of affective negativity was synonymous with the concept of neuroticism in the five-factor model of personality (McCrae & Costa, 1986, 1987). Research has shown that most descriptors of personality can be condensed to the five factors of neuroticism, extroversion, openness to experience, agreeableness, and conscientiousness. Most of the measures of emotions that make up the higher order factor of negative affectivity correlated with measures of neuroticism. Anger was the exception. Anger scores were related to both high neuroticism and low agreeableness. However, only anger was measured, not hostility. Surprisingly, Watson and Clark (1992) finally concluded that anger functions differently from other negative emotions, perhaps because it involves an outward rather than inward focus and attribution for blame. These conflicting results of course are limited by the definitional confusion discussed in the previous chapter. Hostility and anger may have different relationships to the general factor of negative affectivity. An anger measure, as opposed to one for hostility, might yield different results.

Recent factor-analytic studies suggest that anger may not be part of general negative affectivity with anxiety and depression but is a separate emotion. For example, McGough and Curry (1992) factor analyzed the responses of adolescent inpatients on the SCL–90 (Degrogatis, 1975, p. 539), a measure of psychopathology, and found two major factors. The first factor, which they labeled *dysphoria,* was a negative affectivity factor and included items on depression, anxiety, and other emotions. The second factor, which they labeled *anger and mistrust,* did not include the negative affectivity items. Similarly, Duckitt (1994) reported the results of a factor-analytic study of the items of the Psychiatric Symptoms Index with a nationally representative sample of almost 800 white South Africans. Anger emerged as a separate factor from depression, anxiety, and psychotic symptoms.

We conducted two separate studies on early versions of our Anger Disorders Scale (ADS; DiGiuseppe & Tafrate, 2004). In addition to the ADS, psychotherapy outpatients and college students completed the Beck Depression Inventory (A. T. Beck, 1987), the General Health Questionnaire (D. Goldberg, 1972), the General Psychological Well-Being Scale (McDowell & Newell, 1987), the Satisfaction with Life Scale (Diener, Emmons, Larsen, & Griffin, 1985), and a measure of irrational beliefs (DiGiuseppe, Leaf, Exner, & Robin, 1988). In one study, the State–Trait Anger Expression Inventory (STAXI; Spielberger, 1988) was also given to several hundred college students. The subscales of the ADS and the STAXI consistently loaded on an anger factor that was separate from a negative affectivity factor and a factor for positive well-being and life satisfaction. More research on the relation of anger to other emotions is needed. Contrary to clinical wisdom, some research supports the idea that anger is an emotion separate from negative affectivity. Anxiety and depression appear more closely related to each other than to anger.

Anger in the English Language

This section discusses how anger is understood in the English language. Various perspectives used in differentiating anger from other emotions are reviewed.

Most theoreticians support the idea that there is a set of basic emotions that all humans experience. Besides these emotions, derivatives of the basic emotions exist. For example, Ekman (1994) refers to families of emotions. Thus, secondary emotions can be considered subcategories belonging to one of the families of basic emotions. Researchers differ concerning the number of emotional words they believe exist in English and the proper classification of different emotions in the overall schema of emotions. The estimates of the number of emotion words in English range from 500 and 2,000 (Averill, 1975; Wallace & Carson, 1973), to the more conservative estimate of 99 (Ortony, Clore, & Foss, 1987). According to the traditional view, all such words are either basic emotions (joy, anger, fear, guilt, shame, disgust, and sadness) or subcategories of the basic emotions (Ekman, 1984; Izard, 1971; Johnson-Laird & Oats, 1989; Tomkins, 1962).

One controversy concerns the classification of basic and secondary emotions. For example, *annoyed* is a word viewed within the higher category of anger, yet it differs from *anger* in intensity or degree of disturbance. Thus, annoyance is in the anger family but under a subclass of a less intense or less disturbed anger state, along with irritated or peeved. According to the classical view, each basic emotion has one or more essential characteristics, and each member of that family of emotion will share those characteristics.

According to the classical view of emotions, all words in the anger family should have similar characteristics. Those researchers and theoreticians following the classical view have proposed several characteristics that are essential features to the anger family of emotions.

Physiological Activation

Many have suggested that anger differs from other emotions primarily by its physiological reaction. This is supported by the view that each basic emotion has a unique physiological response. According to this theory each emotion evolved for a different survival strategy, and therefore, each emotion will have a separate physiology that is consistent with the particular strategy. Although this notion has face validity, currently there is insufficient evidence to support the idea that each emotion has a specific physiology (see Ekman & Davidson, 1994, for a discussion). Some classical theorists who have defined anger by its physiological reactions include Ausberger (1986), Ekman (1992), Izard (1977), and Novaco (1975). Although substantial research on direct physiological measures of anger in comparison to other emotions is lacking, anger does differ from anxiety in some aspects of its physiological reaction (Ax, 1953).

Causes or Triggers

The next, and perhaps most popular feature, used to define the anger family is its eliciting stimuli. One of the oldest theories, the frustration–aggression hypothesis (Dollard, Doob, Miller, Mowrer, & Sears, 1939), posited that aggression and anger result when an organism's goal-directed behaviors are blocked or thwarted. Since then, many activating events have been proposed as the cause of anger. A list of these causes, along with the articles discussing them, appears in Table 3.1 (for reviews see Russell & Fehr, 1994; Ekman & Davidson, 1994).

These activating events range from general causes such as frustration, to more specific causes such as perception of blameworthiness or threat to self-esteem and low self-esteem. Many of the proposed causes are not events but perceptual or evaluative cognitions. Defining anger according to the type of activating event or related cognition has several limitations. To define all anger as frustration or threats to self-esteem and then to provide research to show that these variables cause anger would be tautological. The cause-and-effect relationship would be inevitable since the causal variable was used to define the effect or dependent variable. Researchers ensure they will find evidence supporting their theories when the variables are defined this way. T. Smith (1989) cautioned cognitive theorists about this type of definition. He notes that if cognitive theories are to be tested, one must have separate definitions and measures of the causative cognitive variables that are distinct from dependent variables.

Table 3.1
Proposed Causes of Anger and the Articles Discussing Them

Proposed Cause	Authors
Injury	Alschuler & Alschuler, 1984
Harm and injury	Schimmel, 1979
Serious or personal threat	Averill, 1982
Stress or danger	Gaylin, 1989
Perception of blameworthiness	Clore & Ortony, 1991; Clore, Ortony, Dienes, & Frjida, 1993
Appraisal of immorality	de Rivera, 1977
Thwarted goal	Berkowitz, 1990
Frustration	Hunt, Cole, & Reis, 1958; Berkowitz, 1990
Threat to self-esteem	Feshback, 1986; Izard, 1977; Kemper, 1991
Low self-esteem	E. Anderson, 1994; Jankowski, 1991; Renzetti, 1992; Gondolf, 1985; Levin & McDevitt, 1993; Long, 1990; MacDonald, 1975; Oats & Forrest, 1985; Toch, 1969/1993; Schoenfeld, 1988
Interference, threat or insult	Kliewer, 1986
Appraisals of novelty, pleasantness, goal significance, coping potential, social and self-standards	Scherer, 1993

Several researchers explored which categories of the stimuli elicit anger (Averill, 1979; Shaver, Schwartz, Kirson, & O'Connor, 1987; C. A. Smith & Ellsworth, 1987; Torestad, 1990). Mabel (1994) constructed a questionnaire that appears to have the broadest sample of anger-provoking stimuli. He reviewed more than 900 stimuli and reduced these to 360 items. He administered the questionnaire to a wide range of people from high school students to senior citizens. The resulting factor analysis suggested that the items could be reduced to the following 10 factors:

1. interruption of goal-directed behavior when time is important;
2. experiencing personal degradation or unfair treatment (and being powerless to stop it);
3. being treated unfairly, unkindly, or in a prejudicial way whether or not one is present;
4. being the object of dishonesty or broken promises, or being disappointed by others or even oneself;
5. having one's authority, feelings, or property being disregarded by others;

6. being ignored or treated badly by a significant other;
7. experiencing harm because of one's negligence toward oneself;
8. being shown by others' behavior that they do not care;
9. being the object of verbal or physical assault; and
10. being a "helpless victim." (We would interpret the items that load on this factor as representing things one cannot control despite a desire to do so.)

In considering the potential number of variables related to triggering events, it may not be possible to accurately characterize and describe anger as a unique emotional experience according to causes. Most of the proposed causes of anger fail to discriminate between the events that elicit anger and cognitive factors such as perceptions, inferences, and evaluations about the actual events. An additional problem is that while these proposed causes often lead to anger, they do not always do so, and sometimes lead to other emotions. For example, frustration or perception of blameworthiness often leads to anger. However, some clients may become depressed. These clients believe they are helpless to overcome their tormentor or are anxious because they are afraid the frustration will continue. Even if these variables always "caused" anger, trying to define anger by its causes fails to tell us about the experience of anger, or what makes the emotion of anger different from other emotions.

Focusing on the triggering events of anger may also have limited clinical utility. In a survey of anger episodes in high-trait-anger and low-trait-anger adults, Kassinove, Tafrate, and Dundin (2002) found no discernable differences in the trigger patterns reported by the two groups. Differences were found in other areas of the anger experience including cognitive appraisals, expressive patterns, and outcomes related to anger episodes. Those with everyday anger experiences and those with more disordered anger may share similar struggles and challenges.

Context

Another perspective that can be used to discriminate anger from other emotions is the context under which it occurs. Assessing both American and Russian college students, Kassinove and Sukhodolsky (1995) found that anger occurs more frequently at home than any other location. People we like or love are more likely to hurt us because they have more opportunities to disappoint us or do things of which we disapprove. In turn, the target of anger is most often a person one likes or loves. This is consistent with the blameworthiness hypothesis. This data suggests that for many people anger is more commonly experienced toward those close to the heart. However, context is not sufficient in describing anger since anger occurs in other locations and toward other people besides those people whom we like or love, and we feel additional emotions toward those we love. Also, this aspect of anger is not a cultural universal. Scherer (1993) reported that although people from Western cultures get angry with those they know, Japanese subjects reported getting angry more often with strangers.

Cognition

Berkowitz (1990, 1993) recently reformulated the frustration–aggression hypothesis. According to his cognitive-associative theory of anger, an aversive event first produces general negative affect or discomfort, primarily without cognition. Shortly after this initial "frustration," thoughts, attitudes, and memories enter the picture as the person contemplates what has occurred, why it has happened, and what possible consequences might follow. The purpose of this second stage is to define more fully and elaborate the emotion. Thus, certain types of cognitive variables elicited by the initial emotional upset will determine which emotion is experienced. This theory states that anger is always a secondary emotion to arousal and that some cognitive variables trigger only anger. Issues related to this theory are discussed in greater detail in chapter 8, which focuses on cognitive models of anger.

Behaviors

A third definitional feature of anger is its behavioral reaction. Several authors defined anger by the desire to behave aggressively toward, or do harm to, an imagined or real transgressor, or to plan to behave aggressively (Frijda, 1986; Rubin, 1986). This definition does not link anger with aggressive behavior but with the desire or plan to behave aggressively. Initially this definition seems plausible. Even people who score high on anger-in can plot to retaliate against the target of their anger; however, they may fail to implement their plot for lack of courage or opportunity. Those who score high on Spielberger's anger-control scale may also experience an initial desire to harm their transgressor but employ coping strategies to reduce the affect or to control their behavior. Although revenge ruminations often occur in angry episodes, they need not occur in every case of anger. Research on the retrospective experiences of anger (Averill, 1982; Kassinove & Sukhodolsky, 1995; Vaughan, 1996) includes reports where people experienced anger and did not want to do harm or act aggressively. Wanting to resolve the conflict between themselves and the perceived transgressor was a common response. Despite this disclaimer, it is possible that the desire or plan to do harm may be a defining feature of someone with an anger disorder. An empirical investigation of those with disordered anger experiences could explore this possibility. We recommend that a comprehensive clinical evaluation of angry clients should always include a thorough assessment of such intentions. Clearly, people can choose many possible responses when angered. Perhaps the desire to harm is a universal aspect of anger but is controlled when people choose other behavioral reactions. The universality of the desire to do harm has yet to be confirmed.

It is possible that the behavioral manifestation of anger distinguishes anger from other emotions. Anxiety usually leads to escape or avoidance, and depression usually leads to reduced motoric output. Anger may have eluded a clear definition because so many behavioral reactions are associated with it. J. Deffenbacher and his colleagues (J. Deffenbacher, Oetting, Lynch, & Morris, 1996; J. Deffenbacher, 1997) recently developed an anger-expression inventory by collecting 99 items representing subjects' reactions to anger. A combination of cluster- and factor-analysis techniques of the items revealed 14 separate anger-expression subscales. These 14 ways of expressing anger are as follows:

1. Anger control. This includes all calm and patient responses that attempt to control one's own behavior.
2. Direct expression of anger. This reflects the clear, direct expression of how one feels.
3. Reciprocal communications. This includes listening and problem solving with the target of one's anger to resolve the conflict.
4. Considered response. This entails cognitively reflecting on the consequences of anger expression before engaging in any activity.
5. Time-out. This means removing oneself from the conflict until one calms down.
6. Physical assaults of people. This manifests itself when a person strikes out at the target of his or her anger by hitting, slapping, pushing, or punching the person(s).
7. Physical assault of objects. This includes throwing, slamming, hitting, or banging things.

People can express anger verbally three separate ways. In terms of the next three items, Deffenbacher's research does not clarify whether they represent one negative verbal anger-expression factor or three separate factors. He recommends that they be considered separately until further research addresses this issue.

8. Noisy arguing. This includes loud arguing and disagreements with the target of one's anger.
9. Verbal assault. This involves making intimidating or threatening verbal insults against the target of one's anger.
10. Verbal put-downs. This entails using subtle insults, cynical comments, sarcasm, or put-downs against the target of one's anger.

Anger can also be expressed through body language. Deffenbacher reported two separate nonverbal styles of communication.

11. Dirty looks. This involves making facial expressions that communicate anger or contempt.

12. Body language. This involves making bodily gestures that express anger or contempt.

Spielberger's anger scale has long included an anger-in scale, and this construct is important for understanding the different styles of anger expression. Deffenbacher noted that anger-in could be further broken down into two separate reactions.

13. Anger-in/suppression. The person experiences anger but keeps it in, avoids expressing anger, or avoids people.
14. Anger-in/critical. The person is critical of others, or has negative opinions of others without expressing anger.

Other expressions of anger not mentioned by Deffenbacher but specified by Tangney et al. (1996) include:

15. Malediction. The person says bad things about the target of his or her anger to a third party. This may be the most frequent reaction of anger, and it is often safe from reprisal.
16. Corrective action. The person changes his or her behavior to avoid conflict with the target of anger.
17. Diffusion or distraction. The person releases the anger tension through an avoidance activity that distracts him or her from the anger without requiring facing the problem.
18. Passive-aggressive sabotage. The person behaves in a way that fails to help or passively sabotages the target of his or her anger or that resists completion of assigned tasks or agreed-upon tasks, thereby blocking the goals or compromising the well-being of the target of anger. Most researchers avoid studying this anger behavior, possibly because it is a broad class and therefore constructing items that address this behavior may be difficult.
19. Relational victimization or social isolation of the target. The person encourages, cajoles, or bullies others to isolate the target of his or her anger socially. This behavior has been primarily studied in adolescents. Adolescent young women do this more than adolescent boys, and the recipients of the isolation feel victimized (Crick & Bigbee, 1998). Currently no research exists on the degree or frequency with which adults engage in this behavior when angry. However, our anecdotal experience suggests that this reaction is not limited to adolescents and that gender differences with adults may not exist.
20. Displacement. The person behaves aggressively toward people or targets other than those at whom they are angry. Thus, a person angry at work may come home and yell at his or her family. This is a robust phenomenon (Novaco, 1993; Robins & Novaco, 1999). Although explanations have been proposed, none seem adequate to explain this phenomenon. Excitation transfer theory (Zillmann, 2003) provides one explanation. Emotional arousal dissipates slowly and a person may be

still aroused from a previous anger-provoking event. When a new event is encountered, its arousing potential is additive and boosts the person's anger arousal to a level that excites aggression. Perhaps people remain aroused by previous anger events and behave aggressively only when they encounter those whom they believe will tolerate their aggression or who are less powerful and cannot punish anger expression. Similarly, Robins and Novaco (1999) have discussed a systems approach to conceptualizing anger. Prevailing stressful conditions can create arousal that lingers, thus lowering the threshold to react to future provocations with anger. In addition, individuals who experience anger-related conflicts often create a more negative environment where future anger experiences are more likely to occur.

Clearly clinicians and researchers are challenged by the many possible ways people can express anger. Unfortunately, clinicians and researchers have avoided assessing some of these possible expressions in favor of investigating only the most frequent or salient anger reactions such as aggression or verbal expression.

The failure of the classical theorists to define anger does not mean their work fails to tell us a good deal about anger. Perceived threat, blameworthiness, threats to self-esteem, and desires to do harm may be frequent characteristics of anger. Averill found that more than 85% of the angry episodes recorded involved a perceived voluntary injustice or a potentially avoidable accident. He concurs that "anger is a response to some perceived misdeed" (1983, p. 1150). Perhaps for most people what determines how they label their emotional experience of anger is the perception of injustice and attributions of blame.

In summary, most of the theories generated from the classical view of emotions have failed to define anger and how it differs from other emotions. Most of the attempts to define anger to date have proposed that eliciting stimuli, cognitive appraisals, or behavioral consequences are the distinguishing characteristics of anger. Such definitions can lead only to tautology and fail to describe the experience of anger. All these variables are not ubiquitous features of anger but frequently coexist with the experience of anger.

Culture, Language, and the Universality of Anger

Rage, anger, and indignation are exhibited in nearly the same manner
throughout the world.
—Charles Darwin

Research on the universality of emotions has focused primarily on subjects' ability to recognize the facial expressions that correspond with the basic emotions. This research comes directly from Darwin's (1872/1965) classic work *The Expression of Emotion in Man and Animals*. Darwin proposed that emotions are biologically universal across each species. Members of a species express emotions in programmed muscle movements that are recognized by other members of the species. The ability to send and recognize emotions results in communication. Darwin thought his ideas also applied to human emotions since our emotions have their origins in our ancestral species. However, we humans differ from other animals in the degree to which our behavior is controlled by learning influences rather than instinct. To what extent does evolution and genetics determine our emotional experiences and expression and how does the primacy of learning over instinct apply to basic emotions? This debate still flourishes about all emotions, including anger.

Most research supporting the universality hypothesis comes from cross-cultural studies on recognition of affective facial cues or voice intonations. In these studies, research subjects are asked to identify the emotion that is being expressed by a confederate from a different culture who has been asked to express an emotion through facial muscles or voice intonations. The subjects choose the emotion they observe from a list of emotions. Critics of this methodology point out that the various words for emotions are translated from English into the respective languages of the research subject. It is possible that the researchers' translations do not accurately reflect how the subjects would label the emotions they perceived in their own language. This could be avoided, however, by using an open-ended format. The methodology of choosing emotions from a list restricts the research subjects' choices to words translated from English and does not allow the subjects to choose from their own vocabulary. Also, not all subjects in these experiments accurately perceive the emotion that the confederate expresses. Perception is subjective and not universal. Thus, learning may influence the process.

The support for cultural influences on emotions comes not from empirical research, but from in-depth studies of a culture by anthropologists living among the group studied, or from linguistic analyses of the meaning of emotional words from a culture's language. These research methods rely on native informants, in-depth interviews, and logical analysis. Also, they often focus on exotic cultures. These research methods do not show whether the different vocabulary words represent the same emotional experience.

Ekman (1974, 1994) listed anger as one of the six basic prototypical human emotions along with sadness, happiness, fear, surprise, and disgust, which all humans experience, whatever their culture. Kemper (1987, 1991) identifies four emotions as universal: anger, satisfaction, fear, and sadness. However, all theorists who posit sets of universal human emotions consider anger a universal emotion.

Despite the volumes written on emotion, precious little cross-cultural research exists that explores how people experience emotions across cultures. The one exception has been the programmatic research by Scherer and colleagues (Scherer, 1988; Scherer & Wallbott, 1994; Scherer, Wallbott, & Summerfield, 1986). These researchers attempted to explore the similarities of phenomenological experiences across emotions and across cultures. Their methodology included asking people to answer questions concerning particular incidents involving their experiences of each of the basic emotions of anger, fear, sadness, disgust, shame, guilt, and joy. The questions entailed rating each emotional experience on the following dimensions: the time since the emotional episode occurred (which the researchers believed implied the frequency of the emotion), the duration of the episode, the intensity of the episode, their attempts to control the experience of the emotion, the emotion's effect on their relationships with others, sympathetic-arousal sensations, parasympathetic-arousal sensations, the sensation of temperature while feeling the emotion, whether they approached or avoided the eliciting stimulus, types of changes in their nonverbal expressive behavior, and changes in the paralinguistic aspects of their voice while experiencing the emotion. Their most recent study (Scherer & Wallbott, 1994) questioned more than 2,900 participants in 37 countries. The results indicated a very large statistical main effect on the dependent measures for the type of emotion. The main effects for country and the interaction of emotions by country were significant but accounted for very little of the variance compared with the main effect for emotions. They interpreted this to mean that a diverse sample throughout the world describes emotions in very similar ways. The similarities found in the experiences of the emotions are much greater than the influencing factor of culture on emotional experiences.

A summary of Scherer and Wallbott's (1994) results appears in Table 3.2. The columns compare various emotions to anger, and the rows represent the dependent variables by which the participants rated their emotional experiences. The description of anger that results from these comparisons reveals more about the nature of anger than all the definitions previously discussed. This research describes a number of characteristics of anger as follows:

Frequency
Participants were asked how long ago the emotional event occurred. Scherer and Wallbott inferred that one's choosing recent emotional episodes meant that such emotions occurred more frequently than if one chose events from further back in time. From Table 3.2 it appears that anger is more frequent than fear, shame, or sadness. Given the greater frequency of anger, it is surprising that anxiety and depressive disorders have received more attention. Perhaps anger occurs too frequently for people to consider it a disorder. Anger is as frequent as joy, guilt, and disgust.

Duration
Anger episodes are shorter than episodes of sadness, guilt, or joy but longer than fear episodes.

Table 3.2
The Relationship of Anger to Other Emotions

					Anger is						
Frequency	Duration	Intensity	Control Attempts	Effects on Relationships	Sympathetic Arousal	Para-sympathetic Arousal	Felt Temperature	Approach or Avoidance	Verbal Expression	Paralinguistic Expression	than
more frequent	longer than	equally intense	fewer attempts	more negative	less aroused	less aroused	hotter	less withdrawal	more expressive	more change	**than fear**
more frequent	shorter than	less intense	fewer attempts	more negative	more aroused	less aroused	hotter	less withdrawal	more expressive	more change	**than sadness**
equally frequent	shorter than	more intense	fewer attempts	more negative	more aroused	less aroused	hotter	less withdrawal	more expressive	more change	**than guilt**
more frequent	equal to	more intense	fewer attempts	more negative	more aroused	equally aroused	colder	less withdrawal	more expressive	more change	**than shame**
equally frequent	longer than	more intense	fewer attempts	more negative	more aroused	equally aroused	hotter	less withdrawal	more expressive	more change	**than disgust**
equally frequent	shorter than	less intense	more attempts	more negative	more aroused	more aroused	less warm	less approach	less expressive	more change	**than joy**

Note: These findings are based on the cross cultural research of Scherer and Wollbott (1994).

Intensity
Anger and fear are equally intense, but anger is less intense than sadness or joy and more intense than shame or guilt.

Attempts to Control the Emotion
Participants in this research reported fewer attempts to control the experience of anger than all other emotions except joy, for obvious reasons. This implies that people with anger problems may be less likely to perceive the anger as a problem than people who suffer from other emotional excesses. Also, angry clients may not wish to change their anger since they do not see it as a problem, and clinicians may need to persuade them that their anger needs to be controlled. This finding is similar to our clinical experience, and we discuss this topic at greater length in chapter 17 and 18.

Effect on Interpersonal Relationships
People describe anger as more likely to have a negative influence on interpersonal relationships than any other emotion. The clinical implications of this finding are that angry persons may need to rebuild their relationships because of the acrimony that has resulted. One aspect that we propose distinguishes those with anger disorders from normal people is a failure to perceive the negative effect of anger on relationships.

Sympathetic Arousal
Anger results in more sympathetically aroused sensations than any other emotions except fear. Given the intensity of sympathetic arousal in anger, relaxation techniques may be a crucial part of any treatment program. Relaxation is a successful treatment for anxiety but not recommended for depression or guilt since these elicit little sympathetic arousal. Other researchers have found that experiences of anger produced greater cardiovascular reactivity than did fear, joy, or sadness (Sinha, Lovallo & Parsons, 1992).

Parasympathetic Arousal
Anger is associated with less parasympathetic arousal than fear, sadness, or guilt. It results in an equal amount of parasympathetic arousal as shame and disgust but less arousal than joy. Perhaps the pattern of physiological arousal explains the medical complaints that result from excessive anger. Anger resulted in high sympathetic arousal and lower parasympathetic arousal, whereas fear resulted in higher physiological arousal but also high parasympathetic arousal. This pattern of high sympathetic arousal with low counterbalancing parasympathetic arousal may help explain why anger is associated with cardiovascular disease more than anxiety is. It may also explain why the anger literature fails to mention gastrointestinal complaints, even though gastrointestinal disorders such as ulcerative colitis have frequently been associated with anxiety.

Felt Temperature

Physiologically, anger is experienced "hotter" than all negative emotions except shame. Subjects felt warmer when experiencing joy. Although the scoring system used by Scherer and Wallbott (1994) resulted in a numerical score indicating greater felt temperature for joy, participants used different words to describe their sensations. The word *hot* was used to describe anger, whereas *warm* was used to describe joy. Fear and sadness, conversely, were described as feeling *cold*.

Approach–Avoidance of Eliciting Stimuli

Anger is experienced as less likely to lead to withdrawal from the eliciting stimuli and more likely to lead to approaching the eliciting stimuli than all emotions except joy. Obviously, people prefer to approach joy-causing stimuli. The tendency for anger to lead to approach behaviors and not withdrawal clearly differentiates anger from other emotions that are the targets of psychotherapy. This finding suggests that angry clients may more likely respond to triggering events impulsively, and intervention to promote response inhibition may be an important component of anger treatment.

Verbal Expression

This quality refers to the desire to talk and actual talking about the emotional experience. Anger is a very expressive emotion. It is more expressive than all emotions except joy. Thus, when people experience anger they are more likely to engage in expression and discuss the feeling or its activating events than with most other emotive experiences.

Paralinguistic Expression

This quality of an emotion refers to changes in the paralinguistic qualities of a person's voice when they speak. Anger results in more paralinguistic changes in one's speech than any other emotion. These qualities of verbal expression and paralinguistic expression, taken together, are likely to be perceived by the listener as negative or intimidating and therefore may contribute to angry persons' interpersonal difficulties. Clinically, this implies that teaching new forms of responding, such as assertiveness training, may be a necessary treatment component for those with anger problems.

Surprisingly, Scherer and Wallbott's (1994) findings indicated that some variables show anger is closer to joy than to any other emotion. This is evident by the ratings on expression variables, control, duration, temperature, and approach–withdrawal tendencies. On the other hand, anger is similar to fear in only two respects: its intensity and the degree of sympathetic arousal. Thus, anger more closely resembles joy than fear. This may explain why some authors have described anger as a positive emotion (e.g., Danesh, 1977; Schimmel, 1979). Scherer and Wallbott did not ask their participants to rate the emotional experiences as positive or negative. Comparisons of a semantic differential across a variety of cultures would be helpful.

The research by Scherer and his colleagues (Scherer, 1988, 1993; Scherer & Wallbott, 1994; Scherer, Wallbott, & Summerfield, 1986) has been more beneficial and informative than any other research to help us define anger and understand how it differs from other emotions. They caution, however, that their results could be biased since they used university students in all their samples. Some aspects of Western culture might be communicated by a shared academic culture and thus influence the results. Because the academic community in any country is more likely to be exposed to Western culture, the selection of subjects may have over-represented Western influences. The possibility exists that uneducated persons from different countries might show greater differences in emotions than subjects selected from universities. Research using the Scherer methodology would also be useful with clinical samples and would aid in the development of a profile for disordered anger.

Another research strategy that would help determine the universality of emotions would be rating emotional words on the semantic differential dimensions of evaluation (*pleasantness* versus *unpleasantness*), potency (*powerful* versus *powerless*), and activity (*fast, lively* versus *slow, quiet*). Many emotion theorists propose that a two-dimensional model of emotional experiences best accounts for the research data. These dimensions are pleasantness and activity. MacKinnon and Keating (1989) asked American and Canadian college students to rate 99 emotional words on three dimensions of the semantic differential. They concluded that a two-factor model of pleasantness and activity could account for the variance in ratings of most emotions. Anger and fear were similar on these dimensions. Potency accounted for little variance in the rating of all emotional words but appeared to distinguish anger from fear clearly, with anger words receiving ratings of higher potency. This study is limited to two similar cultures. A sample of subjects from a wider variety of cultures could strengthen the relationship between anger and potency. Such a study could provide preliminary evidence that an additional characteristic of anger in comparison to other emotions is high power or potency.

All do not share the opinion that anger or any other emotion is universal. Some sociologists and anthropologists would propose that culture, not biology, influences the nature and extent of our emotional experiences and expression. The development of social constructivism within psychology (Gergen, 1985) has extended the idea that emotions are socially constructed as well (see Averill, 1980).

Wierzbicka (1992a, 1992b), a linguist, entered this debate through her search for linguistic prime concepts. A *prime concept* is similar to a prime number in mathematics. It is an idea that cannot be divided into two smaller concepts. Wierzbicka identified several cultures that have no word for anger. She demonstrated how the words initially translated as *anger* represented emotions that have no translation in English. Wierzbicka argues that emotions are private experiences that are difficult to translate from one language to another. Even the notion of differentiating emotions from other feelings or sensations may be a uniquely English concept that does not necessarily emerge in other languages (1992a). For example, Polish and other Eastern European languages make no distinction between the types of feelings that English calls *emotions,* such as anger or fear, and types of feelings that are *sensations,* such as cold or pain. She concludes that the evaluation of emotion as some special category of feeling is an English-language concept and not a human universal.

Wierzbicka (1992b) also attempts to break down the meaning of emotional words in different languages. She concludes that the only prime concept that refers to feelings is *good versus bad.* All other emotional words do not differ greatly by denoting different sensations or phenomena. They define only (a) the different situations or activating events that elicit the emotions, (b) the different behavioral reactions that accompany the emotion, or (c) the evaluations of the activating event that lead to the emotion-arousing state. Emotional words convey little about our phenomenology and more about the situation, appraisal, and behavioral reaction that accompany the emotional state. It is not surprising, therefore, that psychologists following the classical view have attempted to define emotional states according to preceding events or behavioral reactions. Because we define them this way in English, we assume this is the way people define them in other languages.

Wierzbicka (1992a, 1992b) concludes that anger is not a prime concept linguistically and "there is no reason to think that the English word *anger* represents a *pan-human prototype.*" She takes an extreme constructivist approach that emotions are idiosyncratic to cultures.

Substantial literature exists on the sociology of emotions that psychologists and psychotherapists rarely read or reference (see Kemper, 1991, for a review). Accordingly, emotional scripts consist of socially derived schemas that include the eliciting stimuli, the evaluations and beliefs about those events, culturally sanctioned emotional experiences, the physical reactions, social expression, and behavioral reactions to the emotions (Abelson, 1981; deSousa, 1980; Fehr & Russell, 1984; Sabini & Silver, 1982; Tomkins, 1979). We have found the script theory of emotions helpful in understanding anger.

Hochschild (1983) presents the most complex theory. She posited that people choose, often unconsciously, from the culturally available and sanctioned options of emotional states according to four categories of perceptions. These include the perceptions of motivation, agency, value, and the relationship between the self and the agent. Emotions are experiences that match prescribed combinations of perceptions. For example, in one culture anger could be the emotional experience tied to these five perceptions: "I want to be treated with respect; I do not have X's respect; not having X's respect is terrible; X is wrong for not respecting me; X is a less worthwhile person than I am." Kemper points out that such theories can help psychologists because the mechanisms by which the culture has its effect, the five categories of perceptions (or cognitions), are similar to the mediating variables that cognitive behavioral therapies hypothesized cause emotions.

The sociological theories of emotions also provide some clues to suggest when people are motivated to change their emotions. Hochschild (1979) proposed a concept called *emotional deviance*, which represents the person's perception that the emotion experienced differs from one that is socially proscribed or sanctioned. Thoits (1985, 1989) proposed that people are motivated to change their behavior, physiological reactions, situation, or emotions when they experience emotional deviance. The recognition that one's emotional reactions are inappropriate or socially unacceptable becomes a primary motivation for emotional change.

Several hypotheses about the diagnosis and treatment of anger result from these sociological perspectives on emotion. First, cultures and subcultures have rules about which affective states the group sanctions and which it does not. Second, people in subcultures may fail to recognize that their emotions are regarded as deviant by the larger culture or by members of other subcultures. One's subculture may proscribe an angry feeling while the mainstream culture does not. For example, responding with anger to perceived disrespect in a gang environment may be reinforced. However, a similar anger reaction to negative feedback in the workplace would be viewed as deviant. Third, people may have failed to learn through their family's socialization or other acculturation experiences the scripts that guide the emotional reactions proscribed by the mainstream culture. They may be perplexed and frustrated by their inability to perceive others' emotional reactions. Such individuals may experience confusion because they do not know what to feel. Fourth, people may be surprised when they respond emotionally with a script sanctioned by their subculture and this emotional experience is perceived as deviant by the mainstream culture. Consequently, they may believe their emotional reactions are invalidated by members of the mainstream culture.

Another implication of script theory concerns the number of scripts people learn from their family group or their subculture. Individuals may have learned culturally unacceptable scripts or failed to learn accepted ones because of deviant socialization through their family, clan, or subgroup. Since emotional scripts evolve in a culture across time, cultures may contain many or few scripts for each emotional family. That is, there may be several variations of scripts for anger, guilt, sadness, and so on. Cultures could fail to contain a script or schema for an adaptive form of anger. We believe that the emotional-script concept is helpful in understanding maladaptive anger reactions and in treating anger disorders. We would hypothesize that American culture possesses too few scripts concerning the prototype of anger and as a result many people respond with an anger script that is maladaptive. Chapter 14 provides a more detailed discussion of the implication of this topic for clinical practice.

Cultures and their languages vary greatly in their distinctions between affective states. Therapists need to be aware of how the emotional script for anger (or any other emotional state) is valued in a patient's culture or subculture and what alternative scripts are available from that culture. If the patient's cultural, subcultural, or family group has no alternative script for a functional emotional response, the therapist should attempt to build a schema for them.

The sociological challenges to the idea that emotions are universal suggests that groups will not experience anger equally because anger is not an idea they all share. People may express anger differently because their scripts for anger may differ in their subculture. These theories suggest that looking at cultural differences in anger should yield large differences in how people define, experience, and express what we call anger.

A Description of Anger

We believe that anger is a universal emotion, experienced more similarly around the world than differently. However, there are many ways to express anger, and as Wierzbicka pointed out, affective words seem to differ in the situations that elicit the emotion or the intensity of the emotion. Although humans experience the basic emotion anger, the scripts for its expression may be cultural. Perhaps a compromise is warranted. To quote Lewis Carroll, "All have won and all must have prizes."

However, cultures differ in the number and variety of prototypes they have for secondary emotions in the anger family. Since prototypes are individualistic and "fuzzy," cultures may differ in the number of reactions described in their language. Some cultures or subcultures may have few words or scripts in the anger family, and therefore people have limited scripts to choose from when anger is experienced. Other cultures may have abundant scripts in the anger family, giving people many alternatives to choose from to adapt their emotional experience to the provoking event. Different scripts affect which circumstances elicit anger, how intensely anger will be experienced, and what mode(s) of anger expression the cultural group sanctions. Persons with limited scripts for anger might be predisposed to experience more intense than moderate anger. Also, people may be predisposed to express anger aggressively if the only scripts sanctioned by their culture are aggressive ones.

Based on all the research reviewed, we can describe how anger differs from other emotions. What follows is not so much a definition of *anger*, in the classical sense, but a description of anger.

1. Anger is a relatively frequent emotion (Scherer & Wallbott, 1994).
2. Anger is a negative or unpleasant emotion (MacKinnon & Keating, 1989).

3. Anger is as intense as fear but less intense than sadness (Scherer & Wallbott, 1994).

4. Anger lasts longer than most other affective states (Scherer & Wallbott, 1994).

5. Anger includes high sympathetic arousal (Scherer & Wallbott, 1994; Sinha, Lovallo & Parsons, 1992); though not as high as fear, it is higher than most emotions.

6. Anger includes lower parasympathetic arousal than all other emotions (Scherer & Wallbott, 1994).

7. Anger is experienced as "hot" (Scherer & Wallbott, 1994).

8. There may be a wide variety of behaviors to express anger, and it is associated with greater variability of behavioral expression than other emotions are (J. Deffenbacher, 1997; J. Deffenbacher, Oetting, Lynch, & Morris, 1996).

9. It leads to verbal expression more than any emotion except joy (Scherer & Wallbott, 1994).

10. Anger elicits the strongest paralinguistic changes in one's voice of any emotion (Scherer & Wallbott, 1994).

11. People feel little desire to change or control their experience of anger. The only emotion that people are less likely to want to change is joy (Scherer & Wallbott, 1994).

12. Anger produces a strong tendency to approach rather than avoid the eliciting stimuli, surpassed in the approach tendency only by joy (Scherer & Wallbott, 1994).

13. Anger includes an experience of greater power or potency than either the eliciting threat or the object of the anger (MacKinnon & Keating, 1989).

14. People perceive anger as negatively affecting their interpersonal relationships more than any other emotion (Scherer & Wallbott, 1994).

15. One's anger can be displaced and targeted at persons other than the anger-provoking person.

Other aspects of the description are more tentative and may not apply to all anger experiences but are usually part of most people's anger prototype. Therefore, one can say that anger often includes one or all of the following:

16. Thoughts concerning perceived threats to high, unstable self-esteem (Baumeister, Smart, & Boden, 1996);

17. The perception of an injustice or grievance against oneself (Tedeschi & Nesler, 1993);

18. The perception of another's blameworthiness (Clore & Ortony, 1991; Clore, Ortony, Dienes, & Frjida, 1993); and/or

19. A desire to harm the transgressor (Rubin, 1986; Tedeschi & Nesler, 1993).

Classical Categories, Definitions, Cultural Universals, or Prototypical Scripts

This chapter ends where it began. Attempts to define the subcategories of anger either logically, rationally, or empirically have led to a series of conflicting and contradictory classification schemes. Russell and Fehr (1994) proposed an alternative view of how people classify anger and other emotions. People may fail to label emotional experiences the same way. Each of us, however, has a prototype or schema of what each word means. Prototypes, rather than definitions, may provide the meaning of emotional words. The use of prototypes rather than definitions allows for inconsistencies in the data.

Russell and Fehr (1994) proposed that people know what emotion they are experiencing from prototypical experiences that they use as references. A prototype differs from a template or a logical definition because a prototype defines the best example of something. Templates or logical definitions require that each feature or some essential feature of the template or definition be present for a specific case to be included in the category. Prototypes are "fuzzy." A prototype does not have to have all the characteristics of the concept to be considered in the same class. For example, the prototype of a bird would be an animal that has wings, a beak, and feathers, and that flies and lays eggs. While an eagle or a robin fits every characteristic of the prototype, a kiwi or an ostrich fits several characteristics of the prototype but has some distinguishing features—yet they are still birds. A person's anger prototype might include situations that elicit the emotion, the experience of the emotion, the physiological reactions accompanying the experience, and action tendencies to cope with the experience. A person's schema or construct used to describe an emotional experience may fail to include all the characteristics of the prototype and still be a member of the prototype. Also, each person may have his or her own prototype. One's culture or language assumes some degree of overlap in the features each person uses to express the prototype, but each person may have a different prototype. Thus, the long list of features used to define anger may be a legitimate part of some people's experience to be included in the prototype for anger. This theory suggests that people share a prototype of the characteristics of the anger experience. The characteristics people share may not be the same in each case, but some crucial elements of the prototype will be present in each case.

Prototypes need not be related in a hierarchical order to each other. Rather, people's definitions for affective states have "fuzzy" boundaries (Russell & Fehr, 1994). People may use different words to describe the same emotional experience. The emotional vocabulary in a subculture may not be learned to the extent that all people share the same prototypical schema for all these words. Rather, one learns prototypes and some idiosyncratic scripts that one can experience in place of anger. "To know the concept of anger is to know a script (to be able to simulate a scenario) in which prototypical antecedents, feelings, expressions, behaviors, physiological changes, and consequences are laid out in a causal and temporal sequence" (Russell & Fehr, 1994, p. 202).

Russell and Fehr's prototype theory explains how speakers of English (and we assume other languages) use words in the anger family inconsistently. It also suggests that people may have several emotional scripts that they can employ in a given anger-provoking situation. This prototype theory better fits the data than the classical categories theory and has clinical utility. However, it does not clearly define anger, indicate what characteristics comprise the prototype of anger, or explain what characteristics differentiate the prototype of anger from the prototypes of other emotions. The characteristics of the prototype, like the words in our language and the classical theories, have focused on eliciting stimuli, evaluations, and behavioral consequences.

In our work with angry clients, we have noticed clients' difficulties in finding consistent accurate words to express their anger. Our discussion of emotional word definitions and prototypes suggests the reasons clients have such difficulties. Clinicians can consider several important strategies while interviewing angry clients.

First, people may not share the same prototype for the same emotion. Therefore, practitioners must ask careful questions to understand what a particular client means by any emotional word. Second, the words clients use to express their anger may reflect only one characteristic of the prototype of anger, such as the eliciting events, the behavioral consequences, or the intensity of an emotion. Other aspects of the prototype may not be represented for them with the word they used. Thus, *envy* and *jealously* convey the eliciting event, *revenge* refers to the desired reaction, and *annoyance* or *rage* indicates the intensity. To know one of these aspects as a practitioner does not ensure you know the others. For example, can one simultaneously experience annoyance and revenge with the intent to seek damages? Can one experience annoyance and envy simultaneously, versus rage and envy? Clinicians need to help clients identify other aspects of the script for the emotion they experience and not assume that clients' words share all the characteristics of the anger prototype.

Conclusions

The lack of a consistent definition of anger and its related concepts has hampered scientific inquiry into the subject area. In these first three chapters, we have examined the definitional confusion surrounding anger and have proposed several definitions that will form the foundation for discussions presented in the remaining chapters of this book. We realize that the definitions proposed in chapter 2 may still be inadequate as a means by which to describe some types of experiences and behaviors encountered in clinical practice and research. This may be especially true regarding the differentiation of anger from aggression—the demarcation line is not always clear. The complex relationship between anger and aggression is taken up more thoroughly in Part II.

In spite of the challenges involved, we believe that in order for our understanding of anger to progress, it is crucial for researchers to consider definitional issues carefully. As noted, practitioners would also benefit from a careful consideration of definitions used in identifying problems and from the development of a consistent, shared vocabulary with their clients.

Part II

Anger and Aggression

4

Theories of Anger and Aggression

As mentioned in chapter 1, scientists, clinicians, and laypeople frequently confuse the constructs of anger and aggression. Professionals often use these words interchangeably. When you hear the word *anger,* the two words *and aggression* usually follow it. The behavioral sciences, and the field of cognitive behavior therapy in particular, separate human experience into thoughts, feelings, and behaviors. The relationship between emotions and behaviors becomes muddled because of the attempt by professionals and theoreticians to separate these constructs. As we said in chapter 2, anger is an emotion, and aggression is a behavior. One possible link between anger and aggression is motive. For several generations psychology has paid little attention to motives. This lack of attention has contributed to the confusion between anger and aggression.

Emotions are not defined only by the way one feels. Most emotion theorists (see Ekman & Davidson, 1994) define emotions as complex structures of thoughts and feelings that prepare one for action. Emotions prepare and motivate organisms for action in response to changes in their environment. As LeDoux (2002), the famous researcher of emotions and the brain, puts it, "incentives do their motivating by activating emotional systems. Actions motivated by emotional arousal have a purpose—to deal with the emotion being aroused" (p. 236). Thus, every emotion produces a motive, and the motives produce action potentials. Therefore, people cannot consider emotions without reference to what motives they arouse and what actions people take to satisfy those motives when they feel or experience emotions. The next three chapters will explore the relationship between anger and aggression and the motives that mediate the two constructs.

Anger may lead to aggression, but it is not aggression. Averill (1983) used the metaphor of a blueprint for the relationship between anger and aggression. Having a blueprint makes it easier to build a house, but you have to want to build the house. The blueprint provides information concerning which aggressive behaviors are acceptable and when. This we learn from our social environment. However, the blueprint does not build the house. Getting angry does not necessarily lead to aggression. You can build a house without a blueprint, but it is more difficult; you can be aggressive without being angry. Conversely, you can have a blueprint and not build a house; you can be angry and not behave aggressively.

Despite this close correspondence between what people feel and their desire to act, and the ubiquitous verbal linking of *anger* and *aggression,* all anger episodes do not lead to aggressive responses. While anger may prepare the body for the fight, it usually does not lead to aggression. In the present chapter influential theories of aggression are reviewed. The status of the relationship between anger and aggression will also be discussed and the limitations of the hostile–instrumental aggression distinction will be introduced.

Influential Theories

Evolutionary Theory

Charles Darwin (1872/1965) may have been the first modern scientist to propose a direct, necessary, and adaptive connection between the arousal of anger and the expression of aggressive behavior. For Darwin, the arousal of anger led to involuntary muscle movement involved in its expression. All members of a species share a common expressive pattern of emotions and the ability to recognize such patterns in others. Similarities in emotional expression allow for inter- and intra-species recognition of affective states. This recognition has survival value and enables animals to freeze, flee, or fight when they recognize anger in others. Therefore, the expression of anger communicates to potential enemies that the animal or person is angry and preparing for aggression. The communicative features of anger may drive off potential intruders. The automatic link among anger, its expression, and the desire to attack ensured the enemy that signs of anger were associated with and likely followed by aggression. Thus, for Darwin, defending against and repelling attackers is the primary motive behind anger. The likelihood that expressing anger would threaten the enemy is anger's crucial function.

> But animals of all kinds, and their progenitors before them, when attacked or threatened by an enemy, have exerted their utmost powers in

fighting and in defending themselves. Unless an animal does thus act, or has its intention, or at least the desire, to attack its enemy, it cannot properly be said to be enraged. (Darwin, 1872/1965, p. 74)

While the experience of anger did not ensure an aggressive response, it did ensure the aggressive desire or drive. Aggression motives then became a biological or instinctual reaction. Darwin did not label this drive or discuss its characteristics very much, but he did believe that the aspects of anger that he described were universal. Perhaps Darwin's description of anger leading to an aggressive impulse accounts for the behavioral sciences' failure to separate the constructs of anger and aggression. If a desire to aggress is part of the experience and excitation of anger, aggression may be seen as part of the same construct. However, the impulse to act does not require action, and animals and people may evaluate the potential for harming their enemy, the chances for successfully repelling them, or the possibility of receiving greater retaliation. Such evaluations, along with social and learning history, will determine if the impulse leads to action. The idea that humans have universal and automatic impulses to aggress is enticing and is included in other models of anger.

Instinctual Theories

William James's functionalist approach to psychology was strongly influenced by Charles Darwin's adaptation. However, James's view of emotions differed from Darwin's in that James emphasized the emotional experience more than behavioral potentials aroused by emotions. Both Darwin and James thought of emotions primarily regarding the physical body. Although James believed physical sensations came first, he did believe cognitive processes recognized these physiological changes. However, he believed that these physical changes were the most important element of emotion and were largely biologically determined. James (1890) also believed that anger and aggression were related and that aggression was primarily instinctual. He endorsed the hydraulic model by which anger created an energy that fueled aggression and had to be diverted into instinctual behavior to be discharged or released. When that failed, it would manifest itself as aggression. Therefore, James recognized anger in reference only to aggression. He believed that aggression had been bred into the human race and that it would be nearly impossible to "breed it out" (James, 1890).

S. Freud (1917/1963) shared the belief that anger was instinctual and was a less intense expression of aggression. Similar to James, Freud believed aggression would result if we did not release the energy produced by anger. This notion of a hydraulic buildup of energy that required draining or releasing differed from Darwin's idea that, for survival value, anger and aggression were aroused by threat. Freud cited yet another internal construct responsible for aggression, the "death instinct," which was composed of "impulses aiming at destruction [or] death" (S. Freud, 1915/1963). However, the purpose or survival value of Freud's Thanatos drive remains unclear and differs considerably from Darwin's evolutionary approach to emotions. Like James, Freud insisted that an instinct must be redirected. However, Freud believed that the death instinct moved us toward suicide. To prevent suicide, the organism had to aim its aggression outward. Thus, the instinct turned outward to become aggression (S. Freud, 1915/1963). This has led many to assume aggression comes from a negative view of self. However, scientific research has failed to support this hypothesis, and controversy remains only among those unfamiliar with the data (Baumeister, 1997; Bushman, & Baumeister, 1998).

Unlike Darwin, James and Freud failed to discuss the survival value for their version of the aggressive drive. Darwin's model appears to have obvious survival value. The impulse to strike and repel an attacker has a protective consequence, hence the survival value for humans and animals. Neither James nor Freud presented the survival value of the hydraulic build up of an aggressive drive. The ethologist Lorenz (1966) attempted to rectify this problem in his influential book *On Aggression.* Lorenz proposed a similar aggressive drive. From his observation of animal aggression, Lorenz concluded that aggression had many useful functions in the competition between species and within species. By showing the adaptive value of aggression in so many species, Lorenz presented a convincing argument that the aggression motive evolved to ensure survival. Lorenz, like Freud and James, used the model of biological drives like food and hunger as a basis for the aggressive drive. This involved the build up of aggressive energy and the need to release that energy.

Darwin, James, Freud, and Lorenz, four monumental figures in the history of psychology, viewed anger as instinctual and something to be controlled, lest it manifest itself as aggression. Thus, the nineteenth- and early-twentieth-century scientific community relegated anger to be a part of the construct of aggression. Even though anger is more common than aggressive actions (Averill, 1983; Tafrate, Kassinove, & Dundin, 2002), this model, in part, was integrated into behaviorism (Dollard, Doob, Miller, Mowrer, & Sears, 1939; Salzinger, 1995).

Frustration–Aggression Hypothesis

Influenced by Darwin, James, and Freud, Dollard et al. (1939) proposed the frustration-aggression hypothesis. This model stated that frustration, the blockage or interference of a goal, automatically produced an urge to aggress against the source of the frustration. Although Darwin saw the function of anger expression and the desire to harm others as adaptive, Darwin's model did not specify how animals perceived attack or whether other stimuli would excite anger and its concomitant urge to aggress. The frustration–aggression hypothesis is more specific than Darwin's theory. Stimuli that represent an obstacle to one's goals can elicit anger. The frustration–aggression hypothesis has not been in favor in recent years because the theory is misinterpreted as a stimulus—response model with no mediating or moderating variables such as appraisals, thoughts, or evaluations—variables that became popular after the cognitive revolution in psychology. However, the frustration–aggression hypothesis was more complicated than a simple stimulus–response theory. Dollard and his colleagues believed that only the frustration of goals that people hoped for and expected led to an aggressive response. Aggression followed only when one wanted and expected that a goal was achievable. The frustration–aggression hypothesis also stressed the role of resentment in the development of aggression. And, the model recognized that expectations of retaliation or punishment for using aggression would produce fear that could inhibit aggression. It hypothesized a process called displacement, where the person aggresses against a safer target to achieve the desired retaliation.

A sociological theory consistent with the frustration–aggression hypothesis is social strain theory. It proposed that property crime resulted when elements of the social structure, such as prejudice or unequal access to societal resources, prevented people from realizing their hopes and desires. If society prevented a person from reaching their financial, material, or social goals, a person would resort to aggression to take those things for which they strove and to which they were entitled (Cloward & Ohlins, 1960; Merton, 1957). A revision of social strain theory by Agnew (1992) stated that the frustration must be sufficiently strong to produce political rebellion or social deviance along with aggression.

Historical analyses of the American, French, and Russian revolutions have supported social strain theory and are consistent with the frustration–aggression hypothesis. All three major social and political revolutions occurred when sudden economic downturns dashed rising expectations among the populace (Davies, 1962). Improving economic and political conditions increased people's expectations for a better life. The denial of these expected advancements caused frustration and violent overthrows of the respective governments. Using the frustration–aggression hypothesis, Caplan (1970) hypothesized that black men who participated in the riots of the 1960s had better educations than their nonparticipating peers. Their education had led to increased expectations that were then unrealized and increased their resentment and willingness to participate in the riots.

More recent analyses of Muslim extremists' involvement in the September 11, 2001, attacks on the World Trade Center and Pentagon and other terrorist acts (Krueger & Maleckova, 2003, 2002) supported the frustration–aggression hypothesis. The poor, uneducated, and displaced youth do not join modern terrorist groups as often as suggested by the media. Members of the educated class with higher expectations for economic and social advancements who encountered obstacles to achieving their hopes have joined terrorist groups and committed violent acts. Islamic countries that produce terrorists have higher education rates and better economies than those that do not.

The frustration–aggression hypothesis did not attempt to explain aggression as an unconscious reflex for minor discomforts and frustrations. The theory recognized the cognitive variables of raising expectations and the probability of achieving outcomes. It leads to the understanding of cataclysmic social changes that occur when people's hopes for a better life, through economic and social equity, evaporate. Although Dollard et al. (1939) presented the urge to aggress (that emerges from frustration) as a motive, they did not describe the motive in much detail. The motive was to eliminate or overcome the frustration.

Although the frustration–aggression hypothesis and the revised social strain version in sociology and criminology (Agnew, 1992; Caplan, 1970; Cloward & Ohlins, 1960; Davies, 1962; Merton, 1957) focused on how the frustration of major goals led to aggression, they failed to account for how more–mundane frustration leads to aggression. Psychology needed a theory that explained how stimuli such as pain, temperature variations, and discomfort, in addition to denied economic advancement and social status, led to aggression. Berkowitz's (1983, 1993, 2003) more-comprehensive theory attempted to explain how such a wide array of stimuli could result in aggression. Berkowitz proposed that frustration, pain, discomfort, or social strain also produced negative emotion, and the negative emotion mediated the relationship between frustration and aggression. Berkowitz did not believe that experiencing anger was a prerequisite for aggression. In his view, the arousal of negative affect occurs very early in the affective process, even before the person has sufficient time to make appraisals that differentiate the various emotions. Thus, the aggressive impulse or urge occurs early in the sequence of psychological events. Also, in Berkowitz's model, any negative affect, if strong enough, can lead to aggression. This model sharply contrasts with the traditional models of anger and aggression. In most other models (Averill, 1982; Baumeister, Smart, & Boden, 1996; A. A. Lazarus, 1989; Tedeschi & Nesler, 1993) people experience frustrations followed by attributions and appraisals concerning injustice, fairness, and the appropriateness of others' behavior. It is the anger that then produces a motive for aggression. For Berkowitz, anger has no greater relation to aggression than any other negative affect, all of which can produce aggression. Frustration leads to aggressive urges because it arouses anger, and anger is just a negative emotion. Any stimulus unpleasant enough to generate any negative emotion can produce aggressive urges (see Figure 4.1).

Berkowitz's model proposed that an unpleasant stimulus will elicit simultaneously an urge to escape and an urge to attack. Once these experiences are recognized, cognitive processes such as attributions, appraisals, and problem solving are activated. At this point a person's cognitions determine which emotion is experienced and what course of action he or she will take. Berkowitz's model relegates cognitive factors to a secondary role in emotional arousal. However, they play a central role in determining which emotion is aroused. Berkowitz's model does not propose that aggression is a consistent, required, or necessary reaction to unpleasant emotions or anger. The urge to aggress, although present, will have its intensity determined by biology and learning history. These components will interact cognitively,

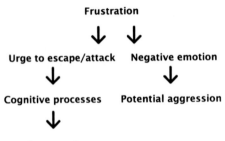

Frustration

Urge to escape/attack   Negative emotion

Cognitive processes   Potential aggression

**Awareness of
specific emotion**

Figure 4.1. Berkowitz's (1990)
Frustration-Aggression Model

emotionally, and motorically to determine whether aggression will occur or be inhibited. If Berkowitz's theory is correct, the desire to do harm to others is an integral, common part of the anger experience.

Although Berkowitz's theory sounds easy to understand, a critical component is the definition of the term *unpleasant stimulus*. Defining unpleasant stimuli by the behavior they elicit results in a tautology: that unpleasant stimuli cause aggressive behaviors, and we know the stimulus is unpleasant because it triggers aggression. How do we know that stimuli are unpleasant, independent of the behavior? This has not yet been worked out by behavioral scientists.

General Aggression Model

Considerable research exists in the social–psychological literature providing us with many facts about the variables that influence the occurrence of human aggression. Several theories have emerged from this research concerning human aggression. These include social learning theory (Bandura, 1977),[1] script theory (Kemper, 1991, p. 553),[2] excitation transfer theory (Zillmann, 2003),[3] and social interaction theory (Felson & Tedeschi, 1993).[4] Some of these theories, such as social learning theory fail to identify anger as

---

1. *Social learning theory* proposes that the origins of aggressive behavior are related to observational learning and that such behavior is maintained through external and self-reinforcement.

2. *Script theory* suggests that habitual behaviors are initially developed through social learning processes and when repeated successfully are stored in memory as programs that guide behavior in response to certain classes of events.

3. *Excitation transfer theory* identifies three factors that explain aggressive behavior: (a) activation of emotional arousal, (b) reinforcement history, and (c) higher order cognitive processes that monitor and inhibit behavior.

4. *Social interaction theory* views individuals as decision makers who impose harm or engage in coercive actions to achieve valued outcomes.

having a role in aggression. Others, such as script theory and social interaction theory view anger as increasing the likelihood of aggression.

Several cognitive theories of aggression identify cognitive variables proposed to arouse anger and elicit aggression. However, the theories fail to identify whether these variables' effect on aggression is mediated by anger being aroused first. Also while many of these theories have research support, they focus on one set of variables and fail to account for other variables that have been shown to influence aggression.

Anderson and Bushman (2002) attempted to condense all these theories and the information on the causes and correlates of anger into the General Aggression Model. They proposed that aggression occurs because of a number of personal, situational, social, biological, and psychological factors. Person variables such as traits, gender, attitudes, beliefs, values, and long-term goals contribute to the occurrence of aggression through the makeup of the person who is brought into a potentially aggressive situation. These traits interact with situational variables such as aggressive cues, provocations, pain, frustration, drugs, biological states, and incentives to cause aggression. Anderson and Bushman (2002) indicated that cognitive variables associated with stimulus cues and biological states will influence a person's emotional state and autonomic arousal. At this point the person evaluates the short-term and long-term outcomes associated with aggression and alternative responses. As a result of all these processes, aggression will or will not occur.

Anderson and Bushman (2002) suggested five reasons why anger can increase the probability of aggression. First, anger arousal will reduce a person's inhibitions to aggression. This occurs because the experience of anger provides a justification for aggression and the belief that the other person "deserved it." Also, anger may interfere with the higher order cognitive processes and reappraisal that might have led the person to focus on moral restraints or possible negative consequences. Second, the anger experience allows the person to remain primed to aggression over time. The continued rumination returns the person at least cognitively to the provocation and reactivates the emotional states associated with aggression. Third, like all emotions, anger provides an informational context that influences how ambiguous stimuli will be interpreted. During anger episodes people are more likely to perceive the target of their anger as attempting to harm them, and so focus on retaliation and view the target as blameworthy and condemnable.

Fourth, anger is likely to trigger or prime aggression-related thoughts, sensations, action potentials, and a whole knowledge structure that brings aggression into the person's mindset. The angry person will attend to anger-related and aggression-related aspects of the environment and thus selectively focus on aggressive solutions to problems. Fifth, the anger experience activates high emotional arousal. Thus, anger and aggression associations and knowledge structures are energized to action by the arousal.

This general aggression model integrates many scientific findings concerning aggression. The model acknowledges that variables may trigger aggression without a necessary pathway to anger. However, anger plays a central role in the model and many of the variables that the model postulates as influencing aggression also effect anger and may influence aggression through anger arousal. The General Aggression Model acknowledges the combined and unique contribution of anger in leading to aggression. We see the General Aggression Model as a general anger model as well. Most of the personal, situational, biological, and psychological factors that effect aggression also influence anger arousal. Clearly researchers have focused more on predicting aggressive responses and have paid little attention to whether or not stimuli affect aggression by first arousing anger.

Treatment Utility of Separating Anger and Aggression

Because many clients with both anger and aggression are coerced into treatment by the courts, their employers, or their families, we have found that psychotherapeutic interventions can produce a very quick decrease in aggressive behavior. However, our clients' anger remains. Defining anger and aggression separately has treatment utility. Separating the concepts encourages practitioners to target treatments at both aggression and anger. Consider a client who frequently offends others with obnoxious statements and occasionally pushes others out of his way to get what he wants. This client may behave aggressively because he has poor social skills or a selfish desire to attain his goals at others' expense. The client's aggression does not involve angry revenge motives. Such a person may experience negative feedback and be ostracized. Treatment for him may focus on making him aware of the consequences of his responses, and modeling, coaching, and rehearsing new responses. If, however, our hypothetical client enjoys pushing others because he is angry, resents people, and wants revenge, treating his social skills-deficits will be futile. However, resolving the anger could greatly improve his willingness to display the social skills he may already possess. We contend that differentiating aggression and anger, as outlined above, has significant treatment utility for clinicians.

Criminal courts throughout North America now commonly refer men arrested for domestic violence to domestic-violence groups. As addressed in more detail in the next chapter, there is disagreement as to whether or not anger management is an appropriate treatment for such individuals. Some practitioners focus treatment on issues related to power and control, while others focus on teaching clients emotional-control skills. While anger-management skills are important for many perpetrators, not all spouse abusers are angry. Jacobson and Gottman (1998) reported that one group of perpetrators had no physiological arousal associated with anger when they assaulted their victims. In fact, they appeared to have the response that predatory animals do when stalking their prey. We frequently see the referral of this type of offender to anger-management groups because it is assumed that anger and aggression are the same thing. Such referrals usually result in failure to control the offender's aggression, while misleading the legal system into thinking that some effective intervention has occurred. Our clinical experience suggests that aggressive individuals who do not experience significant anger episodes connected with their aggressive actions do not do well in anger-management groups and have a negative influence on other members of the group. Such people enjoy their aggression and usually distract other group members from focusing on anger control by extolling the benefits of aggression. The failure to make the distinction between anger and aggression in such cases results in ineffective treatment.

Another reason for targeting anger separately from aggressive behaviors is clients' consistent failure to improve their interpersonal relations even after they successfully eliminate their physical aggression or angry verbal expression. Our clinical experience suggests that clients can often reduce aggressive behavior in a few sessions. However, such angry–aggressive clients often maintain their anger, and even hatred, after they have stopped behaving aggressively. This residual anger leads to unsatisfactory marital, parental, peer, and work relationships. Reducing anger seems necessary to facilitate prosocial behavior. For example, one of us recently treated a family with a 15-year-old daughter who experienced intense anger at her parents for divorcing. She displayed violent outbursts such as punching holes in walls and throwing plates. A behavior-management program that reinforced periods of non-aggressive behavior and introduced costs for aggressive behavior quickly eliminated the violent outbursts. However, the adolescent remained extremely angry, showed no improvement in prosocial behaviors and communication with her parents, and continued to suffer from tension headaches. Interventions targeted at her anger were necessary before the young woman could mend her relationship with her parents. Most people we see in treatment with anger problems come because of family or relationship issues. The anger continues to poison their relationships even if they learn to control their aggression.

If the goal of therapy focuses on aggression reduction, the client, the courts, or the third-party payer may seek to end the therapy because the goals have been attained. However, we have found that in such cases the residual anger that we did not address in therapy is a good predictor of relapse of aggressive behaviors. If the anger contributes to the aggression, only temporary decreases in aggression may occur until the anger is successfully treated.

How Frequently Does Anger Lead to Aggression?

Factor Analytic Research

Aristotle (Loomis, 1943) was the first to notice that some people held their anger in and seethed while others let fly insults and missiles. Seneca (Basore,

1958) later expounded on this idea. The first modern scientist to support this notion empirically in the development of his anger-expression scales was Spielberger (1988). He found that factor analysis supported separate anger-in and anger-out scales. Since then, most attempts to measure anger have found that factor analysis has extracted different means of anger expression corresponding to this distinction. This includes the Buss-Durkee Hostility Inventory (Buss & Durkee, 1957), the Novaco Anger Scales (Novaco, 2003), the Multidimensional Anger Inventory (Siegel, 1986), and the Multidimensional School Anger Inventory (Furlong & Smith, 1998). Our work in designing an anger-assessment device supports the idea that anger and aggression are different constructs. Factor analysis of our Anger Disorders Scale (ADS; DiGiuseppe & Tafrate, 2004) found three higher order broad factors representing reactivity–verbal expression, vengeance–physical aggression, and anger that is held in. Also, J. Deffenbacher, Oetting, Lynch, and Morris (1996) developed an anger-expression scale and found support for an anger-in rumination and an anger-in suppression scale. They also found many other nonaggressive means that people use to express their anger. Although researchers have found scales supporting different types of outward anger expression, they have uniformly found support for a factor of the non-outward expression of anger. Thus, we can safely conclude from this research that not all anger leads to aggression.

Epidemiological Studies of Anger Episodes

Research by Averill (1982, 1983), Kassinove (Kassinove, Sukhodolsky, Tsytsarev, & Soloyova, 1997), Meltzer (1933), and Vaughan (1996) had people report on a single recent anger episode and asked them to provide details of the components of the experience. Among their questions they asked about their actual behaviors while angry. Although these researchers found some minor differences between men and women, and among cultural groups, their results found that people rarely react with aggression when angered. Verbal responses such as yelling and screaming were the most common and were reported in 43% (Meltzer, 1933) to 58% (Kassinove et al., 1997) of anger episodes. Physically aggressive responses were less common and were reported only 2% (Meltzer, 1933) to 10% (Kassinove et al., 1997) of the time. Thus, serious physical aggression following anger arousal is a rare occurrence. These findings are restricted to community and student samples who do not report problematic anger reactions. In a similar descriptive study, Tafrate and Kassinove (2002) found that high-trait-anger adults reported negative verbal responses in 74% of anger episodes. Physical aggression was reported in 22% of anger episodes examined. Those predisposed to have problematic anger experiences appear to engage in higher rates of both verbal expression and physically aggressive behaviors.

The conclusions drawn from these studies are tentative because of two limitations in their method. The first related to how they defined aggression, while the second concerns the populations they studied. The manner in which these researchers measured aggression is consistent with the way most researchers and clinicians label an aggressive episode. Averill (1982, 1983), Kassinove and colleagues (1997), and Vaughan (1996) all used physical assaults on objects and people to define aggression. However, such a limited definition of aggression may under-represent the occurrence of aggressive behavior elicited by anger. Think of yourself or those people closest to you. Most of the time that people experience anger they do nothing. Perhaps they tell a close colleague or friend how upset they are. They may tarnish the reputation of the person at whom they are angry. They may even refuse to do things that the target of their anger expects from them. Also, they may purposefully but secretly damage the person's reputation or sabotage the person's goals. We believe that most researchers and clinicians have attended almost exclusively to the dramatic, physical, and loud aggressive responses. However, other incidences of aggressive reactions, such as relational (sabotaging social networks), passive (not living up to others' expectations), or indirect (covert property destruction) aggression appear more common to us. These types of responses fit the definition of aggression discussed in chapter 2: behavior that is enacted with the intent to do harm and with the expectation that harm will occur. These additional expressions of anger could eventually produce just as much damage to the angry person's quality of life and might also do serious harm to his or her interpersonal relationships.

The Averill (1982, 1983), Kassinove et al. (1997), and Vaughan (1996) studies used college populations, not people suffering from clinical anger. As supported in the Tafrate and Kassinove (2002) study, perhaps people with anger disorders behave aggressively more frequently than the average person when angered. That is, as the intensity and frequency of anger increases so does the proportion of anger–aggression episodes. As mentioned above, most conceptualizations of anger use Spielberger's (1988) distinction between anger-in and anger-out. Spielberger (1988) has maintained that these two types of anger expression are statistically "orthogonal" or independent. However, our research suggests that few people with exclusively high anger-in exist. Anger-in appears to lead to greater aggression or anger-out in an exponential function (DiGiuseppe & Tafrate, 2004). Thus, people with higher anger may have a higher proportion of anger episodes that include the outward expression of anger. Research by J. Deffenbacher supports this idea. He found that the higher one's trait anger, the higher the score on anger-out (J. L. Deffenbacher, Oetting, Thwaites, Lynch, Baker, et al., 1996). Thus, the degree of anger-related aggression may depend on the absolute level of trait anger. Besides physical aggression and verbal expression, higher scores on measures of anger-in also increase the degree to which people use relational, indirect, and passive-aggressive strategies (DiGiuseppe & Tafrate, 2004).

Although higher trait anger and higher anger-in does increase a person's potential to display anger outwardly, it appears that anger episodes infrequently involve physical aggression. Even for clients with clinical anger problems, most of their anger episodes do not involve physically aggressive behaviors. However, our knowledge in this area is sketchy and we need more research. We suspect that people express their anger through other subtler and less-direct means of expression more than they do through the means usually assessed (e.g., verbal and physical). We also suspect that persons with anger disorders may have a higher incidence of anger episodes associated verbal expressiveness and physical aggression including other more-subtle and indirect means of anger expression such as relational, indirect, or passive-aggressive. The important issue for practitioners is to assess anger and aggression directly with specific questions on each topic or to use a multidimensional anger-assessment instrument such as the ADS (DiGiuseppe & Tafrate, 2004).

Predicting Aggressive Behaviors From Anger

Several practical implications follow from the above discussion and research findings. Clinicians frequently need to assess their client's potential for violence. Often they are prepared to consider a client potentially dangerous because of the level of anger the client experiences or expresses. Our view, and the models presented by Baumeister, Smart, and Boden (1996) and Tedeschi and Nesler (1993), suggests that anger is often present in the violent individual and acts as a mediator of violence. However, existing research fails to prove a relationship between anger and aggression that warrants the use of anger measures alone to predict dangerousness to others. The existing measures of anger do not assess anger disorders and may not yield adequate information to confirm the relationship between anger and aggression. Predicting aggressive behavior by the level of anger will produce many false positives because highly angry people display a wide range of behaviors and are not necessarily violent. To predict violence in people with high levels of anger, clinicians need to assess the individual's behavioral response patterns when anger is experienced, and the ratio of anger episodes to aggressive acts. In addition, they should evaluate the internal and external discriminative stimuli that differentiate nonaggressive anger episodes from aggressive anger episodes within the individual.

Actuarial prediction still results in fewer false positives and false negatives than clinical prediction (Gardner, Lidz, Mulvey, & Shaw, 1996). Hughes (1996) argues that mental health professionals are expected to predict dangerousness, though most studies in the area have failed to confirm the knowledge base or the ability of practitioners to make accurate predictions. Most studies to date have attempted to predict violence based on history of aggression rather than on the presence of the emotion of anger, the cognitive aspects of resentment, or the motivation for revenge. Perhaps the hit rate would improve if these variables were added to the regression equation or the clinicians' interviews.

Hostile Versus Instrumental Aggression

Most books and articles on aggression make the distinction between instrumental and hostile aggression (Buss, 1961; Feshbach, 1964; Geen & Donnerstein, 1998; Hartup, 1974; see Bushman & Anderson, 2001, for a review). Psychologists sometimes call hostile aggression *affective* or *reactive aggression,* or *rage.* They sometimes call instrumental aggression *predatory* or *proactive aggression.* In this chapter we have been discussing aggression mediated by anger experiences. *Hostile aggression* has been described as having anger present, being motivated by causing harm to others, and being characterized by a cognitive style of impulsivity or lack of planning. Although theorists describe hostile aggression as showing the motivation or intention to harm the victim, the word *revenge* is rarely used. These theorists have been unclear concerning whether the motive in hostile aggression is restricted to the immediate harm of others as a means of repelling them, and therefore represents an attempt at self-defense, or whether they are to include vengeance and "evening the score" as the motive.

Theorists have described *instrumental aggression* as not having anger present and lacking an intention to harm others. The motive for instrumental aggression is coercing others to cede resources or things wanted by the aggressor. Positive outcomes, which aggressors acquire from their victims, motivate instrumental aggression. Thus, the rewards garnered by aggression provide reinforcement that motivates more aggressive behavior in the future. Instrumental aggression also differs in cognitive style. It involves calculation of the cost and benefits of the aggression and planning to attain the desired goals. These distinctions are presented in Table 4.1.

The strongest support for the distinction between hostile and instrumental aggression comes from neuroscience. Examination of the neural pathways of the mammalian brain that control aggression reveals three

Table 4.1
Characteristics of Hostile Versus Instrumental Aggression

	Anger	Motivation	Cognitive Activity
Hostile Aggression	Present	To harm the victim	Impulsive—no planning
Instrumental Aggression	Not present	To acquire the victim's possessions	Calculates the costs and benefits of behavior—planning present

discrete paths for aggression (Carlson, 2003; Panksepp, 1998). One corresponds to hostile aggression and is often referred to as the *rage path.* Another is the *predatory pathway* that, when activated, elicits hunting behavior. A third pathway controls inter-male competition for mating. Most aggression theorists believe that these categories explain human aggression.

As noted in chapter 2, Bushman and Anderson (2001) have argued that this distinction, though a popular explanation, fails to describe adequately the different types of aggressive reactions for several reasons. First, anger may motivate aggression. However, angry, retaliative, vengeful behavior does not have to be impulsive. Planning is not restricted only to people who use instrumental aggression to prey on others. Consider some of the high school shooters who have killed their peers or teachers: Kip Kinkle from Oregon, the trenchcoat mafia from Columbine High School in Colorado, or from Jonesboro, Arkansas. Also, consider the perpetrators of the September 11th attack on the New York World Trade Center and the Pentagon. Consider the Palestinian suicide bombers who strap on bombs, move among their enemies, and wait till they position themselves to inflict the most damage. After reading about the people who commit such attacks, one cannot deny that they experienced intense anger and hate. However, none of these people acted impulsively. In fact, planning seems obvious. They experienced outrage at perceived insults and seethed with resentment. They longed for retaliation and planned, sometimes for years, a strategy that would inflict maximal pain on their targets. Psychology and psychiatry seem to have ignored planned, deliberate aggression when it occurs in people filled with anger and hatred and motivated by revenge. The hostile versus instrumental-aggression distinction fails to account for the most-dangerous people, for whom revenge is the primary motivation.

The concept of hostile aggression has dominated the attempt to identify and describe anger and aggression in the present diagnostic system in psychiatry. The presence of impulsive aggression or the failure to resist impulsive urges to aggress defines Intermittent Explosive Disorder almost exclusively (American Psychiatric Association, 2000; Coccaro, 1992; Coccaro, Harvey, Kupsaw-Lawrence, Herbert, & Bernstein, 1991). This distinction has hampered our understanding of psychopathology. Anger and revenge, or planned aggression, are not recognized as disorders by the present *DSM–IV–TR* (American Psychiatric Association, 2000).

The description of hostile aggression as impulsive has led to treatments of anger that aim at increasing impulse-control skills. One of the earliest interventions, Novaco's (1975) self-instructional training procedure, was designed to teach self-statements that inhibit anger arousal and aggressive responses and guide new more adaptive responses. It remains one of the most popular and well-researched anger-management strategies. However, this procedure may fail to help angry people who commit deliberate, vengeful acts. Over the past decade we have seen an increase in the popularity of various forgiveness-based interventions (Enright & Fitzgibbons, 2000; Kassinove & Tafrate, 2002; McCullough, Pargament, & Thoresen, 2000).

This development may reflect researchers' and practitioners' awareness of the role of revenge in sustaining anger disorders and aggressive behaviors. Presently, we do not have a model to explain how anger can lead to both deliberate and impulsive aggression. We will present such a model in chapter 6.

Another problem with this dichotomy involves the idea that instrumental aggression involves coercion without anger. To test this idea we included a subscale measuring the motive of coercion in our ADS (DiGiuseppe & Tafrate, 2004). Coercion could be considered a measure of the motive in instrumental aggression, since it involves anger and aggressive acts compelling others to do what one wants. Factor analysis of all the ADS subscales resulted in a higher order factor of subscales including verbal expression, coercion, high physiological arousal, enduring anger problems, and other subscales measuring aspects of anger. This pattern supports Bushman and Anderson's (2001) criticism of the instrumental–hostile aggression distinction because the coercive or instrumental motive was associated with high affect arousal, thus providing affective–instrumental aggression. In many cases, when people get angry, they expect their anger to serve the function of getting what they want.

Bushman and Anderson (2001) proposed that the hostile versus instrumental-aggression dichotomy also fails to account for people with mixed motives for their aggression. Thus, the very nature of a dichotomy may be false. Often, more than one motive drives a person's aggressive behavior. As noted above, separate neural pathways may mediate hostile and instrumental aggression. However, Panksepp (1998) reported that each of these two pathways have subcortical nuclei that lay next to each other. When one is activated, it inhibits the other. Thus, only one aggressive system is activated at a time. He points out that what starts as a predatory aggressive act can easily turn into a rage reaction, and vice versa. The system can then move back again to the originally activated system. Consider a mugger who has planned to snatch someone's purse. When the mugger makes his move, the victim fights back fiercely and insults the mugger. The mugger's pride is hurt because the victim has put up such resistance and the victim's insults have threatened his ego. As a result the mugger becomes angry and the rage system is activated and inhibits the predatory system. The fight continues and the mugger prevails, knocking his victim to the ground. As the victim cringes in pain and the mugger revels in his triumph, seeing the hurt he has inflicted and having accomplished his revenge, he notices that the victim's wallet is lying within reach. He kicks the victim, and as the victim recoils from the blow, the mugger grabs the wallet and is off. In this actual case, the attacker's motive was both predatory and retaliative. Such cases support Bushman and Anderson's (2001) notion of complex aggressive motives. In this case, the mugger vacillates between instrumental motives and revenge motives. Each motive appears discrete but also gives way to the other. Thus, each is separate but the other is also present in the exchange. For other people the two motives are not so distinct and may be merged, and the desired outcome satisfies both motives.

Consider the case of George, a man referred to our anger group when his wife left him. Many of his wife's behaviors triggered George's anger. These included what she bought, how she cleaned, and how she raised their children. When George became angry, he reported that he had an uncontrollable desire to vent his frustration. He hated her for her defiance of his wishes and wanted to hurt her. When angered he would immediately yell, throw things, or bang on the nearest table or counter. He reported that the motive for these outbursts was to hurt her for being such a bad homemaker. However, these aggressive outbursts scared his wife and she would immediately comply with whatever her husband wanted, just to stop his loud intimidating rants. Thus, his wife's compliance reinforced George's anger and expressive venting. When confronted with this reinforcement of his anger, he agreed that he knew his anger "worked" for him and that he could control his wife by using it. Obviously, cathartic release, revenge, and coercion motivated George's angry and aggressive acts. This is clearly a case of mixed motivations and is difficult for the hostile–instrumental theory of aggression to explain. We believe that the anger present in most dysfunctional couples and family relationships, especially involving perpetrators of domestic violence, has such mixed motives. The angry person's desire for tension release and revenge are achieved. However, the victim's compliance and submission reward the person for his or her intimidating behavior. This behavior usually destroys the relationship with the intimidated partner over time, as it did with George and his wife. Anger outbursts can be viewed as social traps with the short-term reward of compliance and the longer-term consequences of resentment. We will return to this issue in chapter 18, which discusses establishing the therapeutic alliance with anger clients.

Our research with the ADS (DiGiuseppe & Tafrate, 2004) supports the idea that there are usually multiple motives operating in angry people. A cluster analysis of more than 990 clinical cases revealed a group of people who scored high on verbal expression, coercion, and affective arousal of anger but had a somewhat lower score on the revenge subscale. Thus, becoming angry and letting one's anger out can relate to the desire to coerce another person to comply with one's desires with a still strong, but somewhat less strong, desire for revenge. Thus, mixed motives were present, as Bushman and Anderson predicted. We have found this cluster of scores in people who come for couples counseling, parents involved in family therapy for their disruptive children, and ineffective managers in business settings.

Another problem with the description of hostile aggression is the linking of anger with the cognitive style of impulsivity. A reading of neuroscience literature fails to present a reason that the *rage* neural pathway must involve impulsive action. Panksepp (1998) pointed out that the rage pathway starts in the prefrontal lobes. This area controls one's consideration of the costs and benefits of one's behavior or problem solving in achieving one's goal of inflicting harm. This area of the brain compares expectations with actual outcomes and appears active in the rage neural pathway. Panksepp (1998) also noted that many connections exist between the neural pathways of rage system and the brain's "seeking" system. When activated, the seeking system searches for rewards and initiates behaviors to attain rewards. It is possible that once the rage system arouses the revenge motive, connections to the seeking system allow the person to consider the best way to achieve revenge.

Bushman and Anderson (2001) have noted that our legal system has long distinguished between murder committed in a state of passion or rage, second-degree murder, and murders that involve premeditation, which usually carry the greater punishment. However, the legal system does not consider motives in the definition of this crime. One is guilty of first-degree murder whether he or she carried out a premeditated murder to avenge a past wrong or to acquire another's possessions. Second-degree murder involves the taking of another's life when the perpetrator acts impulsively in the state of an intense emotion when they could not have anticipated the event that provoked the emotion. Western society and law recognizes the distinction between planned and impulsive acts of violence. We do not deny this distinction. However, we believe that the present model of aggression popular in the behavioral sciences leaves two questions to investigate. To what degree do those who commit premeditated aggression experience strong emotion (anger) and vengeful motivation? And to what degree do people guilty of impulsive aggression experience the emotion of anger and hatred toward their victim before they engage in the final act of explosive violence?

The distinction between hostile and instrumental aggression appears flawed. Much of what we call instrumental aggression may in fact result from multiple motives or include anger arousal. Perdition without anger appears much less likely. Anger can elicit multiple motives that can generate aggression, and these motives may be consistent with the rewards of instrumental aggression. The possibility exists that much aggressive behavior is motivated by strong passions or emotions that blind aggressors to the likely negative consequences of their acts. Perhaps much of what people label as instrumental aggression is anger-motivated aggression. The criminal group most associated with instrumental aggression is psychopaths, who are often described as emotionless, acting without guilt, and having few close personal attachments. However, descriptions of psychopaths also recount that they are easily aroused to anger (Cleckley, 1976; Hare & Hart, 1993).

Despite the popularity of the hostile–instrumental aggression distinction we think anger facilitates aggression in many cases considered purely instrumental aggression. Although some researchers suggest that anger is a direct causal link to aggression (R. Baumeister, Smart, & Boden, 1996; Konecni, 1975; Tedeschi & Nesler, 1993), other researchers propose that anger is only a precursor to aggressive and violent behavior (Bandura, 1973; R. S. Lazarus, 1991; Novaco, 1975). In the next chapter we will present evidence that anger plays a role in some forms of aggression often considered examples of instrumental aggression: war, murder, rape, and domestic violence.

5

Anger as a Mediator of Violence

As presented in the previous chapter many theories have attempted to explain the relationship between anger and aggressive behavior. The present chapter examines specific categories of violence perpetrated by individuals and groups and how anger may be a contributing factor.

Criminologists usually exclude studying anger as a variable that contributes to crime. Military historians usually fail to include anger in their analyses of why countries wage war. Scholars usually portray crime and war as instrumental aggression. However, some theoretical work has addressed anger in acts of violence that have traditionally been considered motivated by instrumental factors. Baumeister, Smart, and Boden (1996) presented a model of aggression and violence that posited that unstable, positive appraisals of the self lead to intense anger arousal, which then leads to aggression (see Figure 5.1). These authors link threats to high self-esteem with various types of aggression, including murder, rape, terrorism, spousal abuse, child abuse, racial violence, assassination, and war. However, the evidence that the threat to self-esteem first mediates this relationship by arousing anger is only hypothesized and not yet proven. This lack of evidence for this aspect of their model exists because researchers directly measure aggression but rarely measure anger. Their model strongly suggests that anger leads to violence.

A similar theory was proposed by Tedeschi and Nesler (1993). They posited that aggression results from grievances that the aggressors believe are unjust and avoidable. In this model, the attributions of avoidability, blameworthiness, and unfairness cause aggression through their effect of first arousing anger. Tedeschi and Nesler (1993) presented evidence that

Figure 5.1. Baumeister, Smart, &
Boden's (1996) Model of Aggression

attributions of blame and avoidability lead to aggression. However, they
provide no evidence that anger mediates this relationship.

Both Baumeister, Smart, and Boden (1996) and Tedeschi and Nesler
(1993) presented little data that the hypothesized variables that cause aggression do so through the arousal of anger. However, both groups show the
relationship between the cognitive variables and aggression. Does either of
these cognitions first arouse anger, as they theorized, or do the cognitions
separately arouse anger and aggression? Perhaps researchers fail to use
measures of anger directly because they believe that the connection between
anger and aggression is already well established, or they just assume that
anger and aggression represent the same construct. We would advance our
knowledge about the relationship between anger and aggression if theoreticians and researchers would not assume that these constructs are the same
or that anger is necessarily the mediator of aggression. We recommend that
researchers and practitioners measure each of them independently.

If acts of crime and war represented instrumental aggression, they
would include the cognitive style of planning and balancing costs and
benefits. However, it is unlikely that rational planning and problem solving
determine such aggressive behaviors exclusively. First, they so rarely succeed
in achieving their ends, and second, inflicting harm on others is so often the
purpose. This suggests that violent acts, both at the individual level and in
larger regional conflicts, are less the result of dispassionate deliberations and
more the result of passionate deliberations.

Murder and Anger

Although murder is often considered a legal concept, one could see it as a
form of disturbed behavior if viewed through the harmful dysfunction
model. Murder rarely achieves its desired ends, and its perpetrators usually

regret their actions (Gilligan, 1996; Gottesfried & Hirschi, 1990; Sampson & Laub, 1993), so it is often dysfunctional. It usually leads to harm for the perpetrator.

Resentment is a crucial component of what Spielberger (1988) calls *anger-in*. It is an attitude that one has received the worst treatment in life and deserves better. As noted below, several authors have identified resentment or anger-in as a key factor in prompting aggressive acts such as murder, rape, and assault. Although most acts of aggression do not engender the extreme consequences caused by murder and rape, perhaps understanding these forms of extreme aggression could enlighten us as to how anger leads to aggression.

Pincus's (2001) investigation of the psychiatric status of convicted murderers uncovered three variables common to most of the convicts. First, most murderers suffered from some neurological dysfunction that resulted in impaired impulse control. Second, most murderers suffered from some serious mental illness such as Schizophrenia, Bipolar Disorder, or Schizoaffective Disorder. Third, most had a history of severe child abuse. Pincus's explanation highlights the key role of hatred and resentment about severe abuse experienced in childhood. Pincus proposed that these early experiences created in such individuals a bitter resentment about being unloved and poorly treated. Because the effects of the abuse lingered for many years after the trauma, these early experiences set the stage for a strong motive to seek retribution. It is also hypothesized that personal histories of abuse left murderers with a strong sense of doubt about their personal worth. An enduring sense of worthlessness and, more specifically, shame, was the legacy of the abuse and influenced the murderer's interactions with their victims. According to Pincus (2001), seething resentment over the early abuse created a vulnerability to perceive the slightest indifference as total disrespect and rejection. Their serious mental illness helped them misinterpret or distort cues from their victim's behavior as shameful rejection. Finally, their neurological impairment reduced their capacity for self-control.

These three factors coexist to increase the likelihood of a fatal outcome (see Figure 5.2). Without the serious mental illness or neurological injury, the men in Pincus's study might not have killed. However, that does not mean they would have been good citizens. Many had histories of less fatal aggression before the total loss of control that ended a life. Pincus sees the roots of their violence as stemming from the enduring resentment over their rejection and abuse. Resentment is a crucial component of the anger-in construct. Thus, long-term, held-in anger played a crucial role in crimes committed by these men. Other people with better impulse control and better-functioning synapses may have chosen other, less fatal means of revenge, or they may have used better planning for a means of revenge that involved less chance of discovery and incarceration. For our purposes it seems that long-term, intense resentment about being abused and shamed

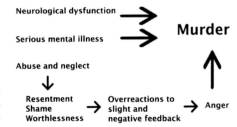

Figure 5.2. Pincus' (2001) Model
of Variables That Potentially
Contribute to Murder

and an inability to control impulses are key variables that may lead to anger in and an angry and aggressive episode.

Similarly, based on 25 years as a forensic psychiatrist, Gilligan (1996) proposed that reactions to a sense of shame and worthlessness are the primary psychological causes of murder. He found an extremely high rate of child abuse in the histories of murderers. Many had been physically or sexually abused or had histories of abandonment or rejection. Gilligan argues that most murderers have an intense sense of shame that causes deep enduring hurt. This shame leads to a sense of worthlessness and the belief that one is unlovable. Most times, he reports, the pain of shame is so great that the murderer feels numb. For Gilligan, murder is a crime of retribution. The murderer has a strong desire to hurt others in an attempt to even the score for the pain and suffering that he or she has experienced. Murderers ruminate about making things right and see violence as the only means of achieving equity. Gilligan also noted that many murderers killed over minor provocations. Stories of murder usually shock us because we cannot imagine that such trivial provocations can lead to such drastic outcomes. Gilligan believes that rage over failure to get "respect," even in minor social interactions, is often the "last straw" for such individuals in a life filled with disrespect and shame.

Gilligan (1996) and Pincus (2001) both see murder as a violent act that occurs after years of anger, resentment, rumination, and a desire for retribution over the pain from abuse, neglect, and rejection. Their analyses reinforce the idea that most murderers do not clearly fit the model of instrumental aggression but instead represent affective aggression. Pincus more than Gilligan believes that another variable accounts for a murderer's inability to control the desires to avenge past mistreatment. Serious mental illness and neurological deficits result in the murderers' inability to follow society's strong censure of taking another's life. However, both authors, who have studied murderers up close and personal, recognize that these desires and impulses to harm others rarely emerge from nowhere. Years of resentment and attempts to resist a desire for revenge break down and end in a failure to resolve the pain or overcome the urge to strike back. Also, these studies show that enduring anger often leads to displaced aggressive behaviors. The ultimate victim of the murderer's rage may not be the person who caused the greatest pain. Instead, a mild rejection that was the last in a long line of perceived insults results in an extreme response. The victims are often irrelevant in the larger context of the murderer's life. How the victims are chosen is little understood. Gilligan and Pincus both stress the role that shame plays in the murderers' lives. These are often men on the fringe of society who feel worthless. If they do maintain mainstream lives, they feel unworthy. They have experienced abuse and rejection and feel shamed by their past. Clearly, they interpret their abuse as an attack on their ego.

Rape, Sexual Assault, and Anger

Anger may also motivate rape. Although researchers have not questioned rapists about their emotional states or anger directly, the thoughts and attitudes that rapists report coincide with those that generate anger. Similarly, serial killers (Douglas & Olshakher, 1995, 1997, 1998) often feel a sense of anger, yet this aspect of their emotional life generally receives little attention. Perhaps researchers pay less attention to criminals' affective states because their crimes are so violent and their aggressive acts grab our attention.

Ideological feminist theories of gender have dominated the discussion of rape in the social sciences in recent years, although they lack empirical support (see Brownmiller, 1975; Petersen, 1999). These theories define rape as a coercive act by men to continue the power imbalance between men and women in society. Rape is considered a demonstration of power and not a sexual act. These models present rape as an act of instrumental aggression and focus little on the affective experience of the rapist. Many predictions based on feminist theories of rape are inconsistent with empirical findings (for a review see Baumeister, Catanese, & Wallace, 2002). Feminist theories focus on the experience of rape more from the victims' perspective and from a sociological perspective. Although this larger level of analysis may prove helpful in some ways, such an analysis fails to provide an understanding of the individual psychology of rapists.

Several researchers have identified clusters or subtypes of rapists. Tirrell and Aldridge (1983) purposed that they could classify rapists' motives along two separate but correlated dimensional variables. They defined the first continuous dimension as anger, hostility, and aggression, and the second as sexual arousal. They concluded that most rapists display some degree of each motive. However, as a rapist's motives increase along the hostility dimension, the sexual motivation declines. As the sexual motive increases, the hostile motive declines. They concluded that some evidence of anger and sadistic aggression exists in most rapists.

Also using continuous dimensions, Groth, Burgess, and Holmstrom (1977) hypothesized that power, anger, and sexuality explain the rapist's behavior, and that elements of all three issues operate in every rape. However, the proportion might vary and one or another motive might predominate.

The authors ranked accounts from 133 offenders and 92 victims for the dominant issue and found that they could categorize the offenses as either a power rape (sexuality used primarily to express power) or an anger rape (sexuality used to express anger). In no case was sex the dominant issue. Rapists pursued sex in the service of other, nonsexual motives. In a further analysis of these cases, Groth and Burgess (1977) concluded that most rapists did have alternative, appropriate sexual outlets. A third of the rapists reported experiencing some type of sexual dysfunction during the assault. They concluded that only two psychological determinants influenced rape: anger and power.

Other studies have reported that rapists often project on their victims a sense of superiority. Rapists perceive themselves as rejected and believe their victims' sense of superiority is a threat to their egos. Rapists need to disavow their perception of the victims' superiority by controlling them (Scully & Marolla, 1985; Groth, 1979). Rape may be an attempt through anger to restore their diminished ego and retaliate for perceived ego insults. Thus, feminist theories are partly correct in attributing rape to power motives. However, to understand the individual rapist's behavior fully, we need to consider anger as well.

Using a categorical approach to classification, Knight and Prentky (1987, 1990) reviewed the records of more than 100 rapists and found four subtypes: opportunistic, pervasively angry, sexual, and sadistic or vindictive. Two of these types, the pervasively angry and sadistic or vindictive, support the role of anger in rape. Research shows that these subtypes differ on measures of psychopathology and that the pervasively angry and sadistic vindictive groups score highest on measures of expressed anger (Darcangelo, 1997).

Rapists may be high on trait anger. Hudson and Ward (1997) found that rapists had more-insecure attachment styles and experienced more anger than child molesters, violent nonsexual offenders, and nonviolent nonsexual offenders. Acceptance of rape, or the failure to see it as a despicable behavior, also predicted rape (K. Anderson, Cooper, & Okamura, 1997). However, even the acceptance of rape and the failure to condemn it may result from anger and hostile attitudes. In a meta-analytic review of 72 studies of rape attitudes, K. Anderson, Cooper, and Okamura found that, along with gender-role beliefs, adversarial sexual beliefs, needs for power and dominance, conservative political beliefs, aggressiveness, and trait anger predicted rape acceptance.

Other studies have related rape and other types of sexual assault to a central aspect of anger—revenge. Scully and Marolla (1985) interviewed 114 convicted, incarcerated rapists to explore the function of sexual violence in their lives and their motives for rape. Findings revealed that a substantial portion of rapists used sexual violence to get revenge. In another study, Nathan and Ward (2002) examined the personality profiles of a small sample ($N=12$) of women prisoners convicted of sex offenses against children. Women sex offenders is a group that has been rarely studied until recently. Results showed that the majority of these women were co-offenders with men. Only a few appeared to have been coerced and motivated by fear. Revenge motivated these women more than rejection.

Even false allegations of rape by women have been linked to revenge. Kanin (1994) studied 45 consecutive, disposed, false rape allegations covering a nine-year period. These false allegations served three functions for the complainants: providing an excuse, seeking revenge, or obtaining sympathy and attention. Kanin further concluded that filing false allegations with the police did not appear premeditated but represented non-reflective, impulsive, and desperate efforts to cope with situational stress.

The researchers' findings—that men rape because of power and anger motives—partially support feminist theoreticians' claims. However, the power motive that emerged in these studies may not be concerned with men's attempting to enforce stratified and rigid sex roles and power differentials in society as suggested by feminist theories. Rather, a rapist's power motives might represent the selfish desire of the rapist to reach his personal goals, as proposed by Baumeister, Catanese, and Wallace's (2002) reactance–narcissistic theory of rape. According to this model, two psychological processes greatly increase the probability of rape. The first, reactance theory, suggests that people whose goals are frustrated will perceive those goals as more desirable and have a negative emotional reaction to the deprivation. Reactance also leads to people's attempting to reassert their freedom and attempting to deny the blocked goal, and to attack or aggress against the person responsible for blocking the goal. Although reactance leads to increased desire of the forbidden object and the desire to aggress, most men do not commit rape when denied sex. The frequency of denied sex for heterosexual men is staggeringly large compared with the incidence of forced sex. Baumeister, Catanese, and Wallace believe that the characteristics of narcissism are the important ingredients that lead to aggressive rape. Narcissists regard themselves as superior to others, require a constant need or desire for ego gratification or approval, have an exaggerated sense of entitlement, and have low concern or empathy for others. The narcissist believes he is special and that women should want to have sex with him. Rapists therefore take the refusal of sexual access as an insult to which they respond, based on their sense of entitlement and superiority, with aggression. Thus, while the rape may be about restoring one's power, it started over sex. Baumeister, Catanese, and Wallace's theory appears to explain research findings on rape better than other theories. However, they do acknowledge that this theory does not explain all rapes. The emotion of anger generated by the cognitive distortions that accompany narcissism may be the relevant emotion that activates this aggressive behavior.

Although rapists may be angry, it is possible that their anger results from their arrest, conviction, and incarceration. Does their anger at their victims or women usually lead to increased sexual arousal or does state anger when aroused lead them to engage in sexual behavior forcibly? Taking men convicted of sexual crimes as their subjects, Proulx, McKibben, and Lusignan (1996) investigated the relationship between sexual aggressors and emotions following conflicts. To measure sexual behaviors, their subjects completed logs of sexual fantasies and their masturbatory activities during such fantasies. The emotions most frequently reported by convicted rapists were anger, loneliness, and humiliation. Also, for rapists and heterosexual pedophiles, their negative moods coincided with strong deviant sexual fantasies and increased masturbatory activities during such fantasies. Thus, the arousal of anger appears to increase deviant sexual fantasies, arousal, and orgasm. Of course, one could hypothesize that such deviant sexual behavior provides the individual with a mechanism to regulate mood or distract himself from negative emotions.

In a controlled laboratory study, Yates, Barbaree, and Marshall (1984) explored how an anger-producing insult from a woman confederate influenced sexual arousal to rape cues in 24 college men. After the insult or a period of exercise for the control group, the men were presented with two-minute descriptions of both mutually consenting sex and rape while penile plethysmography monitored their sexual arousal. Descriptions of rape scenes evoked significantly less sexual arousal than descriptions of mutually consenting sex in subjects who had not been insulted, whereas rape and mutually consenting sex evoked similar levels of sexual arousal in subjects who had been insulted. The authors concluded that anger either disrupted the discrimination between mutually consenting sex and rape that occurs in normal men's sexual arousal or increased the power of rape cues to elicit sexual arousal. Although we need more research to explore these possibilities, attempts to arouse anger did produce greater sexual arousal to rape scenes.

It also seems plausible that the variables of shame, rumination, self-worth, and anger-in, described in the previous section discussing murder, would also apply to some rapists. In our clinical and consulting experiences we have observed that sex offenders have frequently suffered harsh treatment, neglect, and rejection at the hands of family members and others. Thus, rapists may be particularly sensitive to perceived rejection, leading to shame and anger. Sexual offending may be a behavior pattern that is used to restore a sense of worth and perceived control. This would seem consistent with some aspects of the power motive while also acknowledging the potential role of anger.

Domestic Violence and Anger

Anger may have a profound role in domestic violence. However, researchers in this area have historically failed to include anger measures in their studies. As a result, explanations of why men behave violently in intimate relationships have been incomplete and have led to intervention programs with limited effectiveness (Babcock, Green, & Robie, 2004). Recent research that has included anger measures finds that maritally violent men are angrier than nonviolent though maritally dissatisfied men (Babcock, Costa, Green, & Eckhardt, 2004). This finding also seems to extend to younger men in dating relationships that report higher anger scores than their nonviolent counterparts (Eckhardt, Jamison, & Watts, 2002). In a meta-analytic review of 33 studies, Norlander and Eckhardt (2005) found that perpetrators of intimate-partner violence consistently reported higher levels of anger and hostility than nonviolent men.

Despite the lack of attention to anger, domestic violence has been a topic of intense research interest (Stover, 2005). Particularly alarming is the prevalence of spousal abuse. In the United States, an estimated 2 million women annually are battered by their husbands or mates (Straus & Gelles, 1986). This number probably underrepresents the actual occurrence (O'Leary, Barling, Arias, Rosenbaum, Malone, et al., 1989). More than twice as many women were shot and killed by their husband or intimate acquaintance than were murdered by strangers (Kellermann & Mercy, 1992). Twelve to 18% of all murders are spousal assaults. Forty percent of women murdered each year die at the hands of their husbands (Sigler, 1989). Although women engage in physical violence (O'Leary et al., 1989), men are more likely to commit acts of extreme violence or to murder their spouses (Gillian, 1996). The lack of clarity concerning who is likely to abuse remains.

Early studies focusing on the distinguishing characteristics of maritally violent men investigated the effects of alcoholism, low self-esteem (Goldstein & Rosenbaum, 1985), poor assertiveness skills (O'Leary, Curley, Rosenbaum, & Clarke, 1985), and, ironically, the aggressors' wives (Gellen, Hoffman, Jones, & Stone, 1984). Several studies in the 1980s first indicated that anger may have a critical role in partner violence. For example, spouse abusers were reported to have significantly higher levels of self-reported anger, hostility, and depression than those in the control group (Maiuro, Cahn, Vitaliano, Wagner, & Zegree, 1988; Maiuro, Vitaliano, & Cahn, 1987). Similarly, Margolin and colleagues (Burman, Margolin, & John, 1993; Margolin & Wampold, 1981) found that in a structured laboratory setting, husband–wife conflicts that contained frequent expressions of anger and hostility differentiated physically abusive men from the nonabusive control group. As noted above, Eckhardt and colleagues have made the link between anger-generating cognitions and marital violence (Eckhardt, Barbour, & Davison, 1998; Eckhardt & Kassinove, 1998). Initial studies compared the articulated thoughts of maritally violent men to those of maritally dissatisfied men and to those of maritally satisfied men during simulated situations (Davison, Navarre, & Vogel, 1995). They asked all the men to imagine scenes that generated anger and then to report into a microphone the automatic thoughts that entered their consciousness. Research assistants recorded, transcribed, and then coded these thoughts for cognitive distortions (A. T. Beck, 1976), irrational beliefs (Ellis & Tafrate, 1997), hostile attributions (K. Dodge, 1985), problem-solving strategies (Spivack, Platt, & Shure,

1976), or anger-coping strategies (Novaco, 1975). The results showed that the maritally violent men expressed more cognitive distortions, irrational beliefs, and hostile attributions, and had fewer problem-solving and anger-coping strategies than either of the two other groups. This suggested that spouse abusers' aggression might be mediated by the thoughts that cognitive behavior therapies typically address. Anger may mediate the effect of these thoughts on aggression since the men generated the thoughts in an anger-induction task. One might conclude that anger management would be an important component in intervention programs.

In spite of the evidence for the link between anger and partner violence, strong controversy exists regarding the appropriate targets of treatment. Most treatment programs are focused on issues related to male coercive control over women (Cavanaugh & Gelles, 2005). The underpinnings of this approach are that partner violence is a result of societal messages and cultural norms that male violence against women is acceptable to obtain compliance and control in intimate relationships. Thus, the majority of programs are focused on changing attitudes related to gender roles. An alternative view is related to skills deficits. In this model, perpetrators are viewed as lacking the ability to reduce anger, resolve problems, and communicate effectively. From this perspective, treatment focuses on fostering skills designed to decrease arousal and increase competencies. In a study of attitudes and behaviors presumed to mediate partner violence, Date and Ronan (2000) found little support for the role of sexist attitudes and beliefs in differentiating partner abusers from other violent or nonviolent offenders. They concluded that, "indeed, we are not aware of any published research that has found antifeminist attitudes to differentiate domestically violent offenders from other violent offenders or non-violent offenders" (p. 1140). They found that partner abusers shared with other violent offenders the characteristics of high trait anger and deficits in problem solving.

Taking a different tack, the role of shame resulting from a history of abuse and rejection, as described in the previous sections, may again play a role in partner violence. Dutton's (1998) studies of spouse abusers suggest that these men restore their egos by physically abusing their partners to control them. Most abusers have a history of having been abused themselves. They feel shame over the abuse they suffered and have fragile egos that are easily bruised. Other researchers have reported that many child abusers have histories of having been abused and harbor great resentment against those who abused them. Although not all spouse and child abusers were abused, a substantial number were. It surprises people that victims of abuse perpetuate the cycle.

Finally, a growing body of evidence suggests that not all perpetrators of partner violence are alike. In their review of domestic violence offender typologies, Holtzworth-Monroe and Stuart (1994) found that existing subtypes can be classified along three dimensions: (a) severity and frequency of violence, (b) scope of violence (family only versus extrafamilial), and

(c) the psychopathology of the offender. The first group, family only, is considered to be the least violent of the subgroups, reports little or no psychopathology, and does not tend to engage in violence outside the home. The second group, dysphoric borderline, is viewed as the most psychologically distressed, and these individuals are likely to experience anger and jealousy. The third group, generally violent and antisocial, is considered to be the most violent, to have extensive criminal histories, and to have features of antisocial personality disorder. We hypothesize that anger would play a more significant role in mediating violent behavior among the more psychologically disturbed second group. Gottman, Jacobson, Rushe, Short, Babcock, et al. (1995) identified two distinct groups of offenders. *Type I* men showed decreases in physiological arousal during angry verbal exchanges, engaged in violence outside the relationship, and exhibited antisocial characteristics. In contrast, Type II men were described as more emotionally needy and dependent and tended to engage in lower levels of violence than the first group. The role of anger may be more important for the Type II offenders. Several other typologies have also been described in the literature and are reviewed in more detail by Cavanaugh and Gelles (2005).

It may be that anger plays an important role in intimate-partner violence for specific subgroups of offenders. The obvious implication of this literature regarding typologies is that a one-size-fits-all theory of intimate-partner violence and subsequent treatment programming may not be effective. A more targeted approach that considers the role of anger as a cause of violence in relationships would likely have greater potential for success.

Anger and Group Conflict

Another approach to exploring the relationship between anger and aggression is to examine theories of violence between groups. As we write this chapter, fighting is occurring in more than 25 places around the globe. Violence continues in the Middle East between the Palestinians and Israelis. Civil war rages in Liberia and other African countries. The United States has troops in Afghanistan fighting the regrouping of the Taliban. In Iraq, U.S. troops are constantly under fire. The Filipino government is battling terrorist groups. These are the conflicts that get the most news coverage. In all these conflicts, hate or anger promotes violence. What variables promote the type of intergroup conflict that is too common in the world?

Eidelson and Eidelson (2003) reviewed the research on five attitudinal domains that individuals and groups share when they engage in conflict or aggression. They believe that these "five dangerous ideas" can each alone contribute to violence or aggression, and when they exist together, they greatly increase the chance that violence will occur. Although Eidelson and Eidelson do not directly address anger as a mediator of group violence, the ideas they discuss have similarities with those that generate anger (and hate), and when held strongly seem to increase the likelihood of aggression. The first dangerous idea is superiority. Individuals or groups who believe they are better than others can justify violence or expropriation of other people's land or resources. There is the belief that one, or one's group, is special, deserving, or entitled. This idea seems to conflict with the ideas of Gilligan (1996), Pincus (2001), and Dutton (1998) in the area of individual aggression. How can anger and aggression result from both a sense of worthlessness and shame, and from a sense of superiority and entitlement? This conflict has remained in the psychological literature for many years, and we will propose a resolution in chapter 6.

The second dangerous idea concerns injustice. Angry individuals and hostile groups believe they are the recipients of unfair treatment. They attribute their failure to achieve or to effect positive outcomes not to their own efforts but to others' unfair treatment of them. Although many individuals and groups truly are victims of injustice, it appears that dwelling on one's victimization and defining oneself as a victim leads to externalizing blame for failures and justifying retribution for attacks.

The third ingredient in producing aggression is a sense of vulnerability. As Darwin noted, anger and aggression are part of the protective mechanism that evolved to react against threats. Individuals and groups do not get angry or respond aggressively unless they perceive some degree of threat. Eidelson and Eidelson (2003) also pointed out that the individual psychology of emotions has shown that exaggerated perceptions of threats often lead to another protective emotion, anxiety.

A fourth dangerous idea is distrust or suspicion. Angry, aggressive people attribute hostile intentions to others for neutral acts. We have often heard embattled people say that others are either with them or against them. They perceive no middle ground and interpret failure to join their attack as a sign of ill will.

Finally, helplessness is the fifth dangerous idea. Most emotion theorists see anger as an emotion of strength and effectiveness. Again, we have another controversy. How can anger (and aggression) result from effectiveness, when the person perceives they are hopeless? When individuals or groups believe that they have no other recourse, that no one will come to their rescue, and that no means of negotiation will be effective, aggression may appear to be a more likely option.

Eidelson and Eidelson (2003) see a combination of cognitive elements as leading to aggression. Aggressors believe that they are superior to others, have experienced some injustice, are vulnerable to attack, cannot trust others, and are helpless, and that no other options will be effective.

As noted in chapter 3, Sternberg (2005) developed a theory of hate that attempted to explain what factors lead to the hate involved in genocide, terrorism, and massacres. Based on a review of the psychological and political literature, he proposed that three psychological elements lead to hate and then violence. The first factor was a negation of, or complete lack of intimate or warm feelings toward, the target. Sternberg notes that hate does not always cause extreme violence, but it often does. Hateful violence usually results when people feel disgust and are repulsed by their enemy. A second element of hateful violence is either passion or some intense feeling to motivate such extreme behavior. Thus, Sternberg proposes that intense anger or fear generated by a perceived threat would also be present. The third element of hateful violence is the cognitive devaluation of the target. Sternberg believes that individuals make an appraisal of the worth of the target. He sees these three aspects of hate as independent. People can have various types of hate depending on which factors are operating. The danger of violence increases with the number of aspects of hate. Thus, if one feels disgust toward another person or group and feels threatened and appraises the other as worthless and subhuman, violence is more likely to occur.

War and Anger

Violence against nations is usually considered the ultimate example of instrumental aggression and rarely viewed as a psychological problem. Nonetheless, war can represent a harmful dysfunction. Wars harm both attackers and defenders (Keegan, 1993). Terrorism and assassinations rarely achieve their desired political ends (Ford, 1983). Consider the recent terrorist attacks on the United States on September 11, 2001, which caused an increase in group cohesion among Americans. As one colleague said to us, "They made us a country again." Similarly, other aggressive tactics such as torture and brutal interrogations fail to elicit useful information (Scarry, 1985).

Warfare is usually described as instrumental aggression because land and resources are conquered and acquired with little regard for the emotions of the combatants. The desire to acquire resources, rather than harming the vanquished, supposedly motivates the conquerors (Keegan, 1993). However, who can watch news of the continuing hostilities in the Middle East, the former Yugoslavia, or Central Africa and not perceive the anger each side has for the other? Can one read Hitler's book, *My Battle*, and not see an angry man (see J. W. Gerard, 1933/1996, for a review)? A. T. Beck (1999) points out that the propaganda and rationales that perpetrators of war use to describe the citizens of their rival countries include the same attitudes of superiority and justification that angry individuals use when speaking about the targets of their anger.

We concede that some leaders may sometimes wage war for resources and thereby engage in instrumental aggression. However, what of the general population and the soldiers who fight and die? They require another motivation to keep fighting. An important historical question concerning the American Civil War revolves around just this issue. Why did the average Confederate soldier, usually not a slave owner, fight to ensure the existence of slavery when only the Southern aristocracy owned slaves? The idea of instrumental aggression fails to explain the dedication of Confederate soldiers. McPherson (1996), a historian specializing in the American Civil War, points out that Southern politicians promoted anger toward the North to encourage their war effort. They falsely suggested that the Federalist anti-slavery policy would take jobs from whites and give them to blacks, and that Federalists' threats to states' rights and home rule would compromise individual freedom. These allegations stirred the passions of the populace to continue the war. Keegan (1976), a military historian, argues that his field usually focuses on the brutality of war and the tactics and strategies of war, and often avoids the emotional perspectives of the soldiers.

There is disagreement about the effectiveness of anger's role in warfare. Some believe that effective soldiers must eschew anger. For an angry soldier may impulsively charge rather than follow a more effective strategy. An angry soldier will lack the discipline for an effective campaign. The Roman philosopher Seneca perhaps best expressed this view as he debated Aristotle.

> "Anger" says Aristotle "is necessary, and no battle can be won without it, unless it fills the mind and fires the soul not as a leader, but as the common soldier." But this is not true. For it is no longer anger, of which the chief characteristic is willfulness. If, however, it resists and is not submissive when ordered, but is carried away by its own caprice and hurt, it will be an instrument of the mind as useless as is the soldiers who disregard the signal for retreat. The useful soldier will be one who knows how to obey orders; the passions are as bad subordinates as they are leaders. (Basore, 1928, p. 129)

Perhaps Seneca is correct. However, we suspect that Seneca also was an adherent of the instrumental versus hostile dichotomy of aggression. Seneca describes angry soldiers as unable to follow orders and likely to abandon the regimentation of strategy. For Seneca, an angry soldier is an impulsive soldier. However, if one abandons the notion that hostile aggression cannot be premeditated and organized, perhaps angry soldiers with sustained hatred could develop and follow planned strategies to kill their enemies. The high frequency of ethnic wars of hatred that involve planned, organized killing suggest that Seneca and the dichotomy between hostile and instrumental aggression present a false picture of human aggression.

Social Sanctions and Inhibitions Against Aggression

People may behave aggressively when angered because familial or cultural norms sanction or proscribe aggression. Considerable evidence exists to support the idea that modeling and reinforcement of aggression increases aggression (Bandura, 1977; Dishion, McCord, & Poulin, 1999). Cultural groups that believe people must defend their honor when disrespected or insulted are more likely to support the idea that aggression is an appropriate response when one becomes angry. The idea that one must be aggressive when angered would increase the relationship between anger and aggression (Fives, 2003).

People will be less likely to aggress if they have moral restraints on aggression. The more they believe that aggression is wrong, or will result in social censure, the less likely they are to aggress when angry. People inhibit their aggression when they fear that their aggression will lead to an escalation that will result in their own injury or harm. The person does not have to believe that he or she will lose the fight, only that the harm caused by their opponent would be greater than they care to bear. Mutually insured destruction, or fear of retaliation, was the defense strategy of both the United States and the Soviet Union during the Cold War. Such fears inhibit aggression in individuals as well. People may not aggress because they have developed thoughts that expressing anger physically is dysfunctional and will only continue the discomfort of anger and the displeasure of conflict.

Conclusions

Anger appears to be a critical mediator in many forms of aggression. Treating only the aggression without treating the anger that mediates it will likely lead to a relapse of the aggressive behaviors. However, the relationship between anger and aggression remains complex and is likely to be influenced by several variables. It is still unclear when anger leads to verbal expression or physical aggression, when it leads to adaptive behavior, or when people just hold it in. We will attempt to address this issue in the next chapter.

6

A Proposed Model of the Relationship
Between Anger and Aggression

Given the research and theories presented in the previous chapters, we now propose a model to explain how anger leads to aggression. Darwin, James, Freud, Lorenz, Dollard, and Berkowitz all suggested that humans feel some type of urge, drive, desire, or motive to strike out aggressively when attacked. Berkowitz's theory and supporting research has shown that any unpleasant stimuli may spark this urge. Although all these authors suggest that this desire to aggress is instinctual, the notion of human instincts has fallen out of fashion. Humans appear to possess few instincts (Pinker, 2002). The idea that some instinctual connection exists between unpleasant stimuli and the urge to be aggressive suggests that human's are primed to be aggressive and undermines the view that humans are a reflection of their environment.

If Darwin, Dollard, and Berkowitz are correct, and if anger, negative emotions elicited by unpleasant stimuli, or a perceived unpleasantness arouse a desire to hurt the perceived initiator of the emotions, this reaction most probably would have evolved for survival. Yet, if the desire to aggress exists in humans, what kind of psychological construct is it? Is this connection an instinct? The concept of instinct requires that a specific behavior pattern become activated by a specific stimulus. Given that so many possibly unpleasant stimuli can trigger aggression that can be manifested in so many ways, the concept of instinct does not seem to fit here (see Buck, 1988, for a review). This chapter will try to resolve how we learn to become angry and aggressive.

The Drive-Reduction Model

William James and Sigmund Freud proposed that aggression is a biological drive. Biological drives, such as the drives for air, food, water, sleep, temperature regulation, pain avoidance, and sex, cause internal bodily disturbances that result from a lack of the needed stimuli. These stimuli are usually required for survival, and the acquisition of the required resource is reinforcing. The sex drive is different in that a failure to mate eliminates the chance of leaving progeny but does not compromise the individual's own survival. The positive reinforcement of sex itself increases the chance of leaving offspring. Whenever one of these drives is unmet for a period of time, some type of stimulation in a specific area of the brain occurs. As this stimulation increases, excitement increases in the motivational centers of the brain that direct the person to satisfy the drive. Doing so reduces the drive and the stimulation and excitement in those areas of the brain. Learning determines how and where the person finds what is needed to satisfy the drive (Buck, 1988). Does the desire to aggress fit the drive-reduction model? We think not. The neurological pathways of drive-reduction motivational systems that compel humans to get those things necessary for survival and reproduction are clearly identified by science (Buck, 1988; Carlson, 2001; Panksepp, 1998). The brain pathways identified in aggression do not follow the same patterns as those pathways that control the biological necessities of life. All biological drives have a brain site specific to that drive that senses whether the drive has been satisfied. If it has not been, the brain activates the motivational system. No one has yet proved that the desire to aggress produces a biological-based drive similar to these basic survival drives. Science has identified no area of the brain that monitors the discharge of aggression and then triggers the motivation system when aggression gets too low.

Thus, aggression does not fit the hydraulic-system model suggested by James, Lorenz, or Freud's aggressive drive or Thanatos. In addition, no evidence has emerged that the urge to attack accumulates in strength over time when no aggression is expressed, like the hydraulic metaphors used by Freud and James. To our knowledge, no theoretical rationale or empirical evidence has appeared in the literature to support the value of a hydraulic-drive model. Also, the aggressive-drive model fails to fit the drive-reduction model of motives necessary for survival. The aggressive urge described by Darwin, Dollard, and Berkowitz is a temporary state that easily dissipates once the threat or the target is removed.

The phenomenon of displacement in aggression suggests that aggression does act like a drive. If one cannot find rice or water to survive, bread and wine will do. When the target of one's urge to aggress proposes a mighty threat that makes attack unwise, attacking a safer target may be more likely. If a person becomes angry with someone of higher social status, power, or strength, and the angered party wants to strike back but fears retaliation, he or she often picks a different target (Novaco, 1993). However, displacement does not work in some of the ways that Freud and Lorenz postulated. They believed that symbolic representations of aggression, such as watching an aggressive sport or violent film, would reduce the aggression drive. Thus, people could reduce the aggressive drive that was initially aimed at a high-status or stronger opponent by going to the coliseum to watch gladiators in ancient Rome, or by tuning in to Monday night football in modern America. Freud believed that such symbolic aggression was good for society because it allowed for the discharge of the aggressive drive and would reduce the degree of actual aggression. However, research has shown that just the opposite is true. Observing aggressive entertainment increases the probability that aggression will occur in the future. Thus, the existence of aggression displacement may not support the aggressive-drive model.

Displacement of aggression is poorly understood. Other mechanisms besides the discharge of accumulated energy might explain it. Possibly, people satisfy a revenge motive when they displace their attacks onto another person. They convince themselves that they have "evened the score." Somehow, causing harm to another, even if it is not the person at whom one is angry, seems like justice. Another possibility is that the arousal in the anger-aggression system provided by one set of stimuli lowers the threshold necessary to trigger aggression in a new stimulus. Although we need more research to understand the process of displacement, its existence fails to support a drive-reduction model of aggression.

Attempts to propose an innate aggressive motive have failed because they have all proposed models analogous to the motivational systems involved in biological needs. As we have pointed out, no evidence exists to support such models. James, Freud, and Lorenz all believed that our biological motive for aggression was based on a hydraulic model of energy. The aggressive drive created a reservoir of energy that needed draining. This energy could be "discharged" by engaging in cathartic or symbolic activities, such as viewing others' aggressive actions or even fantasizing. Freud created this hydraulic metaphor in his attempt to make psychology a science. When Freud attended medical school at the University of Vienna, a leading center for physics, that field was making great strides in hydraulics (Gay, 1988). Perhaps in a state of "physics envy," Freud borrowed the ideas of hydraulics to explain human motivation. Emulating the models used in physics, he felt, would make the new field of psychoanalysis more scientific. The notion of cathartic release and behaviors designed to reduce negative energy is frequently employed in the treatment of anger. However, research has consistently failed to show that cathartic release of energy reduces a person's anger or aggression. In fact, engaging in cathartic activities increases the probability that one will become angry or behave aggressively (Bushman, 2004). The drive model also fails to explain what we know of the RAGE system, the neural pathways of affective aggression. The RAGE system starts by activating areas of the frontal cortex that detect differences in what the person expects to happen and what has occurred (Panksepp, 1998), not by activating brain sites similar to those that the hunger drive monitors.

Aggression as an Acquired Motive

If the model of biological needs and hydraulic drive does not explain the desire to aggress, what mechanism explains it? Could aggression be an acquired drive? Acquired motives develop when we pair the reinforcers that satisfy basic motives with other stimuli. These stimuli then reinforce and become desirable on their own, and people will work to attain them (Buck, 1988). Thus, if a person ate while viewing a certain boring TV program, the TV program might become a secondary reinforcer because of its consistent pairing with food. Eventually the person might work to watch that program, and the program could be a reinforcer capable of strengthening other responses, even though the program was originally boring and not reinforcing. Although people learn to aggress, we believe that it is unlikely that the desire to aggress develops solely as an acquired motive paired with a biological drive. Such a mechanism would leave the development of aggression solely to associative learning and not guarantee its occurrence when needed. If aggression did develop this way, we would find more cultures without aggression. Although cultures differ in their degree of aggression, anthropologists have not yet found the utopian aggression-free culture (Konner, 1982).

Perhaps aggression is developed as an acquired drive through learning to avoid pain and frustration. Activation of the RAGE system may be related to our instinct to escape pain. The presence of stimuli that produce pain impedes survival. Humans are motivated to remove such stimuli, and this removal is reinforcing. Thus, people learn to anticipate pain in the frontal cortex, and this anticipation triggers the RAGE system. The successful removal or avoidance of pain reinforces the connections between the anticipation of such stimuli and anger arousal and aggression. Perhaps, to enable one to avoid the unpleasantness of frustration, frustration arouses the same areas as pain—those that trigger the impulse to aggress. In this way, anticipating frustration is associated with arousing anger and aggression. The frustration that leads to the urge and any resulting aggressive acts may remove the frustration. Thus, the urge and the aggressive behavior are negatively reinforced. If the resulting aggressive act leads one to get the desired object, the aggression may be positively reinforced as well.

Aggression as an Effectance Motive

Emotions and motives are strongly linked. This connection has received much attention in psychodynamic models of clinical disorders and therapies. However, the link between emotions and motives has received less attention in more modern clinical psychology. Experimental or scientific psychology still studies affective motivational systems. We propose that anger is part of an affective motivational system that generates several strong motives that drive or influence the occurrence of aggressive or adaptive behaviors. One motivational idea that might explain aggression is effectance motivation. Psychology has long noticed that humans do many things that are not immediately necessary for survival. Interacting with the environment and developing competencies or control over the world are important behaviors for growth and reproductive fit. Effectance motives are those intrinsic motives to interact and master the environment (Buck, 1988; R. W. White, 1959). Such motives influence exploration and stimulus seeking and motivate effective ways of dealing with the environment. This theme appears to build on achievement motivation. Through studying this motive, psychology has discovered that a sense of control and agency is reinforcing to people. We propose that the desire to aggress may be classified as an effectance motive that develops a sense of self-efficacy, control, and accomplishment.

Aggression may be a fundamental behavior in the repertoire of the effectance motives. The basis for developing aggression may be the mechanism in Berkowitz's model. The experiences of unpleasant or painful stimuli, or stimuli associated with them, motivate a reaction to repel or remove the source of pain (Buck, 1988). Striking out and attacking is the first thing one does to stop an unpleasant stimulus. Such behaviors are not elegant and ignore the long-term consequences. Nevertheless, they do make unpleasant things go away and provide the illusion of control, and as such they are reinforced. Initially, aggressive behaviors are used to repel unpleasant stimuli or escape or avoid pain. However, the lesson may be that anger arousal and expression and physical aggression help one achieve goals. Unpleasant stimuli are associated with and then activate areas of the brain involved in the effectance motives that seek to control the environment. This explains Berkowitz's finding that any unpleasant stimuli or any emotional state can trigger aggression or the desire to control the environment and stop the unpleasantness.

Crucial to our model is how effectance is initially acquired. We suggest that the model starts with Berkowitz's theory (Berkowitz & Harmon-Jones, 2004) that unpleasant stimuli motivate an urge to strike out or aggress. Berkowitz believes that such a response is innate. This theory stands in contrast to cognitive models of anger arousal. Berkowitz does not deny that cognitions can arouse anger or that they can augment the experience of anger once aroused by unpleasant stimuli. There is considerable disagreement among emotion theories on this issue. Cognitive theorists (Clore & Centerbar, 2004; Smith & Kirby, 2004) point out that it is hard to define a priori what is an unpleasant stimulus; one needs an organism's response to it. Also, they question whether all humans experience any given stimuli as unpleasant. They would argue that some appraisal process is required for stimuli to be experienced as unpleasant. We would argue that some stimuli, such as pain or loud noises, would be classified as unpleasant stimuli and may instinctively trigger responses to repel or remove them. However, the majority of unpleasant stimuli may be learned or may involve some type of appraisal.

Developmentally, simple and direct aggressive behaviors may be the first actions a young human takes to expunge negative stimuli. If the success of these early behaviors is rewarded, then the desire to aggress becomes stronger. As the child grows up and more stimuli are evaluated as unpleasant and successfully repelled, the strength of this association will increase. We propose that social-learning factors such as modeling and reinforcement can influence whether this initial desire grows to a strong motive or whether it remains weak and other methods of coping with negative stimuli and states are reinforced. Also, the reinforcement history of this learned reaction might depend on the parents' tolerance for aggression as a means of resolving conflict. Parents who tolerate such behaviors may produce more aggressive children. Also, the successful reinforcement of the urge to repel or remove unpleasant stimuli may relate to physical strength. Children who are physically larger or stronger relative to their peers may attain more reinforcement. The unpleasant feelings that arise from failing to get what they want may also be removed by aggressive behavior. Thus, in our view the distinction between affective and instrumental aggression becomes blurred.

We think it is important to discriminate between healthy and adaptive motives generated by adaptive, or nondisturbed anger, and destructive motives generated by disturbed anger. Adaptively, anger generates a motive to change the environment. Aggression is sometimes necessary to change the environment. Healthy people may have no option to change their environment besides aggression and may choose aggression reluctantly. Here the motive is to control not to harm. Harming or punishing others for failing to follow social rules may, however, work to ensure conformity and a stable community. Humans harm others to ensure equity in resources or to punish those not following social rules. Such harm is believed to be appropriate and just and may even be satisfying to those who carry it out and to those who observe its practice. This is referred to in the evolutionary-psychology literature as vicarious punishment (Knutson, 2004). Humans recognize that if others do not see a penalty for rule violation they too will break the rules. Some harm to others, in the service of achieving conformity and honesty, is desirable. Humans spend quite of bit of energy allotting just enough harm to maintain the social order. This task is difficult and is the ultimate province of our justice system. Disturbed anger, however, may include a desire to harm others over and above what is necessary to maintain social order. Here, aggression or the infliction of harm is the motive. These two motives are distinct. Failing to distinguish them will result in a failure to differentiate between healthy and disturbed anger.

To follow our model so far, the presence of frustration, unpleasant stimuli, the perception of an attack, or the perception that another person might take one's resources or status arouses an undifferentiated emotional state that activates simultaneously two motives. (In addition, some form of cognitive appraisal may be necessary for certain stimuli to be considered frustrating.) The first is the motive to flee or avoid the negative stimulus, and the second motive is the *effectance* motive to control or eliminate the frustration or threat.

Once a person recognizes the negative emotion and the desire to flee or aggress, appraisal processes are activated that focus on the relative strength of the threat and potential resources to repel or deal with the threat. These appraisals can lead to fear, anger, or depression. That is flight, fight, or freeze. Once the appraisal process determines which emotion is experienced, motives consistent with that emotion are strengthened, and those that are inconsistent with that emotion dissipate. Thus, if a person makes the appraisals that lead to anger the motive to control or attack increases and the motive to flee dissipates. Also the stronger the emotional experience the greater the strength of the motive. As the level of trait or state anger increases, this urge will increase. The satisfaction of this urge has great reinforcement value. It feels good. The flow chart in Figure 6.1 illustrates this model.

Revenge is the term most often used for the desire to strike out and harm another. This desire to harm others or seek retribution is strongly reinforcing. We think the role of this reinforcer is presently underrepresented in current models of aggression. Our experience with angry clients shows that they sometimes enjoy striking out at others. We propose that anger generates motives to control the environment or aggress. Genetic, developmental, and learning factors and the intensity of state anger will increase the strength of this motive. Learning plays a crucial role in determining the strength of this motive. The original desire may be no more than an urge to control the environment and drive away aversive stimuli. However, if this desire results in the infliction of harm on others, a person can learn to enjoy

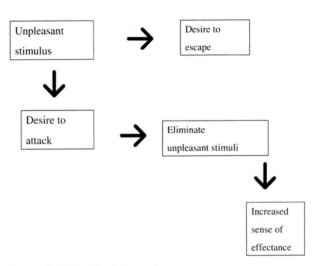

Figure 6.1. Model of Aggression

inflicting harm. Consider the development of secondary reinforcers in learning theory. Whether through pairing a primary reinforcer with another stimulus or through repeated rehearsals of the act, a person can cultivate a desire. Just as people can cultivate tastes for wine, foods, or entertainment, people can cultivate a taste or motive for hurting others. Clinically we have seen this type of progression described by aggressive-conduct-disordered adolescents and antisocial adults.

The level of state and trait anger will also influence the strength of these motives. The greater the state anger, the stronger the motive becomes. Trait anger reflects the frequency, intensity, and duration of the person's anger and the number of stimuli that trigger anger. The higher the trait anger, the more the person has practiced the response and rehearsed thoughts that intensify the urge. Therefore, the urge will be stronger in those with higher trait anger. Consider people who have high trait anger, frequently want to hurt others, and have a history of acting on those desires, versus those who rarely experience anger, do not tend to desire to hurt others, and commit fewer vengeful acts. The first group has experienced the reinforcement of hurting others. They have learned to enjoy the nuances of seeing the pain in another's expressions or gestures. Or perhaps they have learned to wait and see another person embarrassed after a well-planned assault on their social standing. Our point here is that just as experience helps develop a taste (motive, urge, or desire) for wine, certain cuisines, music, literature, or clothes, people can nurture the urge to hurt others. In the development of all tastes, experience helps educate one as to the nuances of the enjoyment.

Also, the greater the empathy a person has, the less likely it is they will enjoy inflicting harm. Humans as a rule have difficulty causing pain to others or killing them (Baumeister, 1997; Grossman, 1995). Again, we note that from clinical observations anger episodes inhibit empathy.

The idea that people experience a motive to aggress when angry and that such a desire can be nurtured suggests that the desire to aggress develops early in life when anger is first experienced. This idea conflicts with the present popular ideas about the development of aggression. The official view of the National Academy of Sciences (Reiss & Roth, 1993) states that children learn aggressive behavior primarily through imitation and operant conditioning. The social-learning perspective has suggested that as children progress through life, they are exposed to a greater number of aggressive models. They learn from these models that aggression is rewarded. The children's levels of aggression increase from the observations that one can acquire desired rewards through aggression. Aggression in this model is an operant and has no reinforcing value in and of itself. The harm, retribution, or control achieved by aggression is not seen as part of the reinforcement.

This social-learning model suggests that levels of aggression should be low early in life and will increase as one has more opportunity to observe aggressive peers or receive social rewards for aggressive behavior. Our model suggests that the desire to aggress occurs early in life when the emotion of anger first develops. Thus, aggressive behavior should be highest when people first experience the emotion of anger but have not yet experienced socialization to inhibit aggression and learned nonaggressive alternatives to control their environment. Aggression should decrease when infants learn to inhibit these urges.

Research models of aggressive behavior in children often portray aggression as developing later in childhood or even in adolescence. Tremblay (2003) has questioned the traditional social-learning model. He has suggested that it is not aggression that is socialized but the inhibition of aggression. Research has demonstrated that anger occurs early in infancy, as early as eight weeks. At this age, infants appear to recognize an association between the means and ends of their aggressive behavior (Lewis, Sullivan, Ramsay, & Alessandri, 1992). Longitudinally, most infants experience a decrease in anger and aggressive behavior from 14 to 33 months of age (Kochanska, 2001). Developmental studies of aggression show that aggression actually peaks in the preschool years and declines over time (see Tremblay, 2003, for a review). Even chronically physically aggressive youths, who have higher absolute levels of aggression than their peers, have a developmental reduction in their aggressive behavior across time, peaking at the same age as nonaggressive children.

Thus, the most commonly accepted theory of aggression fails to explain the data on the developmental trajectory of aggressive behavior, and some alternative model is necessary to account for the early peak in aggression. High levels of early aggression can be explained by the development of anger and a corresponding motive to control the environment in infancy. This motive provides a sense of agency to cope with frustration and, when reinforced, can become stronger. Socialization teaches people to regulate their anger, learn alternative means of dealing with frustration, or inhibit the desire to aggress.

Survival Value of an Effectance Motive

It is useful to understand the adaptive value anger has for humans and what functions it may have evolved to serve. The field of evolutionary psychology has discussed the survival value of anxiety and other emotions more than anger (see Barkow, Cosmides, & Toobey, 1992; Pinker, 1997, 2002). Anxiety inspires the flight response that has obvious survival value—our ancestors had to escape dangerous predators that sought to eat them. A. T. Beck and Emery (1985) pointed out that escaping all possible threatening situations or creatures was adaptive for earlier mammalian and human species.

Anger's ability to arouse an aggressive urge that repels attackers has obvious adaptive value. However, anger has other adaptive functions. The experience of anger signals that some conflict exists or people have not achieved some goal or not attained some resource or that some competitors are getting more or better resources. Resolution of such problems requires attention and effort. Thus, anger may motivate not only the immediately defensive acts of repelling attackers but also the attaining of competitors' resources or achieving equity in resources.

Neuroscience, Anger, and Effectance Motives

Recent findings from neuroscience partially support the notion that the activation of anger may generate *effectance* motives. Three major theories exist to explain the control of human emotions in the brain. The first and oldest theory proposes a single, unified neural system, the limbic system, which controls all emotional functioning. Second, neural theories of emotions have proposed that emotional functioning is organized around a small number of dimensions. These have included the valence of the emotion (positive versus negative affect), pleasure (pleasurable versus unpleasant emotions), level of arousal (calm versus excited), and action tendencies (emotions that prompt approach versus withdrawal). In this model, most negative emotions are associated with avoidance tendencies, whereas positive or pleasurable emotions are associated with approach tendencies. Anger is unique because it is described as a negative emotion with approach tendencies (Henrique & Davidson, 2000; Henrique, Glowacki, & Davidson, 1994; Lane, Reiman, Ahern, Schwartz, & Davidson, 1997). The third neurological theory, based on Ekman's (1974, 1992) notion of basic emotions, developed when neuroscientists searched for specific "affect programs" representing the respective basic emotions, each represented or controlled by a unique area of the brain.

A recent meta-analytic review of more than a hundred neuroimaging studies of emotional functioning in the brain tested these three theories (Murphy, Nimmo-Smith, & Lawrence, 2003). No support emerged for the limbic-system theory. Partial support emerged for the dimension theory, especially for the dimension of action tendencies that assessed approach versus withdrawal motives. Also, support emerged for the specific affect *program* model. Most important to our present discussion concerns the results for the dimensional model of emotions. The dimension that received the most support was an action tendency. The approach emotions of happiness and anger showed more activity in the anterior portions of the left than right hemisphere. Thus, emotions do appear organized in the brain around action tendencies with anger and happiness representing the approach action tendencies. Approach tendencies and anger appear in the left side of the orbital frontal cortex. Fear and depression are associated with avoidance motivations, which are represented in the right orbital frontal cortex. A recent study that specifically tested this hypothesis confirmed that state anger is associated with left orbital frontal cortex activity (Harmon-Jones & Sigelman, 2001).

The left orbital frontal cortex corresponds to the area damaged in the famous case of Phineas Gage described by Damasio (1994). Gage was a railroad construction engineer who suffered a frightful accident in 1848. While excavating rock for a new line of track Gage used a long metal rod to set explosives in the rock. The explosives ignited prematurely, sending the tamping rod like a rocket through Gage's skull. Gage miraculously lived but had substantial damage in the left orbital frontal region of the brain. Gage's skull was preserved, and descriptions of his personality and behavior were recorded. Among the many personality changes that occurred in Gage after the accident: he became more irritable, angry, and aggressive. This dramatic case study suggests that among other functions, the orbital frontal cortex also controls anger and irritability. The fact that the brain area that controls anger also is involved in controlling approach behaviors supports our theory that anger is related to effectance motives. Anger, when aroused, seems to stimulate brain areas that guide people to pursue or accomplish things rather than to avoid them.

In a related line of research, additional data from de Quervain, Fischbacher, Trever, Schellhammer, Schnyder, et al. (2004) suggests that getting revenge activates the reinforcing areas of the brain. Their research involved a laboratory task in which people could choose whether or not to cooperate, while their brain activity was assessed using positron–emission tomography. When subjects encountered uncooperative partners, the subject could choose to administer a punishment. In another experiment the subjects would have to spend money for the opportunity to punish the uncooperative partner. The punishment and even the anticipation of punishment of the uncooperative partner coincided with activation of a subcortical area of the brain called the *striatum*. The striatum is also activated when people cooperate or anticipate monetary rewards or pleasant tastes. Thus, anticipating or getting revenge seems to activate brain areas also involved in other types of reinforcement.

This area of research is new, and the results and methods require further study before firm conclusions can be drawn. However, the present conclusions appear to support the notion that anger arouses "effectance" motives or generates action tendencies to accomplish some goal.

Types of Effectance Motives

Anger is the emotion of strength and self-efficacy. Anger helps people get what they want. Without some degree of appropriate anger, people become doormats who are submissive, unassertive, and unsuccessful in attaining their goals. Thus, we propose that the desire to aggress differentiates into three motivational states. The first motive is *repelling attacks* to self, kin, or colleagues. The resulting defense has obvious self-protective and survival value. This motive for anger appears self-evident. Those with high trait anger may respond to perceived attacks that fail to represent any real threat. Those people with anger disorders may behave more aggressively because they perceive neutral stimuli as threatening to themselves or their ego and respond with attempts to neutralize the perceived threat. The more options the person has in thwarting perceived threats, the less likely they are to act aggressively. However, if their options are limited and they feel the need to defend themselves, they will become aggressive.

The two other angry motives are concerned with maintaining or surpassing the attainment of resources relative to one's peers. These include *revenge* motives, which are connected to notions of fairness and equity, and *envy*, which is related to power and domination. Evolutionary psychologists have focused on the social nature of humans and the importance of cooperation versus dishonest strategies for success. Most of the time humans can survive better if they cooperate with each other. However, some humans have adopted a strategy of cheating without getting caught that can benefit them at the expense of the group. At its extreme, we call this strategy *psychopathy* (Kinner, 2003). Anger has been called one of the moral emotions (R. S. Lazarus, 1991), and it can be instigated by the recognition that others are cheating, not following the agreed-upon rules, competing, or threatening to attain more resources. The motives aroused by anger would rectify these situations. We call this motive *revenge,* which has as its goal retribution or the reestablishment of resources according to social mores. This motive seeks a redistribution of resources. In some cases people feel revenge and so want transgressors to pay or suffer for their behavior. It attempts to redress the unfairness of other people's cheating or taking more than their fair share of resources. Revenge is the motive that seeks to take resources from the "haves" so they are equal to the "have nots." In some cases the angry person seeks justice and wants the person to suffer to the same degree that the angry person has suffered. In other cases, the angry person wants the transgressor to suffer, and any sense of equity is lost. The suffering induced by the revenge motive may be well beyond that inflicted by the transgressors. We have found that in people with serious anger problems their desire for revenge is insatiable. No degree of suffering satisfies their revenge.

Equity is not often desirable. Sometimes peers possess a superiority of resources that people wish to expropriate for themselves with no sense of equitable distribution. We call this *envy*. The envious strive to attain for themselves others' resources. These motives may seem contradictory. Revenge redresses the cheating of others, whereas envy strives to increase one's share of the pie. The human species is inconsistent in its logic. Humans want other people to live by the social rules and not cheat. However, they also want to exploit an opportunity to get things for themselves when possible.

Revenge as a Motive for Aggression

Revenge functions to attain restitution or equity. People seek revenge when they believe they were unjustly treated at the hands of others. Revenge need not be pathological and may have evolved in humans as a means of fostering equity and fairness in social relationships. Revenge appears central to humans' sense of justice in social groups because it attempts to remedy or prevent injustice or unfair treatment. Thus, revenge can be rational and moral (Bies & Tripp, 2001; W. Long & Brecke, 2003) when not taken to extremes or used to inflict excessive, undue penalties. Making perpetrators of injustice pay with the loss of resources would be a rational revenge.

All too often revenge includes the desire to inflict physical pain on the perceived attacker. Also, people wish to extract more pain by revenge than they have received. Baumeister (1997) has suggested that the Old Testament quote concerning equity in revenge, "an eye for and eye" underestimates humans' desire for revenge. We usually want an eye and a half. Although mental health professionals have paid little attention to revenge motives in anger or aggression, it has remained a staple of good drama for more than three millennia and is a common motive associated with anger and aggressive behavior.

Only a few anger or aggression measures include a subscale for revenge: our Anger Disorders Scale (ADS; DiGiuseppe & Tafrate, 2004), Deffenbacher's Angry Thoughts Questionnaire (Deffenbacher, Petrilli, Lynch, Oetting, & Swaim, 2003), the Hostile Automatic Thoughts Scale (C. R. Snyder, Crowson, Houston, Kurylo, & Poirier, 1997), the Organizational Revenge Scale (Sommers, Schell, & Vodanovich, 2002), and the Vengeance Scale (Carraher & Michael, 1999; Stuckless & Goranson, 1992), which assesses revenge in the work environment. Spielberger's (1999) state-anger measure includes some assessment of this motive in some of the state-anger scale items. The epidemiological studies of anger by Averill (1982), Kassinove, Sukholdolsky, Tsytarev, & Soloyova (1997), and Vaughan (1996) did not question their subjects about revenge or the desire to strike out. Research on the experience of anger needs to focus on the presence of revenge or the desire to hurt the target of one's anger to determine whether this drive is ubiquitous, as Berkowitz suggests. In reviewing the professional literature, we found few citations when searching *PsycInfo* and *Medline* with the term *revenge*. Doing a keyword search for *revenge* on *PsycInfo,* searching all publications, articles, chapters, or books for all years for which records were kept, through 2006, yielded just 124 references. When the search was performed to find the word anywhere in the citation or title, among the keywords, or in the abstract, 708 references were found. Using *Medline* to search for the word *revenge* anywhere in the citation, title, keywords, or abstract, only 242 references emerged.

The citations for revenge fell into several categories. Some were experimental or social–psychological studies employing college students and investigating variables that effected the desire for or actual behavioral revenge. The largest group consisted of studies from organizational psychology interested in predicting aggression in the workplace. Only a small number were associated with clinical problems. Most of these investigated the role of revenge in persons who had experienced posttraumatic stress disorder (PTSD). Such studies generally concluded that the presence of thoughts or desires for revenge were associated with worsening PTSD symptoms. Some studies investigated forgiveness and measured revenge as the starting point for the failure to achieve forgiveness. Finally, several studies in forensic science investigated the role of revenge as a motive for violent crime. Revenge was found to be one of the most common motives for crimes, including arson (Fritzon, 2001; Prins, 1995). We applaud these researchers' attempts to investigate revenge. But we still know little about this aspect of anger. If the reader is interested in learning about the anguish brought on by revenge, we suggest reading some Greek tragedies such as Sophocles's *Ajax,* or Homer's *Iliad,* Shakespeare's *Merchant of Venice,* or Verdi's opera *Rigoletto,* and Soundheims's *Sweeny Todd,* all enduring tales about the strong yet destructive human tendency for revenge.

Spielberger's (1999) revision of his state-anger scale could be used to explore this issue. This scale includes three correlated subscales of items that form three separate factors. These include the experience of anger, the desire to verbally express one's anger at the target, and the desire to physically hurt the target. In our validation of the ADS, we administered Spielberger's state-anger scale to more than 600 people, including prison inmates, psychotherapy outpatients, and a community sample. The degree that the person felt angry correlated with the desire to strike out verbally ($r = 0.82$; $df = 605$) and with the desire to physically strike back ($r = 0.72$; $df = 604$). These relationships were not linear and fit an exponential curve, meaning that as the degree of experiencing state anger increased, there was an increase in the rise of the curve. Graphs of the data suggested that at a certain intensity of state anger, all research subjects had a desire to verbally or physically strike out. Our analysis showed Spielberger's (1999) trait-anger score and the total score on the ADS (DiGiuseppe & Tafrate, 2004) significantly increased the prediction of vengeful desires made by the state-anger feeling scale. The degree of trait anger a person has adds to their desire to strike out when in an angry state. We know relatively little about the proposed readiness, desire, or drive of people to hurt others when they are angry. How widespread is this desire? What factors relate to its intensity?

We anticipate several objections to our proposal that revenge is a motive. In the operant-conditioning literature, a motive is something that people (or animals) work to satisfy. Some researchers see revenge as an automatic thought that occurs with anger (Haney, Maynard, Houseworth, Scherwitz, Williams, et al., 1996). Both the Angry Thoughts Questionnaire

(Deffenbacher, Petrilli, et al., 2003) and the Hostile Automatic Thoughts Scale (C. R. Snyder, et al., 1997) conceptualized revenge as stream-of-consciousness cognition rather than a motive.

If revenge were a motive rather than a thought, it would have reinforcement properties. Animals or people would perform tasks or operant behaviors to get revenge or enable themselves to harm others. Getting revenge is powerfully reinforcing and people will undergo pain or costs to do it. Listen to the words people use when speaking about revenge. Revenge is something people wish for as if it were a possession, albeit a fleeting one, and something that they will pay or exert energy for.

Research supports the idea that many species of animals will work for the opportunity to aggress, including fish, birds, mice, rats, cats, and monkeys (see Fish, DeBold, & Miczek, 2002; Portegal, 1979). In this research paradigm, operant conditioning occurs when the opportunity to attack an intruder serves as the reinforcement. What of humans, will they work or expend energy or resources for the opportunity to get revenge? In an interesting study that suggests revenge is a motive people will work to satisfy, Fritzon (2001) explored how far arsonists traveled to commit their crimes. When an arsonist targeted a specific individual for revenge, he or she traveled the greatest distance to commit the crime. Some individuals pay the ultimate price to achieve their revenge: life itself. In several studies, revenge was found to motivate suicide (Shader, 2003; Zilboorg, 1996). Even when unsuccessful, those who attempted suicide still relished the rewards of their revenge and continued to dream about it after their failed attempt (Maltsberger, 1993).

In our practice we often pose the question "How much would you pay in actual dollars to achieve revenge if you knew you would not get caught or receive any societal censure?" Respondents always give a number, usually in the hundreds of dollars. Thus, revenge appears to be a motive that people are willing to work for, pay for, or exchange resources to achieve. It often appears "worth it" for the person to suffer legal or social penalties to get even. Aggressive behavior does not seem so "crazy" when you calculate the reinforcement that the hedonic act provides.

We recently evaluated a 28-year-old man, Ralph, who was arrested for stalking his ex-girlfriend. Ralph reported that he knew stalking his ex-girlfriend upset her and that was the reason he did it. The stalking resulted in Ralph's arrest, jail time, and large legal bills. When we asked Ralph to consider how much his actions had cost him, Ralph responded with the familiar, "I don't care what it cost. It was worth it." How often have you heard angry, vengeful people say that they "do not care" what their aggression cost them? Clinicians and law enforcement officers often take this statement to reflect the "craziness" of such people. Obviously, they are deranged to make such a comment, since the cost appears to be so much higher than whatever they accomplished by aggression. Such hedonic calculus does not appear to make sense when you assume that relatively little is gained by revenge. But for the angry, vengeful person, the cost is often worth it.

Although revenge may have some adaptive features, it can function like a symptom of psychopathology and lead to tragic outcomes, as befalls the characters in *The Iliad, The Merchant of Venice, Sweeny Todd,* and *Rigoletto.* In relationships between nations and ethnic groups, revenge and retaliation have produced profoundly counterproductive results (Pettigrew, 2003). As well, revenge has been shown to impair the normal grieving process. Stuckless (1998) found that people who believed that a perpetrator was responsible for the death of a loved one and experienced a strong desire for revenge found life less comprehensible, manageable, and meaningful. Studies of revenge and the big-five personality dimensions showed that revenge was negatively associated with *agreeableness* (McCullough & Hoty, 2002; McCullough, Bellah, Kilpatrick, & Johnson, 2001) and positively associated with *neuroticism* (McCullough, Bellah, et al., 2001). Revenge has also been associated with lower satisfaction with life (McCullough, Bellah, et al., 2001). In studies of elementary schoolchildren, pursuing revenge on a friend was strongly associated with lacking friends and having poor-quality friendships (Rose & Asher, 1999). When psychological interventions have targeted revenge, improvements in anger and adjustment have resulted (Holbrook, 1997). Some research suggests that cultures may differ in the degree of desire for revenge their people typically exhibit (Kadiangandu, Mullet, & Vinsonneau, 2001), and future investigations should focus on how a desire for revenge is transmitted within a culture so that we might learn to prevent its negative influences.

Power and Domination as a Motive for Aggression

The third motive, *envy,* concerns domination or competition. It focuses on acquiring the target's resources. Envy motivates competition to attain the limited resources that others may have or to dominate another person in social status or rank. Anger that motivates competition focuses the person on acquiring things that the person believes are necessary for his or her survival. Our model suggests that envy is an emotion within the anger category. Can we consider envy a part of the anger experience? Words for emotions convey information beyond the feeling aspect of the experience. Words for emotions sometimes reflect the events that arouse the emotion or the reaction and thoughts one has with the emotions. *Jealousy* and *envy* are two such emotional words. The *Oxford English Dictionary* defines *envy* as the hostile feeling provoked when a person covets the resources or positions of others. Envy differs from anger not because it feels different from anger but because the stimuli are different. *Anger* is a word that reflects the feeling, regardless of the eliciting stimuli. *Envy* tells us that a person has an aroused state about someone else's having some resources the person desires. *Jealousy* can be the same feeling state; it differs not in the state but in the provocation. Jealousy is aroused by the possibility that another can take that which you already possess. Thus, we propose that envy and jealousy are not separate human emotions. We use these words to describe a state of anger that a person has toward a target having something the person wants, or toward a target wanting to take away what the person has. The experience of envy and jealousy will depend on the degree to which the person is satisfied with having achieved his or her goals compared with what others have attained in competition, or the degree to which other people express an intention to usurp his or her possessions. Envy and jealousy motivate domination. Of course, not all motivation to achieve a goal is part of the domination motive. Some people achieve for the joy of effectance motives. We hope all our readers recognize the positive experience that comes from the sense of agency felt when one completes a task one enjoys doing. But not all people achieve because they enjoy the task. Motivations may include outdoing a specific competitor, being perceived positively by others, or just experiencing the joy of winning.

A stronger objection could be raised concerning our linking competitive behaviors and domination to a motive aroused by anger. What evidence do we have that anger evokes such a motive? If anger arouses a motive to compete to reach a goal, it could be its own reinforcement. However, consider how often you have seen or heard people despise or hate a competitor. Hate and contempt may be the facets of anger more relevant to such a motive. As mentioned in chapter 3, these emotions are variants of anger, with hate having less physical autonomic arousal and contempt having the arousal of disgust. Can you recall someone's relishing the achievement of a goal, not in its absolute sense, but in achieving it over a rival? A good example is the anger and competition aroused by athletic rivalries. Consider the case of Joe, an avid New York Yankees fan. He hated nothing more than a New York Mets fan. For non–New Yorkers or those unaware of American baseball, these are two professional teams in New York City. Joe was referred to treatment after his arrest for assaulting a Mets fan seated near him at a Yankees-versus-Mets game. Joe wanted his team to win. He had strong negative arousal toward the Mets and toward their fans. What was the real threat to Joe? He did not gamble, so no money would be lost or gained by the game's outcome. However, if the Mets won, he did lose bragging rights to the best baseball team in the city, that is, his symbolic position in social rank. Watching the game, he became very angry with the Mets and their fans, who were competing for the same "bragging rights" as he. Joe had an intense desire to dominate those who supported the Mets, which eventually led to his assaulting a Mets fan. Change the city: Chicago White Sox versus the Chicago Cubs; change the game: the football teams the Giants versus the Jets; change the country: Manchester United versus London Arsenal—and the emotions, motives, and behaviors are the same.

Adaptive anger may lead to the motive of repelling threats. However, revenge and domination encourage the person to achieve equity in resources, conserve resources, or attain resources. Disturbed anger, however, can lead to intensification of these motives to the point that they dominate a person's life and are unfulfilled. For example, continued suspiciousness represents an attempt at sustained vigilance in order to repel threats. Excessive revenge focuses on hurting a specific person for the pain they caused the vengeful person. Prolonged desires for revenge require a tremendous amount of energy and divert one from other productive goals. In its more disturbed form, revenge makes the vengeful person want to hurt almost anyone to somehow bring the degree of suffering in the world to the level they think their own is. Excessive envy may result in an excess focus on the accumulation of resources well beyond those held by any competitors. Such a lifestyle keeps one in a continuous state of aggressive competition, to the exclusion of life's other goals and pleasures.

Additional Variables That Influence Aggression

Several variables moderate the effect of the motives of repelling attack, revenge, power, and domination that are aroused by anger. For example, the degree of resource inequity may increase the sense of moral indignation and unfairness and increase the urge to aggress. High trait anger or an episode of particularly high state anger will also increase the desire to aggress. Also, the longer a person ruminates about the injustice and remains in an angry state, the stronger the motive to aggress becomes.

Other variables influence whether one acts on the desire to aggress. If one's family or social group sanctions aggressive behaviors to achieve one's goals, the desire to aggress may increase. If one's culture and family has prohibited aggressive behavior, one develops moral restraint and inhibits aggression. Neurological impairments that interfere with self-control and inhibition may also make one more likely to give in to aggressive urges. However, it remains unclear why people respond to some provocations with controlled anger but explode with aggression at others. As noted in chapter 5, Gilligan (1996) proposed that murderers often kill people over trivial insults because they think they cannot get enough respect even in minor situations and so the minor insults they receive reflect just how worthless they are. However, most murderers who have killed over trivial insults have withstood similar insults at other times without responding violently. So why do people aggress only sometimes when they are angry?

Self-Control as a Muscle

Angry people often describe their aggression and anger-out as uncontrollable. "I couldn't control myself" is a common refrain of the angry person. We think the work of Baumeister and Muraven (Baumeister, 2003;

Baumeister, Bratslavsky, Muraven, & Tice, 1998; Muraven & Baumeister, 2000; Muraven, Tice, & Baumeister, 1998) on self-control helps explain this process. They suggested three major theories of impulse control. The first theory assumes that self-control is a skill that one can learn. The second assumes that self-control results from knowledge structures. Activation of schema concerning self-regulation and the consequences of behavior leads to self-control. Finally, self-control has been thought to resemble an energy that can be depleted and then restored. Self-control is like a muscle that gets tired from excessive use. Through a series of experiments, Baumeister and Muraven have shown that the energy or muscle model best explains how experimental subjects performed on self-control tasks. Attempts to exert self-control consume mental energy, and excessive attempts at self-control can deplete this energy and result in the failure to regulate behavior. These results apply across tasks. That is, attempts to control either a thought and emotion or a behavior will not only decrease the ability to control a similar task once the energy is depleted, but the person will fail to control other tasks as well. Thus, mental energy that can be used for self-control, like energy in a battery, is a limited resource. Once depleted, it needs to be recharged.

Repeated insults or anger-control tasks may result in a person's resisting the urge to attack. However, as the assaults continue, a person may give in to such urges as his or her resources dwindle. We think that this often happens. Some people may try to remove themselves from verbal conflict because they become aware that they are approaching the limit of their self-control resources. Frank was referred to our anger-management group after being arrested for domestic violence. Frank and his wife, Trudy, had been arguing and exchanging insults for about 30 minutes when Frank felt he could no longer control his anger. He left the room and went to the den. Trudy followed him and continued their discussion. Frank left the room again and went to his workshop. When Trudy followed him again and resumed the argument, Frank shoved her out of the room. This interaction is often a prototype of interactions in dysfunctional marriages. Sometimes men, who are the ones who leave the interaction, are advised to stay and finish the conversation. However, given the findings of Baumeister and Muraven (Baumeister, 2003; Baumeister, Bratslavsky, Muraven, & Tice, 1998; Muraven & Baumeister, 2000; Muraven, Tice, & Baumeister, 1998), we think that it is best that people do remove themselves from conflict when they sense that they are reaching their limit. Although no degree of insult on Trudy's part justified Frank's action, he may have served himself and Trudy best by removing himself from the house rather than acting aggressively. We would also advise spouses like Trudy not to pursue a fleeing partner and force them into continued discourse. Again, while Trudy's behavior did not cause Frank to aggress, she could have recognized Frank's attempt to calm down and not have followed him. Teaching couples to acknowledge when they have reached their respective limit of self-control and to request an argument be postponed until they both are level-headed could prevent serious aggression.

Sleep, rest, and positive emotional experiences restore the mental energy so people can restore their ability to exert self-control. Also, repeated practice of a self-control task appears to strengthen one's ability to exert self-control in that particular activity (Muraven, Baumeister, & Tice, 1999). It is uncertain whether practicing the exercise of self-control increases one's overall ability to control oneself. Exercising self-control in one task appears to strengthen self-control in that task and may not generalize to others. Possibly this occurs because a well-rehearsed self-control task strengthens the synaptic connections in the pathway, requiring less energy in similar situations.

Is Anger-Out Impulsive?

Baumeister and Muraven's muscle theory of self-control explains interesting findings concerning anger and aggression. We found that scores on our ADS Rumination subscale accurately predicted the ADS Impulsivity subscale scores and that such a relationship produced an exponential curve. Also, we found that several measures of anger-in and high trait anger predict scores on anger-out or anger-related aggression exponentially. The longer one ruminates or holds anger in and thus attempts to control the desire to aggress, the more that person depletes the self-control energy necessary for inhibition. When the self-control energy is consumed, inhibition fails and aggression is more likely. Such a rapid decline in self-control feels like a sudden surge of impulse. Thus, rumination may be an important step in the loss of control and the experience that one has behaved aggressively because one has lost control. However, the phenomenon of impulsivity is deceptive. Long periods of rumination and the struggle to hold one's anger in may play a more important role in aggressive impulses than previously recognized.

Consider Jack, who was extremely angry with his boss, Sam, and had a desire to hurt Sam by yelling, defaming Sam to others, and sabotaging Sam's success. Suppose Jack got angry one a day and stayed angry for five minutes. If Jack had one aggressive urge per minute and was 95% successful in controlling his aggressive urges, Jack's chances of succumbing to an aggressive urge would be very low. Suppose Jack had high trait anger and got angry with Sam and others 10 times a day. When Jack gets angry, he ruminates for two hours per angry episode. At one aggressive urge per minute, Jack would now have 1,200 aggressive urges. Given the same success rate of controlling 95% of his hostile urges, Jack might fail to control 60 of those urges and commit that many aggressive acts. The process described by Baumeister (1997, 2003) is much more complicated. The more Jack ruminates, the stronger the urges will be and the greater the strength required to control them. The faster the anger episodes come, the less time there is for Jack to have a restorative experience to replenish his self-control energy, and the greater the chance of reaching a depleted state. Aggression becomes more problematic when other variables are added to the mix. If Jack is also tired, struggling to stay on a low-fat diet, trying to stop smoking, and concentrating on a difficult work task, the drains on his self-control add up. With so many tasks consuming Jack's self-control resources, Jack may become depleted more quickly.

The idea that self-control is a limited resource helps explain one other aspect of anger and aggression. Angry, aggressive episodes often occur when a person is tired, hungry, or stressed in some other area of life. People often reveal to us that although they have often been angry at the target of their aggression, their anger episodes usually did not lead to aggression. The aggressive episode occurred at a time when their resources to control their aggressive desires were depleted because they were under stress in so many other areas. This can create implications for treatment. AA groups advise alcoholics who struggle to inhibit drinking urges to be aware of when they are tired, hungry, and cranky because such states increase the likelihood of a drinking relapse. Angry clients need to assess their self-control fatigue. When they notice they are depleted, they can take time to recuperate or avoid anger-provoking situations.

Some Objections to Our Model

One objection to our model of aggression concerns its heavy focus on the affective, emotional causes of aggression. Our suggestion that anger drives such behavior seems to fly in the face of the popular social-learning approach to aggression (Bandura, 1977). Social-learning theory asserts that early environments teach aggression by modeling and reinforcing aggressive behavior. The lives of many spouse and child abusers are sufficiently filled with models of violence to account for their behavior. Being the recipient of aggression and submitting to the coercive requests of others taught them that aggression works. But what were their emotional reactions to having been abused? Dutton's (1998) research with spouse abusers and Gilligan's (1996) and Pincus's (2001) research with murderers suggest that these people experience intense resentment about their own abusive treatment and have experienced shame and insults to their sense of self-worth. They are overly sensitive to any hint that they are not respected. Thus, anger, resentment, and sensitivity to strike out when they perceive a threat to their self-worth or the withdrawal of affection also play a significant role in explaining the behaviors of certain types of violent offenders. We believe that the social-learning explanation of reinforcement and modeling, and the arousal of resentment and aggressive desires because of the experience of strong emotions are compatible, not competing, explanations of aggression.

We suspect that social-learning factors do more to curb the motive to aggress. If we are correct that the desire to aggress represents an effectance motive, and that it operates early in life, young children may engage in aggressive behavior fairly early. As already noted, charting aggression by age reveals that people are most aggressive in the preschool years. Studies over the last 70 years have demonstrated that a decrease in aggressive behaviors occurs between preschool and elementary school (see Loeber and Strou-thamer-Loeber, 1998, for a review). Thus, aggression peaked early and decreased with age for most people (Tremblay, 2003). The peak appears too early to be accounted for by only social learning-theory variables like modeling and reinforcement. If these variables had such a strong effect on aggression, one might expect aggression to rise over the lifespan with the accumulated influence of reinforcement and successful models on a person's behavior. It is more likely that such early aggression results from the urges associated with frustration and anger. Thankfully, as one matures, social learning has its primary effect, which is to reduce the aggressive desires of most people. We are not suggesting that social-learning theory is wrong but that social-learning variables do not promote aggressive behavior as much as they inhibit our desire to behave aggressively.

We again return to Averill's metaphor of a blueprint. Social-learning theory helps the person draw the blueprint to behave aggressively. It teaches which aggressive behaviors will be sanctioned, censored, or effective. But you do not need a blueprint unless you want to build a house. The angry motives provide one with the incentive to use the blueprint that was learned from models and one's reinforcement history. The two models are complementary and do not invalidate each other. So too is the motivational–affective approach. A person may have learned effective ways of hurting others through modeling and reinforcement. However, he or she has to want to hurt a specific person before he or she will implement these learned behaviors. The affective-motivation system of anger activates and directs these previously learned behaviors.

Conclusions

There are several important observations in this chapter. First, the debate still rages about whether or not cognitive appraisal is necessary for the arousal of some aggressive reaction. Perhaps Berkowitz (1990, 2003) is correct, and some perception of unpleasant stimuli is all that is necessary to trigger an angry response and aggression. The perception of pain or noxious smells may constitute such stimuli. However, cognitive appraisal is a common path to anger arousal and aggression when the triggering unpleasant stimuli are disrespect or failure to achieve social status. Second, our model suggests that the emotional arousal of anger plays a greater role in eliciting many types of aggression than other models of aggression. Third, we contend that anger and aggression appear early in human development, as early as ages two-and-a-half to three. These responses are almost automatic, as Berkowitz has suggested (1990, 2003). Nurturing of these responses or learning how to inhibit them determines whether anger and aggression become well-established behavioral patterns. This differs from the traditional social-learning model that suggests that anger and aggression are learned throughout a life span. Finally, we believe that operant learning plays a central role in establishing both the emotion of anger and the response of aggression, as we will discuss in Part III.

Part III

Cognitive and Behavioral Models of Anger

7

Behavioral Models of Anger

At present, there are two major approaches to explain emotions. The first involves behavioral or conditioning theories, and the second relies on cognitive-appraisal theories (Power & Dalgleish, 1997). Emotions can be aroused by exciting conditioned or learned connections between the activating stimuli and the emotional response. Classical or instrumental conditioning accounts for how these responses are learned. These connections are usually established without our awareness. Cognitive appraisals often involve some type of higher-level mental process that occurs within awareness. However, as noted in the following chapter, some cognitive activity may not be conscious and can be learned through association. Over the past few decades considerable heat has been generated in the debate concerning whether conditioning or cognitive variables mediate emotional and behavioral responses. This debate has more than just theoretical importance. Since the primary theoretical orientation in clinical psychology today is the cognitive behavioral theory, one would expect that therapies in the cognitive behavioral tradition would include explanations that involve both types of mediating pathways. Recent theoretical work by Power and Dalgleish (1997) suggests that the dichotomy between cognitive and behavioral processes needlessly simplifies human psychology. They believe that two separate pathways can lead to emotions. The first is the automatic, modular, effortless, inflexible pathway that uses parallel processes, requires little awareness or attention, and is more difficult to modify. The second pathway is slower, sequential, and dependent on higher-level structures, and requires more effort, awareness, and attention to arouse the emotion. This second pathway is more flexible and easier to modify. Power and Dalgleish (1997) do not hypothe-size about the neuroanatomy of these pathways. However, the first path-way appears to rely on conditioning principles or associative learning. Such connections might be subcortical in the thalamus. The second appears to rely on higher mental processes (Carlson, 2001; LeDoux, 1996, 2002; Pank-sepp, 1998).

This model explains several interesting phenomena. The first concerns people's experience of almost simultaneously having different emotional reactions to the same situation. An understanding of such dual arousal is important in anger since people frequently experience anger along with other emotions such as fear, depression, or shame. Consider our client Hector, who had been traumatized in an automobile accident and experi-enced both fear and anger when he thought about the crash. Hector felt fear automatically when faced with anything that reminded him of the accident or driving. This fear reaction appeared to have been mediated by classical conditioning processes. Hector also felt angry with the other driver who had behaved so recklessly. Hector's anger was driven by the idea that the acci-dent could have been prevented had the other driver operated his vehicle more safely. Hector's fear motivated him to avoid cars in general and the intersection where the accident had occurred. His anger motivated him to repeatedly contact the other driver by phone and e-mail and express his anger verbally and in writing. Thus, conflicting emotional reactions to stim-uli reminiscent of the same event aroused emotions that propelled Hector to both avoid and approach stimuli associated with the accident.

Each emotional–behavioral pathway may best respond to interventions aimed at the processes underlying the particular emotional reaction. For example, Hector's fear and anger would be treated differently. In this case, exposure-based interventions based on conditioning principles would be used to reduce his fear reaction, and cognitive restructuring would be im-plemented to overcome his anger.

Another problem resolved by the Power and Dalgleish model is that slower, cortically mediated processes can become fast, automatically medi-ated processes. Consider the survival value of quicker reactions for emo-tional experiences. One function of emotions is that they have evolved to inform people that problems exist and that responses to such problems are required. In harsh environments, the more cognitive processes required between the recognition of a stimulus, the emotional experience, and the response (fight, flee, or freeze), the greater the chance of harm or death. Quicker reaction time to threats would have been naturally selected in humans. Thus, repeated firing of the slower, sequential, interactive, con-scious connection between a threat and an emotional response can result in associations between the specific stimulus and the emotional response at a lower level in the pathway, thereby eliminating several synapses and short-ening reaction time. What may have originally begun as a slow, cognitively mediated path from some stimuli to anger may, over time, become an automatic response.

This seems to fit well with our clinical experiences. Many angry clients have good insights into the reasons they become angry. They easily become aware and report the automatic stream-of-consciousness thoughts that occur with their anger experiences. They can also access more tacit schematic cognitions that may mediate their anger. However, their anger continues to flare up quickly in response to certain stimuli, and they react before they can consciously intervene to change their thinking and behavior. Consider the case of Charles, who was referred to our anger group because of a 20-year history of anger, hostility, and verbal expression directed at his wife, Audrey. Charles had great insight and reported to us that his anger at Audrey started shortly after their marriage. When Charles returned home from work each day, Audrey would command him to do a long list of chores. Many of these chores appeared unreasonable and related to Audrey's obsessive fears and desires for cleanliness. Charles rapidly identified the automatic thoughts and irrational beliefs that provoked his anger. He recognized his thoughts that their marriage had serious imbalances in power and control because he usually surrendered to Audrey's demands as a means to "keep the peace." The group helped Charles replace these ideas with less negative attributions concerning Audrey's motives, fewer generalizations about her behavior, and a more accepting belief regarding her actions. However, Charles's immediate reaction to any request from Audrey was the same. In addition, it was observed that, in the sessions, the thought or even the mention of her produced a series of angry facial expressions and a surly vocal tone. For Charles, stimuli associated with Audrey connected directly, quickly, and rigidly to anger.

In clients like Charles, both pathways mentioned by Power and Dalgleish may mediate their anger, and aiming interventions exclusively at the cognitive pathway seems only partially effective. Using behavioral interventions aimed at the automatic pathway seems to help resolve their problem more fully. In Charles's case, exposure interventions were used to teach a new response to the stimuli associated with Audrey.

Thus, using interventions aimed at only one pathway may fail to produce the optimal outcome. Using behavioral interventions allows clients to retrain themselves to avoid the over-learned automatic response. However, even when successful, the automatic connections can quickly reemerge or gain strength if clients continue to reindoctrinate themselves with their dysfunctional thinking. Maximum benefit may require a combination of behavioral and cognitive interventions.

In the remainder of this chapter, the theoretical and empirical evidence for how these pathways to anger arousal are formed will be reviewed. The use of conditioning theories and principles to guide behavioral interventions in the treatment of anger disorders will also be addressed.

Classical Conditioning of Anger

Science has firmly established that humans and other animals learn to connect fear and anxiety through the mechanisms of classical conditioning (LeDoux, 1996, 2002). Pairing the arousing stimulus with another dangerous stimulus, or with pain or discomfort, will result in fear being aroused the next time the conditioned stimulus is presented. The question arises, however, as to whether or not anger conditions in this same way. Pavlov believed that organisms could increase their ability to adapt and survive if they could learn to associate conditioned stimuli with innate unconditioned responses (UCRs). Pavlov proposed 13 innate UCRs that could be conditioned. Among them was the desire to aggress (see Windholz, 1987). Given Pavlov's theory, several authors have attributed the learning of anger or aggressive responses to classical conditioning (Berkowitz, 1983; Ulrich & Wolfe, 1969). Despite the popularity of the belief that anger (and aggression) can be classically conditioned, very little research exists to confirm Pavlov's original conjecture. We found not a single study that has directly conditioned anger. Also, in terms of aggression, the empirical literature seriously questions whether animals or humans can learn aggression through classical conditioning. As early as 1945, Seward (1945) concluded from a series of studies that "there was no evidence that aggressiveness occurred as a classically conditioned response" (p. 38). Since then, few studies have appeared on the topic, and Seward's statement may still be true.

A few authors have reported the classical conditioning of aggression in some species of fish: blue gourmis (Hollis, Cadieux, & Colbert, 1995) and fighting beta fish (Bronstein, 1988). These tropical fish are frequently found in pet stores. In both studies, the conditioned stimulus was paired with stimuli that elicited aggression toward other male fish competing for mating territory.

Some studies have attempted to pair a conditioned stimulus with an unconditioned stimulus that elicits an innate aggressive attack in rats (Creer, Hitzing, & Schaeffer, 1966; Farris, Gideon, & Ulrich, 1970; Lyon & Ozolins, 1970; Vernon & Ulrich, 1966). During these aggressive attacks, the rats showed facial features that Darwin (1872/1965) associated with anger. However, these studies involved the pairing of the conditioned stimuli directly with painful shock to the animal. This design is unlikely to account for much of the learning of human anger, except where anger and aggression may be learned when the conditioned stimulus is paired with pain-inducing stimuli. Such a mechanism might account for the high level of anger in some people with Posttraumatic Stress Disorder (PTSD) who have been victims of abuse or combat. However, most people who are angry about abuse suffered in childhood did not respond to their abuse by expressing anger or exhibiting aggression because they were too young and weak to confront the abusive adult. Fear was most likely their immediate unconditioned response.

Therefore, people who experience anger as a symptom of PTSD deriving from a childhood trauma would have learned to associate fear with the abusive stimuli. Their anger would more likely result from appraisal processes that occurred after the abuse.

We found only one study that attempted to classically condition aggression in primates. Using squirrel monkeys, Dunham and Carr (1976) found that in this species conditioning to shock depended on the degree to which the unconditioned aggressive response (biting) was predicted or resulted in a long shock-free period. When they administered the trials randomly, no conditioned response was learned.

We found no studies that attempted to classically condition anger or aggression in humans. Some researchers reported studying the use of angry facial expressions compared with facial expressions for other emotions in fear conditioning. These studies indicated that when the conditioned stimulus was an angry face, the conditioned response had greater resistance to extinction than when learning was associated with human faces expressing other emotions (Dimberg, 1986; Dimberg & Oehman, 1983; Oehman & Dimberg, 1978; Zafiropoulou & Pappa, 2002). These results were interpreted to mean that humans have a greater preparedness to learn to fear angry faces than to fear faces expressing other emotions. However, these studies fail to tell us whether anger or aggression can become a learned conditioned response.

The entire literature on the classical conditioning of anger (and aggression) is minuscule compared with the literature on classical conditioning of the fear response. As the popular books by LeDoux (1996, 2002) have shown, researchers know a great deal about fear conditioning in humans and other species through literally thousands of published studies. The specific neural pathways of fear conditioning and the neurotransmitters that operate these pathways are well established. Researchers have a deep understanding of the urge to flee and how that urge is transferred to other stimuli in adaptive and maladaptive ways. Why then has a scientific literature of classical conditioning discussing the urge to strike out or fight and the emotion that often accompanies it progressed so little? Based on the lack of evidence one is tempted to conclude that classical conditioning of anger and aggression cannot occur. Perhaps many more researchers have tried to establish the classical conditioning of anger or aggression, and our review encountered the "file drawer problem." This refers to the fact that scientific journals rarely publish negative findings, and negative research reports remain in the investigators' file drawers.

Does this have practical relevance? What is at stake besides the ivory-tower ideas of that long-deceased Russian theorist Ivan Pavlov? Well, a lot. The principle of Pavlovian conditioning and the knowledge that has grown in the last hundred years has led to helpful interventions for the treatment of anxiety disorders. Pairing stimuli with relaxation or other incompatible responses and exposure-based extinction interventions have been very effective.

Exposure to feared stimuli is a unifying principle of psychotherapy and has been used across theoretically disparate orientations such as behavioral, psychodynamic, and Gestalt therapies. Based on empirical evidence, exposure treatments are preferred for the full range of anxiety disorders. Should they be used to treat anger problems as well?

Exposure-based treatments for anxiety disorders were originally based on models of classically conditioned responses. Will exposure-based interventions, developed for anxiety, work equally well for anger disorders? For example, in exposure-based treatments for anxiety, the treatment is more effective if clients are instructed to feel fully their emotions and not avoid them. The more that clients attend to their feelings and report feeling anxious while experiencing the exposure imagery, the better the treatment outcome. Also, clients should be exposed to the stimuli until they experience a reduction in their anxiety (see Foa & Kozak, 1986). If clients distract themselves from the imagery or leave the in-vivo stimuli, they successfully escape or avoid the feared stimulus, thereby experiencing negative reinforcement through the removal of an unpleasant stimulus. This strengthens the relationship between the conditioned stimulus and the conditioned response.

Since the inception of behavior therapy and Wolpe's (1958) demonstration of the effectiveness of systematic desensitization and other exposure treatments, a debate has raged regarding the mechanism underlying effective exposure interventions for anxiety. Theorists have proposed that reciprocal inhibition, counterconditioning, habituation, and extinction could account for the effectiveness of exposure, while cognitive theories have emphasized increases in self-efficacy and cognitive restructuring (see Tryon, 2003, for a review). Tryon concluded that research on these proposed mechanisms of learning have failed to support any of the proposed mechanisms for the effectiveness of exposure interventions. Several new explanations for the success of exposure treatments have relied on neural-network theories (Tryon, 2003) and emotional-processing models (Foa & Kozak, 1986), as such explanations may best account for the behavior change that results from treating anxiety disorders.

These new emotional-processing models (Foa & Kozak, 1986) assume that once people experience trauma, all knowledge about the stimuli and responses become part of a memory–fear structure. Emotional-processing models propose that memories associated with or triggered by fear consist of a cognitive network of information. This network links the stimulus situation, thoughts about the situation, meaningful associations about the situation, and behavioral and physiological components of the response to the fear. Changes in the fear structure occur in three stages. First, the fear needs to be aroused through exposure to the provoking stimuli. If the fear structure is not activated, it is presumed that change will not occur. Next the fear should be habituated. The continued arousal for a period of 60 or even 90 minutes within an exposure-treatment session produces habituation of the physiological responses associated with anxiety. Finally, the association of the stimuli with the lowered arousal, which occurs with habituation, provides information concerning the frequency of danger or the valence of a threat. If the stimulus has been present through exposure, and habituation has occurred, the reduced arousal conveys knowledge that danger is infrequent or that the threat is of a low valence. Finally, this new learning should result in a lowering of affect across a session. In the next exposure session, lower arousal should be expected. Research has demonstrated that emotional processing appears to account for the changes associated with exposure treatments of anxiety disorders. Barlow (1988) proposed that this information-processing model could be applied to other negative emotions such as sadness and anger. Given the number of similarities between anger and anxiety, this model would seem promising for the treatment of anger responses.

Interventions for Anger Based on Classical Conditioning

Given the dearth of research in the area, a number of important questions arise. Will exposure interventions work with angry clients? If they do, does the same mechanism account for the change? Should exposure treatments for anger include the same instructions as used for anxious clients (e.g., focusing on feeling the anger and remaining angry for long periods)?

Several interventions designed to treat anger have included exposure elements and have significantly reduced anger. Many clinicians have devised these treatments on the assumption that anger and anxiety are similar emotions and, therefore, interventions used to treat anxiety should work for anger. However, research in anger treatments has only recently focused on exposure-based interventions, and very little research has attempted to devise an exposure-based intervention on a particular theory of learning or emotional processing.

Goshtasbpour (1999) used data from available treatment-outcome studies and effect sizes reported in our meta-analytic review of anger treatments (DiGiuseppe & Tafrate, 2003). An effect size is a statistic that represents a standardized measure of change in a treatment study. She predicted, as shown in the anxiety-treatment literature and based on classical conditioning and emotional-processing principles, that the more clients received instructions to feel their anger, the more they would do so, and the more effective the treatments would be. Goshtasbpour coded each study for whether or not the method section reported that the therapist instructed clients to feel their anger. This dichotomous variable was then used to predict the effect sizes of the treatment. Having clients focus on the feeling of anger resulted in a $-.52$ correlation. The more that clients focused on their anger, the worse the treatment outcome. This study suggests that although exposure remains a crucial part of anger treatments, instructing clients to maximize their degree of anger may lessen treatment effectiveness. Different procedures may maximize exposure's effectiveness, and different mechanisms may underlie its effects. Obviously, this study represents a general snapshot and has several flaws. Assessing clients' experience of the emotional state during the exposure treatment, as is typically done with anxiety treatments, would represent a better test of this treatment principle.

A slightly different conclusion is reached, from the same set of data, when examining the effect sizes of similar interventions with and without an exposure component (see Table 7.1). Interventions that focus on the development of relaxation skills and those that use relaxation skills plus imaginal exposure seem to show different levels of effectiveness. For example, in anger-management training (AMT; Hazaleus & Deffenbacher, 1986; Suinn, 1990) the client practices relaxation skills in response to anger scenes that the client develops. Clients are asked to feel their anger in response to the scenes, thus providing a context for the use of relaxation skills. Several meta-analytic reviews compared AMT to progressive muscle relaxation and noted increased effectiveness in protocols that included an exposure component.

In an attempt to explore the feasibility of using imaginal exposure for anger reduction, Grodnitzky and Tafrate (2000) provided a better test of the mechanism of action proposed by Foa and Kozak (1989). Using a small group of adult outpatients, Grodnitzky and Tafrate (2000) measured state anger within and across sessions while participants rehearsed imaginal scenes of anger-provoking stimuli. Over the course of the study, the majority of patients met a criterion for clinically significant improvement on important indices of anger. They believed that visual analysis of the process measures, which included patient reports of daily-exposure sessions, suggested the pattern of habituation within and across sessions. This is consistent with the emotional-processing model (see Figure 7.1 for an example of the visual data from two patients). However, due to the small sample size ($n=6$), they reported no analyses that indicated that habituation was related to more successful outcomes. This study represents an initial attempt to use an imaginal-exposure strategy to treat anger and awaits replication with a more rigorous design.

Another attempt to assess whether emotional processing accounted for the effects of imaginal-exposure interventions was done by Walley (2002). Her treatment and research were designed to correspond to work done with

Table 7.1
Effect Sizes (d) of Relaxation Alone (PMR) and Relaxation
With Imaginal Exposure (AMT)

Meta-Analytic Reviews	PMR	AMT
Tafrate (1995)	.48	1.01
DiGiuseppe & Tafrate (2003)	.59	.82

Reprinted with permission from Elsevier.

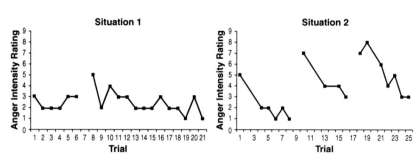

Figure 7.1. Two Clients' Anger Ratings to Imaginal Exposure Trials of Anger Scenes (From Grodnitzky & Tafrate, 2000). *Note:* Boxes represent distinct anger situations, and breaks in the line indicate a shift to a revised version of the same situation.

exposure interventions for anxiety. The treatment included the development of a hierarchy of anger-provoking situations. Participants were instructed to imagine the scenes and to report the level of their anger every five minutes throughout the exposure imagery. They held the image for at least 30 minutes, or until they had a substantial drop in their angry feelings. The participants were instructed to focus on the feelings but not to respond with aggression. Walley had research participants rate their level of state anger. The hypothesis that habituation within and between sessions, as measured by clients' ratings of state anger, would correlate with outcome measures of anger and aggression was not supported. Again, exposure was a successful intervention for anger (clients showed improvements), but the mechanisms of emotional processing did not seem to account for the effect. So far, these two early attempts at using imaginal exposure to treat anger, and the review by Goshtasbpour (1999), have not fully supported the emotional-processing theory as the mechanism responsible for treatment effects.

Using a more in-vivo strategy, Tafrate and Kassinove (1998) developed an exposure treatment for anger that involved presenting angry men with verbal insults or barbs. They created a pool of insults or negative statements that were associated with angry outbursts. In the individual treatment sessions, the therapist read a list of these barbs to the subjects in an angry tone over the course of fifteen 30-minute sessions. In each session, 10 barbs were directed at the client and then repeated. While experiencing the insults, the men were instructed to rehearse rational, irrational, or irrelevant self-statements. The authors devised their experiment primarily to examine whether the content of different self-statements were associated with differential treatment effects. A secondary focus was whether cognitive change or classical-conditioning extinction accounted for treatment effects. If anger were under cognitive control, the group that recited rational self-statements would benefit more from the exposure than those who recited irrational or irrelevant self-statements. If the three groups fared equally well, exposure alone would have accounted for the positive treatment effects. Thus, extinction of a conditioned response would be a plausible explanation for any treatment gains. The results indicated that all three self-statement groups benefited from the barb technique, suggesting that exposure alone could reduce anger. However, the men who rehearsed the rational statements improved significantly more on some dependent measures. The barb technique may not have been a good test of extinction or of Foa and Kozak's emotional-processing model. In each case the participants rehearsed some type of statement. This would have distracted the participants from focusing on the anger-arousing stimuli and the experience of anger. In addition, new stimuli, in the form of a variety of barbs, were continually directed at the participants. Thus, extinction or emotional processing would have had to occur with a class of stimuli, as opposed to one stimulus scene, as happens in exposure treatment of anxiety. This may be an advantage. Although exposure to a class of stimuli may encourage generalization to situations outside therapy much better than exposure to one stimulus at a time, this procedure deviates from the traditional use of exposure interventions, which usually expose the client to one emotionally arousing stimulus at a time for a prolonged period. Since the individual sessions lasted only a half hour, Tafrate and Kassinove's (1998) intervention did not last long enough to test the emotional-processing model, and they did not measure anger arousal within and between sessions to assess if high arousal followed by habituation predicted change.

A study by McVey (2000) from the same laboratory tested the barb technique in one three-hour massed learning trial under three conditions. One group received the barb exposure with response prevention. Participants were instructed to "focus on the feeling," and to "experience the anger." Another group was exposed while rehearsing rational self-statements. A third group was exposed while rehearsing irrelevant self-statements. The prolonged exposure trial and the instructions to focus on the feeling in this design provided a much better test of the emotional-processing hypothesis. The inclusion of a group that rehearsed rational statements provided a test of the cognitive-processing model. The rehearsal of rational and irrelevant self-statements would have diminished arousal. The rational statements were incompatible with anger arousal and the irrelevant statements would have distracted participants from focusing on the barbs or their own feelings. Participants in all groups showed statistically and clinically significant reductions on the measures of anger from pretreatment to follow-up. Also, none of the three treatments was different at follow-up. The fact that the group instructed to focus on their angry feelings failed to improve significantly more than the other groups receiving exposure suggests that the emotional-processing model fails to account for the benefit of exposure treatments for anger. Another interpretation of these results is possible. Perhaps the only real active ingredient was the exposure without affect arousal. Or, even in the cognitive-rehearsal groups, enough arousal was achieved to get the effect. The emotional-processing model may be different for anger, and any type of arousal might be sufficient for emotional processing, while in anxiety the higher levels of arousal are required.

In a third study from this group using the same technique, Terracciano (2000) compared research participants who were insulted while rehearsing rational self-statements to participants who were insulted but did nothing. He found that exposure produced a significant pre- to post-test reduction in anger, but there were no differences in outcome between the groups. Thus, the barb technique worked regardless of the presence of cognitive rehearsal.

There have been no studies using the barb technique while measuring anger arousal within and between sessions to observe habituation. Thus, they have not provided a direct test of the emotional-processing model as the mechanism of change. However, since exposure to barbs works with all types of cognitive rehearsal that distracts the client from feeling the emotional arousal, it seems that the existing research on the intervention does not support the hypothesis that emotional processing accounts for the change. As noted above, emotional processing might be different for anger and anxiety. Perhaps high levels of affective arousal are not necessary for emotional processing with anger.

The studies reviewed above show that exposure can be an effective intervention for anger. However, no consistent pattern of results emerged concerning what mechanism accounts for this success. Although Grodnitzky and Tafrate (2000) present some support for habituation as the mechanism of change, their study included only six subjects, and no direct link between anger arousal, habituation, and anger-outcome measures was made. Walley's (2002) study most directly tested the emotional-processing hypothesis and failed to find support that emotional processing accounted for the change. In the studies by Kassinove and colleagues (Kassinove, et al., 1997; McVey, 2000; Terracciano, 2000) using the barb technique, a general pattern of support was found for exposure but not for the emotional-processing model specifically. Several reasons may account for this failure. The anger-provoking barbs may not be equivalent to the stimulus used in exposure treatments for anxiety. The barbs are usually delivered every couple of minutes. Each new barb may start a new trial of exposure, which is then ended when a new barb is presented. Thus, clients were not exposed to one stimulus for a long time but to many examples of a class of stimuli. Possibly, emotional processing might have occurred with anger if clients were exposed to one long image or the presentation of one barb. Perhaps the presentation of barbs was not long enough for habituation to occur. Although early attempts to use exposure techniques have helped clients reduce anger, most of the research reported above failed to present anger-provoking stimuli for a sufficiently long period as recommended by Foa and Kozak (1986). Longer exposures may produce habituation. However, there is also the possibility that focusing on anger may produce cognitive ruminations that blame the perpetrator pictured in the stimulus, and these self-statements may reinforce angry attitudes and counteract any decrease in anger produced by habituation.

Perhaps people do not learn to associate anger with eliciting stimuli in the same way they learn to become anxious. Several researchers who have used exposure to reduce anger report they are reluctant to have clients focus for long periods on one anger-provoking stimulus while instructed to focus on their experience of anger. Such instructions may increase anger (Brondolo, DiGiuseppe, & Tafrate, 2003; J. L. Deffenbacher & McKay, 2000). As mentioned in chapter 3, anger is an emotion related to approach behaviors, while anxiety is most associated with avoidance. Perhaps avoidance is best learned through classical-conditioning processes. Anger is more associated with the brain's seeking system (Panksepp, 1998), the area of the brain that searches out positive reinforcers and directs approach behaviors. Perhaps these aspects of behaviors are best learned by instrumental or operant learning paradigms. When people become angry, they experience thoughts of justification and self-righteousness. These thoughts could provide reinforcement for the anger arousal. Also, when angry, people may rehearse vengeful images that can be experienced as rewarding. Finally, some expressions of anger may be reinforced because they are effective in getting compliance from others. Although exposure interventions do appear to work, more research is needed to learn what characteristics of the intervention will maximize its effectiveness. We do not recommend that practitioners use prolonged exposure with instructions to focus on the angry feelings until more research appears to support its usefulness.

Since exposure models have been effective, perhaps constructing exposure interventions on operant models of learning may lead to more-successful interventions. In this next section we review the literature on operant models of conditioning and their possible application in the treatment of anger.

Instrumental Conditioning of Anger

Hundreds of research articles have documented the role of reinforcement and modeling in the learning of aggressive behaviors, and a review of this literature is beyond the scope of this book (see Connor, 2002, for a comprehensive review). Despite this voluminous literature, we know little about how these same variables affect the arousal of angry emotions. Two factors seem to account for this. The first is the lack of separation of anger from aggression, and the second is the questionable distinction between instrumental and affective–reactive aggression (discussed in more detail in chapters 4–6). In the literature concerning learning and anxiety, psychologists conceptualize avoidance or escape behaviors as motivated by fear. Anxiety occurs and the behavior follows to relieve the negative experience of fear. Would we study escape and avoidance without the emotion of fear, or could we study fear without considering the behaviors that it motivates? We think not. Anger and aggression have been more easily separated because, as noted previously, people become angry much more often than they behave aggressively. In addition, anger may lead to a whole host of behaviors such as pouting, appropriate problem solving, bodily expressions, passive-aggressive actions, verbal expressiveness, withdrawal, and physical aggression. We propose that the focus on extreme forms of anger expression, usually physical aggression, has led to a poor understanding of the relationship between anger and behavior and how these are learned.

The distinction between instrumental and reactive aggression has promoted this separation of anger and aggression. The operant models of aggression popular in psychology today best explain instrumental aggression. If a person wants a goal and sees that others can attain the goal through aggression, that person is likely to use aggressive means to acquire the goal as well. If the person has attained goals with aggressive behavior, he or she is more likely to do so in the future. Factored into this model of aggression is the probability of punishment or retaliation from the victim or his or her group, or criminal detection and prosecution by society. Such theories explain how the person learns to behave aggressively but do not explain what they want to achieve by aggression. If the aggression is aimed at achieving some object, the explanation works. The same principles of reinforcement and modeling explain how people and other animals learn to get food. They do things that they observe others doing to get food or they rely on behaviors for getting food that have been reinforced. Such a model fails to explain exactly when people display these behaviors to get food. For that we need the construct of hunger and the brain mechanism that arouses hunger, food seeking, and reinforcement for getting food.

Operant psychology has long made the distinction between acquisition and performance. How people learn a behavior does not predict under which circumstances they will display that behavior. Operant models of aggression appear to have failed to make this distinction. An operant model works less well in explaining when the person uses aggression for other types of rewards such as power, status, revenge, or compliance. In these situations, affect is usually involved. Does the reinforcement of aggression also reinforce the experience of anger?

Several stages are necessary for the learning of aggression to occur. Harold was referred to us for infecting his company's computer network with a virus. Harold, a 51-year-old Caucasian man, was a computer programmer for a large insurance company. Despite being the most senior member in his department, Harold was passed over for promotion several times. Harold became quite angry when his company hired someone from outside to head his department. Managers had told Harold that they did not consider him management material. Although he would continue to receive regular raises and bonuses, they would not promote him. Harold felt that the company did not appreciate his years of loyalty and hard work. He felt angry and strongly wanted to get revenge. Although Harold was an excellent programmer and knew a great deal about the workings of the company's system, he had little experience with computer viruses. Harold had learned about viruses and virus detection from talking to colleagues who worked in that area. Once Harold became angry he decided to seek revenge and use his knowledge of computer viruses to disable the company's system.

Learning occurred along the way to Harold's successfully implanting a virus in his company's computer system. First, Harold had learned to use computers and did so for many years in his job as a computer programmer; he had learned about viruses by talking to others. Second, Harold had learned that a failed computer could cost a company both financially and in terms of embarrassment to the vice president of information technology. Third, Harold learned to feel excessively angry about his failure to reach a certain level of success. He had to learn to think of himself as unappreciated and treated unjustly. Fourth, Harold had learned that anger was associated with a desire to "even the score" and bring harm to the target of his anger. Fifth, although Harold had learned items three and four above, he still needed a target at which to direct his anger. His learned responses required a specific motive in order to be activated. Harold needed to be angry enough with someone to want to harm them. Sixth, once angry and vengeful, Harold further instructed himself on the finer details of computer viruses to accomplish his goals.

We propose that people learn anger primarily through operant rather than classical conditioning. Anger has many positively reinforcing characteristics. As mentioned above, anger is a "moral" emotion in that it is associated with self-righteous attitudes. This alone has some self-reinforcing components. Anger also gives a sense of power and control over the perceived indiscretions of others. Angry outbursts may result in others' compliance. In addition, anger promotes a desire for revenge. People enjoy revenge and will spend time, money, and effort to achieve it. When they get it, they savor it. These are characteristics of positive reinforcement.

Despite the distinction between affective–reactive and instrumental aggression, the arousal of anger and the resulting display of angry facial and bodily gestures, verbal intonations, angry content, and angry behaviors often have the effect of coercion. As mentioned above, the human species seems prepared to learn to fear angry facial expressions. Getting angry thus arouses fear in others, often resulting in the angry person's getting what he or she wants in the short run. Anger arousal can also be negatively reinforced. Negative reinforcement occurs when some behavior results in the cessation of an aversive stimulus. Displays of anger often succeed in silencing others or compelling them to cease behaviors we find unpleasant, distracting, or annoying. Examples of this can be found in many families, where an anger outburst stops a spouse or child from behaving in a way that annoys the angry person.

Becoming angry can also encourage others to avoid certain topics or issues. Such negative reinforcement may explain the lack of introspection and insight usually attributed to angry clients. Psychoanalytic theory (S. Freud, 1920) and Gestalt therapy (Perls, 1969) have proposed that people lack awareness and keep things out of consciousness. Barlow (1991) and Ellis (2003) proposed that avoiding negative emotions is a major cause of psychopathology. Recently, Hayes and Gifford (1997) proposed to link this process, which they call *experiential avoidance,* to many forms of behavioral disorders. Anger may be one way that people successfully avoid facing unpleasant situations and keep psychological pain out of consciousness. Becoming angry and expressing it through facial or bodily gestures or tone of voice may intimidate another person to avoid talking about uncomfortable topics. Thus, successful anger leads to intimidation, which then leads others to avoid topics and allows them to remain out of consciousness.

Janis came to our anger group because she feared that she would hurt her two-year-old son. She frequently got angry when the child did not sleep or made demands on her. Janis had several other stressors in her life that depleted her coping resources. She had been physically abused as a child, moved often, and, for financial security, married a man she did not love. Janis had little insight into her reasons for marrying, her frequent moves to new cities, or any of her life choices. She failed to understand why she was so angry with her son, who she reported loving very much. Whenever a group member questioned her on aspects of her life, Janis snarled or looked away in anger and pouted. Group members quickly stopped asking her about herself, and no demands were placed on her to confront uncomfortable topics. Eventually, Janis reported that she responded with sarcasm and insults when her husband approached her about the distance in their relationship and her relationship with her abusing parents. Janis was aware that she did not want to talk about these issues and resented other people's attempts to meddle in her life. We eventually helped Janis recognize that her anger intimidated others to avoid all criticism of her or mention unpleasant topics. This had allowed Janis to avoid facing important issues in her life.

Conceptualizing anger as controlled by operant rather than classical conditioning has several implications for treatment. First is the focus on problem solving. Our experience is that angry people often focus on the short-term positive consequences of their anger. Helping clients become aware of all the long- and short-term consequences of their anger often produces a dramatic change in their emotional and behavioral responses. As mentioned in chapters 17 and 18, this is an important component in the early stage of anger treatment. Teaching the consequences of anger makes one aware of the contingencies. If angry clients focus on getting revenge or compliance with their short-term goals, anger will prevail. Focusing on the quality of life instead of inflicting pain on one's enemy, or focusing on the long-term quality of intimate relationships instead of one's immediate desires, allows for other reactions besides anger. Teaching alternative-solution thinking allows for new responses to develop that are likely to lead to more desirable outcomes.

Using an operant model to understand anger also changes the way we implement exposure interventions in anger treatment. Exposure interventions should instruct the client to learn to associate a new competing, and often –incompatible, response with the triggers of one's anger. An operant model would pair the previous anger trigger with a new response, even if that response were to relax, cognitively accept, make an effective assertive response, or remain calm in the face of challenging triggers. Repeated pairings of the stimuli with the new response will make for more effective learning. Such repeated pairings may account for the success of the barb technique. In this treatment, a class of stimuli (barbs or insults), are paired with calm non-responding, rather than typical angry responses (e.g., menacing gestures, verbal retorts, stomping out of the room). Relaxation, assertiveness, and social skills are all new behaviors that we recommend teaching angry clients. Once taught, these responses also require rehearsal. Rehearsing new responses in the context of the actual anger triggers disrupts the associations at the direct automatic-pathway level proposed by Power and Dalgleish (1997). With repeated practice and reinforcement of the new behaviors, in and out of sessions, new behavioral reactions can be established in connection with original anger-inducing stimuli. A demonstration DVD showing this type of exposure procedure for anger can be found in Kassinove and Tafrate (2006). Since anger reactions may become established early in life and rehearsed over many years, people may not be aware of the reinforcers that have existed or presently exist for their anger. Thus, the arousal of anger may be well rehearsed and automatic.

Conclusions

Although classical conditioning has been enormously helpful in understanding fear and anxiety disorders, at this time it has shed little light on how people learn to become angry. Operant models, commonly studied in relation to aggressive behaviors, are also limited in explaining anger arousal. Nonetheless, preliminary results from treatment studies using exposure methods to reduce anger provide encouraging evidence for the effectiveness of this approach. The development of a comprehensive exposure model for the treatment of anger requires a far greater understanding of the process of conditioning in anger than now exists. Additional research on the precise mechanisms of how exposure works with angry clients will ultimately yield greater understanding and more effective treatment development. Since it is unclear whether instructions designed to maximize habituation, such as focusing on the anger and prolonged exposure, are essential mechanisms for change, we recommend a focus on the operant model in treatment. This approach emphasizes the development of new skills while exposing clients to existing anger triggers.

8

Cognitive Models of Anger

Anger is a moral emotion. Philosophers such as Plato, Aristotle, Seneca, Aquinas, and Descartes have proposed that appraisals of misbehavior or wrongdoing that are perceived as intended, preventable, avoidable, or at least the result of negligence arouse anger. For thousands of years people have discussed the thoughts, attributions, and evaluations that elicit anger. The long history of a connection between appraisal and anger suggests that something in the way humans think, appraise, or evaluate their environment, and specifically the misdeeds of others, has something to do with anger. Cognitive theories of emotion have gained popularity in recent times in psychology as a whole and in clinical psychology in particular.

This chapter will first highlight three areas of debate that remain unresolved in understanding the role of cognition in anger arousal. How these issues are understood has relevance for clinical practice. Several influential theories related to cognition and anger will then be reviewed. As defined in chapter 2, *anger* is an emotional response to threat. As noted in this definition, the notion of threat is viewed in a broad sense (e.g., physical well-being, property, present or future resources, self-image, social status, maintenance of social rules that regulate daily life, and physical comfort). Such a broad use of the term encompasses both the evolutionary adaptation of accurately perceiving and reacting to threats related to safety and also the complexities of the types of threats more common to humans in modern times. Thus, the remainder of this chapter is organized around the evaluation of threat. A variety of thinking styles have been proposed to be instrumental in the development and maintenance of anger reactions. These will be discussed in terms of two broad themes: perceptions of threats to physical well-being and resources, and perceptions of threats to self-efficacy and self-esteem. Certainly, given the lack of research in this area, other ways of organizing relevant cognitions may be equally valid. Specific cognitive processes are identified and may prove useful in formulating cognitive interventions. The traditional conceptualizations of cognitive distortions and irrational beliefs proposed by A. T. Beck (1999) and Ellis (1977; Ellis & Tafrate, 1997) are integrated into these themes. Evidence for the relationship between anger and self-efficacy and the self-esteem hypothesis is critically reviewed.

Anger and Cognition: Unresolved Issues

Great debate still exists in psychology concerning the way cognitions and appraisals influence human emotional arousal in general (Davidson, Scherer, & Goldsmith, 2003) and anger in particular (for the most recent debate, see Berkowitz & Harmon, 2004; Clore & Centerbar, 2004; and Smith & Kirby, 2004). It is important to keep in mind that appraisals are not always conscious. People make instant appraisals that are learned through association and that result in emotional arousal before a person becomes aware of the appraisal. This has clinical implications for practice. Most cognitive theorists do not assume that all anger-arousing thoughts are in a person's awareness. The clinician and the client still have to work to discover them. Clients often comment on the automatic nature of their anger experiences. In applying cognitive interventions with angry clients, practitioners may need to spend more time identifying thoughts that are outside a client's immediate awareness and that precede or are concurrent with anger experiences. This issue of whether thoughts always precede anger experiences is discussed further in the next section.

Another caveat concerns general cognitive theories of emotion and those theories focusing on disturbed emotions. The majority of theories of emotional arousal focus on normal, nondisturbed emotions. If we know that a certain appraisal process leads to nondisturbed sadness or anger in normal people, does the same appraisal process operate to produce depression and dysfunctional anger in clinical samples? What processes or cognitions, if any, need to be added to account for the arousal of dysfunctional anger in clinical populations? Is it simply that the same cognitions are activated more often or more strongly to produce disturbed anger, or are some other additional cognitive variables necessary? As of now we have no clear answer to these questions.

The third issue is that several clinical theories of emotional arousal suffer from a uniformity myth. They do not so much focus on the unique cognitive aspects that arouse anger but on the difference between disturbed and functional emotions. The work of A. T. Beck (1999) and Ellis (1977; Ellis & Tafrate, 1997) are examples of this. Ellis (1977) hypothesized that the construct of being demanding causes not only disturbed anger but also all human emotional disturbance. The cognitive errors related to low self-esteem that A. T. Beck (1999) identified as associated with dysfunctional anger are similar to those he proposed as arousing anxiety and depression (A. T. Beck, 1976). However, Beck's models focus on cognitive factors that are shared in the arousal of disturbed affect in general and others that are unique to anger. The same can be said of Novaco's (1975) coping-skills approach. However, Novaco's (2003) more recent clinical anger-assessment scale focuses on cognitive variables such as anger justification, rumination, and hostile attitudes that are unique to the arousal of disturbed anger. Descriptive research into the types of thoughts that are characteristic of and also unique to dysfunctional anger episodes would be of great value as clinical models continue to develop.

Influential Cognitive Theories

Any cognitive theory of anger arousal must first encounter Berkowitz's reformulation of the frustration–aggression hypothesis. Originally, the frustration–aggression hypothesis stated that all aggression resulted from frustration and that all frustration would lead to some type of aggression (Dollard, Doob, Miller, Mowrer, & Sears, 1939). Berkowitz's (1962) earliest revision of this theory stated that anger played a mediating role between frustration and aggression. His theory stated that frustration aroused anger. Anger included a strong desire or urge to harm the target of one's anger. Various appraisals such as the relative strength of the person versus the target and the probability of retaliation determined whether one acted on the urge to harm. Berkowitz (1990, 1993, 2003) later revised his theory to suggest that any unpleasant stimuli, in addition to frustration, led to a negative affect that included the urge to flee and the urge to aggress. The person's appraisal after this initial arousal of negative affect led to fear, sadness, or anger. Berkowitz's model has prompted considerable research indicating that unpleasant stimuli do precede thoughts, feelings, and behaviors that are usually associated with anger (Berkowitz & Harmon-Jones, 2004).

As we mentioned in chapter 4, several criticisms have been leveled at Berkowitz's (1990, 1993, 2003) later theory. Are there stimuli that are unpleasant to all humans? Can there be an instinctual reaction to fight or flee without appraisal or any association with other stimuli? Do emotional reactions require some type of appraisal that is registered in the brain through learning an association between two stimuli, one of which has been linked to anger? While the jury may still be out on Berkowitz's theory, this theory has nevertheless forced anger theorists to acknowledge that some quick-acting pathway to anger arousal or some type of undifferentiated negative-affect response does exist and that this response is followed by further appraisal, clarity of affective arousal, and action. Even if Berkowitz's model does not ultimately prove an automatic connection between unpleasant stimuli and anger, a two-process model of anger arousal will be needed to account for his research results.

Novaco's (1975) work has lead to the most widely used clinical intervention for anger, self-instructional training, and is based on a theory similar to that of Berkowitz (1990, 1993, 2003). In Novaco's model, a person appraises external events and this results in a general state of physiological arousal. People then label the arousal as anger, fear, guilt, or something else, based on contextual cues. People then choose a path of action based on their appraisal of the situation and what their experience tells them they can expect as an outcome. Appraisals occur after an initial stage of arousal. Self-instructional training teaches clients to become aware of anger-provoking stimuli and to rehearse appraisals and instructions for new behaviors.

We believe Power and Dalgleish's (1997) SPAARS model is the most comprehensive cognitive theory of emotions. SPAARS stands for *S*chematic, *P*ropositional, *A*ssociative, *A*nalogue, *R*epresentation *S*ystems. These systems represent the cognitive processes involved in appraisal before an emotion is aroused. As discussed in chapter 7, Power and Dalgleish proposed that two separate pathways could arouse all emotions. This first pathway is the direct-access or automatic route. It may involve innate prewired pathways; however, it is most likely to consist of over-learned associative responses that are learned in the course of development. The direct pathway is fast, effortless, and inflexible. It relies on parallel processing, involves little or no awareness, requires little or no attention, and changes with difficulty. The direct pathway is modular in that different stimuli may trigger specific emotions. The second pathway is the appraisal route. This pathway involves first evaluating a situation for goal relevance. The appraisal pathway is effortful, slow, and flexible. It uses sequential processing, requires attention, is conscious, and is interactive and easier to modify.

When a person enters a situation, he or she may have one emotion activated by the automatic route and a separate emotion (or the same emotion) activated by the appraisal route. According to this model, stimuli set off an analogue system associated with the sensory system involved with that stimulus (e.g., visual, auditory, olfactory). Once stimuli are registered in the analogue system, they are sent to three semantic-processing systems that operate in parallel. First, is the *associative system*. This involves the direct, automatic route. If the stimuli are associated strongly with any specific emotional reaction, that emotion is triggered. The second system is the *propositional system*. This is a language-based processing system that requires a great deal of awareness and linguistic processing. If the linguistic propositions activated by the analogue sensory system are associated with a specific emotion, then that proposition triggers the associative system. If propositions lead to stimuli associated with deeper, more schematic structures, the schematic system is triggered. The third system, *schematic processing,* is the most cognitively advanced. It can receive input directly from the analogue areas of the brain or from the propositional system. This is the system that involves all higher-level appraisals and contains the schematic information and structures usually associated with emotional arousal in cognitive approaches to psychotherapy. In Power and Dalgleish's (1997) model, stimuli can cycle through the three levels of processing. That is, a stimulus may first activate the direct automatic route. As this association is being processed, the stimuli may then trigger the propositional route. Even if both these systems are activated, the stimuli could still trigger the schematic system. Thus, three parallel routes can activate one emotion, or different routes can activate several different emotions.

The SPAARS approach differs from Berkowitz's (1983, 1990, 1993, 2003) and Novaco's (1975, 1985, 1997) model in that SPAARS does not propose that the automatic, direct route arouses a general negative affective state or a general undifferentiated physiological arousal. The automatic route arouses specific emotions. Also, the SPAARS model asserts that direct, automatic associations can arise through any type of learning process. Conditioning processes can allow stimuli to trigger the associative processes in emotions. Also, schematic-level appraisals that once aroused emotions at a higher level can be transferred to the associative level with repeated activation. Thus, a stimulus that once activated only the schematic pathway can, over time, trigger the direct, automatic pathway.

The three models presented above share some similarities. They all propose a dual-pathway approach to anger arousal. They point out that some anger is aroused by quick, almost immediate, associations. Once this pathway is aroused, higher-level appraisals may intensify, weaken, or change the anger arousal. The SPAARS model has one proposition that is more hopeful. It suggests that cognitive change at the schematic level that is repeated may disrupt and realign the associations at the direct, automatic-pathway level. All three models have important implications for clinical practice. Clinical interventions based only at a schematic level may fail or take longer to work if a client's anger is mediated by the automatic-processing level. Angry clients who behave aggressively may need interventions to immediately disrupt the direct-pathway connections before they cause serious problems for themselves or others. Since schematic-only cognitive interventions fail to disrupt the more direct associations, angry or aggressive reactions may continue to be triggered and get reinforced.

We suggest that all future analyses of anger focus on at least a dual-pathway approach to anger and develop interventions aimed at both pathways. Although the models of Berkowitz (1990, 1993, 2003), Novaco (1975), and Power and Dalgleish (1997) have great validity, we have not yet focused on which cognitions arouse anger compared to other emotions.

Evaluations of Threat

To arouse anger, a person must first experience some appraisal process around the theme of threat. In this way, some appraisals or thoughts that arouse anger may be most similar to anxiety. Many types of cognitive distortions and processes can contribute to or exaggerate a person's perception that a threat to desired goals exists. Also, a variety of historical experiences, such as abuse, neglect, or the development of maladaptive schemas of trust, acceptance by others, and entitlement may make it more likely that an individual will engage in such cognitive errors. Figure 8.1 shows the relationship between cognitive errors, the perception of threat, and anger arousal. Because emotions may be reactions to threat, cognitive theories of emotional disturbance may propose similar cognitions as leading to the arousal of different emotions. This section will explore how people can reach false conclusions that they are under threat.

Both A. T. Beck (1999) and Ellis (1977; Ellis & Tafrate, 1997) believe that a *catastrophizing* thinking process—in which the person has an exaggerated view of the probability or degree of threat—causes both anger and anxiety. Thus, targeting catastrophic thinking in therapy could reduce the perception of threat and so reduce the anger arousal. The cognitive distortions originally identified by A. T. Beck (1976, 1999), such as *arbitrary inference, selective abstraction, all-or-nothing thinking,* and *overgeneralization* may lead people to conclude that they are getting less than their fair share of resources and status. A variety of thoughts (e.g., "I never get any respect around here." "You always get to watch what you want on TV. When is it my turn?" "My colleagues at the office are always against me." "We always go to the movie that you want to see.") may therefore represent exaggerated and untrue thoughts concerning unfairness and the distribution of resources and status. These cognitive distortions will increase the perception of a threat. However, the perception of threat will likely increase the presence of

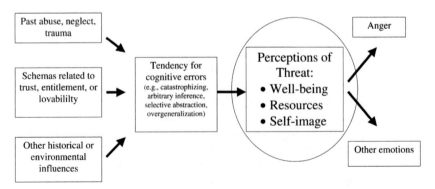

Figure 8.1. The Perceptions of Threat as a Central Construct in Anger Arousal

several negative emotions. The perception of threat alone appears insufficient to differentiate the negative emotion into anger. We suggest that cognitive distortions concerning the perception of threat that are more concerned about fairness and the relative distribution of resources and status are more closely associated with anger than anxiety. Nonetheless, any psychotherapeutic intervention that reduces *catastrophic thinking, arbitrary inference, selective abstraction, all-or-nothing thinking,* and *overgeneralization* will reduce the perceptions of threat and, therefore, reduce the likelihood of an anger episode.

In addition to the perception of threat, other specific appraisals differentiate the experiences of anger, depression, and anxiety. The fact that anxiety, depression, and anger share an exaggerated perception of threat may explain why clients often vacillate among these emotions. Some other appraisal process that is unique to each emotion is necessary to distinguish among the three emotional experiences. If a person changes the unique appraisal process without changing his or her exaggerated perception of threat, he or she will change the emotional experience but not go from a disturbed to nondisturbed state. That is, the person will go from disturbed anger to anxiety or depression. Thus, we see the vacillation among these emotions not as evidence that one emotion is secondary to another but as evidence that the person has changed or shifted the emotion-unique cognitions but maintained the exaggerated perception of threat.

Lazarus proposed that, following the appraisal of a threat, people appraise whether they have the resources to overcome the offense by attack. If one believes that he or she is strong enough to repel the offender, then anger and attack are more likely to occur. If the offender is perceived as stronger, then anger is less likely, and fear and escape more likely. Lazarus's idea overlaps with Bandura's construct of self-efficacy. Anger is facilitated when people perceive themselves as strong enough to mount a successful attack on their adversaries. This idea seems in conflict with the notions that anger comes from low self-esteem. We will return to this idea later in this chapter.

Another type of thought, related to evaluations of threat that may differentiate anger from other negative emotions, is *condemnation.* Many theorists have recognized that angry people condemn or denigrate those at whom they are angry. Ellis (1977; Ellis & Tafrate, 1997) mentions condemning others as a primary cause of anger. The belief that the other person is worthless or less than human generates anger. Ellis takes an extreme position in therapy and encourages clients to adopt unconditional other acceptance (UOA) for countering their anger. UOA involves accepting that one's transgressor may have committed an uncomfortable or horrendous act, but no one is a truly terrible or worthless human. No humans are evil, and to evaluate them as worthless or all bad ignores the fact that even if they have done bad things to us, they most likely have done some good to others. Thus, condemnation is an overgeneralization.

Social–psychological research supports Ellis's claim that thoughts about the worthlessness of others provoke anger, hatred, and aggression. In an examination of the human ability to act cruelly, Baumeister (1997) reviewed the empirical psychological research and many historical accounts of torture and genocide. The belief that others are less than human is found throughout the psychological, sociological, and historical literatures. Armies know that an effective way to encourage soldiers to kill the enemy is to portray the enemy as less than human (Grossman, 1995; Keegan, 1993).

A second thought that may also differentiate anger from anxiety and depression is *suspiciousness*. The information-processing model of angry and aggressive children proposed by Dodge (1985) and Crick and Dodge (1994) focuses on the perceptions and cognitive representations people have when they confront a problem. After they encode external and internal cues, they attempt to interpret the cues and form a mental representation of them. They then select goals and strategies to resolve the problem. Research has shown that hostile children behave maladaptively because of their initial misinterpretation of the situational cues. Perhaps because they project their own hostility onto others, angry and aggressive children seem to believe that other people harbor negative feelings toward them. These suspicious thoughts take the form of attributing hostile motives for others' behaviors. We have found that this characteristic is not unique to angry adolescents but also seems to apply to angry adults. However, there has been little research on the thinking styles of adults. Angry people believe that others act in a purposeful negative way to hurt or frustrate them. Although hostile attributions for intentions are sometimes accurate, angry people are likely to make these hostile attributions even when people behave in neutral ways. Items assessing suspiciousness have been included in anger inventories such as the Buss–Durkee Hostility Inventory (Buss & Durkee, 1957), the Aggression Questionnaire (Buss & Perry, 1992), the Novaco Anger Scale (Novaco, 2003), and the Multidimensional Anger Inventory (Siegel, 1986). Items in our Anger Disorder Scale (DiGiuseppe & Tafrate, 2004) that assess suspiciousness include: "I suspect that friends talk about me behind my back," "I believe that you cannot trust other people," "I think that people I know may turn on me," and "I believe that if you let people get close to you they will let you down or hurt you." Suspiciousness is not paranoia. Angry people lack the delusional thinking that characterizes paranoia. However, those with paranoid ideas are very likely to be angry.

Consider Eileen, who came for treatment after she threw a cup of coffee at her husband during an argument. Eileen had been married for more than five years, and she reported that her husband had been kind and generous to her most of those years. However, she always suspected he would leave her. She also knew that he would not do his share of the household chores. During one session, Eileen reported a fight with her husband after she arrived home from work and found that he had left work early, come home, cleaned the house, made a great dinner, and greeted her affectionately on her arrival. She wondered just what did he want from her? He must be doing this to butter her up for something. Perhaps he had lost his job, or spent too much money. Eileen could not take the behavior at face value and enjoy it.

Thoughts related to suspiciousness are difficult to replace in angry people. Clients often interpret challenges to these thoughts by a therapist as siding with the enemy. We suggest developing a good therapeutic alliance in which there is clear agreement on the goals of changing the client's anger before the therapist attempts to challenge these dysfunctional ideas. Also, using a standardized anger measure such as the Anger Disorders Scale (ADS) and providing feedback to clients on areas in which they score high will allow for a discussion of the role of suspicious thinking (assuming that is such an area) in a way that is acceptable to most clients. Once the area is identified as a problem, a collaborative approach to monitoring and changing the thoughts can be implemented. Several of the specific distorted automatic thoughts identified by A. T. Beck (1976, 1999) and others (Leahy & Holland, 2000), such as mind reading, fortune telling, arbitrary inference, selective abstraction, dichotomous thinking, or overgeneralization may be useful clinical targets in reducing suspicious thinking.

Threats to Physical Well-Being or Resources

Because angry people often believe that they have been threatened or harmed, the justification for harming the transgressor is built in. Any anger experience or any anger-motivated aggressive actions a person takes to conserve his or her threatened resources or repel the transgressor are "justified." Even thoughts about revenge and "getting even" include themes of justification. Angry people are always right. Their anger is righteous. The revenge they wreak is deserved. Their hatred or disdain of others is earned. Novaco (2003) included a justification subscale in his anger inventory and has empirically demonstrated this aspect of thought as crucial to anger. This emphasis on correctness often prevents angry people from negotiating and resolving conflicts. Justification thoughts also hinder the establishment of a therapeutic alliance, which is discussed in more detail in chapters 17 and 18.

Responsibility for the perceived threat or blame is an important appraisal that may also determine which emotion is experienced. Internal attributions place responsibility on the self and lead to anger at oneself, shame, depression, or guilt. External attributions place responsibility or blame on others and result in anger at another person. Clore and Ortony (1991; Clore, Ortony, Dienes, & Frjida, 1993) and the information-processing model proposed by Crick and Dodge (1994) have shown that the

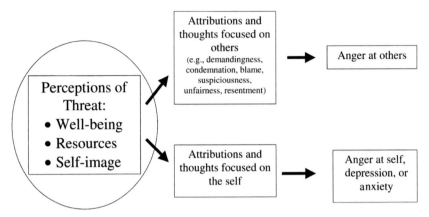

Figure 8.2. The Perceptions of Threat and Self- Versus Other-Directed Attributions and Emotions Arousal

perception of another's blameworthiness leads to anger. Figure 8.2 shows how perceptions of threat and internal versus external attributions may lead to different emotions.

As the opening line for this chapter says, anger is a moral emotion. People become angry when they perceive or believe that they may lose resources that they deserve or to which they are entitled. Anger results from the perception of an injustice, lack of fairness, or grievance (Tedeschi & Nesler, 1993). Thinking about and proclaiming that one's competitors have violated the moral code clogs the angry person's stream of consciousness. As we mentioned in previous chapters, anger appears to have evolved as a way to ensure the attainment of adequate resources for survival and reproduction and to drive away threats to resources already acquired. Humans are social animals who have developed moral codes to allocate resources, protect their resources, and maintain social cohesion. Violations of moral codes represent a threat to one's position in society and the resources that one has attained by the societal rules or that come with one's status. Fairness represents the fulfillment of the moral–legal system for the distribution of resources and status. A person's failure to follow the rules is a threat to the future flow of resources and suggests that the person would need substantial energy to enforce or renegotiate the rules. So a threat to one's moral code sends off an alarm. An angry response may coerce the transgressor to follow the rules and return to the agreed-upon system of resource allocation.

Because anger works so well in getting other people to follow the rules, people may be reinforced to perceive a threat to their resources or status as "unfair" and a violation of the moral order. People believe that they have attained their positions and possessions because they deserve them. Few of us think that chance has favored us. A person's claim that his or her possible loss of resources violates a moral code may intimidate the transgressor just enough to back off. Vocalizing such thoughts may represent an attempt by the angry person to have the social group come to his or her aid, reinforce the moral code, and restore or protect the angry person's resources and status from any competitors. Thus, rumination and verbal discussion about moral rules and "unfairness" often work to enlist a stronger person to intervene on the angry person's behalf, which reinforces these thoughts. Humans prone to seeing threatened resources in moral terms may have been reinforced over the centuries and passed their thinking along genetically. People who are particularly rigid in their thinking about morality should be more prone to anger. Also, those whose resources and status in society are the most threatened will use the existing moral rules to defend their position and will claim the rules were violated by their competitors when a loss of resources or status seems possible. This explains why those just a step above the lowest class in a society harbor the greatest prejudice against the lowest class.

Thoughts of unfairness do not lead only to disturbed anger. They may arouse appropriate adaptive anger in those who are exploited, and they have often led to revolt and social change. Such moral anger may lead people to renegotiate their business or interpersonal relationships. The recognition that one deserves better treatment than one has received and that one has been in an unfair and imbalanced exchange of resources may arouse suffi-cient anger for one to behave assertively to renegotiate the relationship and the exchange of resources. The evaluation of unfairness may explain why depressed people or anxious people often become angry when they get better. Once they surrender their self-effacing and denigrating beliefs, they see they have not deserved their bad treatment and believe they have not been getting their fair share. Anger and assertively asking for what they want may follow these revelations.

Related to the theme of unfairness is the proposed irrational belief of *demandingness.* Demands reflect beliefs about the way the world should be or what people expect the world to be. As such, they represent an ex-pectation. Ellis's (Ellis, 1962, Ellis & Dryden, 1988) and Walen, DiGiuseppe, and Dryden's (1990) rational emotive behavior therapy (REBT) approach posits that people become disturbed because they demand that people or the world be as they wish. Thus, REBT asserts that rigidly held expecta-tions could lead to anger. Ellis calls this rigid thinking "hardening of the 'oughteries.'" He believes words like *should, must,* and *ought,* and the phrase *have to* can represent rigid expectations of the world. Believing that one's desires or preferences must be realized or be met by others reflects what Ellis means by *demandingness.*

Several preliminary investigations on thinking styles lend support for the relationship between demandingness and anger. DiGiuseppe and Froh (2002) found that the endorsement of demandingness, relative to other cognitive constructs, correlated higher than any other items with the level of state anger in psychotherapy outpatients and office workers. In a second study, Tafrate, Kassinove, and Dundin (2002) examined anger episodes among adults with both high- and low-trait anger. Participants reported an individual episode of anger and answered questions related to the following anger dimensions: triggering stimuli, appraisals, subjective experiences, behaviors, and outcomes. In an analysis of appraisals it was found that the REBT construct of demandingness was the most commonly reported thought for both high- and low-anger adults. Close to 90% of the subjects acknowledged demanding that the target of their anger should have acted differently. This finding was interpreted to indicate that demandingness is a central theme in most anger episodes.

A better way to understand the REBT theory of demandingness and its effect on emotions is to consider wants and demands as schemata or cognitive expectancies about reality. Emotional disturbance results from "Expectancy—Reality—Discrepancy." Such discrepancies arouse negative affect in people (Eells, Fridhandler, & Horowitz, 1995; Horowitz, 1997). Piaget proposed that people can resolve this discrepancy in one of two ways. The first is assimilation. Here a person keeps the schema intact and incorporates from their experience information consistent with the schema while ignoring the inconsistent data. People can also use accommodation. In this process the person changes the schema because of the "Expectancy—Reality—Discrepancy." Assimilation is easy. Accommodation requires greater cognitive energy. Anger results from assimilation, which is failing to change a schema about the world when it fails to match reality. Not all schemata lead to anger. The most problematic schemata concern the existence of things people want. When angry, we confuse what we want with the reality of what is.

We ask the reader to perform this thought experiment that we use in our anger groups. Imagine a long-term loved one—a parent, sibling, spouse, mate, child, or friend. Imagine something this loved one does regularly that really angers you. Imagine that person engaging in that act. Now think about if you have ever had these thoughts while angry with this person: "I cannot believe that he or she did it again," or "How could he or she do it again?" These cognitive responses show surprise. When we do this thought experiment people often chuckle at this point because they recognize these thoughts. Now count how frequently in a week or month the person has done the act that angers you. Multiply that frequency by the number of weeks or months in the year. Then multiple that number by the number of years you have known the person. Probably, the person you love has done the thing that angers you hundreds or thousands of times. Yet you cannot believe "they have done it again." The fact that people register shock and are incredulous that an event that has occurred hundreds or thousands of times before has occurred yet again suggests that they have used assimilation and not accommodation to cope with the discomfort caused by the "Expectancy—Reality—Discrepancy." We do not base our expectation of what our loved ones will do on what they have done in the past in similar situations. We form our expectations based on what we want them to do, despite their many failures to do what we wanted. We used the following thought experiment with Hank, a happily married college professor.

Hank had been married for more than 20 years. Anger, however, haunted his marriage. Hank's wife, Lisa, taught high school. Her classes started at 7:30 A.M. Each morning she jumped out of bed, quickly got dressed, and ran for her cup of coffee. She inevitably left the milk on the counter. Hank awoke hours later, since his first class was not until 10:00 A.M. When he sauntered downstairs for his breakfast of cold cereal and milk, he found the milk had been left out and was warm. All he asked was that his wife put away the milk each morning. He did not think that was too much to ask. When we asked Hank what he thought when he came down to the warm milk he said, "I cannot believe she did it again. How could she do it again after I asked her so often?"

Next, we asked Hank how often his wife left the milk out on the counter. He said every morning before work. How many mornings does she go to work? Five times per week; she teaches. Schoolteachers work about 180 days per year in his state, so he estimated that he got warm milk 180 times per year. Next, we asked how many years she left out the milk. He replied 13 years. She has done it 180 times a year times 13 years for a total of 2,340 mornings. So, why was Hank so surprised? He was a smart man, a college professor. If he based his expectations on what she did, not what he wanted her to do, he would bet on the milk being out and warm, not in the refrigerator and cold. When we asked Hank to change his thoughts and expect warm milk, he objected. Hank liked cold milk with his cereal.

Two cognitions occur here. The first is that Hank wanted something. The second was the expectation that he would get it. When we challenge clients' beliefs, they often feel invalidated. Clients fail to separate their desire (preference) and the expectation or demand. As a result, the client can misinterpret a challenge to the expectation as a challenge to their preference. For Hank, when we challenged his expectation, he thought we misunderstood that he liked cold milk. He told us how good it was, as if we did not understand his preference. It is as if the client has merged his or her desire with the expectation that it occur. Desires and the probabilities that they occur are independent.

In using cognitive interventions with anger-disordered clients it is necessary to overcome this roadblock. First, we teach the client the distinction between the preference or desire and the schema or expectation that something will or must occur. Second, we posit or reinforce the preference. Therapy is not interested in changing Hank's preference for cold milk with his cereal. We agreed it was better. Third, we challenge the schema, expectation, or demand that the preference must be met. Just because people like something does not mean it must happen. Fourth, we help the client develop a rational replacement idea such as: "Just because I want Lisa to put the milk away so it is cold when I come downstairs does not mean that she will do it. Lisa felt guilty about all this. She had good intentions, but in her rush to leave for work it did not happen." The realization that things do not have to happen because we wish them to often leads to problem solving. People do not try to solve problems they believe should not exist. People must first acknowledge that a problem exists before they will attempt to think of a solution. Hank did just that. Once he acknowledged that Lisa was just rushed in the morning, he bought two cartons of milk. She left one out and the other remained in the refrigerator for him.

Thoughts about the unfair distribution of resources over the long-term frequently haunt angry people. *Resentment* refers to the attitude that life has treated one poorly or worse than most other people. Grudges over past maltreatment drive many people's anger. Our ADS (DiGiuseppe and Tafrate, 2004) includes such items as: "I resent that life has treated me badly," "I feel bitter and think that I have had more bad breaks than others," "I think I have had a harder life than most people," and "I feel jealous that life seems to go easier for other people." Items assessing such attitudes have been part of anger scales such as the Buss–Durkee Hostility Inventory (Buss, & Durkee, 1957), the Aggression Questionnaire (Buss & Perry, 1992), the Novaco Anger Scale (Novaco, 2003), and the Multidimensional Anger Inventory (Siegel, 1986).

Grudges can last for decades. We once treated a 60-year-old client who held a grudge against a fellow high school student who had teased and bullied him at the age of 14. Forty-six years later, our client was still angry. The client still lived in the same community with his tormentor from adolescence and they occasionally crossed paths. On these occasions our client, still obsessing about the past events, thought about revenge and believed that he could have had a better life if he had been treated differently by his tormentor.

Crosby (1976) proposed that four specific cognitions lead to resentment. First, people perceive a desired outcome as obtainable. Second, they believe that they are entitled to that outcome. Third, they do not attribute the failure to achieve the outcome to themselves but hold others or even a system responsible. Finally, they make a social comparison to others who possess or have achieved the outcome. The resentful person believes he or she is, in relevant ways, like those who possess the desired outcome.

Folger's (1997) referent-cognitions model notes that resentment is a counterfactual emotion. Resentment is a feeling about what could have been. The term *referent cognitions* refers to mental simulations about alternative circumstances. Referent cognitions take the form of a narrative involving a story about what happened and what could have been different. The alternatives for the narrative come from three possible sources: the observations that other people have been treated better, observations that the person had been treated better in the past, or imagined scenarios in which the person could have received better treatment. The referent or imagined outcomes involve some social comparison, as in Crosby's model.

Another aspect of referent or imagined cognitions involves the differences between the actual outcomes and the referent or imagined outcomes. People are less likely to feel resentment when they experience a bad outcome that occurs because the person responsible has behaved in a morally acceptable way. However, resentment will occur if people imagine that the responsible person could have kept a higher moral standard. Even if the two processes mentioned above, those of imagined outcomes and those of imagined actions, occur, resentment may not result. If people believe that the responsible person will make some restitution for the disparity between real and imagined outcomes, resentment is thwarted.

There is considerable research in industrial psychology to support both theories. However, it is unclear how applicable these models are to clinical anger. Both theories focus on resources that people failed to attain or the perception that better resources went to others. Such theories are applicable to situations in which a peer gets a promotion, a raise, or better working conditions.

In terms of clinical approaches to combat resentment, as well as other thinking styles such as condemnation and long-term perceptions of injustice, the work of Robert Enright (Enright & Fitzgibbons, 2000) has broken new ground in the psychological study of forgiveness. Forgiveness is often considered a topic for theologians and philosophers. Nonetheless, those who experience resentment and blame suffer greatly. Enright proposed that forgiveness fosters psychological health and the lack of it causes pain and suffering. Enright believes that people are healed when they forgive. We have found among clients who have suffered extreme losses (e.g., death of a child, loss of a spouse) that continued anger and rage interfere with social functioning, impede healthy self-care, and disrupt careers. The few clients who have been able to forgive, even under extreme circumstances, seem better able to move forward in their lives. It must be noted that forgiveness is a process that can take years to achieve. For a detailed discussion of the use of forgiveness in the context of an anger-treatment program, readers are referred to Kassinove and Tafrate (2002). For clinical demonstrations of the use of forgiveness in treatment we recommend the demonstration DVD created by Kassinove and Tafrate (2006).

Threats to Perceptions of Self-Efficacy, Self-Worth, and Self-Esteem

The idea that a threat to a person's self-image sets the stage for experiencing anger is widely expressed in the literature on anger and on aggressive behaviors. R. S. Lazarus (1991) proposed that perceived threats to a person's ego identity or self-esteem arouse anger. He believes that threats that undermine a person's representation of his or her self to others will almost invariably activate anger. Psychologists generally refer to a person's view of his or her self as *self-esteem*. However, self-esteem can be differentiated into a sense of global self-worth, and self-efficacy (Bandura, 1977). Although these two constructs are related, we will discuss their effect on anger separately. We have found the literature in this area rather confusing. Some theorists have suggested that anger results from appraisals of high self-efficacy. Others see anger resulting from low self-esteem. Many theorists see anger resulting from ego threat or social rejection. The theoretical, research, and clinical literature seems to have failed to distinguish between self-efficacy, self-worth, or self-esteem, and rejection of the self.

Self-Efficacy and Anger

Early attempts to distinguish anger from other emotions focused on the high self-efficacy associated with anger. Consider the words of Charles Darwin (1872/1965) in his classic book on the expression of emotions.

> Few individuals, however, can reflect about a hated person without feeling and exhibiting signs of indignation or rage. But if the offending person be quite insignificant, we experience merely disdain or contempt. If, on the other hand, he is all-powerful, then hatred passes into terror. (p. 237)

At the end of the nineteenth century, G. Stanley Hall (1899), the founder of modern psychology, had a similar notion:

> Anger is an expression of egoism, and vanity and hyperself feelings intensify it. The greater and more formidable the foe, the more fear expels anger and prevents its ebullition. The weakness, which instead of hitting back turns the other cheek, is at a certain stage an advantage. Weak people cannot hate or be very angry. (pp. 524–525)

Consistent with Darwin and Hall, Richard Lazarus (1991) proposed that anger followed from a secondary appraisal that one was stronger than one's threat. As the disparity between coping resources shifts in favor of the threat, anger fades to fear. Several other theorists (MacKinnon & Keating, 1989; Roseman, 1984) have made similar claims focusing more on perceived power, and they concluded that anger includes an experience of having greater power or potency than the eliciting threat. Izard (1977, 1991) reported that anger is associated with a sense of strength and self-assurance. These reactions result in the angry person's feeling brave and courageous and facing or confronting problems. Frijda (1986) suggested that a belief in the ability to cope with a potential threat causes anger. That is, if the threat is stronger than the person, one experiences fear. Conversely, if the person is stronger than the threat, he or she experiences anger. He said, "Anger implies hope." This follows from the idea that one is strong enough to favorably change the threat. Roseman (1984) says that when people experience anger they believe, "aversive events are not necessary or uncontrollable." Still others believe that anger triggers problem solving around obstacles that frustrate goal attainment (Averill, 1982; Mikulincer, 1998; Scherer, 1984).

Exploring the relationship among various cognitions (including self-efficacy) thought to elicit anger, DiGiuseppe and Froh (2002) asked adults recruited from employment settings and an outpatient-therapy clinic to report retrospectively on an anger-provoking experience. The participants rated their state anger intensity and the intensity of cognitions during the anger experience from 0 to 100. The cognition items were in the following areas: high self-efficacy to reflect the work of those mentioned above, thoughts of revenge, Ellis's notion of demandingness (Ellis & Tafrate, 1997), thoughts of unfairness, external attribution of blame, and condemnation of the responsible person. DiGiuseppe and Froh found that the ratings of self-efficacy were strongly negatively skewed. No subject provided a rating below 50 on the 100-point scale of self-efficacy. Thus, all the subjects when imagining a previously anger-provoking situation had at least a moderate level of self-efficacy. No participant reported having low self-efficacy when feeling angry. This study supports the idea that some degree of belief in one's strength or resourcefulness is associated with anger, and low levels of self-efficacy are absent in the experiences of anger.

Thus, the perception that one has greater resources than the perceived threat may increase the chance that the person will experience anger and approach the threat in an attempt to exert control. This appraisal of one's strength compared with the strength of a threat may be the primary determinant of what emotion people experience after they perceive a threat. Consider one of our primordial ancestors on the open African savannah who has just successfully killed an antelope and then sees a competitor approaching. If our ancestor believes he is stronger than the rival, anger is aroused and an attempt is made to drive him away. Our ancestor would have experienced fear if he believed that the competitor was stronger than he and escape was possible. He would have experienced depression if he believed no escape was possible. In the last case, because he cannot flee or repel the threat, he could act submissively and hope the threatening competitor would take the antelope and go away. Submissive gestures toward the competitor would signal that our ancestor did not have the ability to harm the competitor. Most species of mammals have developed submissive rituals that they display when two members of a species are in conflict. The submission ritual sends a signal to the dominant party that he or she has won the conflict and that no further aggression is necessary. This may have survival value. Lorenz believed that humans had failed to develop such genetically programmed submission rituals and this accounted for our high level of intraspecies aggression.

In their evolutionary perspective, Stevens and Price (1996) maintain that depression is the human equivalent of the submission ritual in competition for social rank. Depressive behavior sends a clear signal to the aggressor that the depressed person acknowledges defeat and that no further aggression is necessary. Dominance displays are related to strength and result in anger expression. Anger leads to a motive to dominate and approach. As depression is the human equivalent of submission, Stevens and Price (1996) claim that anger is the human equivalent of the dominance display. Self-efficacy, or the belief in one's strength and resourcefulness, may drive some anger experiences and the display of dominance.

Some researchers have explored people's sense of power with anger. Power is a similar construct to self-efficacy. More equivocal findings emerged when researchers explored the notion of anger with power and dominance. Russell and Mehrabian (1974) proposed that all emotions vary along three dimensions: pleasure, arousal, and dominance. The dimension of *dominance,* which they defined as "the degree to which a person feels powerful or in control of a situation" (p. 79), differentiated anger and depression. In their research, high ratings of dominance were associated with anger, whereas low ratings of dominance correlated with depression.

Some researchers, like Novaco (1975, 2003), believe that anger results from feelings of powerlessness or low self-efficacy not low self-worth. Strachan and Dutton (1992) examined the influence of power on anger responses. Participants in a low-power experimental condition reported higher levels of anger than did high-power participants following an experimental manipulation. The highest anger ratings were found in low-power participants when the antagonist was of the opposite sex. These findings suggest that an interaction of the antagonist's power and gender might contribute to one's level of anger. Strachan and Dutton's findings contradicted those of Russell and Mehrabian (1974) concerning dominance and anger, while offering support for Novaco's notion that anger results from feelings of powerlessness or low self-efficacy not low self-worth.

More recently, Byrne and Carr (2000) investigated differences in power among a sample of married couples in which the women suffered from depression. The authors identified many characteristics that distinguished such couples from non-depressed couples, including a notable difference in power between the spouses. The couples with a depressed woman partner typically featured a pattern in which the man maintained most of the power in the relationship. Though the study was correlational, the results suggested a link between low power and depression, not anger, thus failing to support Novaco's (1975) hypothesis.

In an experimental study, Barrett and DiGiuseppe (2001) randomly assigned African American adolescents in foster care to either a high- or low-self-esteem mood-induction task. Participants imagined rejection experiences. Embedded in the mood-induction instructions were either low- or high-self-esteem statements. The low-self-esteem induction included self-denigrating and low-self-efficacy thoughts. The high-self-esteem condition included thoughts of high self-efficacy and confidence. They measured state depression and state anger before and after the induction procedure.

Participants in the low self-esteem condition had elevations in both depression and anger after the induction. Thus, low self-esteem elicited both depression and anger. Participants in the high self-esteem condition had significant increases in anger but not depression. Clearly, ego threats produce anger whether the threats were in a context of high or low self-esteem. It remains uncertain how low self-esteem can produce anger and depression since these two emotions have such opposite characteristics. Furthermore, this study failed to provide an explanation about how low-self-esteem induction could produce both depression and anger, whereas high-self-esteem induction produced anger exclusively.

In a similar study, Carmony and DiGiuseppe (2003) investigated the effects of power, attributional style, and gender on anger and depression using a series of narrative mood inductions with undergraduates. Participants in the external-attribution and low-power conditions demonstrated significantly higher levels of post-induction anger than those in other conditions. Thus, low power seemed to arouse anger in combination with external blame of others but not when blame was focused inward. The perception of low power may lead to anger when another thought process such as other-blame projects the cause of the powerlessness onto others.

We take the results of these studies to indicate that high self-efficacy is not necessary to arouse anger; it increases the likelihood, but anger can occur without it. Low power in some conditions may elicit other cognitions that also arouse anger. However the person's appraisal of their relative self-efficacy or power can dictate the mode of anger expression. A recent study by Marchetti (2006) with adolescents found that high self-efficacy correlated with reports of physical aggression but not with other types of anger expression. We hypothesize that those who experience low self-efficacy are more likely to hold anger in and let it percolate. In some cases, the anger will be expressed later as the person seeks revenge. This is a common occurrence. People who score high on anger-in are of course angry but fail to express it because they fear reprisals and retaliation from others. If they had high self-efficacy, they would believe in their ability or strength to cope and would be less inclined to hold their anger in. Thus, other thoughts must generate their anger besides high self-efficacy. Beliefs concerning unfairness and external attribution for blame are also part of the appraisal process and interact with thoughts concerning self-efficacy. The potential relationship between self-efficacy in response to perceived threats and the mode of anger expression chosen is presented in Figure 8.3.

We have used the terms *more likely* and *less likely* to describe the nature of the relationship between thoughts about self-efficacy and anger arousal. While high self-efficacy contributes to anger, we believe it is neither necessary nor sufficient to do so. It often does not. For many people their perception of high self-efficacy arouses emotions of commitment and resolve. They know they can triumph over adversities, and will exert their effort and skills to do so. Therefore, in such confident individuals, high self-efficacy fails

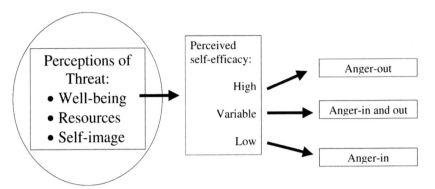

Figure 8.3. Perceived Self-Efficacy in Response to Threat and Modes of Anger Expression

to arouse anger but arouses confidence, commitment, and dedication. Perhaps their self-efficacy is so high that they become confident that they will prevail, which diminishes the perception of a threat. So the presence of very high self-efficacy may serve to diminish the threatening nature of some triggers and lead to adaptive problem solving.

R. S. Lazarus (1991) claims that the appraisals of coping resources make anger and anxiety opposite emotions. However, the experience of anger-in presents a problem for this hypothesis. People who hold in their anger are resentful and suspicious of others, and they ruminate about injustices and transgressions committed against them. However, lacking self-efficacy, they fail to change the situation. Such anger experiences require a different path to anger that does not include high self-efficacy. Thus, high self-efficacy often leads to anger. A path independent of high self-efficacy, perhaps through perceived injustice and external blame, would also arouse anger.

Self-Worth, Self-Esteem, and Anger

The term *self-esteem* sometimes denotes self-efficacy and sometimes global self-worth. Considerable confusion exists among psychological theories concerning the role of a person's self-esteem in eliciting anger. Many theorists (E. Anderson, 1994; A. T. Beck, 1999; Levin & McDevitt, 1993; Oats & Forrest, 1985) have suggested that those with anger problems have low self-esteem, meaning low general self-worth. For the remainder of this discussion we will use the term *self-worth* when discussing theories and research to avoid confusion with the literature on self-efficacy discussed above. Many clinical interventions for anger rest on the assumption that low self-worth causes anger, hate, and aggression. Correcting the malady of low self-esteem represents the most recommended intervention for anger and aggression across many populations including African Americans (E. Anderson, 1994), adolescent gang members (Jankowski, 1991), adopted children who murder their parents (Kirschner, 1992), child-abusing mothers (Oats & Forrest, 1985), domestic-violence perpetrators (Gondolf, 1985; Renzetti, 1992), terrorists (D. E. Long, 1990), and perpetrators of hate crimes (Levin & McDevitt, 1993; Schoenfeld, 1988).

However, there is a dearth of empirical evidence that low self-worth causes anger and aggression. Surprisingly, many of the authors who have proposed a connection between low self-esteem and anger also described their research samples as arrogant, self-centered, or narcissistic (see discussion by Douglas & Olshakher, 1995; Toch, 1969/1993). They have not reconciled how arrogant, self-centered people suffer from low self-esteem. Also, typically no data is presented to support the claim that low self-worth leads to anger or aggression. Direct empirical tests of this hypothesis usually produce negative results. Olweus (1994) found that children who bullied their peers did not suffer from low self-worth. Jankowski (1991) failed to find evidence that members of violent gangs suffered from low self-perceptions. Researchers on spouse abusers have also failed to find that members of this group suffer from diminished esteem (Christensen, Brayden, Dietrich, McLoughlin, Sherrod, et al., 1994). In several papers, Baumeister and his colleagues (Baumeister & Boden, 1998; Baumeister, Smart, & Boden, 1996) failed to find support for a link between low self-worth and anger, hostility, or aggression. We also searched extensively for research to support this hypothesis yet failed to find supporting evidence for a link between low self-worth and anger.

Besides the lack of empirical support, the low self-worth–anger hypothesis presents another problem. Low self-worth has been associated with depression (A. T. Beck, 1967, 1976). Theorists who have proposed that low self-worth plays a role in anger arousal have failed to discuss how self-denigrating appraisals can elicit two opposite emotions—anger and depression. In fact, A. T. Beck (1976) long ago proposed that unique cognitions aroused each emotion. Specifically, attributions of blame or responsibility and beliefs that a transgression was unreasonable, unjustified, or arbitrary aroused anger. Despite these assertions, A. T. Beck (1999) recently joined the many theorists proposing that anger results from low self-worth without resolving the issue of how low self-worth can produce both anger and depression. As mentioned in the previous section, some dysfunctional cognitions identified by clinical theories, such as catastrophizing and arbitrary inference, can play a role in arousing several dysfunctional emotions. However, low self-worth has not been proposed to affect anger in such a way.

If low self-worth does facilitate the arousal of anger, some mediating variables needs to account for how low self-regard can sometimes lead to depression and at other times arouse anger. Circumplex models of emotions characterize anger as a negatively labeled emotion with high-energy activation and high physiological arousal, as opposed to depression, which is characterized by low-energy activation, low physiological arousal, and is also negatively experienced (Larsen & Diener, 1987; Plutchik, 2003; Russell, 1983). Because anger and depression are such different emotions, another variable must mediate the effect of low self-worth on affect arousal to cause either anger or depression. No author who has proposed that negative views of the self can cause anger or aggressiveness has attempted to resolve this paradox.

Alternately, other emotion theorists have proposed that anger results from high, unstable self-esteem. Baumeister (Baumeister & Boden, 1998; Baumeister, Smart, & Boden, 1996) suggested that high self-esteem might cause hostility. To support this view Baumeister notes several conclusions from the research literature. People with high self-worth often respond poorly to failure and ego threats. Groups who have high self-worth engage in aggressive behavior more than those known to have low self-worth. Incarcerated offenders in America (Wilson & Hernstein, 1986) and Britain (Berkowitz, 2003) who have committed aggressive crimes are more egotistical and confident than people in general. The same holds true for rapists (Scully, 1990). Most tyrants of the last century, such as Hitler, Stalin, Pol Pot, Saddam Hussein, Chairman Mao, and Osama bin Laden, felt contempt for others and saw themselves as the heads of superior nations, political systems, or religious movements. Ethnic hatred and aggression spawned by the Ku Klux Klan relied on white-supremacist doctrine that assigned higher worth to whites and denigrated African Americans and other groups (Wade, 1987). Even heads of organized crime families, such as the Mafia, perceive themselves to be superior to others (Anastasia, 1991). The same holds true for members of youth gangs (Bing, 1991). Evidence suggests that one runs a greater risk of being victimized by the anger, contempt, or hatred from a person with high, rather than low, self-worth.

Despite the frequent calls for treating angry clients' low self-esteem, we found no treatment-outcome studies that successfully reduced anger (or aggressive behaviors) by attempting to remedy low self-esteem. Some data from our meta-analytic review of anger treatment studies (DiGiuseppe & Tafrate, 2003) found that when self-esteem was measured, successful anger interventions produced no change in self-esteem.

Stability of Self-View and Narcissism

Several variables concerning the self have empirical relationships to anger and may account for the perception among so many theorists that low self-esteem leads to anger. These include the stability of a person's self-esteem, the presence of narcissism, and the role of shame. The absolute level of a person's self-esteem may be less of an issue than the stability of one's esteem. People who have unstable views of their self-esteem react with greater anger and aggression (Kernis, Cornell, Sun, Berry, & Harlow, 1993; Kernis, Granneman, & Barclay, 1989). Some readers may interpret this well-established finding as supporting the role of low self-esteem in anger. If people's self-esteem is low, then they might try to bolster it by attempting to compensate with something to convince themselves that they are worthwhile. Because they do not really believe this, their attempts to bolster their self-esteem result in unstable high self-esteem. The obvious question is, do these people really have low self-esteem? We do not think so. Angry people with unstable self-esteem appear to vary from high to average on self-evaluations. They have high expectations about their own competency and status. They become upset when they encounter a discrepancy between their self-views and others' views of them. Opinions from others in the form of negative feedback or criticism result in a temporary reevaluation of their self-view that is emotionally painful. However, they do not revise their self-identity downward to view themselves as average but continue to hold an unrealistically positive view. In our experience, angry people almost never consider themselves below average. They find being average distasteful and reject the notion that they are merely as competent or worthwhile as most others.

Consider the case of Mark, a 37-year-old white man who came to our anger group because of arguments with his wife and boss. Mark had worked for many years in the financial district. He believed he had made a successful name for himself but had received inadequate monetary compensation. His marriage of two years was having problems. Mark hated to be corrected. Whenever his wife or boss suggested that he had made the slightest error, Mark responded with sarcastic and insulting comments out of proportion to the feedback. He would rattle off his good points as a husband or employee. "Can't they see the good in me?" he would say. Mark believed that he was an excellent husband and employee and beyond reproach or criticism. The many examples Mark gave about the unfair criticism from his wife and boss suggested that they were not overly critical. Their comments to Mark fell well within the normal range of corrections someone might receive from people in their respective roles. Their comments intruded on and challenged Mark's perfectionistic self-image. This created self-doubt that Mark was not the person he thought he was. Thus, Mark displayed the unstable self-esteem reported in the research. Mark aspired to be perfect and vacillated between perfection and mediocrity, the latter being unacceptable to him. Mark never entertained the idea that he was below average on anything. We taught Mark to accept himself as an above-average person but not a spectacular guy. Being perfect would be pleasant, and he could strive toward it. However, his wife and boss meant no insult if they recognized that he was human. He learned to reinterpret their comments as means to self-improvement. Also, they still liked and respected him even if they noticed his occasional human foibles. Once we lowered his self-esteem and made it acceptable for Mark to be fallible, he no longer had to defend against comments that showed he was imperfect.

Besides self-image stability, another variable that might mediate or moderate anger and aggression in people like Mark is narcissism. *Narcissism* is a personality trait characterized by a sense of specialness and superiority, along with an exaggerated entitlement and a propensity to exploit others. In its extreme form, narcissism represents a personality disorder in the *DSM–IV–TR* (American Psychiatric Association, 2000). Narcissism has been positively correlated with hostility (Hart & Joubert, 1996; Rhodewalt & Morf, 1995) and anger (McCann & Biaggio, 1989). People with high self-esteem and narcissism report high levels of anger and a propensity for anger expression, whereas those with high self-esteem and low narcissism produced lower levels of anger (Papps & O'Carroll, 1998). Highly narcissistic people produced the highest degree of hostility when criticized (Bushman & Baumeister, 1998) and when they received negative feedback (Smalley & Stake, 1996). Narcissism is more strongly related to anger, hostility, and aggressiveness than to self-esteem.

Anger results from perceived threats to high, unstable self-esteem (Baumeister, Smart, & Boden, 1996). It is not high self-esteem but narcissism that leads to anger and aggression. Narcissism involves passionately wanting to think well of oneself. Not all people with high self-esteem are narcissistic, but narcissists appear to have high self-esteem. Threats to self-esteem in narcissists challenge their self-image as well as the social image projected to others. This threat triggers anger and aggression (Bushman & Baumeister, 1998).

Past Abuse or Mistreatment, Views of the Self, and Anger

Not all perceptions of threat are current. As already noted in the discussion of resentment, anger can be maintained based on thoughts about past actions. The relationship between self-worth, anger, and violent acts such as murder and rape were discussed in more detail in chapter 5. As noted in that chapter, it has been hypothesized that early experiences of abuse may cause "injury" to the person's sense of self-worth or self-esteem. It is widely believed (Kohut, 1978) that victims of abuse may compensate with an inflated sense of self-esteem or a narcissistic self-view. The narcissistic self-view in turn causes the person to overreact to threats. Getting angry with others gives them a sense of power that inflates a weak sense of self-esteem. This theory proposes that *compensating narcissism* is the basis of anger and some types of aggressive actions (Kohut, 1978).

As discussed earlier, research has not supported the idea that anger results from low self-esteem. Nonetheless, in conceptualizing past mistreatment at the hands of others, we believe that there is some truth in this theory. Approximately half of our angry clients report a history of physical or psychological abuse, parental neglect, or some emotional alienation by family or peers in their childhood. Angry people who have experienced abuse experienced hurt, and their anger and sometimes-aggressive behaviors compensate for this hurt.

However, we believe they are attempting to compensate for injustice not narcissistic injury and diminished self-esteem. Anger emerges from beliefs about lack of fairness not low self-esteem. These mistreated clients want to be treated with respect to counter their earlier negative experiences. Their resentment emerges from real injustice. However, typically no amount of special treatment is enough to compensate for their hurt. No matter who treats them with respect or how much they accomplish, they believe that the scales of justice have not been righted. Thus, they have great difficulty tolerating any disappointment or disrespect. Consider the following two cases.

Achilles, a 60-year-old Greek American, ran away from home at 16 to escape a physically abusive father. Achilles completed high school, college, and graduate school at night while supporting himself as a manual laborer. He had married and divorced by 30. Achilles reported that he had been angry for most of his life and would "not take crap from anybody." His struggles in life had been much harder because he had to leave home, and he had awful memories of beatings from his father. Achilles believed that others owed him respect and life owed him no hassles because he had suffered enough at the hands of his father and he had worked harder than anyone he knew to establish his professional status. Resentment over the past colored all of Achilles's interactions.

Sam, a 55-year-old Caucasian man, came to our anger group after an arrest for disorderly conduct at the local grocery store. He had yelled and pushed other customers in the checkout line so many times that the store manager had banned Sam from entering. The encounters occurred when Sam stood behind a customer in the express checkout line. The sign read "12 items or less." Customers in front of Sam with more than 12 items triggered Sam's anger because Sam had to wait longer than he believed he should. Interviews with Sam and his wife revealed that he had never been angry or abusive at home. However, he had a long history of confrontations in stores, on the roads, and in parks. Whenever people did not do what they were supposed to do and it involved some inconvenience for Sam, an argument followed. Sam later revealed that he was a Vietnam combat veteran. He reported having memories of this military service up until the Tet Offensive but no memories of his service after this event. He said, "I must have killed many people because they gave me many medals." When we tried to get Sam to talk about his war experiences, he refused. However, when asked if his anger and attitudes toward frustration were related, he became angry. He said, "I have been through enough shit, and I should not have to put up with any more." As time went on it became clear that Sam thought he had suffered enough in the war and could not and should not have anyone else inconvenience him.

Not all cases of trauma and abuse lead to anger. Many people who suffer trauma do have Posttraumatic Stress Disorder (PTSD) without angry symptoms. Perhaps those who do experience trauma and have PTSD with anger have more referent (imagined) cognitions about better possible outcomes and imagine more moral, justifiable behaviors by those responsible for the trauma. Referent- or imagined-cognition theories suggest that anger should be less likely to occur in trauma occurring to a group of people. Here the victim is not singled out as an individual. Anger would also be less likely to occur when the source of the trauma is a natural disaster such as a hurricane or earthquake.

Directly challenging the automatic thoughts of trauma victims, that others should not have treated them unfairly, often results in clients' feeling invalidated by the therapist and withdrawing from treatment. Obviously, it is important to validate reports of injustice and suffering. Nonetheless, clients often remain bitter for many years longer than they experienced the transgressions about which they ruminate. Consider the case of Achilles. Although he lived with an abusive father for only the first 16 years of his life, he angrily badgered others and demanded special compensatory treatment for three times as long as he had suffered at the hands of his father. We have found it helpful to ask clients when they will have or receive enough resources or affection to compensate for the loss or pain that they experienced. We asked Sam, the Vietnam veteran, how long he has to avoid the hassles of daily life to make up for the pain he experienced in war. Most clients cannot answer this question; they have never even thought about it. When they do reply, they usually conclude that no payback is sufficient. Thus, they are forever trapped in a cycle of trying to compensate for past pain that they will never escape. Getting them to see the price of their anger is the primary intervention we recommend. They cannot undo the past. Continually focusing on what could have been different prevents the client from accepting what has happened and moving on to make the most of his or her life.

Conclusions

A dual-pathway approach consisting of quick and immediate associations and higher-level cognitive processes seems necessary to explain the complexities of human anger experiences. The first step to arousing anger is the perception of some type of threat. Specific cognitive processes related to threat include catastrophizing, condemnation, suspiciousness, justification, blame, lack of fairness, demandingness, and resentment. The traditional cognitive distortions identified by A. T. Beck (1999) and the irrational beliefs proposed by Ellis (Ellis, 1962; Ellis & Dryden, 1988) and by Walen, DiGiuseppe, and Dryden (1992) erroneously increase the probability that threat will be perceived and also reduce confidence that the threat can be managed effectively. It seems there is no one cognitive path for anger and people can experience anger by many different routes. Thus, practitioners need to assess for the specific themes unique to each client.

In terms of views regarding the self, high self-efficacy seems to be implicated in some anger episodes but not all. High, unstable self-esteem and narcissism are more associated with anger than low self-esteem. Finally, anger related to past experiences of abuse may be more associated with philosophical views about life's fairness rather than with views of one's self-esteem, efficacy, or self-worth.

Part IV

Anger and Comorbidity

9

Anger and Axis I Pathology

As noted in chapter 1, anger rarely appears in the *DSM–IV*; however, several diagnostic categories include anger as a possible symptom in their criteria. As discussed in chapter 2, the term irritability appears more often in the *DSM–IV–TR* (American Psychiatric Association, 2000), possibly because this term has been linked with biological theories of emotion as mentioned by Born and Steiner (1999). The disorders in the *DSM–IV–TR* that include anger (or irritability) include manic episodes in bipolar disorders, Generalized Anxiety Disorder, and Posttraumatic Stress Disorder. Several personality disorders mention anger or irritability: Borderline, Antisocial, and Paranoid. Irritability is also mentioned as a common symptom in neurological impairments such as epilepsy, head trauma, endocrine dysfunction, Huntington's chorea, delirium, and dementia. It also appears as a criterion for Oppositional Defiant Disorder (ODD). Yet it is not present in Conduct Disorder (CD), or Attention Deficit–Hyperactivity Disorder (ADHD). This is surprising since most children develop Oppositional Defiant Disorder before they misbehave sufficiently to be classified as conduct disordered, and a high comorbidity rate exists between ADHD and ODD. Several *DSM* disorders in Appendix B (in need of further research to establish validity) include anger or irritability: Postconcussional Disorder, Premenstrual Dysphoric Disorder, the proposed alternative criteria for Dysthymic Disorder, and Mixed Anxiety–Depressive Disorder. Also in Appendix B, the criteria for Passive-Aggressive Personality Disorder do not mention anger or irritability, but include resentfulness, which we have found to be a key component of anger. Resentfulness represents an extreme form of anger-in.

Anger (and irritability) symptoms appear across a wide range of categories in the *DSM–IV–TR,* from affective disorders, personality disorders, and neurological conditions. Table 9.1 provides an overview of how anger appears in the *DSM–IV–TR* across different diagnostic categories, and Table 9.2 represents how anger appears in Appendix B of the *DSM–IV–TR.*

For both these tables the columns classify a construct as a disorder representing depression, anxiety, anger, or aggression. That is, the disorder primarily represents a dysfunction on one of these constructs. An additional column represents disorders that include either anger or irritability as a symptom. However, anger and irritability are neither necessary nor sufficient to meet the criteria for the disorder. The primary focus of the disorder is often a symptom other than anger or irritability.

More than 18 disorders describe depressive conditions. A person with anxiety problems could receive any of 24 possible diagnoses. Disturbed aggressive behavior can fit in one of five diagnostic categories. The *DSM–IV–TR* includes no disorders in which anger is the primary problem. As previously noted, seven disorders include anger (or irritability) as a symptom, but the primary focus in these disorders is on some other problem. In Appendix B eight additional disorders representing depression are under consideration, four disorders under consideration focus on anxiety problems, and two disorders with primarily aggressive behaviors are included. No potential anger disorders appear in Appendix B.

The *DSM–IV–TR* fails to consistently or systematically address the presence of anger. Anger does not appear in the index. One could conclude that anger is a generalized symptom that occasionally appears across divergent disorders. This inconsistency is also true of most abnormal psychology or psychiatric textbooks (J. L. Deffenbacher & D. M. Deffenbacher, 2003). Although anger may not appear formally as a potential symptom, it is frequently described in research and clinical case descriptions as a characteristic of other disorders such as schizophrenia, eating disorders, substance-abuse disorders, and especially depression. The remainder of this chapter reviews the research and clinical literature on the occurrence of anger in patients with common clinical problems, and the theoretical and clinical implications of such patterns of comorbidity. In addition, some preliminary findings, from several samples, on anger and Axis I comorbidity patterns are provided. The relationship between problematic anger and personality disorders is covered in chapter 11.

Anger and Impulsivity

Since many practitioners are likely to use the diagnostic category Intermittent Explosive Disorder (IED) to diagnose angry clients, and this diagnosis is categorized as an impulse-control disorder in the *DSM–IV–TR,* anger may be viewed as an impulse-control problem. Unfortunately, as discussed in

Table 9.1
DSM–IV–TR Diagnostic Categories for Depression, Anxiety, Anger, Anger-Related, and Aggression Disorders[1]

Depression Disorders	Anxiety Disorders	Anger Disorders	Disorders With Anger or Irritability	Aggression Disorders
Mood Disorder due to GMC[2]	Separation-Anxiety Disorder		Oppositional Defiant Disorder	Conduct Disorder
Amphetamine-Induced Mood Disorder	Anxiety Disorder due to GMC[2]		Posttraumatic Stress Disorder	Personality Disorder due to GMC[2]
Cocaine-Induced Mood Disorder	Amphetamine-Induced Anxiety Disorder		Paranoid Personality Disorder	Sexual Sadism
Alcohol-Induced Mood Disorder	Cocaine-Induced Anxiety Disorder		Borderline Personality Disorder	Intermittent Explosive Disorder
Hallucinogen-Induced Mood Disorder	Alcohol-Induced Anxiety Disorder		Bipolar I Disorders (Most Episodes Depressed or Mixed[3]	Antisocial Personality Disorder[3]
Inhalant-Induced Mood Disorder	Cannabis-Induced Mood Disorder		Bipolar II Disorders[3]	
Opioid-Induced Mood Disorder	Hallucinogen-Induced Anxiety Disorder		Cyclothymic Disorder	
Phencyclidine-Induced Mood Disorder	Inhalant-Induced Anxiety Disorder			
Sedative-Hypnotic-Axiolytic Mood Disorder	Phencyclidine-Induced Anxiety Disorder			

(continued)

Table 9.1 (*continued*)

Depression Disorders	Anxiety Disorders	Anger Disorders	Disorders With Anger or Irritability	Aggression Disorders
Other (Unknown) Substance-Induced Mood Disorder	Sedative-Hypnotic-Axiolytic Anxiety Disorder			
Schizoaffective Disorder	Caffeine-Induced Anxiety Disorder			
Major Depressive Disorder[3]	Other (Unknown) Substance-Induced Anxiety Disorder			
Bipolar I Disorders Most Episode Depressed or Mixed[3]	Panic Disorder Without Agoraphobia			
Bipolar II Disorders[3]	Panic Disorder With Agoraphobia			
Cyclothymic Disorder	Agoraphobia Without Panic			
Adjustment Reaction With Depressed Mood	Specific Phobia			
Adjustment Reaction With Mixed Depressed & Anxious Mood	Social Phobia			
Adjustment Reaction With Mixed Disturbance of Emotion & Conduct	Obsessive-Compulsive Disorder			
	Posttraumatic Stress Disorder			
	Acute Stress Disorder			
	Nightmare Disorder			

Adjustment Reaction With Anxious Mood

Adjustment Reaction With Mixed Depressed & Anxious Mood

Adjustment Reaction With Mixed Disturbance of Emotion & Conduct

Avoidant Personality Disorder

---

[1]Anger related disorders are those in which anger may be present but is not necessary.

[2]GMC = General Medical Condition

[3]These disorders include a criterion of "irritability" but not anger.

Table 9.2

DSM-IV-TR Appendix B Diagnostic Categories (Provided for Further Study) That Mention Depression, Anxiety, Anger, and Aggression

Depression Disorders	Anxiety Disorders	Anger or Irritability Symptoms Present	Aggression Disorders
Postconcussional Disorder	Postconcussional Disorder		Postconcussional Disorder
Caffeine Withdrawal	Caffeine Withdrawal		
Postpsychotic Depression Disorder of Schizophrenia			
Premenstrual Dysphoric Disorder	Premenstrual Dysphoric Disorder	Premenstrual Dysphoric Disorder	
Minor Depressive Disorder			
Recurrent Brief Depressive Disorder			
Mixed Anxiety-Depressive Disorder	Mixed Anxiety-Depressive Disorder		
Depressive Personality Disorder			
		Passive-Aggressive Personality Disorder	Passive-Aggressive Personality Disorder

greater detail in chapter 14, IED fails to mention anger at all and does not seem to adequately describe the characteristics of clients with anger difficulties. Nonetheless, anger, irritability, and aggression are common characteristics of many people with impulse-control problems and neurological conditions (see Raine, 1993). Much of the research and clinical literature on externalized disorders such as Attention-Deficit–Hyperactivity Disorder (ADHD), Oppositional Defiant Disorder (ODD), and Conduct Disorder (CD) describe these children as angry (e.g., Garbarino, 1999, Green, 1998). Impulsivity is often listed as part of a child's angry and aggressive reactions. Because not all these children grow up to have serious adult problems such as Antisocial Personality Disorder, we wonder whether many of them are never identified as needing mental health services as adults. The experience of impulsivity remains part of the anger experience for many people. However, it may be caused by excessive rumination, as mentioned in chapter 5. Thus, we need more research to determine when and how frequently impulsivity (without rumination) is a characteristic of disturbed anger. This section discusses anger and ADHD. Anger and CD and ODD are examined in the next section.

In a descriptive investigation, Lachmund, DiGiuseppe, and Fuller (2005) found that many anger-disordered adults were close to meeting the criteria for Attention Deficit–Hyperactivity Disorder (ADHD). It has been noted by Barkley (1996) that many adults fail to meet the criteria of ADHD, because the symptoms were written for elementary school children. He suggested that a more developmentally sensitive description of the symptoms would result in more adults' meeting the criteria for the disorder. Similarly, Hallowell and Ratey (1994) suggest that anger, rage, and violent behavior are frequently presenting symptoms of adult patients with ADHD. However, little empirical literature exists exploring the relationship between ADHD and anger. Again, this finding raises the question of whether anger problems are secondary to ADHD, or if both problems are related to an underlying impulse problem. We suspect that the ADHD and self-control problems may represent a more primary dysfunction; however, not all people with ADHD-like symptoms will have difficulties with anger expression. Our own research suggests that poor self-control, the outward expression of anger, short episode length, and rumination all load on a similar dimension or higher order factor on the Anger Disorders Scale (ADS; DiGiuseppe & Tafrate, 2004). Thus, impulsivity may be an important aspect that determines the presence of an anger disorder with verbal expressiveness or physical aggression. A subtype of anger and aggression similar to Intermittent Explosive Disorder has been well researched by Coccaro and his colleagues (Coccaro, 1992, 2004; Coccaro, Harvey, Kupsaw-Lawrence, Herbert, & Bernstein, 1991). It is characterized by impulsive, aggressive outbursts. We will discuss this disorder in detail in chapter 14.

Addictive problems and ADHD both share the feature of dysinhibition. The possibility exists that anger problems in patients with these comorbid disorders may be mediated by dysinhibition. Clients with anger problems often have difficulties with impulse control, and many behavioral manifestations of anger reflect impulsivity. Aggression, crime, and delinquency are frequently present in patients who experience head injuries (see Raine, 1993, for a review). Since aggression and anger are frequently confused, it is uncertain whether the effects of head injury may also apply to anger. However, head injuries most often result in damage to the orbitofrontal regions of the frontal lobes and the anterior region of the temporal lobes. Damage to the left orbitofrontal regions leads to hostility and anger (Mattson & Levin, 1990). Raine (1993) reported that there are many pathways by which prefrontal lobe problems could result in aggressive behavior. Again, since researchers often fail to distinguish between aggression and anger, it is uncertain whether these same pathways mediate anger and aggression. However, since anger sometimes precedes aggression, speculating that prefrontal lobe areas may inhibit anger appears reasonable. Thus, deficits in this area may also lead to disregulated anger.

Some conflicting evidence fails to support the idea that impulsivity related to prefrontal lobe areas mediates anger episodes. Although Raine (1993) and Mattson and Levin (1990) identified the prefrontal deficits as leading to aggression and anger, the impulsivity of ADHD might not be mediated by deficits in these same regions (Loge, Staton, & Beatty, 1990). The excessive anger typically displayed by child and adult ADHD patients may result from general affective liability. This is supported by high comorbidity rates of emotional problems such as anxiety and mood disorders (Barkley, 1996; Hallowell & Ratey, 1994). Barkley (1996) pointed out that ADHD children and adults fail to develop "separation of affect," which allows one to withhold affect expression until one objectively evaluates a given situation. This skill deficit results in ADHD patients' displaying greater emotional expressions of any type and making fewer objective evaluations of responses to events. If this is the case, the excessive anger may be caused by the same neurological factors that predispose these groups to experience anxiety or depression. Further research is needed to investigate the role of various types of neurological impairments and dysinhibition on anger arousal.

We encourage clinicians to consider the hypothesis that clients presenting with anger problems may have problems with dysinhibition overall. Exploring the possibility of the presence or history of impulse problems with angry clients appears prudent.

Anger With Opposition and Conduct Problems

Although anger is a possible symptom of Oppositional Defiant Disorder (ODD), it is not necessary for a child to be angry to meet these criteria. It would be interesting to study a group of children and adolescents with ODD to ascertain what percentage of them meet the criteria for an anger disorder. Li, Wellen, Turchiano, Anderson, Jones, et al. (1996) recently presented a meta-analytic review of more than 200 studies of behavioral and cognitive behavioral therapies for externalized disorders of childhood and adolescence. In this review, studies of ODD rarely included an outcome measure of anger. Similarly, adolescent anger-control studies rarely included a measure of oppositional or defiant behaviors. However, studies targeting the treatment of ODD and anger each produce relatively large effect sizes compared to outcome studies aimed at other externalizing disorders of childhood and adolescence. Studies targeting ODD usually employed operant interventions, while those targeting anger used a combination of cognitive restructuring, imagery, and self-instructional training.

To what extent are these two groups of studies treating the same types of children but labeling them differently? Research has failed to address the role of anger in ODD or Conduct Disorder (CD). Is anger just a symptom that co-occurs in these disorders, or could anger mediate the symptomatic behavior in ODD and CD? If anger mediates the production of oppositional and aggressive behaviors in children, then an anger-management treatment package such as that developed by Feindler (1995) would be recommended. However, if anger rarely appears in these disorders, or if when it does occur it is an epiphenomenon unrelated to the behavior, anger-management programs would not be warranted for all clients in these categories. It is possible that for some youngsters with these disorders, anger mediates the behavioral symptoms. In others, anger may play no role. Such a diagnostic distinction could have treatment utility for practitioners in determining which set of empirically validated interventions are best for the individual child.

Therefore, we encourage clinicians treating children to consider the hypothesis that oppositional and conduct problems may be mediated by anger, and to directly assess this possibility. If anger appears to mediate the behaviors, treatment could be targeted at the anger with interventions mentioned in part VI of this book. Feindler's (1995) work is uniquely targeted at children and adolescents, and Kassinove and Tafrate's (2002) guidebook has useful interventions that can be adapted for adolescent clients. However, if anger does not mediate the behaviors, behavioral family therapy and parent management training represent the most efficacious interventions.

Anger in Marital and Family Discord

Lachmund, DiGiuseppe, and Fuller (2005) identified successive outpatients who admitted to having anger problems. Each patient received a computer-administered structure interview for the *DSM–III–R*. Many anger-disordered clients who failed to meet criteria for any other *DSM* disorder reported family-related problems and received *DSM–III–R* V codes. V codes indicate problems that are not mental disorders but that may be the focus of clinical attention. In our experience, the most common V codes with angry clients are V61.20, parent–child relationship problems, and V61.1, partner relationship problems. In fact, it appears that angry clients often seek treatment because of ongoing relationship or family conflicts. We suggest the therapist review his or her caseload to see if anger is the primary emotional excess in cases involving family therapy or in cases in which the individual client has sought help because of family problems. Keep in mind that people experience anger more frequently in the home than in any other place and that anger is more often targeted at loved ones than at unfamiliar persons (Averill, 1983; Kassinove, Sukhodolsky, Tsytsarev, & Soloyova, 1997). This aspect of anger may explain why there are no *DSM* diagnostic categories for anger. People with anger problems frequently seek out family or marital therapy. Insurance companies do not generally reimburse the cost of marital therapy because it is considered an intervention to promote actualization and not the treatment of a disorder. Also, most conjoint therapy arises from family-systems therapies that eschew diagnosing individuals and generally focus on assessing systems. If angry clients present with family problems to therapists using a systems model, the anger of individual family members is unlikely to receive attention because the anger is viewed as an expression of a systemic problem.

There appears to be no research literature that has focused on the role of anger in family or marital problems. Nonetheless, it could be hypothesized that high anger is related to marital discord and family dysfunction. Additional research is needed to confirm this hypothesis. Research presented in chapter 3 suggests that across cultures people see anger as the emotion most likely to damage interpersonal relationships. Therefore, we encourage clinicians to consider the hypothesis that clients presenting with anger problems are likely to have marital or relationship difficulties. We also recommend that when clinicians are confronted with marital and family dysfunctions they consider that anger may be an important factor in maintaining negative interactions. As an additional note, practitioners from different orientations have various opinions about when to involve spouses or family members in treatment. We have found that involving clients with anger-control problems too early in conjoint sessions can lead to a high level of conflict in the treatment sessions themselves. Conjoint sessions tend to be more productive after a client with dysfunctional anger has achieved a level of self-control and trust in the treatment process and the practitioner.

Anger and PTSD

The *DSM–IV–TR* (American Psychiatric Association, 2000) lists anger as a possible symptom of Posttraumatic Stress Disorder (PTSD). However, it is neither necessary nor sufficient for the diagnosis. Not much theory exists to explain why anger may be associated with PTSD; therefore, it is uncertain how frequently one should expect anger symptoms to be present. Exposure-based treatments aimed at reducing the anxiety associated with PTSD are considered the treatment of choice (Foa, Riggs, Massie, & Yarczower, 1995; Foa & Rothbaum, 1998). However, several authors have recommended that treatment for PTSD needs to include anger management with certain groups of PTSD patients. For example, children with PTSD who have witnessed family violence, and combat veterans with PTSD may benefit from an anger-management component (Wagar & Rodway, 1995).

Similarly, when anger management is indicated, it has been recommended that the anger interventions precede exposure-imagery techniques targeted at anxiety symptoms. Anger experiences and expressions and substance use may serve to prevent PTSD veterans from addressing their trauma. Both drug use and anger may serve as a means to avoid imaginal or conversational exposure, thus blocking the potential usefulness of exposure to traumatic memories. Thus, angry ruminations and verbal expressions can serve to maintain PTSD symptoms. Patients should address their substance-abuse and anger-management problems in the first phase of treatment before addressing the PTSD and engaging in exposure-based treatments. Although there are few treatment-outcome studies that have investigated treating anger specifically among PTSD clients, one recent investigation showed promise. Vietnam War combat veterans with severe anger problems who completed an anger-treatment intervention showed better anger-control skills than those receiving just an anxiety-focused intervention (Chemtob, Novaco, Hamada, & Gross, 1997).

On a related topic, some researchers have reported that secondary or vicarious PTSD occurs in the loved ones of up to 30% of crime victims. Anger may prevent the loved ones of primary victims from resolving their problems. It may interfere with their providing support and understanding to the primary victim. A spouse's anger at the perpetrator of a crime against his or her spouse leads to a failure to discuss the effect of the crime on the couple's relationship. This interferes with the support, which helps the primary victim recover from the assault.

Anger and Substance-Use Disorders

Lachmund, DiGiuseppe, and Fuller (2005) investigated the comorbidity of adult outpatients who presented with anger problems, and they discovered that angry clients had a high rate of comorbid addictive behaviors. Since the clients reported anger symptoms after they developed control of their addictive behavior, the question arose as to the relationship between anger and addictive disorders. Is the anger part of the addictive disorder? Is the addiction problem a way to cope with some primary anger-dysregulation problem? Or are both addictive disorders and anger disorders related to an underlying impulse problem? We commonly encounter angry people with a history of addictive behavior that suggests a link between impulsivity and substance abuse or misuse.

The *DSM–IV–TR* includes many disorders reflecting affect disturbance that results from the influence of psychoactive substances (see Table 9.1). These include such conditions as Amphetamine-Induced Mood Disorder and Amphetamine-Induced Anxiety Disorder. Similar disorders exist for alcohol, cannabis, caffeine, cocaine, hallucinogens, inhalants, phencyclidine, and sedatives. It is puzzling that the authors of the *DSM–IV* perceived that so many classes of drugs could induce disorders of depression and anxiety yet none of these substances could induce an anger disorder. Perhaps the angry drunk is such a ubiquitous figure that his pattern is too common to be considered a disorder. Besides alcohol, cocaine has been identified as leading to increased anger and aggression. Some scholars have identified the reduction of cocaine use as a cause for reduction in violent crime. Anger can also be induced by the other substances noted to cause affective disturbance. The omission of anger disorders in this section of the *DSM* reflects the total disregard, or purposeful avoidance, of anger and its disorders by the psychiatric community and its nosological gatekeepers.

The role of emotional disturbance has long been considered a cause of addiction. This has been called the self-medication hypothesis. Accordingly, people abuse drugs because the short-term effect of the drug medicates and relieves the excessive affect they are experiencing (D. I. Gerard & Kornetsky, 1955). Most research in this area, which has focused on adults, has supported the role of self-medication in the relief of depression and anxiety. We have failed to find any studies that have investigated the self-medication hypothesis with anger. This is another surprising oversight in the addictions literature. Khantzian (1985) has reported anecdotal evidence supporting the self-medication hypotheses for anger. He also suggested that a person's drug of choice might be related to which emotional excess the person experiences. He proposed that opiates would be the self-medicating drug of choice for persons with anger and rage because of their calming effect. Accordingly, cocaine would be the self-medicating drug of choice for depressives, because its action compensates for their lethargy. Although this specificity hypothesis of drug effects has not yet been adequately tested, Khantzian has been one of the few authors to acknowledge the link between drug abuse and anger.

There is some evidence for the relationship between substance use and anger in adolescents. Both correlational and path-analysis studies show that anger is linked to adolescent drinking and drug use in both boys and girls of various ethnic groups (Colder & Stice, 1998; Lee, Mendes de Leon, & Markides, 1988; Swaim & Deffenbacher, 1998; Swaim, Oetting, Edwards, & Beauvis, 1989). Swaim and J. L. Deffenbacher proposed that since anger is a multidimensional construct, not all aspects of anger would lead to alcohol use. Through a path analysis they found a causal link between the verbal and physical expressions of anger and the use of alcohol in Hispanic and

Non-Hispanic white boys and girls. Although other strong emotions, such as anxiety and depression, have been associated with increased alcohol use in adolescents, anger appears to have the strongest connection (Leibsohn, Oetting, & Deffenbacher, 1994). Anger predicts alcohol use in high school students better than does anxiety or depression (Swaim & Deffenbacher, 1998). The effect of anger on alcohol use appears to be long lasting and does not represent a correlation that exists at one point in time. Brooks, Whiteman, and Finch (1992) found that adolescent levels of anger and aggression predicted alcohol use eight years later.

Other studies have found a similar relationship between anger and substance use in college students and young adults. Liebsohn, Oetting, and Deffenbacher (1994) studied the levels of trait anger in college students. They found that anger effects existed for all alcohol-consumption measures. High anger predicted more drinking, more intoxication, and more negative consequences, including becoming physically impaired from drinking but not including passing out. Those scoring high on anger were twice as likely to experience physical impairments from drinking as those with lower anger. They were 2–7 times more likely to experience negative emotional consequences, and 10 times as likely to report behavioral consequences from drinking. Those scoring high on anger had more-frequent and severe alcohol-related consequences. Some gender differences were noted: men consumed alcohol more often and in greater quantities than women and also reported that they more often fought and damaged property. Women, on the other hand, were more likely to report damage to relationships.

Walfish, Massey, and Krone (1990) administered the State–Trait Personality Index and the Student Drinking Questionnaire to undergraduate students. They found that, except for trait anxiety and trait anger, most personality variables were not strong predictors of alcohol abuse. They also note that those who were highly anxious were more likely to abuse alcohol, and those scoring high on trait anger appeared to suffer more behavioral consequences from alcohol use.

Other studies have examined the relationship between anger and substance use in adult populations. Potter-Effron and Potter-Effron (1991) evaluated inpatients and outpatients receiving treatment for alcoholism with Spielberger's State–Trait Anger Expression Inventory (STAXI; 1999). They concluded that male inpatients have a more intense experience of anger than the general population but controlled their anger expressions better. The outpatient group was above national norms on both anger-in and anger expression. Although outpatient men appeared to have less intense anger than inpatients, they still had significant anger expressed outwardly. Women in this study were above national norms on trait anger. Inpatient women directed their anger both inwardly and against others, whereas outpatients had lower scores on trait anger but scored higher on anger-out. It seems they directed their anger toward others. Also, female adult children of alcoholics were above national norms on all dimensions of anger. The overall picture supports the idea that men and women with alcohol problems experience more anger than the general population and have difficulties controlling their anger expressions.

In a similar study, Tivis, Parsons, and Nixon (1998) found that men and women diagnosed as alcoholics (*DSM–III–R* criteria) scored higher on trait anger than did a community control group. In a study examining more than 800 adult alcoholics in a residential treatment facility, Walfish, Massey, and Krone (1990) found that trait anger and anxiety were well above average for those populations, compared to the norms of the general population.

Grover and Thomas (1993) examined the relationship between scores on the Framingham Anger Scales and answers to a social-support questionnaire in a study of substance-abusing women ages 35 to 55. These women volunteered to participate in a longitudinal study of mental health, which began in 1982. The women were grouped based on self-reports of alcohol consumption, scores on the anger scales, and their physiological expression of anger. Grover and Thomas found that 61% of the high-anger group drank alcoholic beverages, whereas only 34% of the low-anger group consumed alcohol. Alcohol use was positively correlated with greater education and anger symptoms (tension, shakiness, nervousness) and the use of over-the-counter medications. They concluded that anger symptoms were a major characteristic of substance users and that substance abusers do not manage their anger effectively and need appropriate interventions to do so.

Fishbein, Jaffe, Snyder, Haertzen, and Hickey (1993) investigated the effects of alcohol on negative mood states. They asked subjects to report how they felt and acted when drinking. The emotion scores changed significantly as drinking increased. Severity of alcohol use was significantly related to increases in verbal hostility, physical hostility, internal stress, and self-reported depression. Significant interaction effects suggested that those who had a history of alcoholism, or who could currently satisfy criteria for alcohol abuse, showed increases on depression, physical hostility, and internal stress scales when drunk. In addition, problem drinkers in this study reported more distress and aggression while drinking. They concluded that those who have aggressive or depressive symptoms drank more heavily, which then triggered anger reactions that already existed within them. Therefore angry or depressive feelings are significantly increased by only a small amount of alcohol in these individuals, whereas normal subjects drinking a small amount of alcohol showed little emotional change.

These studies suggest that anger problems are common in adults who seek treatment for drinking or who drink heavily. However, most of this research is correlational and fails to test any theories concerning the functional relationship between anger and alcohol use.

In their anger-episode analysis of adults high in trait anger (HTA) and low in trait anger (LTA), Kassinove, Tafrate, and Dundin (2002) examined the behaviors that subjects reported during or shortly after anger episodes. It was found that HTA subjects reported using substances four times more frequently than their LTA counterparts. Thus, for those likely to have clinical problems with anger, substance use is a common behavior after anger experiences. J. Deffenbacher and colleagues have also studied how people respond when angered and found that alcohol consumption is a common consequence of anger (J. Deffenbacher, Oetting, Lynch, & Morris, 1996).

In several reports, it seems that anger plays a key role in the development of substance use early in life. When people are angry, alcohol may act as a sedative, relieving muscle tension, physical activation, ruminations, and agitation. However, there is an alternative hypothesis concerning the function anger plays in increasing drinking. The reader has probably seen people become angry and express it outwardly when intoxicated. Such cases illustrate that alcohol does not always reduce the effects of anger and may sometimes augment its expression. Alcohol is known to reduce inhibitions and may increase verbal and physical expressions of anger. Therefore, the temporary reduction in inhibition caused by alcohol should increase anger and aggression.

This raises questions concerning the function alcohol plays in anger. Do people drink when angered to benefit from alcohol's self-medicating effect on anger-related symptoms? The use of alcohol could be negatively reinforced because it reduces a variety of negative symptoms (noted above). Alternatively, people might drink when they get angry to benefit from the reduction in inhibition, which would result in freer expression of anger. Anger is associated with thoughts of self-efficacy. A reduction in inhibition would decrease fears and increase self-efficacy. Thus, some people could drink for the effect of getting angrier and having the courage to express it. In this case, alcohol use could be positively reinforced by the increase in self-efficacy and anger expression. At least one psychoanalytic author (Dodes, 1990) has suggested that addiction represents an attempt to establish a sense of control and power; others have seen it as related to narcissistic personality types (Kohut & Wolf, 1978; Wurmser, 1984). Issues of power and powerlessness are persistent themes in 12-step treatment programs. The first step is accepting that one is powerless over alcohol (or the drug of abuse). The psychodynamic authors see narcissism and the use of alcohol and drugs as an attempt to compensate for powerlessness. However, one does not have to feel powerlessness to crave power or have a strong motivation to increase power. One could imbibe power-enhancing substances to have more power without implying a lack of it. Nonetheless, these psychodynamic theories may be correct in asserting that addiction is motivated by an increased sense of power.

In trying to make sense of the overall patterns, these two functions rely on different mechanisms of reinforcement (positive and negative) to strengthen the connection between drinking and anger. Using substances as a method of reducing negative symptoms associated with anger is likely maintained through negative reinforcement. Using substances to enhance feelings and expressions of self-efficacy and power may be more related to positive reinforcement. Research is needed to determine which of these relationships is most accurate and for whom. However, alcohol could serve either function in anger. When we teach continuing-education seminars on anger and discuss this topic, we ask the audience for their experiences concerning which function alcohol serves with anger. The usual response is that they both occur, each about half of the time. If this clinical experience turns out to be correct, and we suspect it will, it raises another question. What variables determine whether alcohol use is positively or negatively reinforcing when one is angry? We suspect that the mediator here is expectation. Research has firmly established that the effects of alcohol are mediated by one's expectancy of alcohol's effect more than by the actual consumption of alcohol. In this research, people's expectations for alcohol are either measured or manipulated before drinking. One group is given drinks that are alcohol-free and misled to believe it is alcohol. Another group is given alcohol and told they have alcohol-free drinks. The expectations influence behavior more than does the actual consumption of alcohol (Brown, Christiansen, & Goldman, 1987; Leigh, 1989). Perhaps people have different expectations concerning alcohol's effect on behavior. Some people have learned that it serves as a relaxant, and others that it reduces inhibitions. Such differences in expectation may account for reported differences in reactions to drinking while angry. Of course researchers need to focus on both the actual and the expected effects of all drugs on anger. Until research explains the functional relationship(s) between anger and drugs and alcohol, clinicians should assess the functional relationship between anger and alcohol or drug use on an individual basis.

In addition to focusing on variables that initiate a drinking problem, researchers and clinicians have focused on variables that relate to relapse. Once people have stopped using an addictive substance, they face the high probability of a relapse. Marlatt and Gordon (1985) investigated the events that occurred just prior to a person's lapsing into alcohol use after a period of control and abstinence. They reported several types of stimuli elicited a return to drinking, such as excessive emotions. Anger not only elicited a relapse to drinking more than any other emotion, but it accounted for approximately 45% of all relapse-related stimuli—more than did any other stimuli. This research suggests that anger control should be a target of intervention if one expects successful long-term results in the treatment of alcohol abuse.

So, what treatments would work best for high-anger alcohol users? Project MATCH was a multisite outcome study of alcohol abusers that compared the efficacy of a 12-step program, cognitive behavior therapy (CBT), and motivational-enhancement therapy (MET; Project MATCH Research Group, 1997). This group made some a priori hypotheses concerning which therapies would work best for different types of alcoholics. They predicted that alcoholics who experienced high anger would benefit most from MET. They based this hypothesis on the idea that highly angry drinkers resist treatment more than those who are not so angry. Thus the MET would best address motivational issues. Because people often do not wish to change their anger, and drinkers usually do not wish to stop drinking, the angry drinker has two problems he or she does not wish to change. Therefore, the angry drinker might display the least motivation for change and the most resistance to treatment. The results supported this hypothesis. With the MET, high-anger clients drank fewer drinks on drinking days and abstained for more days. This group benefited significantly less from traditional CBT. The results were reversed for low-anger drinkers; they did best with CBT and worst with MET. Anger did not influence the effectiveness of 12-step treatments. The authors recommend that those with alcohol problems who are also prone to experience frequent and intense episodes of anger should receive MET but not CBT, and low-anger drinkers should receive either CBT or the 12-step treatment but not MET. This evidence suggests that substance-abuse prevention and treatment programs can be enhanced by considering the level of anger when selecting an intervention. Readers looking for a treatment program that specifically targets anger in clients with substance-use problems are referred to Reilly and Shopshire (2002).

Preliminary Descriptive Findings

This section presents two data sets that examined individuals with anger problems and potential overlapping Axis I diagnoses. The first data set comes from clients who sought help for anger problems at an outpatient psychotherapy clinic. The second is from a descriptive investigation of high- and low-trait-anger adults recruited from the community.

In the first study, 25 consecutive clients who sought therapy primarily for anger-related problems were tracked. Clients were identified as having a clinical problem with anger based on their meeting certain criteria on an early version of the Structured Interview for Anger Disorders. These criteria included anger as the primary reason for seeking treatment, the experience of a disruptive anger episode at least once a week, and reports that anger had interfered with family, social, or work life. Therapists of the clients were then asked to complete a computer-based program to determine the *DSM–III–R* (American Psychiatric Association, 1987) diagnoses. The comorbidity results appear in Table 9.3.

The largest comorbid group included patients with a history of substance-use problems that were, at the time of the study, in remission. Some of these had continued to attend 12-step programs; other had not. They reported that when they stopped using drugs or alcohol their anger problems continued.

Table 9.3
Patients Presenting With Anger Problems, Age, Sex, Comorbid *DSM–III–TR* Diagnoses[1]

Age	Sex	Criteria for a Comorbid Disorder	Type of Diagnosis or Symptom	Anger Independent of Other Disorder	Treatment Utility of the Anger Diagnosis
29	M	Yes	Posttraumatic Stress Disorder	No	Yes
36	M	Yes	Pathological Gambling	Yes	Yes
41	M	Yes	Alcohol Abuse–Sustained Full Remission	Yes	Yes
52	M	Yes	Alcohol Abuse–Sustained Full Remission	Yes	Yes
23	M	Yes	Cannabis Abuse	No	No
38	M	Yes	Cocaine Abuse–Early Partial Remission	Yes	Yes
25	F	Yes	Alcohol Abuse–Early Full Remission	Yes	Yes
17	M	Yes	Oppositional Disorder	No	Yes
16	F	Yes	Oppositional Disorder	No	Yes
35	M	Yes	Narcissistic PD–No Axis 1	No	Yes
55	M	Yes	Narcissistic PD–No Axis 1	No	Yes
63	F	Yes	Narcissistic PD–No Axis 1	No	Yes
33	F	Yes	Major Depression, Single Episode	No	??
44	M	Yes	Bipolar Disorder–on Medication	No	Yes
47	F	No	Specific Anger Disorder w/o Aggression, Family-Related	N/A	Yes
41	F	No	Specific Anger Disorder w/o Aggression, Family-Related	N/A	Yes
33	M	No	Specific Anger Disorder w/o Aggression, Family-Related	N/A	Yes
63	F	No	Generalized Anger Disorder w/o Aggression. Met 80% criteria for Passive-Aggressive PD	N/A	Yes

Age	Sex		Description		
58	F	No	Generalized Anger Disorder w/o Aggression. Met 80% criteria for Passive-Aggressive PD	N/A	Yes
39	M	No	Generalized Anger Disorder w/o Aggression. Met 80% criteria for Passive-Aggressive PD	N/A	Yes
50	M	No	Specific Anger Disorder w/o Aggression. Work Related - Close to Depression	N/A	Yes
30	M	No	Generalized anger disorder w/o Aggression. Met 80% criteria for ADHD-Hyperactive Type	???	Yes
25	F	No	Generalized Anger Disorder with Aggression. Met 66% criteria for ADHD-Inattentive Type	N/A	Yes
40	M	No	Generalized Anger Disorder with Aggression. Met 80% criteria for ADHD-Inattentive Type	???	Yes
22	M	No	Generalized Anger Disorder w/o Aggression. Met 80% Criteria for ADHD-Hyperactive Type	???	Yes

[1]Clinicians rated the independence of the Anger problems from the comorbid conditions and the treatment utility of having an Anger Diagnosis.

A second group included patients who displayed significant symptoms of ADHD as adults. However, many did not have enough symptoms to meet the criteria. As discussed earlier, this may have resulted from the fact that ADHD usually presents first in children and the symptoms are described for this age group. Some researchers have suggested that more adults would meet the criteria for this disorder if the symptoms were written in an age-neutral manner or if separate criteria were written for adults. Again, these results raise the question, are anger problems related to underlying impulse problems?

In terms of Axis II disorders, patients with a diagnosis of either Passive-Aggressive Personality Disorder or Narcissistic Personality Disorder were most common. We review the research more fully on personality disorders and anger in chapter 11. Research in this area has generally focused on identifying those with personality disorders and then examining the presence of anger symptoms. Here we have looked at those with anger problems and examined the presence of personality disorders. Certainly, more research is needed to confirm these results, because of the small sample size. Nonetheless, these results raise the question of whether or not certain personality types predispose clients to have their excessive emotional reactions in the anger sphere.

Clients seeking help for problematic anger reactions often had a co-morbid depressive disorder. We devote the next chapter to discussing the history and current empirical support for the various theories relating mood problems to anger.

We also uncovered some adolescents with Oppositional Defiant Disorder (ODD) who experienced more anger as the primary symptom than is typical of the classic picture of noncompliance. The present version of the *DSM* provides no corresponding adult equivalent of ODD. Recent research suggests that adults with anger problems meet the criteria for ODD (Malta, Blanchard, & Freidenberg, 2005). Thus, ODD may represent an early form of a longer-term anger problem. The identification of this group raises the question of whether subtypes of ODD could be identified. Some people with ODD may be angry and oppositional, and some may have only one of these symptoms.

Another potentially important finding is that many of those who sought help for anger (and met criteria for the proposed anger disorder) failed to meet the criteria for other *DSM* disorders. This confirms the need for a distinct anger-disorder category. These clients usually experienced family-related problems. Ongoing conflicts with spouses, children, parents, and siblings were the most common reasons for seeking treatment.

In the second study, comorbidity patterns were also examined in a sample of 87 adult subjects (over age 25) recruited through weekly news-paper announcements seeking individuals described as either easily frustrated, annoyed, and angered, or easygoing, patient, and laid back. To statistically select high- and low-anger-prone adults, the Trait Anger Scale (TAS; Spielberger, 1988) was administered to all persons who responded to the announcements. Cutoff scores were set at the upper quartile (> 21 for men, > 22 for women) and lower quartile (< 14 for men, < 15 for women). Subjects completed the Millon Clinical Multiaxial Inventory–Third Edition (MCMI–III; Millon, Davis, Millon, 1997). The percentage of HTA or LTA adults who scored in the clinical range on Axis I disorders on the MCMI–III is shown in Table 9.4. Both the number and percentage of clients meeting diagnostic criteria are noted in the table. Base rate scores of 85 were considered the clinical cutoff for subjects meeting the criteria for a disorder.

Based on this small community sample, the first finding to emerge is that HTA adults appear to experience greater overall levels of Axis I pathology than their LTA counterparts. Although the data are presented in terms of the number of subjects who met criteria in each category, an analysis of mean base-rate scores indicated that HTA subjects generally reported significantly more symptoms across each disorder category.

Similarly, this data suggests that angry clients are likely to present with a wide range of Axis I problems. This finding seems consistent with the data from the clinical sample presented above in that clients seeking treatment for anger problems may not be limited to a narrow range of potential overlapping problems. Thus, even in cases where clients indicate anger difficulties as the primary concern, an overall screening to detect other disorders would be warranted.

Table 9.4

Number and Percentage of High-Trait Anger (HTA) and Low-Trait Anger (LTA) Adults Meeting Criteria for Axis I Disorders on the MCMI-III

Axis I Disorder	HTA ($n = 45$)		LTA ($n = 42$)	
	#	(%)	#	(%)
Drug Dependence	16	(36)	1	(2)
Alcohol Dependence	9	(20)	1	(2)
Anxiety	13	(29)	1	(2)
PTSD	4	(9)	0	(0)
Depression	4	(9)	0	(0)
Dysthymia	4	(9)	2	(5)
Bipolar Disorder	3	(7)	0	(0)
Delusional Disorder	3	(7)	0	(0)
Thought Disorder	0	(0)	0	(0)
Somatoform Disorder	1	(2)	0	(0)

Note: Base rate scores range from 0 to 115. Base-rates ≥ 85 are considered clinically significant. An analysis of mean base-rate scores indicates that HTA adults reported significantly more symptoms than LTA adults for every disorder category.
Reprinted from Kassinove and Tafrate (2006) with permission from Springer Publishing Co., Inc., New York.

In terms of specific comorbidity patterns, drug and alcohol dependence appear to be among the most common problems identified by adults prone to high anger. Again, this finding seems consistent with the data presented above from the clinical sample. Thus, practitioners across varied settings would be wise to assess for current or past substance use among clients reporting anger-related difficulties.

Somewhat surprisingly, symptoms of generalized anxiety emerged as a notable area of overlap and were more prevalent than mood-related difficulties. This finding raises the possibility that, among angry clients, anxiety may be a more frequent co-occurring problem than depression. Obviously, this finding is not consistent with the conclusions presented above, which found higher comorbidity with depression among those actually seeking treatment. Certainly, examining larger samples across different settings would allow for stronger conclusions regarding the patterns of overlap among anger, anxiety, and depression.

Conclusions

Disordered anger can exist in the absence of other psychopathology, or it may overlap with a wide range of disorders. As pointed out numerous times in this book, the current diagnostic system does not address anger consistently or systematically. In the current system, anger occasionally appears as a symptom across divergent disorders but is never considered a problem in its own right. In addition, even in cases where it is mentioned, anger is a peripheral symptom and not necessary for meeting the criteria of any disorder.

Unfortunately, for those seeking treatment, our current system does not allow practitioners to conceptualize anger as a critical problem. Nonetheless, those who deliver treatment often recognize problematic anger in their clients. Understanding and prioritizing the complex comorbidity patterns that frequently exist is often a first step in developing a sound treatment approach. In the present review we have found that those likely to have problematic anger reactions may present with a diverse range of comorbid Axis I problems. Nonetheless, the area of greatest clinical overlap appears to be with substance use and addiction. Certainly, more descriptive research would be helpful in understanding the likely comorbid issues that may exist. At the present time we recommend assessing a broad range of general psychopathology when working with angry clients.

10

Anger and Depression

No other emotion or concept has been related more to anger than depression. Because of two of the most prominent figures in abnormal psychology, Emil Kraeplin and Sigmund Freud, anger has been assumed to be part of melancholia and depression for all of the twentieth century. In this chapter we will review the theories about the relationship between anger and depression, propose several hypotheses derived from these theories, and review the supporting research, to shed new light on this relationship.

Before we review these theories, we think it is important to make the distinction between state and trait aspects of an emotion (Spielberger, 1972a, 1988, & 1991). As discussed earlier, states refer to how the person is feeling in the present. Traits refer to the tendency to experience emotions frequently and intensely. Many of the theories concerning the relationship between anger and depression fail to specify whether the relationship being proposed is for state or trait anger, or state or trait depression. The English language uses the same word, *anger*, for both the state and trait of this emotion. However, *sadness* is the word used for the state emotion, whereas *depression* is usually reserved for the trait aspect of that emotion. Thus, most researchers in this area have failed to specify whether they are testing the theory at a state or trait level or whether the instruments used to assess emotions in their studies measure the state or the trait aspect of the emotions. We ask the reader to consider this distinction while thinking about these theories.

Overview of the Theories

Anger Turned Inward

S. Freud (1915/1963) originally believed that people experienced depression as a mix of sadness and anger over the loss of a significant other. Because people expect negative sanctions for expressing anger in such situations, Freud believed that their hostility was aimed toward themselves. This is the depression as anger-turned-inward hypothesis. Psychoanalytic theorists have maintained that the inability to express anger toward the "lost object" results in turning the anger toward oneself (Abraham, 1927; Fenichel, 1945). If this theory is correct, it would appear that depression is secondary to anger. That is, people feel a state of anger first, experience a fear of negative sanctions for the experience or expression of anger, and then become depressed. Following this model, interventions for depression would focus on the repressed or unacceptable anger and aggressive impulses. This theory seems to emphasize the state of anger and depression. However, the continued state of depression about the unacceptable anger could turn to a trait of depression.

According to this theory, one would expect a blend of sadness and anger in people who experience a loss (see Figure 10.1). However, in patients suffering from clinical depression, the theory posits that their anger is unconscious. Therefore, this theory predicts that anger and depression would only be correlated in normal or mildly disturbed people. It would predict no correlation in severely depressed individuals since their anger would be repressed and therefore unconscious.

Loss of significant other

Anger (& sadness)

Fear of negative sanctions for expression of anger

Depression

Interventions for depression focus on unexpressed anger. In cases of clinical depression, the anger is unconscious.

Figure 10.1. Depression as Anger Turned Inward

Defense Against Depression

Many authors relegate anger to a secondary emotion and suggest that depression is the true problem and the most appropriate target of intervention (see Figure 10.2). Several ego psychologists proposed that anger serves as a defense against "masked" or underlying depression (Bibring, 1953; Bowlby, 1961; Cramerus, 1990; McCranie, 1971). For these theorists, anger is truly a secondary emotion, and treatment focuses on the underlying depression that reduces the need for defensive anger. This theory stresses that the initiating factor for the depression is parental loss or separation (see Cramerus, 1990, for a review). Angry and narcissistic adults, and oppositional, defiant, and conduct-disordered children and adolescents "act out" because of the loss. According to this model, their anger is an attempt to regain the affection that they lost (Cramerus, 1990). This theory appears to focus on the traits of anger and depression. Because the anger is a persistent defense, the theory refers to trait anger. The depression that is being defended against is also persistent and is therefore trait depression. An examination of this theory would involve measures of both trait anger and trait depression.

Research into this theory has failed to establish the proposed link between parental loss or separation and depression. Several studies (Bifulco, Brown, & Harris, 1987; Harris, Brown, & Bifulco, 1986) have reported that it is not the loss of a parent that leads to depression but lack of parental care, or affectional neglect. However, these results do not seriously undermine the anger as defense against depression hypothesis. The patients' anger could be just as easily elicited by the lack of care as by parental loss. But a greater blow to this theory is the failure to confirm the link between anger and a lack of parental care or between anger and depression. This theory postulates that normal or mildly disturbed people would not experience a correlation

Parental loss or separation

(Later theorized to be lack of parental care)

↓

Depression

↓

Anger

(Anger is a defense against depression)

Interventions for anger focus on the underlying depression.

Defenses may fail in individuals with severe disturbance. Thus anger

and depression may be experienced together.

Figure 10.2. Anger as a Defense Against Depression

between depression and anger. If anger adequately served its defensive function against depression, people would not experience depression. It would appear that depression and anger would be experienced together only if a person's defenses were failing. Under such conditions one would expect more serious psychopathology because of the failure of the defenses. Thus, this theory would appear to predict no correlation between anger and depression in normal or mildly disturbed populations and a high correlation between the two in severely disturbed populations.

The anger-turned-inward and the defense-against-depression hypotheses are similar in their belief that a significant loss initiates the relationship between anger and depression. However, they differ in the role anger plays. For the anger-turned-inward hypothesis, anger is the primary emotional reaction but it is unacceptable. For the defense-against-depression hypothesis, depression is primary and unbearable, and anger ameliorates the depression.

Depression as Inhibited Anger Expression

Gestalt theory proposes that depression results from inhibiting the experience and the expression of negative emotion, especially anger (Dalrup, Beutler, Engle, & Greenberg, 1988; Perls, 1969). For Gestalt theory, depression appears to be secondary to anger, not the other way around. Treatment of depression, therefore, focuses on the unexpressed anger or the unresolved issues that elicited the anger. Experiential therapists have expanded the Gestalt theory and proposed that when anger is restricted or inhibited it is experienced and expressed as hurt. Hurt is the experience that results when people avoid anger elicited by interpersonal conflict (Greenberg & Safran,

Current or unresolved social conflict

Anger

Fear of negative sanctions for expression of anger

Depression

(Later theorized to be hurt)
Interventions for depression focus on the unexpressed

anger or on the issue that elicited the anger.

Figure 10.3. Depression as Inhibited Anger Expression

1987). In this model, people would experience state anger and inhibit its expression and then experience state depression (see Figure 10.3). The anger that the person feels might also be trait anger. They might be angry a lot and feel unable to express it, or their environment might stress that anger is unacceptable. The repetition of this pattern would result in trait depression as a result of the repeated inability to express anger. We suspect that the inability to express anger and resolve issues would result in high trait anger that is held in.

The inhibited-anger-expression hypothesis shares some elements with the anger-turned-inward hypothesis. Both maintain that anger expression is inhibited because of fear of negative sanctions for its expression. However, the inhibited-anger-expression hypothesis does not link the depression with significant loss but rather with current or unresolved social conflicts. It also posits that the expression of anger frees the individual to resolve the conflict.

Anger-Effort-Failure-Hopelessness

Some behavioral theorists postulate a relationship among anger, failure, and depression. Research suggests that anger elicits a sense of efficacy and motivates attempts to change or correct the negative stimuli that provoked the anger (Lewis, 1993). Repeated failure to produce desired outcomes could lead to helplessness and depression (Berg-Cross, 1993; Ferster, 1973; Seligman, 1975). According to this theory, patients would experience anger, followed by attempts to cope, would then fail at these attempts, and would experience subsequent feelings of hopelessness, and then depression (see Figure 10.4). Such patients would unlikely experience simultaneous anger and depression, since the failure to change one's situation would create depressive cognitions rather than cognitions related to anger. In this model,

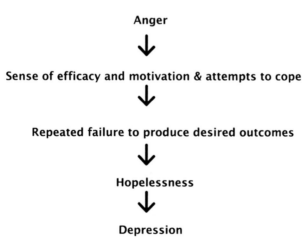

Figure 10.4. Anger-Effort-Failure-Hopelessness

state anger leads the chain of events. Failure to resolve the issue that triggered the anger could result from a lack of skills or the presence of a particularly difficult problem. This failure would first lead to state sadness. However, if the pattern persisted, trait depression might result.

Unique Alternating Cognitions

A. T. Beck (1967) stated that anger rarely occurred in severely depressed patients. He proposed (1967, 1976) that depression resulted from the cognitive schema of self-blame. Anger, according to Beck, results from the opposite schema of other-blame. In this model, separate and distinct cognitive processes elicit depression and anger (see Figure 10.5). People experience anger and depression serially, not simultaneously, because of the shifts in their cognitions. In this model, transient or weakly held beliefs could lead to state emotions, whereas more persistent beliefs and attitudes would predict trait levels of both emotions.

Hypotheses Derived From the Theories

Most research studies investigating the relationship between anger and depression employ simple designs. Most commonly, studies correlate surveys of anger and depression at one point in time. Such a design fails to provide adequate evidence to support any of the above hypotheses. However, it may be helpful to consider what outcome each theory would predict for this type of design.

If the anger-turned-inward hypothesis is correct, depressed individuals would not experience state depression and state anger simultaneously. They would score low on measures of trait and state anger since they would be unaware of their repressed anger. Thus, they might indirectly express anger. It is uncertain what this hypothesis would predict concerning how depressed

Self-blame   *Other-blame*

↓   ↓

Depression   *Anger*

Individuals experience depression and anger serially, not simultaneously, as a result of distinct cognitive processes. Treat each process separately.

Figure 10.5. A. T. Beck's (1976) Unique Alternating Cognitions Theory

individuals would score on measures of anger-in. In fact, this theory raises the issue of what is meant by the term *anger-in.* Anger-in can refer to anger that is directed at the self and that might be expressed outwardly or not. Ask yourself if you have ever made a mistake and yelled at yourself or at an object. Such an experience is anger directed at the self but outwardly expressed. Anger-in sometimes refers to anger that is not expressed. Theories on the relationship between anger and depression and research in the area often fail to make this distinction. Thus, a correlation between anger-in and depression would not necessarily test this theory, because a person might be angry with him- or herself but not have anger-in. The anger-turned-inward hypothesis makes no distinction among the different forms of the anger experience or expression. The vagueness of this hypothesis and the failure of its adherents to provide operational definitions of its constructs have for many decades prevented researchers from directly testing it (see Beck, 1967). However, we believe that this theory would predict no correlation between anger and depression in severely depressed individuals and only a small correlation in normal or mildly disturbed people.

If the defense-against-depression hypothesis is correct, one would expect a negative relationship between patients' scores on depression and anger. People who experience high anger would not experience depression since the anger supposedly defends against depression. Again, it is difficult to deduce predictions from this theory because it is poorly formulated. However, we infer that according to this theory, one might expect correlations between anger and depression in severely disturbed individuals since the severe disturbance results from failure to use anger as a defense.

The inhibited-anger-expression hypothesis proposed by Gestalt and expressive therapies is more easily tested because when people experience anger they should not experience depression. According to this hypothesis, depressed individuals would (a) score high on measures of anger-in or inhibited or suppressed anger, (b) would be unlikely to outwardly express their anger, and (c) could experience high state or trait anger without expressing it.

If the anger-effort-failure-hopelessness hypothesis is correct, it would be unlikely that depression and anger would co-occur. Helplessness is usually associated with depression, and powerfulness is usually associated with anger. Therefore, if the person felt helpless, it would be unlikely that he or she would experience anger. Correlations between state measures of anger and depression at one point in time would not be significant. People would likely alternate between anger and depression over time depending where in the chain of events they fell.

If the unique-alternating-cognitions hypothesis is correct, one would expect no significant correlations between state measures of anger and depression since they would be elicited by very different cognitions. However, according to this theory one might find correlations between trait measures of anger and depression. If the unique cognitions initiated both states frequently, the person could be high on the traits of anger and depression.

The fact that depression and anger are perceived as coexisting appears contradictory since these two emotions seem to be at opposite ends of the continua on physiology, motivation, self-efficacy, and motor behavior. Anger leads to high sympathetic arousal, increased motor activity, and motivation to confront problems. Depression leads to low physiological arousal, motor retardation, and helplessness amid problems. Even if it is established that these emotions are related, a comprehensive theory would be needed to explain how these two seemingly contradictory emotions could co-occur.

Research Findings Related to the Theories

Despite the abundant rhetoric on the relationship of anger and depression, there is little empirical research to support this notion, compared to the large body of literature on the co-occurrence of anxiety and depression (D. Watson & Clark, 1984). Nonetheless, a sufficient number of studies have demonstrated a moderate correlation between depression and anger to establish that some relationship exists between these constructs.

Kellner, Hernandez, and Pathak (1992) hypothesized that inhibited anger leads to depression and then to somatization. Inhibited anger was measured by one Likert item that asked subjects if they tended to keep their feelings "bottled up inside" when they were angry. This item appears to measure the anger-in construct. They found no relationship between anger-in and somatization. However, they reported a significant relationship between anger-in and depression in four different populations. Similarly, Tschannen, Duckro, Margolis, and Tomazic (1992) used path analysis to investigate the hypothesis that anger-in leads to depression, which then leads to headaches. Although there was no relationship between anger-in and headaches, there was a significant correlation between anger-in and depression. These and other studies suggest that depression is related to unexpressed anger or the anger-in construct (Biaggio & Goodwin, 1987; Kendell, 1970; T. W. Moore & Paolillo, 1984; Schless, Mendels, Kipperman, & Cochrane, 1974). These studies lend potential support for the inhibited-anger-expression hypothesis.

Other studies have reported high correlations between the direct and outward expression of anger and depression (Cochrane, 1975; Weissman, Fox, & Klerman, 1973; Weissman, Klerman, & Paykel, 1971). These results fail to support the inhibited-anger-expression hypothesis. Moreno, Selby, Fuhriman, and Laver (1994) administered a measure of anger, hostility, and direction of hostility expression to a clinical-outpatient sample. They found that intropunitive hostility was the only anger–hostility variable to predict depression in a regression equation. The correlations of depression with inward expressions of anger were higher than the correlations between depression and outward expressions of anger. However, they also found significant correlations between depression and subscales of hostile attitudes, hostile behaviors, and anger affect. They maintained that although the inward expression of anger had the strongest relationship to depression, there were strong relationships between depression and other aspects of anger. Moreno et al. (1994) suggested that anger might be a prominent part of the depressive syndrome. Although current theories of depression do not acknowledge this relationship, these researchers recommended that the diagnostic criteria and treatments consider this relationship.

It is possible that the relationship between anger and depression may vary within different populations. Some studies in this area employed college populations or nondepressed adults. Johnston, Rogers, and Searight (1991) reported that depression correlated with anger and overt hostility in normal college students. Other researchers found that depression and hostility are correlated only in certain populations, such as exogenous depressed patients but in neither endogenous depressed patients (Pilowsky & Spence, 1975) nor depressed patients who have not experienced a significant loss (Fava, Kellner, Mainer, Pavan, & Pesarin, 1982). Several researchers failed to find any relationship between anger and depression in clinical samples (A. T. Beck & Hurvich, 1959; Yesavage, 1983). Cullari (1994) reported that anger scores among different diagnostic groups of psychiatric inpatients were high compared to normal subjects. However, depressed inpatients were the least angry and their scores were close to those of normal adults. These studies suggest that for depressed patients who have suffered a loss and for seriously depressed inpatients anger is not related to depression. These studies confirm Beck's early prediction that anger would not be present in seriously depressed patients (A. T. Beck, 1967). These studies are also consistent with the anger-turned-inward hypothesis, which would predict no relationship with anger in seriously depressed patients. The finding that depression and anger do not co-occur in patients who have experienced a loss is consistent with this theory's notion that the depression has rendered the anger unconscious. These studies disconfirm the defense-against-depression hypothesis, which predicts that anger and depression will co-occur only in serious depression when the defenses are not working.

Although most researchers have explored the relationship between anger and depression in adults, few have studied this relationship in children and adolescents. Kashani, Dahlmeier, Barduin, Soltys, and Reid (1995) compared 11 depressed psychiatric inpatient children with matched nondepressed psychiatric controls. They found that the depressed inpatients reported greater difficulty controlling their anger than the nondepressed, yet disturbed, controls. However, there were no differences in the tendency to suppress or deny anger, or to express anger outwardly. This study fails to support any of the major hypotheses relating anger and depression and suggests that although depressed children may lose control of their anger, they are no more apt to get angry or to suppress their anger.

Renouf and Harter (1990) pointed out that depression has often been described as a blend of sadness and anger since S. Freud (1915/1963) made this proposition. They asked a large sample of sixth, seventh, and eighth graders to complete the Depression Emotion Blend Survey. The survey asked subjects to imagine an event within the past year that led to depression and to indicate how strongly they simultaneously experienced six basic emotions (happiness, sadness, love, anger, surprise, and fear). The results indicated that more than 80% of this middle-school population experienced anger while they experienced depression. These results were also similar to a study of 12 normal adolescents who were interviewed about their depression. Eleven of the 12 indicated they also experienced anger or frustration when depressed (Harter & Whitesell, 1988). These results support the psychoanalytic notion that depression is a blend of sadness and anger. However, when Renouf and Harter asked their subjects to indicate who the target of their anger was, only 7% indicated themselves. The majority were angry at others. These results indicate that state anger and state sadness may co-occur quite frequently in adolescents. However, the results fail to support the anger-turned-inward hypothesis. Additional studies have indicated that depression is correlated with anger directed toward others in adolescents (Pfeffer, 1986; Pfeffer, Zuckerman, Pluchick, & Mirzruchi, 1984). It is unclear whether this anger pattern reflects a developmental stage. Perhaps adolescents have not yet learned to inhibit anger expression and therefore fail to turn it inward. Or perhaps the anger-turned-inward hypothesis is incorrect, and anger at others and depression simply coexist frequently. Another explanation is that since most of the children were angry with others, they experienced rapid shifts in cognitions from blaming themselves to blaming others. This would account for the reported combined experience of anger and depression because anger is associated with blaming others, and depression is associated with blaming oneself.

Although research on the potential relationship between depression and anger has focused on normal subjects or patients seeking treatment for depression, no studies have focused on samples that present primarily with anger problems. No research has examined the anger–depression relationship in people with clinical anger problems. Perhaps depressed people sometimes get angry, but do generally angry people get depressed at a higher rate than less-angry individuals? Also, most studies include only clinically depressed clients and fail to assess the relationship of anger with other types of psychopathology. Therefore, it is difficult to determine if the degree of anger associated with depression is unique to depression, or if similar relationships exist between anger and other behavioral and emotional problems.

A few studies have used more complicated designs to test specific hypotheses. For example, Mohr, Shoham-Solomon, Engle, and Beutler (1991) devised a method to test the hypothesis that inhibited anger expression results in depression. If this theory were true, the successful treatment of depression would focus on uncovering inhibited anger in patients and encouraging the experience and expression of this anger. From the paralinguistic and semantic content of patients' in-session verbal responses, they found that hurt and anger resulting from unresolved conflict could be separately measured. However, increasing the clients' expression of anger did not result in a corresponding reduction of their hurt or depression and thus failed to support the inhibited-anger-expression hypothesis.

Other studies attempted to confirm the inhibited-anger-expression hypothesis by examining the effect of cathartic anger expression on depression. The results are inconsistent. Some studies supported this hypothesis in the laboratory (Forrest & Hokanson, 1975) and others supported the hypothesis with a clinical sample (Wadsworth & Barker, 1976). Others failed to confirm a relationship between depression and inhibited anger expression (Atkinson & Polivy, 1976). Although these studies focused on the reduction of depression, they did not assess anger after the cathartic expression of anger. Research strongly indicates that the cathartic expression of anger leads to an increase in anger (see Bushman, Baumeister, & Stack, 1999; Tavris, 1989). Cathartic expression may alleviate depression but leave the person with higher anger. Using this intervention alone may simply replace one excessive affect with another.

Noel (1980) examined the effects of two types of cathartic expression, *cathartic* anger expression and *assertive* expression. Assertive expression led to a decrease in depression while the cathartic anger expression resulted in continued anger and depression. These results fail to support the inhibited-anger-expression hypothesis, and could be interpreted to support the anger-effort-failure-hopelessness hypothesis. Assertion may increase the subjects' sense of efficacy regarding their ability to resolve their conflicts, thereby challenging their hopelessness and lifting their depression.

Some researchers have investigated the relationship between depression and anger by examining whether changes in anger co-vary with changes in depression. Blackburn, Lyketsos, and Tsiantis (1979) demonstrated that hospitalized patients' decreases in depression were related to nurses' ratings of changes in anger-in but not to self-reports or interviewers' ratings of the same construct. The relationship between depression and hostility has also been examined. A. S. Friedman (1970) found changes in hostility were unrelated to improvement in depression. However, the desire for self-punishment and the desire to punish others decreased with the improvement of depression. Fava, Kellnar, and Lisansky (1986) showed a corresponding reduction in hostility for depressed patients successfully treated with medication. If anger and hostility decrease with depression from pharmacotherapy, or if anger and depression respond to the same medications, then both emotions may have similar underlying biochemical or physiological mechanisms.

Depression has long been associated with the risk of suicide (Yesavage, 1983). However, considerable evidence has amassed suggesting that co-morbid anger plays an important role in suicide, especially in adolescents. Suicide is a growing health problem among adolescents and is the third most frequent cause of death among this age group (National Center for Health Statistics, 1991). Adolescents who attempt suicide often report depression, hopelessness, and negative thinking (Mash & Barkley, 1996; K. Myers, McCauley, Calderon, Mitchel, Burke, et al., 1991). They often cope by withdrawing from others and engaging in wishful thinking (Spirito, Over-holser, & Stark, 1989). Although some suicidal adolescents may experience intense depression, others experience less depression with intense aggression and anger (Apter, Bleich, Plutchik, Mendelsohn, & Tyano, 1988; Garfinkel, Froese, & Hood, 1982; Myers, McCauley, Calderon, & Treder, 1991; Pfeffer, Plutchik, & Mizruchi, 1983). Increasing evidence indicates that aggressive behavior may be related to suicidal ideation (Choquet & Menke, 1989; E. Goldberg, 1981) and attempts (Cairns, Peterson, & Neckerman, 1988). Many adolescents report intense anger immediately prior to their suicidal gestures (Hawton, Cole, O'Grady, & Osborn, 1982; Withers & Kaplan, 1987). In one study, a third of the adolescents who completed suicide displayed anger as their predominant mood just prior to their deaths (Hoberman & Garfinkle, 1988). The level of aggression and anger in suicidal adolescents is equivalent to that of assaultive patients (Cairns, Peterson, & Neckerman, 1988). Prior to suicide attempts adolescents may engage in intense verbal attacks or display physical aggression toward objects or people (Gispert, Davis, Marsh, & Wheeler, 1987). Trait anger and anger-out are higher in suicidal adolescents than in nonsuicidal controls, and both variables predict hopelessness. However, the correlation is stronger between anger-in and hopelessness than trait anger and hopelessness (Lehnert, Overholser, & Spirito, 1994). Thus while many forms of anger are related to hopelessness, anger-in predicts hopelessness better than other types of anger scores.

Maiuro, O'Sullivan, Michael, and Vitaliano (1989) reported that suicide-attempting adult patients had scores on anger and hostility equivalent to assaultive psychiatric inpatients. It appears that both overt and covert styles of anger expression as well as depression are related to suicidality. It is unclear which theory is supported by this relationship. Perhaps suicidal attempters escalate their anger and depression because the anger no longer defends against depression. They may also have strong yet inconsistent beliefs about their own efficacy. Although they may have the potential to solve their problems adaptively, a high sense of self-efficacy may lead to an impulsive and drastic problem solution: death. More research is needed to help explain the role of anger and depression in suicidal individuals.

A group of Dutch researchers (Mook, Van Der Ploeg, & Kleijn, 1990) believes that the relationship between anger and depression is confusing and inconclusive because most studies fail to address theoretical issues in their research method. Researchers often fail to examine the relationship between depression and anger in a variety of different populations. Unfortunately, it is common to use normal and subclinical populations to investigate ques-tions and subject matter of a clinical nature. A shortcoming of this approach is that the results for the nonclinical or subclinical groups may not be the same as for clinical groups (Dobson, 1985; Gotlib & Meyer, 1986). Also, as noted earlier, researchers often neglect to distinguish between state and trait measures of an emotion (Spielberger, 1972b; Spielberger, Jacobs, Russell, & Crane, 1983). Mook et al. (1990) point out that the most common research practice has been to correlate a trait measure of anger with a state measure of depression. This continues to be the trend. Additionally, researchers fail to consider the multidimensional nature of anger expression, and use one global measure of anger. Correlations may differ between depression and various characteristics of anger experiences. Finally, few researchers have investigated the possibility that the relationship between anger and depression may be mediated by a third variable that also correlates with both these emotions. Anxiety has been shown to correlate with both anger (Polivy, 1981) and depression (Dobson, 1985). Perhaps the relationship between anger and depression is mediated by anxiety.

Mook et al. (1990) assessed only trait levels of anger, depression, and anxiety in samples of normal adults, medical patients, and psychiatric patients. For normal adults and medical patients, anxiety and depression correlated highly, at about .6. Correlations between depression and anger averaged about .23; however, the correlations between anger and anxiety were higher, averaging around .4. The correlations between trait measures of anxiety and depression with anger-out and anger-control were nonsignificant in the psychiatric patients. However, the psychiatric patients' depression correlated significantly (around .4) with the anger-in subscale.

For all three samples in the Mook et al. (1990) study, the correlation between depression and anger were mediated by anxiety. Partial correlations statistically removed the common variance accounted for by anxiety in the correlation between depression and anger. This means that anger and depression share some relationship with anxiety. When people experience depression, they feel some anxiety; when people are angry, they experience some anxiety. When this common experience of anxiety was removed, depression and anger were negatively correlated in normal adults and medical patients and ceased to exist in psychiatric patients.

This finding was replicated in the data collected in the development of the Anger Disorders Scale (ADS; DiGiuseppe & Tafrate, 2004). In normal adults and college students, anger and depression correlated about .34, and about .2 in a prison sample. When partial correlations were used to remove the shared variance accounted for by anxiety, the correlation between depression and anger in the normal adult and college samples was reduced by half but was still significant. The correlation in the prison sample was no longer significant.

Based on the Mook et al. (1990) and DiGiuseppe and Tafrate (2004) data, the correlations between anger and depression may be overestimated in most studies because of the failure to partial out the common variance accounted for by anxiety. Also, the relationship between depression and anger may disappear altogether in clinical samples when this statistical procedure is used.

Alternating-Cognitions Hypothesis

A. T. Beck's (1976) proposal that emotions are elicited by specific cognitions is a good premise for building a model to explain the comorbidity between depression and anger, yet supporting data is absent. Depression is related to blaming oneself (internal attributions), low self-efficacy, predictions of a negative future, and self-denigration. Anger is related to blaming others (or external attributions), perceptions of moral transgressions by others, high self-efficacy, and high self-evaluation. A person with unstable beliefs concerning their self-efficacy and the placement of attribution for blame could vacillate between depression and anger. One set of cognitions would arouse a state of depression whereas the other would elicit state anger.

> Consider the case of Terry, a 50-year-old woman who divorced her husband after 30 years in an abusive, subservient relationship. As Terry's ex-husband delayed distributing to her the funds from the sale of their home, Terry's mood shifted between depression and anger. As she related her story, she reported that she felt helpless to get him to follow the divorce agreement and hopeless that she would be rid of him. At times, she believed she deserved such treatment for becoming involved with him in the first place. Her mood quickly changed to anger as she focused on his failure to follow the agreement. She became angrier as she discussed the immorality of his failure to follow the agreement, and her anger further intensified as she recounted his past infidelities and mistreatment of her. She became depressed again as she condemned herself for foolishly remaining married to him for so long. Her mood shifted again to anger as she contemplated a plan for revenge by exposing his misdeeds to his professional peers. Terry's cognitive shifts produced shifts in her emotional states and could be easily observed within a 10-minute period in a therapy session.

Since trait measures ask how frequently people experience emotional states, clients such as Terry would score high on trait measures of both anger and depression. Such scores do not reflect the person's experiencing the two emotions simultaneously, however. Unstable cognitions, related to attributions of blame, self-efficacy, and self-evaluation could elicit alternating affective states. Thus, state anger and state depression would be experienced sequentially not simultaneously. The two sequential affective states, each occurring often enough, could warrant the client's scoring high on the respective trait measures. This theory explains how people could score high on two such opposite emotions.

Clients who experience both depression and anger simultaneously may in fact be different from clients who experience each emotion independently. People experiencing these emotions in rapid succession may have unstable attributions of blame or self-efficacy. This theory could be confirmed in several ways. First, clients who score high on measures of trait anger and depression would report experiencing shifting affective states and would not report experiencing both affective states simultaneously. Second, the alternating affective states would each be related to different yet specific cognitions.

The unique-cognitions hypothesis could be tested by collecting data from a client's emotional episodes across time. The person's experiences of anger and depression could be correlated with each other and also with ratings of anger and depression related beliefs at each emotional episode. As an example we collected data on the client Terry, mentioned above, for 10 emotional episodes across four days. We asked Terry to record the day and time of each emotional episode and rate how strongly she felt angry or depressed. For each episode, she also rated how strongly she endorsed a series of thoughts associated with both anger and depression. The thoughts we hypothesized would be associated with each emotion were presented in a counterbalanced order. The client would therefore not be encouraged by the design of the questionnaire to endorse either angry thoughts when angry, or depressive thoughts when depressed. The correlation between her anger and depression ratings was $-.81$.

The ratings of the emotions and their associated cognitions were submitted to an exploratory factor analysis with a varimax rotation. The final solution accounted for 86.5% of the variance and yielded two factors. On the first factor, anger and depression and each emotion's associated cognitions loaded together. However, the ratings for depression and its associated cognitions loaded positively, and the ratings of anger and its associated cognitions loaded negatively. This supports the idea that anger and depression are opposites. The second factor included one item for experiencing frustration that appeared separate from depression and anger.

The cognitive themes that loaded positively with depression were:

- Hopelessness
- Fear for the future
- Self-responsibility for the problem
- Self-inadequacy and worthlessness
- Prediction of mistakes
- Prediction of poor coping in the future
- Low strength and competence

The cognitive themes that loaded negatively along with anger were:

- Other-responsibility for the problem
- Other-blame and worthlessness
- High strength and competence
- Desire for revenge
- Lack of respect
- Other-immorality
- Frustration in finding a solution

This case example suggests that anger and depression were not experienced simultaneously but were quite distinct. Of course, these data represents only one client's experience of depression and anger. More research is needed with clinical populations to determine if these results generalize to most other patients, or whether the pattern of responses differs for different types of patients. The unique-cognitions model would have very specific implications for treatment. It would be unwise to assume that targeting the depression and its associated cognitions would have an effect on the anger and vice-versa. Practitioners would treat clients who alternated emotions by targeting the cognitions associated with anger and depression, respectively. For example, in Terry's case we targeted her self-condemnation and her schema of perceiving herself as an abused and dependent person. However, we also targeted her ruminative beliefs for condemnation and revenge on her ex-husband.

Conclusions

Is anger a preexisting emotion on the path to depression? Is anger a common symptom experienced with depression? Or are anger and depression separate disorders that happen to coexist in some people? Before these questions can be fully answered, research is needed to assess the percentage of patients meeting the criteria for a depressive disorder who also score in the clinically disturbed range for anger or who meet the criteria for the anger disorder proposed in chapter 14. Also, our knowledge would be greatly enhanced by examining individuals with problematic anger reactions and ascertaining the percentage of individuals with dysphoric disorders. Since no diagnostic category yet exists for anger disorders, and there is a limited amount of research literature on anger, it is unclear what the relationship is between anger and depression in patients who primarily present with anger problems.

Some relationship seems to exist between state sadness–depression and state anger. However, the relationship between the traits of depression and anger is complex and differs depending on the population and measures used. Depression may relate more to anger-in than anger-out (Mook et al., 1990). Trait anger appears to be related to depression, but this may be an artifact because of the relationship that both share with the trait of anxiety.

It seems to be common for practitioners to interpret people's complaints of anger problems as representing depression. We propose that the comorbidity between depression and anger cannot be resolved by assuming anger is secondary to depression. The creation of separate diagnostic categories for anger disorders would help resolve this problem. Thus, each emotional problem could be recognized as primary yet coexisting. The comorbidity of anger and depression may in fact have separate dynamics and symptoms from the presence of either problem alone. Perhaps each problem has its own treatment and it should not be assumed that treating one disorder would resolve the other. Appendix B of the *DSM–IV* lists diagnostic categories for further study. One such exploratory category is mixed anxiety–depression disorder. Perhaps a mixed depression–anger disorder is also needed to account for the relationship between depression and anger.

11

Anger and Personality Disorders

Some authors have associated the presence of anger symptoms with personality disorders (e.g., Kaplan & Sadock, 1993; Klein, Orleans, & Soule, 1991). As noted in the previous chapter, Lachmund, DiGiuseppe, and Fuller (2005) found that clinicians frequently diagnosed angry patients with a personality disorder. In their study, clinicians assigned a personality disorder diagnosis 80% of the time when they were asked for a primary and secondary diagnosis. Not surprisingly, men most often received the diagnosis of Antisocial Personality Disorder (ASPD), whereas women most frequently received a Borderline Personality Diagnosis (BPD). Aggressive individuals also frequently receive a personality-disorder diagnosis whether they are psychiatric inpatients (Krokowski, Volvaka, & Brizer, 1986; Miller, Zadolinnyi, & Hafner, 1993), spouse abusers (Hart, Dutton, & Newlove, 1993), or correctional inmates (Yarvis, 1990).

Our proposal that future versions of the *DSM* include anger disorders is often countered with the belief that personality disorders account for most occurrences of disturbed anger. This chapter will explore the theory and research linking anger and personality disorders. We will review some preliminary data concerning the comorbidity of anger and personality disorders, and then review the clinical literature regarding the role of anger in each personality pattern.

Anger and Personality Disorders: The Overall Picture

Very little research has focused on the correlations of personality-disorder measures and anger measures in clinical populations. Most of the literature presented later in this chapter explores the relationship between anger and one personality disorder. Since considerable overlap exists among personality disorders, and patients rarely meet criteria for only one personality disorder, we attempted to explore the relationship between anger and all personality disorders. In the first data set, the third edition of the Millon Clinical Multiaxial Inventory (MCMI–III; Millon, Davis, & Millon, 1997) and the Anger Disorders Scale (ADS; DiGiuseppe & Tafrate, 2004) were administered to 230 psychotherapy outpatients. Overall, most of the correlations were significant and small, supporting the notion that anger and personality psychopathology are weakly related. We had hypothesized that anger should correlate highest with Negativistic, Antisocial, Sadistic, Borderline, and Paranoid Personality Disorder scales. All these personality disorders include symptoms of anger, aggression, or the attitudes associated with anger.

In terms of correlation patterns, the highest were found between ADS scores and Negativistic Personality Disorder. This Millon scale corresponds to the *DSM–IV–TR* Passive-Aggressive Personality Disorder. Such individuals are characterized by periods of explosive anger or stubbornness, intermingled with periods of guilt or shame, frequent disappointment, and passive resistance to demands for adequate performance. These correlations were in the moderate range. Of all the disorders in the *DSM–IV–TR*, this disorder seems to overlap the most with disturbed anger. The next highest correlations were with Borderline, Sadistic, Paranoid, Schizotypal, and Antisocial personality disorders. As discussed in detail later in this chapter, Borderline Personality Disorder scores should have a substantial correlation with ADS scores because anger is a core symptom in this disorder. Sadistic and Antisocial personality disorders represent the most aggressive personality disorders, and again we expected moderate correlations. Suspiciousness is a cognitive symptom of anger and differs from paranoid thinking by degree and the absence of delusions. This explains the potential relationship between anger and Paranoid and Schizotypal personality disorders.

The more internalizing Personality Disorder scales (e.g., Schizoid, Avoidant, Depressive, Dependent, and Masochistic personality disorders) had significant but small correlations with ADS scores. For these personality-disorder scales the correlations were highest with the subscales that comprise the ADS anger-in higher order factor scores. The lowest correlations were found between ADS scores and Narcissistic Personality Disorder. This finding was surprising. The entitlement associated with narcissism should lead to anger when frustration occurs. The correlations with Compulsive Personality Disorder were significant and moderate but negative. Thus, the higher the Compulsive Personality Disorder score the less anger these clients experienced. Millon believes that Compulsive Personality Disorder represents a conforming personality type. Therefore anger may be inconsistent with the interpersonal strategies typical of this group.

In a second study, comorbidity patterns were examined in a sample of 87 adults who were selected and identified as being either high or low on trait anger. This sample is the same one described in chapter 9. Again, subjects completed the MCMI–III. The percentage of high-trait-anger (HTA) or low-trait-anger (LTA) adults who scored in the clinical range on Axis II disorders on the MCMI–III is shown in Table 11.1. Both the number and percentage of clients meeting diagnostic criteria are noted in the table.

Overall, the data suggest that HTA adults experience more personality pathology than their low-anger peers. In addition, those most likely to have

Table 11.1
Number and Percentage of High-Trait Anger (HTA) and Low-Trait Anger (LTA) Adults Meeting Criteria for Axis II Personality Disorders on the MCMI–III

Axis II Personality Disorder	HTA (n = 45)		LTA (n = 42)	
	#	(%)	#	(%)
Cluster A				
Paranoid	6	(13)	0	(0)
Schizoid	3	(7)	0	(0)
Schizoptypal	1	(2)	0	(0)
Cluster B				
Borderline	10	(22)	0	(0)
Antisocial	8	(18)	1	(2)
Narcissistic	8	(18)	7	(17)
Histrionic	1	(2)	9	(21)
Cluster C				
Dependent	8	(18)	1	(2)
Avoidant	2	(4)	1	(2)
Obsessive-Compulsive	0	(0)	6	(14)
Miscellaneous				
Negativistic (passive-aggressive)	11	(24)	0	(0)
Depressive	8	(18)	2	(5)
Sadistic	5	(11)	0	(0)
Masochistic	4	(9)	0	(0)

Note: Base rates range from 0 to 115. Base-rate scores ≥ 85 considered clinically significant. An analysis of mean base-rate scores indicates that HTA adults reported significantly more personality-disorder symptoms than LTA adults for every category except narcissistic, histrionic, and obsessive-compulsive disorders.
Reprinted from Kassinove and Tafrate (2006) with permission from Springer Publishing Co., Inc., New York.

problematic anger reactions tend to present with a wide range of personality difficulties. Thus, the high-anger group was not adequately captured by any one personality disorder. In Cluster A (odd and eccentric), Paranoid emerged as the most common pattern reported by HTA adults. This finding seems consistent with the data presented above. In Cluster B (emotional and erratic), Borderline, Antisocial, and Narcissistic were all strongly represented in the HTA group; however, narcissistic adults appeared to be equally common in the LTA group. For anxious and fearful individuals (Cluster C), Dependent Personality Disorder emerged as the most common in HTA adults. Similar to the finding in the previous data set, problematic anger was not associated with an Obsessive-Compulsive style.

The MCMI–III assesses several personality patterns that are not part of the *DSM* system (i.e., negativistic, depressive, sadistic, and masochistic personalities). HTA adults also scored in the clinical range across these patterns, suggesting that those with anger-related difficulties are not likely to be limited to a narrow range of personality disorder categories. Similar to the finding noted above, Passive-Aggressive Personality Disorder was among the most common disorder experienced by HTA adults.

Other researchers have examined the potential overlap between anger and aggressive behavior and personality disorders. For example, Berman, Fallon, and Coccaro (1998) hypothesized that the presence of anger and aggressive symptoms would predict the occurrence of a personality-disorder diagnosis after they controlled for serious mental illness, gender, and substance abuse. However, they found that the relationships between anger–aggression and all personality disorders were significantly less when they statistically controlled for gender and substance abuse. Thus gender and substance-abuse symptoms more strongly accounted for the relationship between anger and personality disorders. Nonetheless, significant relationships persisted for BPD and ASPD. However, when they statistically controlled the symptoms of BPD and ASPD, significant relationships were found between anger–aggression and both Passive-Aggressive (PAPD) and Paranoid (PPD) personality disorders. This study showed that anger–aggression was not associated with all personality disorders, and that BPD, ASPD, PAPD, and PPD are independently associated with anger. This study is also noteworthy because it demonstrates that the relationship between anger and some personality disorders may be linked to other comorbid conditions. We tried to keep this in mind while reviewing this literature. No study has yet appeared that showed that all or most angry clients have personality disorders.

Across all three data sets reviewed, Passive-Aggressive, Borderline, Antisocial, and Paranoid seem to consistently emerge as the most common patterns likely to be present among those with problematic anger reactions. The potential comorbidity between anger and specific personality disorders poses challenges for practitioners in terms of conceptualization and treatment adherence. For example, engaging PPD clients would likely involve more focus on the therapeutic relationship rather than on specific anger-reduction techniques. A similar focus on the therapeutic relationship and expectations in relationships would be warranted when working with PAPD clients. APD clients may do better with strategies that emphasize long-term consequences related to decision making. Borderline clients are likely to benefit from a broader approach that emphasizes stability in relationships, thinking, and behaviors.

The Role of Anger in Specific Personality Disorders

The information presented in this section reviews both clinical descriptions and conceptualizations about how anger may play a role in different personality-disorder patterns. The various personality disorders are organized in terms of diagnostic clusters presented in the *DSM*. In addition, personality disorders listed in Appendix B of the *DSM*, categories in need of further study, are also reviewed.

Cluster A Personality Disorders

Paranoid Personality Disorder
Paranoid Personality Disorder (PPD) is defined as a pervasive distrust and suspiciousness of people, accompanied by the interpretation of others' motives as malevolent (American Psychiatric Association, 2000). These individuals mistrust ambiguities and have difficulty assimilating reality to fit their preconceptions (American Psychiatric Association, 2004; Hyer, Brandsma, & Shealy, 1995; Swanson, Bohnert, & Smith, 1970). They behave in a guarded, defensive, argumentative manner and experience chronic tension and hypervigilance to perceived threats. Interpersonally, they are secretive and suspicious. They are quick to ward people off and are viewed by others as cold, aloof, and unemotional.

The emotions typically expressed by these individuals are intense jealousy and anger (A. T. Beck, Freeman, Pretzer, Davis, Fleming, et al., 1990; Sperry, 1995). Self-righteousness usually accompanies their anger and functions as a hostile defense against anticipated attacks. Such individuals see the world as a hostile place. Of course, their hostility is often self-defeating and leads to the rejection they fear, or the provocation of further punishment, thereby confirming their hostile worldview (Meissner, 1978; Swanson et al., 1970). To avoid such self-destructive aspects of their anger, some people with PPD sometimes act submissively, though this defense may create feelings of anger (Meissner, 1978).

Few empirical studies have investigated the role of anger in PPD. In Turkat, Keane, and Thompson-Pope's (1990) study, 18 participants with PPD and 18 normal control participants viewed role-plays involving provocation with ambiguous, accidental, hostile, or prosocial intent. Participants identified the intention behind the action and then chose a response. The participants with PPD and normal controls did not differ on intention-cue detection when the intention was clear. However, the paranoid participants had a significantly greater tendency to misread ambiguous situations as hostile and to react with anger. Even when the perceived intention was prosocial or accidental, paranoid participants were more likely to respond with anger and less likely to ignore the event than were normal controls. Although this diagnosis includes the suspiciousness that represents a hallmark of the cognitive style of many angry people, and suspiciousness is considered a key cognitive element of anger, it remains unclear how much anger and Paranoid Personality Disorder overlap.

Schizoid Personality Disorder

Schizoid Personality Disorder (SPD) is described as an emotion-controlled character type with a constricted range of affective response (Kellerman & Burry, 1989). Schizoid individuals have also been described as leading largely unemotional lives (Hyer et al., 1995), having an intrinsic emotional blandness (Millon, 1981a) and an absence of emotional expressiveness (Sperry, 1995). They are difficult to arouse and are generally unresponsive, minimally responsive, or intellectually responsive to stimuli that typically produce intense emotions (Millon, 1981a). They generally have difficulties recognizing and labeling emotional experiences (A. T. Beck et al., 1990; Millon, 1981a), and are rarely introspective since satisfaction in self-evaluation is difficult when deep emotions are absent (Hyer et al., 1995).

Psychoanalytic theorists have proposed that schizoid people fear loving others too strongly. Therefore they choose to shut off emotions and maintain a distant, aloof stance (Guntrip, 1969; Meissner, 1978). Millon (1981a) noted that people with SPD are insensitive to the feelings, thoughts, and needs of others and may be unresponsive when others expect a thoughtful or empathic response. Their lack of interest in communicating and relating affectionately to others often results in few relationships.

A. T. Beck et al. (1990) noted that schizoid people have a vague thinking style and a general poverty of thought. This results in few emotion-based automatic thoughts. Besides having a paucity of automatic thoughts, schizoids have a cognitive style characterized by defective perceptual scanning (Millon, 1981a). Because they often do not perceive cues that trigger affective responses, they experience fewer emotional reactions, including anger (A. T. Beck et al., 1990). Nonetheless, Meissner (1978) and Millon (1981a) have theorized that intense and vindictive anger may occur in SPD patients but will be masked by passivity.

We uncovered only one study on anger and SPD. Coid (1993) showed that anger negatively correlated with a diagnosis of SPD in a sample of 72 women. It seems unlikely that dysfunctional anger experiences and expressions occur with this disorder. Nonetheless, more research is needed to confirm this conclusion.

Schizotypal Personality Disorder

Schizotypal Personality Disorder (STPD) is described as a pervasive pattern of interpersonal deficits and discomfort in social situations, resulting in a reduced capacity for close relationships, and the presence of cognitive or perceptual distortions and eccentricities of behavior (American Psychiatric Association, 2000). Schizotypals are noted for their eccentric, erratic, and bizarre mannerisms and patterns of functioning. Interpersonally, they are loners. Their social isolation may result from intense social anxiety, expressed by apprehensiveness that does not diminish with familiarity. Their thoughts are scattered and ruminative and characterized by cognitive slippage, including presentations of superstition, telepathy, and bizarre fantasies (Sperry, 1995). They tend not to experience full-blown delusions or hallucinations.

Characterized by Kellerman and Burry (1989) as an emotion-avoidant character type, the affect of schizotypal individuals can be completely absent, creating a drab, cold, and aloof appearance. They often reported being neither happy nor depressed. They may realize that others experience a variety of emotions and wish that they did too. Some patients with STPD work actively at controlling emotions, including anger, out of a fear of humiliation and rejection. Their bland appearance may be deceptive as it may conceal underlying anger, anxiety, and depression (Millon, 1981a; Sperry, 1995). When emotion is expressed it is often inappropriate (American Psychiatric Association, 2000; A. T. Beck et al., 1990; Millon, 1981a). Anger triggers for schizotypals often include situations in which they experience humiliation or disappointment (Sperry, 1995). When threatened, they can become more erratic, hostile, bizarre, and even psychotic (Millon, 1981a).

Empirical research on anger in STPD patients is scarce. Schulz, Schulz, Hamer, Resnick, and Friedel (1985) interviewed patients with Borderline Personality Disorder or STPD and their families. Clinicians perceived that anger was the most troublesome symptom for both disorders. Unfortunately, no data was presented on the frequency of anger in the schizotypal group. Future research should focus on exploring both the expression and suppression of anger in people with STPD, as both tendencies have been noted in the descriptive clinical literature. However, no data exists indicating that anger occurs more frequently in patients with this disorder. As noted earlier, correlations between the ADS and the MCMI indicate that anger experiences may be common in individuals with this disorder. The highest correlation between the ADS and MCMI was found on the suspiciousness subscale. Thus, a tendency to be suspicious of others' motives may predispose STPD individuals, as well as paranoid individuals, to experience anger.

Cluster B Personality Disorders

Borderline Personality Disorder

The most notable symptoms of Borderline Personality Disorder (BPD) are a chronic pattern of unstable interpersonal relationships, unstable self-image and emotion regulation, and marked impulsivity (American Psychiatric Association, 2000). Many individuals with BPD often express intense anger. Both the *DSM–IV–TR* (American Psychiatric Association, 2000) and the revised Diagnostic Interview for Borderlines (DIB–R; Linehan, 1993; Zanarini, Gunderson, Frankenburg, & Chauncey, 1989) include anger and angry acts as symptoms. While BPD clients experience a range of shifting emotional episodes, anger is often reported as the most prominent (Gunderson & Zanarini, 1989; H. Stone, 1990). The dysregulation of anger also interferes with treating these individuals (Nason, 1985). Linehan (1993) describes BPD patients as being easily angered by stimuli that others fail to find offensive. Their extreme angry reactions are out of proportion to the stimulus, and they remain angry for prolonged periods. Schulz et al. (1985) found that family members of people with BPD perceived anger as the most troublesome symptom.

In no other disorder is anger as central to its understanding as with BPD. The history of the Borderline construct is one of confusion with at times more than 100 possible symptoms being suggested by authors as describing the syndrome (Widiger, Miele, & Tilly, 1992). However, more recently, considerable progress has been made to define this disorder. For most authors on the subject, anger has remained a key aspect of the disorder. Gunderson (1987) identified the presence of intense affect, either depression or anger, as a key symptom in BPD. Spitzer, Endicott, and Gibbon (1979) included intense, inappropriate anger as a symptom of the disorder, and it has remained in the American Psychiatric Association's *DSM–III* (1980), *DSM–III–R* (1987), *DSM–IV* (1994), and *DSM–IV–TR* (2000). Of course, clinicians perceive anger as a core symptom of BPD. Lively, Reiffer, Sheldon, and West (1987) asked psychiatrists to rate a list of symptoms on a Likert scale indicating how strongly they represented the prototype of a BPD patient. Anger received the third-highest rating after unstable relationships and identity disturbance. Hilbrand and Hirt (1987) asked clinicians to generate the most prototypical symptoms of BPD. Anger was the second-most-noted symptom after impulsivity. Reich (1992) reported an exhaustive review of the research on the assessment of BPD and found that anger was consistently validated as a core feature. Other core symptoms included unstable, intense interpersonal relationships; identity disturbance; affective instability; impulsivity; intolerance for being alone; physically self-damaging acts; and feelings of chronic emptiness and boredom. The association of anger with BPD among clinicians appears strong.

Kroll (1988) believes that clinicians exaggerate the incidence of anger in patients with BPD for several reasons. First, borderlines express anger in a very dramatic and salient manner that clinicians remember. Also, the frequency with which borderline patients express anger at therapists is legendary, and no other diagnostic group expresses anger toward mental health professionals more than borderline patients. Kroll suggested that for such patients anger might result from therapists' promising more than they can deliver. The Borderline syndrome, Kroll points out, is an exaggeration of the hostility and rebelliousness found in late adolescence. Kroll (1988) also notes that anger is incompatible with the primary motivation of borderline patients, which is to please others and avoid abandonment. Thus anger may be a situation-specific emotion in this group and not a personality trait. This notion appears inconsistent with the research reviewed by Reich (1992) and others identifying anger as a core symptom.

People targeted by borderline anger typically withdraw from the borderline person, enhancing the patient's fear of abandonment. Linehan (1993) noted that underexpression of anger and overcontrol of angry feelings are also common features in BPD. Instead of expressing anger directly, BPD clients may display a pattern of passive, helpless, and submissive behaviors when direct assertive behavior would prove more effective. Underexpression of anger may result from an individual's history of over-expression of anger, and a fear that if anger is expressed the individual will lose control, be retaliated against, and ultimately be rejected. It has also been hypothesized that physical or sexual abuse, common in the histories of people with BPD, may lead to resentment that increases anger-proneness.

People with BPD may experience anger as a substitute for other intense and perhaps more painful emotions, such as shame, worthlessness, or despair. Although experiencing anger instead of other feelings can be an effective short-term strategy in that it provides the illusion of control and mastery over challenges, in the long-term, overexpression of anger results in ineffective social interactions and leads to even greater shameful feelings. Anger is also connected to the experience of separation and loss. When those with BPD perceive important people in their lives as abandoning them, being inattentive, or becoming unavailable, they often react in angry ways (Waltz, 1994).

Although anger in BPD patients is often directed toward others, it can be directed toward the self in terms of self-destructive behaviors (Kroll, 1993). Parasuicidal behaviors, such as cutting, can serve a soothing function and reduce intense feelings, which make such behaviors extremely difficult to eliminate (Waltz, 1994).

Biological, psychodynamic, and environmental factors have been proposed to explain the presence of anger in BPD (Millon, 1992). The propensity to anger may represent a biologically lower threshold for emotional reactivity. Another view states that anger is part of cyclothymia. This represents a subclinical condition of bipolar disorder that swings between anger–mania and depression (Akiskal, 1991).

Kernberg's (1975, 1979) work best represents psychoanalytic theories. He proposed that borderline patients vacillate in their reactions from frustrated infantile desires to condemning themselves for having experienced anger. The inability to resolve these feelings occurs because of a parental figure's withdrawal of love when emotions were expressed (Masterson & Rinsely, 1975). This results in a recurrence of anger, self-recrimination, and depression.

Millon (1987, 1992) hypothesized that the increase in the diagnosis of BPD represents a real increase in the base rate of the disorder because of cultural changes in U.S. society. Our culture fosters fewer and less-pervasive family relationships, fewer rituals, and fewer ties to community. These social factors deprive people of a sense of identity and provide fewer reparative social institutions. Although Millon's etiological theory can account for some symptoms of BPD, it fails to directly account for anger symptoms.

An interactional model of BPD etiology has been proposed by Linehan (1993). She maintains that those who develop BPD have a biological predisposition to poor affective regulation. This alone is insufficient to develop the disorder. Invalidating emotional experiences also contribute. In her model, the invalidating experiences teach the person to question his or her own judgments and thoughts. This leads to identity confusion, and since cognitions help regulate emotions, the fluctuating cognitions add to poor emotional regulation. Although Linehan's theory explains much about the disorder, it fails to account for the symptoms of anger specifically.

Considerable research has investigated the comorbidity patterns in BPD patients (see Jonas & Pope, 1992, for a review). Affective disorders, especially major depression, are common. Some clinicians interpret confluence as confusion and believe it casts doubt on the validity of BPD. Since BPD is an Axis II disorder, the possibility exists that patients who meet this diagnosis experience many Axis I disorders. Some borderline patients might have depression, anxiety, or anger disorders on Axis I. Three decades earlier, Rickles (1971) proposed an angry subtype of BPD characterized by unprovoked anger, a critical attitude toward others, a need to excel, perfectionism, suicide attempts, alcohol or drug abuse, and serious marital maladjustment.

Although anger dysregulation is clearly a core symptom, it may not be present in all BPD patients. In their cluster analysis, Grinker, Werble, and Drye (1968) found four subtypes of borderline patients. Only two of these subtypes displayed anger. Thus, an anger-disorder diagnosis on Axis I, in combination with an Axis II diagnosis of BPD, could provide a more accurate picture of some patients.

Because borderline clients express anger so frequently in treatment, strategies to respond to such clients have been developed. Linehan (1993) explicitly asks clients to decrease self-destructive behaviors. Although this is an early goal in treatment, it is communicated that the therapist does not expect that this goal will be achieved immediately. Therefore, the therapist expects that anger outbursts, manipulations, and suicidal gestures will occur. Linehan also encourages clients to contact the therapist between sessions for patient-defined emergencies. Thus, the therapist is available for such contacts to teach the client to resolve problems and to prevent hospitalization. In contrast, the psychodynamic model (Kernberg, 1975, 1977) forbids such contacts, and the patient must rely on scheduled sessions to resolve all problems.

Optimistically, Linehan's dialectical behavior therapy (DBT) approach appears effective in reducing anger in BPD patients (Linehan, Heard, & Armstrong, 1993; Linehan, Tutek, & Heard, 1992; Shearin & Linehan, 1994). Other effective treatments also exist. Certain psychotropic medications may be effective in reducing anger in borderline patients (Cowdry & Gardner, 1988; S. C. Goldberg, Schulz, Schulz, Resnick, Hamer, et al., 1986; Leone, 1982).

We do not believe that angry borderline patients provide a good prototype for individuals with problematic anger reactions or an anger disorder. Linehan (1993) points out that borderline patients display active passivity. They are passive toward problems, but they actively seek out others (like their therapist) to solve their problems. They become angry when others do not solve their problems. Their anger tantrums get others to help them. Nonborderline angry clients are likely to have a greater sense of self-efficacy. They are, therefore, less likely to be angry with therapists for failing to resolve their problems and more likely to be angry about perceived unfairness. Nonborderline angry clients do not have as much therapist-directed anger. No special techniques have been required by us to handle therapist-directed anger because we have rarely encountered this type of problem in research studies or clinical work with nonborderline patients.

Although BPD is the most frequent personality disorder diagnosed in angry patients, we have found that more than 65% of angry patients do not meet the criteria for BPD. Thus BPD does not appear to represent or account for the majority of those individuals with problematic anger reactions.

Narcissistic Personality Disorder

Narcissistic Personality Disorder (NPD) is described as a pervasive pattern of grandiosity characterized by a need for admiration and a lack of empathy (American Psychiatric Association, 2000). Narcissistic patients are seen as conceited and self-centered. Although they may present as pleasant and endearing, beneath the surface they are exploitative and use others to indulge their desires. Expansiveness, exaggeration, and inflexibility characterize their thinking. They may focus on images and themes rather than on facts and issues. They also have an exaggerated sense of self-importance and entitlement. Narcissists may even distort reality and engage in self-deception to be congruent with their inflated sense of self-importance. An aura of self-confidence and nonchalance characterizes their affective style. However, when their confidence is shaken, they are likely to respond with criticism and anger (Sperry, 1995).

Research on NPD patients indicated that they have lower scores on measures of depression, internal angst, and irrational beliefs. They also have higher satisfaction with life and overall well-being compared with patients with other personality disorders, or with patients without a personality disorder (Leaf, DiGiuseppe, Ellis, Mass, Backex, et al., 1990; Leaf, Ellis, DiGiuseppe, Mass, & Alington, 1991). Yet individuals with NPD are more likely than those with other disorders to seek therapy about a negative life event (Leaf et al., 1991).

Psychoanalytic theorists have described the presence of anger in NPD as narcissistic rage (Kohut, 1978). The anger may at times engulf the person with unforgiving hatred and cruelty and the need to hurt others (Kalogjera, Jacobson, Hoffman, Hoffman, Raffe, et al., 1998). Narcissistic rage may be experienced and expressed in indirect ways. Some narcissists work to disguise their anger to avoid having others see their inadequacies and limitations. Anger may also be expressed covertly when one fears being destroyed or abandoned by others. Covert anger functions to make others feel uncomfortable or guilty and to show that the narcissist cannot be controlled. Anger expressions can include acting helpless, demanding attention, criticizing or manipulating others, using power plays, and exhibiting sudden bursts of angry expression (N. W Brown, 1998).

According to psychoanalytic theory, narcissistic rage originates in early childhood from multiple, chronic self-object failures. Such self-object failures refer to a parent's inability to reflect pride in the child's accomplishments in a developmentally appropriate manner, to provide experiences of belonging, and to join the child in activities without intrusion. These failures lead to feelings of inadequacy and emptiness, deficiencies in empathy, and an inability to soothe oneself. These feelings result in narcissistic vulnerability, which can take the form of a hungry, enraged, empty self protected by a grandiose exterior. This vulnerability leads to difficulties depending on others, an increased sensitivity to disappointments, and deficiencies in dealing with real or imagined rejections and failures. This personality structure and related problems are proposed to lead to narcissistic injury and inevitably to narcissistic rage (Kalogjera et al., 1998; B. E. Moore & Fine, 1990).

NPD patients attempt to attain perfection, which they define as achieving admiration and recognition, being independent of everything and everyone, and never being lacking in any way. However, beneath this grandiosity, they are thought to have fragile self-esteem, perhaps because this degree of adoration is unachievable. They are preoccupied with achievement and how others regard them. As a result, they have extreme difficulty managing criticism or challenges to their self-image of grandiosity and perfection (Bromberg, 1986). Under these circumstances, anger serves a protective function, preventing others from seeing what they regard as a hateful, worthless, vengeful, contemptuous self (Kernberg, 1990) and protecting the self from being destroyed or abandoned when it is under attack (N. W. Brown, 1998).

NPD patients are hypothesized to become easily angered when others fail to meet their unspoken needs. They maintain a sense of entitlement, believing that others owe them special favors or have responsibilities to compensate for failed attempts to satisfy them (Cooper, 1986). The narcissistic individual demands that others think, feel, and act according to his or her script. When others exhibit independence, NPD patients feel abandoned and disappointed and become easily angered (N. W. Brown, 1998; Kalogjera et al., 1998; Kernberg, 1986). Although people who are narcissistic long for loving relationships, they fear depending on people. They equate dependency with feelings such as hate and envy and the experience of being exploited, mistreated, and frustrated (Bromberg, 1986).

This theory of narcissistic rage and low self-esteem has had considerable influence on the way anger is perceived among mental health professionals. In this view, low self-esteem is perceived as the cause of anger, and treatment necessitates improving the low self-esteem. We dealt with this issue in chapter 8. For now, let us say that research has failed to find a causative link between low self-esteem and anger or aggression. However, a link does exist between narcissism and aggression and, most likely, anger (Baumeister, Bushman, & Campbell, 2000) Perhaps these conceptualizations of NPD as resulting from early narcissistic injury and low self-esteem need revision.

Millon (1981a) calls the psychoanalytic view the compensating-narcissism theory, in that at the core, narcissists are trying to compensate for deep feelings of low self-worth and inadequacy. Millon (1981a) presents an opposing theory. He believes that parents of narcissists indulge their offspring. NPD patients are treated as special as they mature, and they learn from their environment that rules do not apply to them. Millon calls this group the convinced narcissists. DiGiuseppe, Szeszko, Robin, and Primavera (1995) performed a cluster analysis on several hundred NPD individuals who sought treatment at an outpatient psychotherapy clinic. They concluded both types of narcissists exist. However, the convinced type is more prevalent.

The role of anger for people with NPD differs according to which theory is applied. Kernberg (1986) believes early and open expressions of "narcissistic rage" represent a poor prognosticator for successful treatment. This may be particularly true in narcissists with borderline or antisocial features and those who engage in open physical violence toward the objects of their sexual exploits. Alternately, Kohut (1978) maintains a more positive view of the anger expressed by NPD patients. He does not identify rage as a problem and believes therapists should not treat it as something that is bad. Instead, rage can reflect a loosening of rigid personality structures and of analytic progress. Kohut (1978) believes this is a positive contrast to the defensive wall of apparent tranquility, which the narcissists have maintained with social isolation, detachment, and fantasized superiority. Therapists can use rage to allow grief, sadness, and regret to be more deeply felt and available for the therapeutic tasks of recognition, acceptance, and integration (Nason, 1985).

Other theorists also view narcissistic rage in a positive light and believe it maintains homeostasis. Anger can help restore a needed feeling of omnipotence and internal power (Dodes, 1990; Stolorow, 1984), decrease feelings of helplessness, increase feelings of entitlement to survive (Buie & Adler,

1973), and restore self-cohesiveness when a person feels a sense of imminent fragmentation (Kalogjera et al., 1998). Clearly, the anger of NPD patients is not always targeted in treatment. To date we have found no empirical evidence supporting this treatment approach to anger with NPD patients (see Littrell, 1998, for a review of reexperiencing painful emotions in therapy). We would caution therapists not to allow angry clients to ventilate their anger in the pursuit of these goals since a large literature exists showing that ventilation and expression of anger increases the probability that people will become angry in the same situation.

A few studies have investigated the comorbidity of anger in NPD patients. McCann and Biaggio (1989) investigated gender differences in the mode of anger expression in college students high in narcissism. Students high in narcissism reported greater expression of anger than those who were low in narcissism. However the narcissists did not express more anger than those high on trait anger. The primary mode of anger expression was verbal. However, college men high in narcissism were more likely to express anger physically compared to women high in narcissism or subjects of either gender low in narcissism.

The trait of narcissism has been shown to have three subcomponents: entitlement, perceived authority, and superiority. Witte, Callahan, and Perez-Lopez (2002) examined the correlation between global narcissism scores and these three subscales of the Raskin and Hall (1981) Narcissist Personality Inventory. They found that anger was not correlated with the global score or the superiority scale, but it did correlate highly with the entitlement and authority subscales. Thus, not all aspects of narcissism may be related to anger.

We have encountered a subgroup of NPD patients who have high-status occupations, experience few negative emotions (e.g., depression and anxiety), score low on measures of self-deprecation and catastrophizing, and seek therapy because of negative life stressors about which they feel indignant. Clinicians should consider the possibility that clients who present with NPD may also have an Axis I anger disorder when they are frustrated by others' failures to meet their demands. Assessing for anger problems and targeting NPD patients' intolerance of an unjust world and their inflated self-esteem might be an effective intervention and may help temper their predisposing personality. Despite a rich descriptive and theoretical literature on the relationship between anger and NPD, few studies exist to confirm this link. Our clinical experience and preliminary data reviewed at the beginning of the chapter suggest that they may not, as a group, have high anger scores.

Antisocial Personality Disorder
People with Antisocial Personality Disorder (ASPD) are characterized by anger, impulsivity, aggressiveness, deceitfulness, and cunning. They have a long history of violating rules and engaging in risky and thrill-seeking behaviors. Antagonism and a reckless disregard of others' safety, needs, and

suffering characterize their interpersonal style. They can appear as slick and calculating and can be highly competitive and distrustful of others (American Psychiatric Association, 2000; Sperry, 1995).

Although a rich theoretical literature exists on the overlap of anger and ASPD, few studies confirm this relationship. One study found that antisocial personalities experienced more anger than people in the general population (Sanderlin, 2001). The overly righteous anger experienced by people with ASPD is thought to result from several irrational beliefs and cognitive distortions (A. T. Beck, 1976; Nauth, 1995; Sterling & Edelmann, 1988). ASPD patients have been described as becoming angry when they perceive others trying to control them or not showing them the respect they feel they deserve. Such individuals feel that anger in these situations is justified and that aggressive behavior toward perceived offenders is acceptable (Meissner, 1978). Anger may also result from a sense of injustice, as when other people have possessions that the ASPD individual believes he or she deserves (A. T. Beck et al., 1990). ASPD patients may mask anger either through a superficial charm or by impulsive acts displaying a disregard for consequences. However, Meissner (1978) believes ASPD patients often commit aggressive and criminal behaviors without anger, emotional distress, or provocation. Perhaps their aggression arises from predatory motives, and no anger is involved. Descriptions of angry emotions may be a post hoc rationalization of perdition.

Hyer et al. (1995) suggested that therapists incorporate coping skills, choice reviews, and problem solving into therapy to help people with ASPD manage their anger. One approach to treating anger in ASPD patients focuses on resolving early attachment problems. Levy and Orlans (1999) believe that during the first three years of life the disruption of the primary attachment figure bond can prevent the formation of meaningful emotional relationships. This leads to chronic anger, poor impulse control, and lack of remorse. By age eight, such children begin to display aggressive and controlling behaviors. They may also exhibit a lack of conscience, self-gratification at the expense of others, dishonesty, and a blatant disregard for the rules and standards of family and society. These behaviors contribute to the development of ASPD and a thinking style that leads to anger experiences and aggressive behaviors. Some proposed solutions to the problems of antisocial behavior in children and adolescents include attachment-focused assessment and diagnosis, specialized training and education for caregivers (corrective-attachment parenting), treatment for children and caregivers that facilitates secure attachment (corrective-attachment therapy), and early-intervention and prevention programs for high-risk families.

Some research has assessed the presence of anger in ASPD patients. Studies with ASPD spouse abusers (Lohr, Hamberger, & Bonge, 1988) found that these patients endorsed irrational beliefs associated with depression and anger. Else, Wonderlich, Beatty, and Christie (1993) found that male spouse batterers had elevated scores, compared with controls, on several dimensions of hostility. A study of those who committed intimate-partner abuse, compared to a demographically matched control group, found that offenders had higher scores on an antisocial personality scale and exhibited more frequent anger than the control group (Dutton, 1995). Chase (1999) evaluated the Reactive–Proactive Categorization System for Partner-Violent Men, a system for categorizing partner-violent men as either reactive or proactive aggressors, and found different results. Chase assessed the anger exhibited during a 10-minute interaction with the participants' partners. Specifically, he found that participants categorized as proactive scored higher on antisocial and psychopathic indices compared with those categorized as reactive.

Our clinical experience supports Dutton's (1995) finding that domestically violent men, and some chronically angry nonviolent men with long-term relationship problems, often report histories of rejection, abuse, and neglect in their childhoods. Many hold long-term resentment for these past events, which they view as unjust and arbitrary. However, many of these mistreated, resentful men fail to meet the criteria for ASPD. Also, some patients with ASPD were not abused or neglected and might even have had doting parents. Therefore, resentment or attempts to seek restitution for past abuses do not drive anger or motivate aggressive behaviors for all ASPD patients. We need more research to learn which ASPD patients have early-attachment problems and whether treatments aimed at these early experiences lead to improvement. In addition, we know very little about anger patterns and characteristics among different offender groups (e.g., sex offenders, those who have committed assaults, substance abusers, murderers). Clearly, more descriptive investigations would help clarify the extent to which different types of ASPD clients experience anger-related difficulties.

Histrionic Personality Disorder

People with Histrionic Personality Disorder (HPD) are described as attention-seeking, moody, capricious, and superficial (American Psychiatric Association, 2000). While their behavior may appear charming, dramatic, and flirtatious, they may simultaneously be demanding, manipulative, and inconsiderate. Their cognitive style can be described as impulsive, vague, and field-dependent. They are highly suggestible, dependent on the approval of others, and reliant on hunches and intuition. In addition, they make a clear separation between their real, inner selves and their public, outer selves. They usually put more energy into the public presentation and avoid contemplation and self-awareness. Superficiality and exaggerated emotional displays and excitability, including irrational outbursts and temper tantrums, characterize their affective style (Sperry, 1995). Because this pervasive pattern of excessive emotionality, attention seeking (American Psychiatric Association, 2000), and irrational outbursts and temper tantrums (Sperry, 1995) characterizes HPD patients, this diagnosis is often considered for patients presenting with anger problems. Powers (1972) cites anger as a major theme in such individuals, and Hyer et al. (1995) observed that they are easily angered.

When not angered, such individuals often appear mild-mannered, inhibited, and uncomfortable when asserting themselves. Some people whom they ordinarily treat in a gingerly fashion may, at another time, be the object of a full-fledged anger outburst (Shapiro, 1999). Given this contrasting behavior, it is not surprising that HPD patients have a difficult time acknowledging their anger episodes. They will even disclaim or deny them, and they may have little awareness that they displayed such feelings and may fail to notice that they still feel angry (Lionells, 1984; Shapiro, 1999). A. T. Beck et al. (1990) suggested that clinicians ask HPD patients for specific examples of how they handle anger, fights, and disagreements, thus looking for any signs of dramatic outbursts, temper tantrums, and the manipulative use of anger.

Research studies on the presence and nature of anger in HPD patients are sparse. One study among medication-free depressed outpatients found that anger experiences were related significantly to a higher frequency of HPD and other Axis II disorders (M. Fava, Rosenbaum, Pava, McCarthy, Steingard, et al., 1993). Despite what seems like an obvious link between anger and HPD, our preliminary data presented at the beginning of this chapter failed to confirm such comorbidity. In fact, an individual high in HPD seems to have a pattern of low anger scores. It is certainly possible that HPD clients may be unaware of or not wish to acknowledge anger-related patterns in relationships and thus score low on self-reports. Another possibility is that the relationship between anger and HPD has been exaggerated. Perhaps HPD clients experience relatively few anger episodes. However, when expressed, their anger displays may be of such a dramatic nature as to remain memorable to clinicians and other observers.

Cluster C Personality Disorders

Avoidant Personality Disorder
Those with Avoidant Personality Disorder (APD) are characterized by social inhibition, feelings of inadequacy, and hypersensitivity to negative evaluation (American Psychiatric Association, 2000). People with this disorder often present with social withdrawal, distrustfulness, and aloofness. They control their behavior and speech and appear apprehensive and awkward. They desire acceptance by others, yet because they fear rejection, they keep their distance, test others, and require unconditional approval before interacting with others. Cognitively, they devalue their achievements, overemphasize their shortcomings, and exhibit a perceptual vigilance for potential rejection or acceptance. They may present as shy and apprehensive but may simultaneously feel anger, sadness, or loneliness when their attempts to obtain unconditional approval are unsuccessful. Feelings of emptiness and depersonalization may also be present during times of increased distress (Sperry, 1995).

Although the *DSM* description for APD does not include anger as a symptom, some theorists believe anger plays a significant role in this disorder. According to Kantor (1993), people with APD engage in a vicious cycle that begins with a fear of rejection that leads to withdrawal. APD patients deal with their feared rejection by becoming rejecting themselves. In other cases, their shyness can have a subtle or overt sadistic cast as they use their shyness cruelly to hurt those who could love them. Whether the anger is expressed overtly or passive-aggressively, the expressed anger has the effect of distancing people and creating adversaries. APD clients may subsequently experience a counter-hostile response from others. The negative behavior of others is then taken personally (often for good reason). At this point, fear of relating to others increases. In short, beliefs about potential rejection lead to behavioral patterns that alienate others, confirming original negative core beliefs about risk taking and intimacy.

Many theorists have described the role of anger in APD. Fenichel (1945) viewed avoidance as an anger equivalent. Anna Freud (1946) implied that hostility, not fear of rejection, is the real reason for avoiding others and for being avoided by them in turn. Anna Freud believed that the avoidant's projection of hostility leads him or her to avoid others, based on the paranoid premise that "I hate you" is the same thing as "You hate me." Sullivan (1953) described an asocial personality who avoids others out of a fear that relationships will lead to conflict. He described a somnolent detachment, a disjunctive disintegration of intimacy, which he believed resulted from a variety of factors, including hostility. Sullivan believed that the avoidant function of hostility maintained self-esteem by demeaning the standing of those perceived as rejecting via disparagement and ridicule. In describing social isolation, Thompson (1959) hypothesized that arrogance and/or a hostile, destructive attitude often produced an inability to connect with others. Thompson proposed that people feel so threatened by others that they must either drive them away or destroy them (Kantor, 1993). A. T. Beck et al. (1990) later noted that dysphoric thoughts and negative feelings (in the avoidant) consist of sadness, fear, or anger (p. 273).

Some empirical studies support the presumption that anger is associated with APD. A study of outpatient women with Major Depressive Disorder evaluated whether anger attacks in these patients were associated with higher rates of other Axis II comorbid disorders. Results showed that depressed patients with anger attacks had significantly higher rates of Avoidant Personality Disorder than those without anger attacks (Tedlow, Leslie, Keefe, Alpert, Nierenberg, et al., 1999). In looking at the personality disorder subtypes of male batterers, Tweed and Dutton (1998) found two groups of men: an instrumental group, which had an Antisocial–Narcissistic–Aggressive profile on the MCMI–II, and an impulsive group, which showed a mixed profile on the MCMI–II with passive-aggressive, borderline, and avoidant elevations. The impulsive group, which contained avoidant elevations, exhibited higher levels of chronic anger than the instrumental group. These findings lend weak support to the notion that anger is associated with APD. Anger may only have been present in these patients because they had comorbidity for BPD and Passive-Aggressive Personality Disorder (PAPD).

Some research supports the idea that socially anxious people experience considerable anger. In a study of socially phobic patients, the Axis I equivalent of APD, Erwin, Heimberg, Schneier, and Liebowitz (2003) found that social anxiety correlated highly with anger-in but not with anger-out. Path analysis suggested that people suffering from social phobia resent the cost of their social anxiety. The fact that socially anxious people experience anger-in and suppress anger-out is not surprising and most probably results because they fear reprisals if they express any anger. The model proposed by Erwin et al. (2003) suggests that anger results from, and does not cause, social anxiety. Similar results were found for APD by McDermut, Ahmed, and Zimmerman (2005). APD was the second-most frequently identified personality disorder in patients with anger symptoms.

Although anxiety is traditionally considered the emotion most associated with APD, given these findings, it would be wise for practitioners to also explore the role of anger in this group of patients. Because anger may exacerbate the interpersonal problems of APD patients, treatment should focus on the assertive requests of others and help APD patients overcome their resentment over past social isolation. Another strategy is to help APD patients think more accurately about how people make them angry. This would allow them to avoid making incorrect assumptions regarding others' motives, reduce seeing personal provocations that do not exist, and diminish feelings of rejection.

Dependent Personality Disorder

Dependent Personality Disorder (DPD) involves a pervasive and excessive need to be cared for that leads to submissive and clingy behavior and fears of separation (American Psychiatric Association, 2000). People with DPD are generally passive, docile, nonassertive, self-sacrificing, and in constant need of reassurance. This compliance and reliance on others is accompanied by a subtle demand that others assume responsibility for the dependent patient's life. We can describe their cognitive style as uncritical, unperceptive, naive, and suggestible. Insecurity, anxiousness, fearfulness, and sadness characterize their emotional or affective style. Because they lack self-confidence, they experience considerable discomfort at being alone and focus on fears of abandonment and disapproval. Anger can occur in DPD patients when their dependency needs are frustrated by loss (of a parent or caretaker) or when others do not comply with their demands for care (Sperry, 1995). Anger may also be experienced in these patients because of separation or rejection, especially when it involves caretakers or other people central to the dependent patient's life. When confronted, DPD individuals often justify or deny their dependent and clingy behaviors.

A few correlational studies have explored the relationship between anger and DPD. Blatt, Cornell, and Eshkol (1993) found that dependent people who are concerned with interpersonal relationships and avoid contradiction and controversy have difficulty expressing anger. This study did not focus on the internal experience of anger, however. In contrast, Dunkley, Blankstein, and Flett (1995) administered the Depressive Experience Questionnaire (Blatt et al., 1993) and the State–Trait Anger Expression Inventory (Spielberger, 1991) to 233 university students. They found that a dependent personality style was associated with scores on trait anger, angry reaction, and anger-out.

Other studies have found that DPD is more specifically associated with inwardly directed anger. Studies by Mongrain and Zuroff (1989), Bornstein, Greenberg, Leone, and Galley (1990), and Levit (1991) suggested that the relationship between dependency, life stress, and depression might be mediated by a defensive style of inward-directed (rather than openly expressed) anger. Bornstein et al. (1990) assessed the level of dependency and response to conflict in two mixed-gender samples of undergraduate participants. The results showed that dependent individuals respond to interpersonal conflict by directing anger inward rather than expressing it outwardly. Levit (1991) obtained virtually identical findings in a mixed sample of high school students. These results are similar to those found by Erwin et al. (2003) with social phobics. Thus, those with DPD and APD may harbor resentment at those they are close to and become angry as a result. Their fear of rejection and need for approval prevent them from assertively speaking up or changing their relationships. Consequently, more resentment occurs. Similar to APD individuals, DPD clients engage in a cycle of anxiety, ineffective interpersonal behavior, resentment, and anger. Although anxiety is likely to be the predominant emotion in DPD individuals, anger plays a significant role in dysfunctional interpersonal patterns for some. The descriptive data on high-trait-anger adults reviewed at the beginning of this chapter suggests that, in Cluster C, DPD is the most likely disorder to be experienced by those with problematic anger reactions.

Obsessive-Compulsive Personality Disorder

Obsessive-Compulsive Personality Disorder (OCPD) is described as a pervasive pattern of preoccupation with orderliness, perfectionism, and mental and interpersonal control, at the expense of flexibility, openness, and efficiency (American Psychiatric Association, 2000). People with this disorder are dependable and are often workaholics, yet they can also be stubborn, possessive, indecisive, and procrastinating. They can be doggedly insistent that others do things their way and are unaware of how others may react to such insistence. Authors have characterized their thinking style as constricted, inflexible, and unimaginative. Because they focus on details and miss the larger picture, they have difficulties establishing priorities and perspectives. Emotionally, they are grim and cheerless and have problems expressing intimate feelings.

Many theorists and researchers have recognized anger in OCPD patients. Besides exhibiting anger, the emotional lives of obsessive children may be characterized by defiance, hatred, loneliness, and fear of punishment (Kramar, 1977). Some theorists believe that people who are obsessive-compulsive are not aware of their anger and may feel threatened by hostile forces within themselves that they do not understand (Millar, 1983). Although anger is not often recognized as a key feature of Obsessive-Compulsive Disorder, it is nonetheless associated with specific subtypes of OCD and certain comorbid conditions (e.g., Borderline Personality Disorder; Hollander, 1999). Malan (1979) has noted that people with obsessive-compulsive personalities are often involved in a triangle of conflicts related to anger. Included in this triangle are the hidden feelings of anger, the defense to control or suppress the hidden feeling, and fear of the potential harm of expressing the hidden feeling. Some authors have proposed that obsessive thoughts can be used to ward off angry, anxious, or sexual feelings and to gain a sense of control (Jakes, 1996; Lionells, 1984; Morphy, 1980). Others have hypothesized that ritualistic behavior and the imposition of a rigid, detailed order upon situations are methods of coping with nonverbalized feelings, especially anger (S. Fine, 1973; Jakes, 1996).

Empirical evidence to support the role of anger proposed by these hypotheses has not been forthcoming. A few studies have investigated anger in obsessive-compulsive disorder (Axis I). One qualitative research study that interviewed 10 obsessive-compulsive men revealed that anger was a common theme among the participants (H. L. Gilbert, 2000). Another study compared obsessive-compulsive disordered women, normal-weight women with bulimia, and nondisturbed controls. On measures of anger, depression, and anxiety, participants with OCD and participants with bulimia had similar scores, with both groups scoring higher than did the controls (Rubenstein, Altemus, Pigott, & Hess, 1995). McMurran, Egan, Richardson, Street, Ahmadi, et al. (2000) investigated the hypothesis that anger functioned in obsessive-compulsive behaviors to control situations. Clients referred to a forensic clinical-psychology outpatient service with and without anger problems completed self-report measures of anger, obsessive-compulsive symptoms, anxiety, and depression. Contrary to the hypothesis, the results showed no association between anger and obsessive-compulsive behaviors. The cognitive style associated with OCPD, negatively rating others for not behaving according to high standards, suggests that these patients may be prone to anger experiences. However, the data presented at the beginning of this chapter suggest that anger is not common among OCPD individuals.

Personality Disorders in Appendix B:
Criteria Sets in Need of Further Study

Depressive Personality Disorder

Depressive Personality Disorder (DepPD) is defined as a pervasive pattern of depressive cognitions and behaviors beginning by early adulthood and present in a variety of contexts. Beliefs of inadequacy, worthlessness, and low self-esteem characterize people with this disorder. They are critical, blaming, and derogatory toward themselves and others. Dejection, gloominess, unhappiness, guilt, or remorse characterize their mood (American Psychiatric Association, 2000; Huprich, 2000). However, given that anger is sometimes a feature of major depression, it would appear that anger would also be associated with a diagnosis of Depressive Personality Disorder. Because the cognitions described in this disorder reflect criticism, faultfinding, blaming, and condemnation, and because these thoughts can be directed toward the self or others, either depression or anger may result depending on the attribution of blame. This is similar to the alternating cognitions model discussed in chapter 10.

Many psychoanalytic writers have proposed that anger is an integral part of depression. DepPD is a relatively new disorder and we have found no research directly related to the diagnosis of this disorder and anger symptoms. It may be worth noting that DepPD as measured on the MCMI correlates highest with the anger-in higher-order factor score on the ADS. In line with the conclusions reached in chapter 10, anger-in may be associated most frequently with depressive disorders.

Passive-Aggressive Personality Disorder

The diagnosis of Passive-Aggressive Personality Disorder (PAPD; American Psychiatric Association, 1987) is currently considered of doubtful validity and reliability (M. A. Fine, Overholser, & Berkoff, 1992; Millon, 1993b) and was dropped from the *DSM–IV–TR* (American Psychiatric Association, 2000; Slavik, Carlson, & Sperry, 1998). However, this disorder may be the closest diagnostic category to an anger disorder. Millon (1994) still considers PAPD a personality disorder, and he still includes a scale assessing it on the Millon Clinical Multiaxial Inventory–III. (On the MCMI–III, PAPD is represented as Negative Personality Disorder.) He describes PAPD patients as experiencing, "anger [and] stubbornness intermingled with periods of guilt and shame" (p. 13). This pattern of coexisting emotions appears paradoxical, since high, unstable self-esteem, and other-blame have characterized anger, while low self-esteem and self-blame characterize shame.

We have chosen to review passive-aggressive personality disorder here, given the important role that anger plays in passive-aggressive behavior and the ubiquitous nature of passive-aggressive actions in everyday life. It is not surprising that the *DSM–IV* dropped PAPD, given its empirical basis and the lack of research. What seems surprising to us is that our field had for so long failed to study passive-aggressive behavior.

The main affect in PAPD is unexpressed anger, which is associated with rebellion against an authority. People with this disorder become angry when required to fulfill obligations at work or school and when confronted with authority figures. In these situations, they feel they are unable to deny assertively or modify a request. Thus, the combination of resentment of external demands with a lack of assertiveness leads them to respond passively and provocatively (A. T. Beck et al., 1990). Their anger is expressed indirectly and nonviolently. Their anger expression might lead to appearing ingratiating, friendly, agreeable, or even submissive (Slavik et al., 1998). Thus, they design the behavior to express anger while simultaneously concealing their anger (Hoffmann, 1995). The possibility of one's anger being discovered can lead to great anxiety. Passive-aggressive behavior occurs when the person may not have a repertoire of assertive behaviors or believes that assertion would be undermined, disregarded, or disqualified in some fashion.

The expression of anger indirectly provides the actor the advantage of avoiding being criticized, undermined, or disregarded (Kantor, 1993; Slavik et al., 1998). Moreover, being passive-aggressive can effectively garner attention (Slavik et al., 1998). However, covert passive methods of expressing anger can still create interpersonal problems. Passively expressed anger is much harder to recognize, and the targeted person often questions his or her perception of reality (Kaslow, 1983) and feels uncomfortable (Kantor, 1993). Because people intend passive-aggressive behaviors to remain undetected, and they fail to communicate the issue directly, present conceptualizations have failed to discuss the motive of passive-aggressive behavior. We believe that revenge or retributive justice motivates passive-aggressive behavior. Thus, a desire for revenge is a key element of this syndrome.

Cognitive-behavioral theories have suggested that people with passive-aggressive personalities have a negative cognitive bias and often search for flaws, mistakes, and injustices in themselves and others (Slavik et al., 1998). They see the actions of authority figures as arbitrary and unfair, blame others for their problems, feel misunderstood or unappreciated, and are unable to see how their own behavior contributes to their difficulties (A. T. Beck et al., 1990). They often display their negativism through incessant complaining and grumbling. They frequently complain of being unappreciated, unloved, overworked, and abused. Besides negativism, ambivalence characterizes their cognitive style. Their ambivalence leads them to feel angry, moody, dissatisfied, and oppositional (Slavik et al., 1998).

Empirical studies designed to investigate the role of anger in Passive-Aggressive Personality Disorder are scarce. In comparing the ability of the Millon Clinical Multiaxial Inventory (MCMI) personality scales (Millon, 1983b) to predict accurately anger and psychosis in White and Black psychiatric inpatients, Greenblatt and Davis (1992) found that the passive-aggressive scale of the MCMI predicted anger for both races equally well.

Farber and Burge-Calloway (1998) investigated self-reported anger, hostility, interpersonal aggressiveness, and self-confidence in Type A and Type B adolescent boys. Results indicated that Type A boys were more likely than Type B boys to engage in physically aggressive, verbally expressive, and passive-aggressive behaviors. Thus, it appears that in Type A male adolescents, anger and passive-aggressive personality features occur together. In their investigation of male batterers, Tweed and Dutton (1998) identified two groups of men: an instrumental group, who had an antisocial–narcissistic–aggressive profile on the MCMI–II, and an impulsive group, which showed a mixed profile on the MCMI–II with passive-aggressive, borderline, and avoidant elevations. The impulsive group, which contained passive-aggressive elevations, exhibited higher levels of chronic anger than the instrumental group. As noted earlier in the section on APD, these findings are limited because any one of the three personality patterns found among this group may account for elevations in anger.

In both of the data sets presented at the beginning of this chapter, PAPD emerged as one of the patterns frequently associated with high anger scores. We believe that PAPD is the pattern most prevalent among those with problematic anger reactions.

Conclusions

A review of the clinical and theoretical literature suggests that several personality disorders include anger as a symptom or can be characterized as having dysfunctional anger as part of the profile. The most common appear to be Passive-Aggressive, Borderline, Antisocial, and Paranoid. However, the notion that anger problems are primarily a result of an existing personality disorder does not have empirical support. Those with anger-related difficulties often present with a wide range of self-defeating personality styles. In addition, anger problems exist for many individuals who would not receive a personality-disorder diagnosis. Nonetheless, consideration for the potential relationship between anger reactions and long-term personality patterns is recommended. For example, conceptualizing anger reactions as part of a larger personality pattern may be useful for both clients and practitioners. In addition, contemplation regarding how a client's specific personality pattern may influence treatment receptivity and adherence may help in the development of programs more likely to succeed.

This chapter ends where it began. Axis II disorders do not adequately account for anger problems. More research on anger is certainly needed to better understand the relationship between anger and long-term personality patterns. Researchers should also consider attempting to support or refute the theoretically proposed hypotheses regarding the types of conflicts, cognitions, and events that produce anger in people with these various disorders.

Part V

Diagnosis of Anger Disorders

12

Objections to Formalizing Anger Disorders

Anger dwells only in the bosom of fools.
—Albert Einstein

Throughout this book we have identified the dearth of information regarding anger conceptualization and diagnosis that negatively affects research and practice. We have also attempted to explain that the explicit diagnosis of anger disorders provides advantages to scientists and professionals, which outweigh the disadvantages. However, accepting this fact does not necessarily mean that present or future nosologies would be improved by adding anger disorders. Some clinicians and researchers may believe that the present diagnostic system handles the problem of anger adequately. Perhaps the formal classification of anger disorders presents disadvantages that exceed the advantages. This chapter will address what we know about how mental health professionals diagnose clients presenting with anger problems. We will also review some arguments against including anger diagnostic categories. The chapters that follow in this section discuss differentiating functional from dysfunctional anger experiences, developing a criterion set for an initial anger-disorder diagnosis based on our current knowledge, and considering the possibility that several specific subtypes, under the heading of anger disorders, may need to be developed through descriptive research.

How Clinicians Diagnosis Angry Clients

Because the *DSM–IV–TR* includes no anger disorders, we explored how clinicians diagnosed people who presented with complaints of strong anger. To investigate this problem, Lachmund, DiGiuseppe, and Fuller (2005) constructed four clinical case vignettes and mailed them to practitioners. The first vignette was for a client that met the criteria for social phobia; there were two versions, one a man and the other a woman. The cases were the same in all details except gender. Two additional vignettes were created by changing the word *anxiety* to *anger*. This resulted in four cases: a socially anxious woman, a socially anxious man, a socially angry woman, and a socially angry man. We asked research participants to develop a primary and a secondary diagnosis and to answer some questions about the case they were given. The case descriptions were randomly assigned, with one mailed to each subject. Vignettes were mailed to 1,000 psychologists or psychiatrists in private practice in the 50 largest U.S. cities; 318 psychologists and 224 psychiatrists responded.

Practitioners showed widespread agreement on the anxiety cases. About 80% correctly identified the diagnosis. Another 18% diagnosed some anxiety disorder. Only 2% gave unlikely diagnoses. Practitioners were much less in agreement on the diagnosis for the angry clients. The largest diagnostic category chosen, Intermittent Explosive Disorder, was selected by 20% of the clinicians. The diagnosis was made even though no aggressive behavior was described in the vignette. Other participants made diagnoses such as organic brain syndrome, psychosis, and personality disorders. More than 80% of the respondents identified an Axis II personality disorder as either the primary or secondary diagnosis. There was considerable gender bias in the assignment of Axis II diagnoses. Both men and women professionals diagnosed significantly more angry women with Borderline Personality Disorder and diagnosed angry men with Antisocial Personality Disorder. We expected this finding and so constructed the case descriptions to include no symptoms of either disorder—only anger. Just switching the word *anxiety* to *anger* created diagnostic confusion. Interestingly, all groups rated the case they received as equally pathological on the *DSM–IV–TR* global assessment of functioning scale, indicating that the symptoms contributed equally to impaired functioning.

The participants also rated how adequate they found the information presented to make the diagnosis. Those receiving the anxiety cases thought that sufficient information was provided to diagnose each case. Those receiving the anger cases found the same amount of information inadequate for diagnosis. Finally, we asked the practitioners how frequently they encountered clients in their practices that were similar to those in the vignettes. Those receiving the anger vignettes reported seeing just as many clients with similar symptoms as did those who received the anxiety cases. It appears that clinicians see as many angry clients as they do anxious clients, but they could not reach a consensus on the diagnosis of the angry clients. Practitioners will assign more serious diagnoses to angry clients and will require more information to make these diagnoses. These results are consistent with our experiences consulting with mental health professionals across a variety of settings. Widespread disagreement and confusion regarding the conceptualization of anger reactions ultimately offers little hope for many individuals seeking services. Formal diagnoses of anger disorders would help professionals more accurately identify client problems and develop effective treatment plans.

Arguments Against Anger Disorders

There are several objections to the development of formal anger-disorder categories. Five of the most common arguments that we have encountered are presented below.

Anger Is Secondary to Depression

The main argument against the inclusion of anger disorders is that people who display anger problems experience depression as the core problem. This argument rests on the notion that anger is not a primary or basic emotion but is secondary to depression. This view, developed by Kraeplin (1899) and S. Freud (1915/1963) and still popular today, directly confronts all scientific theories of emotions. Theories of human emotions disagree on the number and content of the basic emotions. However, they all agree that anger ranks among our core affective responses.

Chapter 10 reviews the research on the relationship between anger and depression in greater detail. This research is vast and confusing. Most of it fails to distinguish between trait and state emotions. When researchers have included clinical populations, they have chosen depressed patients and explored their anger. They have not chosen primarily angry patients and discussed their depression. Taken together, this body of research has failed to support the premise that anger is subsumed under depression. Circumspect theories of emotions view both anger and depression as negative emotions yet as opposites on the continuum of energy. Explorations of the cognitive components of anger and depression show that different cognitions mediate these two emotions. Those proposing that anger is secondary to depression promote psychosocial treatment recommendations that have failed to ameliorate either anger or depression.

The only area that supports a relationship between anger and depression is psychopharmacology. Some evidence exists that selective serotonin re-uptake inhibitors (SSRIs) reduce both depression and anger. SSRIs were originally designed to work with the synaptic sites associated with the emotion of depression. However, they appear to work equally well with anxiety disorders. The reactivity of anger to the same medications that improve depression cannot be taken as evidence that depression and anger are the same. They may share some neurological pathways or synaptic receptor chemicals, as do anxiety and depression, but that does not make one primary and the other secondary. In fact, serotonin may be less involved in anger pathways than other neurotransmitters (Panksepp, 1998). Thus, this argument against the existence of anger disorders appears without merit.

Our research on the comorbidity of anger and depression has also supported differentiating anger from depression. We explored the presence of anger symptoms in a sample of more than 1,700 psychiatric outpatients from the Rhode Island Hospital MIDAS (*Methods to Improve Diagnostic Assessment and Services*) project directed by Mark Zimmerman (2005). All patients underwent structured interviews by trained interviewers to determine whether they had an Axis I or Axis II diagnosis. Anger symptoms occurred more often alone than in the presence of a depressive disorder. Also, anger was more frequently comorbid with anxiety disorders than with depressive disorders. Also, Bipolar I and Bipolar II Disorders accounted for a very small percentage of patients with anger symptoms (Ahmed, DiGiuseppe, McDermut, & Zimmerman, 2005). In another study of more than 400 psychotherapy outpatients, we identified angry clients as scoring in the top 10% on the Anger Disorders Scale (DiGiuseppe & Tafrate, 2004) and as having a depressive disorder if they scored high on the Dysthymic or Major Depression scales of the MCMI–III. Once again, the majority of patients with anger problems did not have a depressive disorder (Cannella, Fuller, & DiGiuseppe, 2005).

While some correlations exist between measures of anger and depression, and many depressed clients have angry symptoms, anger appears more strongly related to anxiety. In addition, anger occurs more often alone as a disorder than in combination with depression. These data suggest that S. Freud (1915/1963) and Kraeplin (1899) were incorrect in identifying anger as part of depression.

Conflict With Societal Values

Raine (1993) identifies two characteristics of crime that mitigate against considering anger a disorder. The first is the idea of "free will," and the second is empathy. Our culture, and the Judeo-Christian tradition on which it is based, relies on the idea of free will to assign blame and punishment. Aggressive behavior is seen as an act of will to hurt others and acquire their resources. The ideas of sin, punishment, forgiveness, and salvation in our culture revolve around free will. Because of anger's link to aggression, anger disorders challenge these foundations. People worry that a psychiatric diagnosis will exonerate perpetrators of violent crimes. The diagnosis might undermine our cultural morality and lead to more violence. For these reasons, any taxonomy of anger disorders needs to consider the issues of responsibility and the legal definition of insanity. Raine points out that we consider free will a categorical variable. You either have it or you do not. He suggested that free will might represent a continuous variable. That is, a person might have varying degrees of free will. Certain biological and experiential factors might limit free will to some degree at different times. This proposal rocks the foundations of Western philosophical, legal, and religious thought. Perhaps science will eventually enable professionals to judge the varying degrees of free will that individuals possessed when they committed criminal acts. This could allow judges to assign the degree of culpability. Our present knowledge falls far short. However, we can be assured that some members of the legal profession will learn how to abuse this concept. Nevertheless, all good science starts with taxonomy. The development of more precise categories may lead us to a better understanding of emotional and behavioral aberrations and therefore to better prevention and treatment.

Raine's second characteristic concerns a lack of empathy. Aggressive behavior evokes strong emotional reactions not only in its victims but also in those who observe the behavior. Courtroom TV dramas from *Perry Mason* to *Law and Order* remain popular. Viewers are shocked and distressed by the crimes. They strongly identify with the victims and root for the prosecution, angered by the defense counsels' maneuvers to free the perpetrators. Anger and hate are often felt toward the aggressors. Perpetrators rarely arouse our empathy. Baumeister and Boden (1998) pointed out that the media often portrays violence as random and arbitrary. This strengthens the call for revenge, for we could be the next victims. Cool, logical heads are usually replaced with angry or fearful hearts when the responsibility for hate or aggression is debated. This emotionalism mitigates against the pursuit of knowledge and understanding that will help treat and prevent aggression effectively in the future.

In most cases, the imprisonment of violent offenders removes these individuals from the streets only temporarily. Among industrialized nations, the United States has the highest percentage of its population incarcerated. Yet it has not eliminated crime or hate. In prison, criminals are temporarily unable to victimize the public. But sometimes they are apprenticed to criminal masterminds during their incarceration. However, without effectively identifying and treating their problems, we will return them to the world just as violent, if not more so, then when they entered prison. Research on the identification, characteristics, etiology, and mechanisms of various anger disorders can only help us develop more-effective treatment programs. Diagnostic subtypes could help us more accurately identify recalcitrant, persistent offenders who fail to respond to treatment and will offend again. This information will help forensic psychologists and criminal justice professionals keep the more dangerous perpetrators off the streets longer.

Diagnosis Removes Culpability

The most common argument against anger disorders is legal and concerns culpability. Some angry clients will have committed aggressive acts and attacked, abused, or victimized others. The diagnosis of an anger disorder, as we propose, would not meet the legal criteria for insanity. Patients who met the legal standard for insanity would be excluded because they would already have met the criteria for more serious already existing psychotic diagnoses. However, the concern exists that defense lawyers would claim that an anger diagnosis diminished their clients' capacity to act responsibly and should be considered a mitigating circumstance. If successful, such arguments could influence judges to render more lenient sentences to violent offenders. The diagnostic system would then have been misused by the legal system to win leniency for the aggressor. We have most often encountered such arguments among professionals and advocates working in the areas of domestic violence and victimology. Such concerns are real, for we have already been asked to testify that the presence of an anger disorder limited a criminal's responsibility and that the court should assign a lesser punishment. There are, therefore, complex legal and moral objections to anger diagnoses.

Raine (1993) presented the most comprehensive discussion of this issue and reviewed the philosophical arguments in this heated debate. His discussion focuses almost exclusively on the behavior of aggression without considering the effect of the anger that may have elicited the aggression. The idea that angry–aggressive criminals would receive lesser sentences relies on the notion that free will is not categorical and that other variables have been scientifically demonstrated to contribute to the behavior. Raine proposed that many variables that influence depression, anxiety, and other conditions identified as mental disorders also operate to influence criminal behavior. He notes that:

- Many studies have demonstrated a genetic influence on aggressive behavior.
- Some aggressive individuals display reduced central nervous system serotonin.
- Limited evidence from neuropsychological tests suggests a frontal-lobe dysfunction in some violent criminals.
- Neuroimaging studies offer some evidence that anatomical differences in the frontal or temporal lobes differentiate criminal perpetrators from nonoffenders.
- Criminal populations consistently exhibit lower resting heart rates.
- Researchers have identified other biological factors associated with violent behavior. These include having a history of head injury or birth complications, being considered less physically attractive, and having high testosterone levels, hypoglycemia, or a mesomorphic body type.
- Researchers have identified functional-cognitive deficits in aggressive samples. These include deficits in the acquisition of classically conditioned fear responses, passive-avoidance learning, oversensitivity to rewards, low verbal IQ, learning disabilities, and social-information-processing deficits.
- Many family variables increase a person's chances of aggressive behaviors, such as parental crime, child abuse or neglect, maternal

deprivation, parental divorce or separation, poor parental supervision, and erratic, inconsistent punishment.

Since most theories believe that aggressive behavior is mediated by anger, the same variables that Raine believes influence aggression could mediate anger dysregulation. If free will is a continuous variable, and if some neurological conditions are proven to contribute to problematic anger reactions and aggressive behavior (making criminals less morally responsible for their acts), should sentencing guidelines consider this fact? Despite the cause of the angry–aggressive behavior, reducing the culpability and responsibility for the behavior is likely to result in reduced efforts to moderate the emotional reaction of anger and its outward aggressive expressions. Social and legal sanctions often motivate individuals to decide to reduce their anger reactions.

Of course the answer to the question of whether or not an anger diagnosis reduces culpability or enhances rehabilitation also depends on whether one sees the role of correctional facilities as punitive or corrective. We, as psychologists, are less interested in the punitive function or paying one's debt to society than whether the correctional interventions reduce recidivism. We think removing culpability will increase anger and aggressive behavior. O'Leary (1995) concluded that the most important lesson he learned from studying domestic violence was that the primary cause of aggressive behavior was the social tolerance of that behavior. Aggression persists because people tolerate it. In other words, people know someone is behaving aggressively but refuse to comment on it or make it an issue, resulting in the perpetrator's believing he or she is invulnerable. We are reminded of Adolph Hitler's comment when he was asked if the world would tolerate his final solution of exterminating the Jews. He responded, "Who remembers the Armenians?" He was referring to the Turkish attempt to exterminate the Armenians at the beginning of the twentieth century. No nation came to their rescue. Hitler learned that past apathy toward aggressors would allow him to pursue his own brand of violence. Psychotherapy research suggests that consequences are important to reduce aggression. Some of the most successful interventions for conduct-disordered youths are problem-solving interventions that help patients review and increase their awareness of the consequences of their behavior. Wellen (1998) reviewed treatment studies of aggressive adolescents and concluded that negative consequences (response costs or time-out) were necessary to reduce aggressive behavior. Thus, research shows that treatments that deliver negative consequences for aggressive behavior, or help one recall these negative consequences are the most successful interventions (Kazdin, 2000). Therefore, reducing culpability and relieving people of the consequences of their angry–aggressive outbursts would be ineffective. The question remains as to whether or not confinement with other aggressive peers, over a long period, is an effective intervention. Socialization with aggressive peers is an intervention known to increase aggressive behavior through modeling (Dishion, McCord, & Poulin, 1999).

Anger Is Part of the Aggressive Drive

Another argument against anger disorders stems from the psychoanalytic notion of the ubiquitous aggressive drive. According to this model, all humans possess an aggressive drive, and the recognition and expression of anger impulses is functional. The *DSM–IV–TR* (American Psychiatric Association, 2000) describes Intermittent Explosive Disorder (IED) as resulting from the "failure to resist aggressive impulses." Eckhardt and Deffenbacher (1995) pointed out that the *DSM* category of IED rests on this notion that aggressive impulses occur in all people and that most nondisturbed individuals resist them. The idea that all humans possess an aggressive drive has been controversial (Peele, 1989), remains too poorly defined to be tested, and has not been demonstrated (Geen, 2001). The diagnostic category of IED fails to account for most anger disorders, given the persistent finding that the majority (approximately 90%, depending on how records are kept) of anger episodes do not occur with aggression (Averill, 1982; Kassinove, Sukhodolsky, Tsytsarev, & Soloyova, 1997).

Anger Is an Axis II Problem

Perhaps anger disorders are not needed because anger and hostility reflect Axis II personality disorders. Anger does appear in the criteria for Borderline Personality Disorder, Antisocial Personality Disorder, and Paranoid Personality Disorder. Some may argue that the inclusion of anger in these disorders is sufficient to account for the angry clients who present with mental health concerns. As discussed in detail in the previous chapter, none of these disorders describes very accurately the range of people who present with clinical anger problems. In addition, those with problematic anger reactions seem to present with a range of personality disorder patterns and are not just restricted to two or three.

The decision to place anger or any other disorders on Axis I or Axis II is unclear by the way the *DSM–IV–TR* distinguishes these axes. The *DSM–IV–TR* makes no clear distinction between Axis I and Axis II disorders. In the introduction to the discussion of Axis II personality disorders, the *DSM–IV–TR* defines a personality disorder as:

> an enduring pattern of inner experience and behavior that deviates markedly from the expectations of the individual's culture, is pervasive and inflexible, has an onset in adolescence or early adulthood, is stable over time, and leads to distress or impairment. (American Psychiatric Association, 2000, p. 685)

However, the criterion for stability occurs in several Axis I disorders such as Dysthymia, Schizophrenia, and Delusional Disorder. Therefore, a stable pattern of angry responding would not necessarily exclude anger disorders from Axis I. Also, Axis I and Axis II disorders have both been shown to share genetic, biological, and psychosocial etiological factors (W. J. Lively, Schroeder, Jackson, & Jang, 1994). Other Axis I disorders are enduring, such as Attention Deficit Hyperactivity Disorder (Barkley, 1996) and conduct disorder (Kazdin, 2000). Also, Axis I and Axis II disorders have significant diagnostic overlap (Fiester, Ellison, Docherty, & Shea, 1990; Trull & McCrae, 1994).

Axis II lacks validity. The different types of personality disorders do not represent discrete disorders, and there is considerable overlap among them. Several proposals have been made to discard the present notion of personality disorders and replace it with a description of normal-functioning personality such as the five-factor model (P. Costa, & McCrae, 1994). Attempting to fit anger disorders into the confusing, overlapping, nonvalid categories in Axis II provides limited nosological information for describing clients.

Finally, even if one accepts the validity of Axis II, an overwhelming percentage of angry patients does not receive an Axis II diagnosis. As described earlier, we explored the presence of anger symptoms in a sample of more than 1,700 psychiatric outpatients from the Rhode Island Hospital MIDAS project (Zimmerman, 2005). Only 49% of patients with anger symptoms received an Axis II diagnosis. Not surprisingly, the most common diagnosis was Borderline Personality Disorder, with 33% of the angry patients being so diagnosed. This diagnosis is likely to have occurred because anger is a symptom of this disorder. All the other Axis II diagnoses accounted for only 16% of the angry patients. More than half (51%) of angry patients failed to meet criteria for any personality disorder. Thus, we concluded that the level of comorbidity between anger and Axis II disorders is similar to that found between anger and other Axis I problems.

Conclusions

Because anger can present serious problems for individuals, families, and society, it deserves attention from the professional and scientific community. We have shown that mental health professionals cannot reliably diagnose simple cases of clients presenting with anger problems and offer a confusing array of serious and contradictory diagnoses when presented with the same angry client. There is a need for a classification of anger problems to facilitate clear communication and clear thinking among professionals.

There are several arguments against classifying anger as a separate nosological category. These can be divided into two camps: philosophical and scientific. The first group includes those who argue that anger diagnoses would be inconsistent with the Judeo-Christian values of free will and responsibility that form the basis of our society. We do not think the existence of anger disorders needs to undermine these ideas. Blame, punishment, and penal systems have not solved the human problems of anger. The scientific arguments propose that anger is a construct of secondary importance subsumed under the rubric of depression, aggression, or personality disorders. Scientific data disputes these claims. A system that fosters communication, theory development, and treatment options provides a better alternative.

13

Functional and Dysfunctional Anger

Certain wise men, therefore, have claimed that anger is temporary madness (*brevis furor*). For it is equally devoid of self control, forgetful of decency, unmindful of ties, persistent and diligent in whatever it begins, closed to reason and counsel, excited by trifle causes, unfit to discern the right and true—the very counterpart of a ruin that is shattered in pieces where it overwhelms. But you have only to behold the aspect of those possessed by anger to know that they are insane.
—Seneca, *On Anger*

In this chapter we acknowledge and define some adaptive functions of anger from an evolutionary perspective. At the individual level, anger experiences may be constructive; however, for a certain percentage of individuals, anger dysregulation can become harmful and clinically problematic. The disruptive nature of anger and its potential negative effects has been documented across a range of areas from health to work. We will review some of the evidence suggesting that anger can be a harmful dysfunction. Several comments and observations are also provided regarding the self-defeating nature of anger and aggressive strategies in larger-scale social conflicts and world events.

Adaptive Anger

Human emotions evolved to inform people that trouble exists and to sound an alarm to activate coping strategies for those problems. Our ancestors evolved in a world that presented considerable threats and limited resources, and anger is usually considered part of the "fight or flight" response. The field of evolutionary psychology has discussed the survival value of anxiety more than the survival value of anger (see Barkow, Cosmides, & Toobey, 1992). Anxiety inspires the flight response that has obvious survival value because it motivates escaping dangerous predators. A. T. Beck and Emery (1985) pointed out that escaping all possible threatening objects or creatures was adaptive for earlier mammalian and human species. Those individuals who thoroughly investigated whether a growl or heavy footsteps belonged to a predator were lunch! Those who became anxious and fled any sound close to footsteps, whatever beasts produced them, found themselves running from many a nonthreatening animal or wisp of wind but lived to reproduce. The genetic tendency to respond with anxiety to nonthreatening stimuli may have become over-represented in our human gene pool. However, evolution chooses for survival not comfort.

Whenever we talk to groups about the idea that anger can be a disorder, we immediately hear the objection that anger can be adaptive. Anger does have value. However, differentiating between functional, adaptive anger and dysfunctional anger has proven difficult since Aristotle's time. Averill (1993) identified seven characteristics of adaptive anger. Recognizing these characteristics can help individuals and clinicians determine if their own personal anger reactions or those of clients are adaptive:

- Anger is functional if the wrongdoer's deeds are correctable.
- The anger is directed only at the person who can be held responsible for his or her actions.
- Anger is not displaced onto an innocent third party.
- The aim of the anger is corrective and seeks to prevent an offense's recurrence not to inflict harm on the target or attain selfish goals through intimidation.
- The anger response is proportional to the offense and should not exceed what is necessary to correct the situation and prevent its recurrence.
- Anger should closely follow the provocation and not last longer than required to correct the situation.
- Adaptive anger involves commitment and resolve to fix the problem.

Conversely, these characteristics help us identify disturbed anger. *Disturbed anger* is targeted at people who cannot change or are not responsible for their actions. Anger that seeks excessive revenge to hurt the perceived offender or coerce him or her for selfish ends would be disturbed. Excessive retaliation also characterizes disturbed anger. Delayed retaliation and ruminative anger that persists long after the initial trigger is also dysfunctional. Anger that is not intended to restore or correct the offending behavior but that has some other motive would be considered dysfunctional. *Displaced anger* is disturbed since it is not targeted at the perpetrator of the offending actions.

Alarm Signal

Anger has other adaptive functions besides warding off attackers. The experience of anger signals that some social conflict exists, some goal is threatened, or some resource is unattained. Resolving such problems requires attention and effort. Following the cognitive model of anger mentioned in chapter 8, one first perceives a threat. Second, one evaluates his or her resources as greater than the threat and able to cope with the threat. This elicits an emotional reaction that increases one's energy and focus on the problem and that sets in motion problem-solving actions to resolve the threat. If the person evaluated her or his resources as inferior to the threat or unable to resolve the problem, no adaptive response would occur. This is exactly what occurs when people adopt helpless thoughts and experience depression or when they entertain catastrophizing thoughts and experience anxiety. When people believe they have the resources to take on a threat or problem they can (a) consider solutions to resolve the conflict, achieve the goal, or attain the resource; and (b) engage in reciprocal communication or negotiate with their adversary to reach a resolution. Anger responses of excessive intensity and duration may weaken the body, unnecessarily drive off allies, or produce intense emotional reactions that constrict one's attention and lead to ineffectual responses to potential threats.

All's Well That Ends Well

Few theorists have identified adaptive aspects of anger. Anger that provokes thoughts related to problem solving and that leads to behaviors that remediate problems seems most adaptive. The definition of *adaptive anger* is like the definition of *pornography*. The term is hard to explicate, but people know it when they see it. A problem results when we define adaptive anger by its outcome. However, with anger, the short-term outcome may differ from the long-term outcome. Post hoc definitions fail to operationalize a construct before the fact and require the consequence of an action before classifying it.

> Consider Harold, who came for treatment with his family because of disharmony between him and his three adolescent sons. Harold did not think he had an anger problem. He admitted becoming angry and yelling at his sons. Nevertheless, this got them to complete their chores, homework, and other important things. Harold could point to the positive outcome produced by his anger—compliance from his children. However, his children hated him because he was so angry. So while the short-term effect of Harold's anger led to a positive outcome, the longer-term consequences were negative. Although it is enticing to define adaptive anger by its outcome, we would like to avoid such a definition.

Episode Length

Some researchers believe that the mode of anger expression and the length of anger arousal distinguish adaptive from maladaptive anger (Davidson, Stuhr, & Chambers, 2000; Thoresen, 2000). They posit that episode length provides an important marker for functionality. Adaptive anger is short-lived; longer-lived anger decreases the likelihood of adaptive responding (Davison, Stuhr, & Chambers, 2000; Thoresen, 2000). This idea has some support, at least concerning physical health. Longer anger episodes have been found to lead to changes in blood pressure, whereas short ones have not (Thoresen, 2000). However, consider some people's anger at an ongoing social injustice, such as

Nelson Mandela's anger toward apartheid. We could define his anger as adaptive. His anger included a resolve to follow a long and carefully planned path of social disobedience. His anger has also had a positive consequence. However, his anger lasted for decades. While long-lasting anger may be one aspect of dysfunctional anger, the possibility exists that long-term moderate anger that focuses on an arduous task may be necessary to achieve a goal.

Episode length may not adequately define dysfunctional anger. We have noticed that many angry clients have short but intense destructive anger episodes. Harold, the client mentioned above, did not stay angry long yet caused considerable damage to his interpersonal relationships. Perhaps longer anger episodes contribute to health problems, but brief ones are more likely to have interpersonal consequences.

The Assured-Destruction Strategy

The possibility exists that anger may have had some long-term evolutionary survival value. The goal of anger that leads to attacks on others could be the maintenance or acquisition of scarce resources for survival. As noted above, anxiety exists when one perceives a threat to oneself or to one's resources and assesses that threat to be stronger than oneself. If the possibility exists that the threat will overpower and kill one, the logical thing to do is flee. However, what if the person assesses that he or she is stronger than the threat? Fleeing would result in unnecessarily abandoning resources to the attacker. Consider a band of early humans in the Rift Valley of the African savannah. They have found a large carcass and are breaking the bones to get at the nutritionally rich marrow. Along comes a neighboring band, which tries to drive them off and expropriate their food. The members of the first band see that they outnumber the intruders and have larger and stronger people. They decide that they can fight off the trespassers. The members of the first band become angry and yell and jeer at the approaching intruders, possibly charging as the band comes closer. Even if the first ancestral band suffered some losses, the anger display and attack behaviors could have had survival value because food was scarce and large protein-rich prey was difficult to subdue. If they fled, they would have abandoned their food, which could have resulted in more deaths among the band. Anger motivates the defense of resources in the face of a threat that one evaluates as less powerful than oneself. Angry displays may keep our enemies at bay.

Another mechanism through which anger might provide long-term survival is its potential to enhance social status. As suggested by social rank theory (Gilbert & Allan, 1998), a significant loss of status or experiences of powerlessness within social hierarchies contribute to increases in negative emotions (e.g., anxiety, depression, and shame) and may result in involuntary subordination by others. Thus, anger expression may serve as a protective strategy, preserving one's social status and self-evaluation and decreasing the likelihood of being victimized by others. However, in many modern environments, anger displays are equally likely to result in the loss of social status and alienation by others.

A person who persists in defending himself against a larger and more powerful attacker and loses the fight but inflicts some damage on the attacker, may gain a long-term advantage despite the apparent loss. Pinker (1997) points out that such displays of anger and aggression may have evolved as mechanisms to express guaranteed retaliation. The emotional and behavioral displays signal to others that the angry person is not rational and will pursue any threat and inflict damage on the perpetrator despite the outcome. Pinker (1997) suggests this scares off potential predators. Although the predators know they will win, they do not wish to suffer the guaranteed blows that it will cost. Better to seek a meeker victim.

One of us recalls such an example from early adolescence.

Tom had a reputation as a ferocious fighter, despite his small size. He was sensitive to insults or any comments on his height. The slightest disrespectful comment or insult aroused his anger and unleashed a physical assault on the perpetrator even if the latter were larger and stronger. When Tom became embroiled in a fight, he refused to give up. Several times he was observed getting beaten badly. However, each time he was knocked down he rose again and pressed his attacker. The other fighter often wanted to stop, but the little guy kept coming. How do we explain such persistent anger and aggressive behavior when the anger appears out of control and encourages fights, even knowing the poor odds of winning? Tom got respect despite his small size because people knew that to tease Tom meant certain injury.

Consider the above-mentioned hypothetical group of human ancestors defending their food. Suppose that one band member experiences fury toward the approaching competitors. He charges the intruding band alone and attacks them, fighting hard. He might scare the intruders off; but even if the intruders killed him, he might inflict harm on them. The intruders might come to believe that members of the food-defending band are crazy and will fight to the death. The intruders might then retreat and avoid this territory and this band in the future. This consequence was true in Tom's case. Everyone knew that if they provoked him, he would fight to the end. Even if they won the fight, the costs would be high. So Tom got more respect than even larger, more powerful boys.

People can rationally pursue such mutually destructive defense strategies. The relationship between the United States and the Soviet Union during the Cold War involved a similar strategy (Keegan, 1993; Pinker, 1997). Each superpower, on assessing its enemy's arsenal, built larger and better nuclear weapons; this cycle repeated itself again and again. Each country knew that it could not win an atomic war. To fight such a war meant the destruction of its own society. Even if the enemy were to be destroyed, such heavy losses would be incurred on the side of the victor that fear of those losses, even in the face of an overall victory, kept each country from making a first strike against the other. Brinkmanship, whether it is boys' posturing angry responses in schoolyards or countries' facing war, represents the same strategy: to ensure the enemy that attack is too costly. However, this strategy may also prove costly to those who employ it.

A. T. Beck (1999) noted that the use of anger to ward off possible threats varies across cultures. Two subcultures in the United States have adopted values that promote this behavior. These include Southerners' "code of honor" (Nesbitt & Cohen, 1996) and U.S. inner-city youths' "code of the streets" (Anderson, 1994). The code of honor in the South originated before the Civil War, whereas the code of the streets is of recent origin. Murder has always been more common in the South than in the North (Nesbitt & Cohen, 1996), and the highest murder rates in the world occur among African American adolescent men. In both these cultures, men believe that any negative or critical comment diminishes them in front of their peers and community. In some African American subcultures, maintaining eye contact too long is considered disrespectful. If the offended man does not address or avenge the disrespect, his ranking in the community hierarchy is diminished. In certain environments this change in status makes one more vulnerable to attack by others.

Beck (1999) considered that economic conditions might underlie these cultural values. The Scotch Irish ancestors of Southern whites were primarily sheepherders, who would sustain considerable economic losses if they failed to deter poachers. The inner-city environment has few resources, and the code of the streets may deter theft and mugging. Although the violence caused by these cultural mores appears dysfunctional to outsiders, people immersed in the cultures perceive anger displays and aggressive behaviors as reasonable strategies. Novaco (1997) has noted that violent offenders may be reluctant to give up such modes of responding because anger reactions provide an illusionary sense of mastery and control over hardships. Attempts to convince people of the dysfunction and risk of these attitudes are typically unsuccessful. Reactions may change only when the subject experiences a different environment for a significant period of time.

The assured-destruction strategy has a short-term functional outcome but not a long-term functional outcome. Anger displays may scare others away, which can lead to a variety of costs. Seneca (Basore, 1958) believed that anger was always dysfunctional and people should avoid the emotion at all costs. However, other emotions in the anger spectrum may be functional alternatives.

Anger as a Disorder

As discussed in the previous chapter, despite anger's absence from the official *DSM* list of mental disorders, people seeking mental health services seem to present with problematic anger reactions at the same frequency as they report problems with depression and anxiety.

Distinguishing between functional and destructive anger is important in developing a clinical conceptualization of anger. Factors such as the functionality of outcomes, chronicity, intensity, and duration of episodes may help determine if an emotion or behavior represents a clinical disorder. In working with clients, one useful question to ask is, Has an anger episode served a useful function, or has it done harm?

Several investigators have asked individuals to reflect on the outcomes of their own anger experiences. In Kassinove, Sukhodolsky, Tsytsarev, and Soloyova's (1997) study of anger experiences, they asked American and Russian college students questions about a recent anger episode. Forty-five percent of their combined sample said that their anger experiences ended negatively. Thus, anger is as likely to result in a dysfunctional outcome as a functional one. Many of these research participants reported that they took positive action to resolve their problems. Yet, many did not.

J. Deffenbacher, Oetting, Lynch, and Morris (1996) investigated the relationship between the level of trait anger and scores on the anger-expression subscales, and the individuals' self-reports of the consequences of their anger. Not surprisingly, they found positive correlations between trait anger and all negative anger outcomes. Also, the type of anger expression was related to some specific negative outcomes. Verbal-expression scores correlated positively with self-reports of getting into arguments. Physically aggressive anger expression is positively related to damaging property, and anger expression through physical aggression toward people was positively correlated with legal difficulties. Anger-in was positively correlated with experiencing other negative dysfunctional emotions after the anger episode such as depression, guilt, or shame. These results confirm that high anger is associated with more harmful consequences than functional outcomes.

Of course much of what we know about the consequences and functionality of anger episodes comes from research with college students and adults who do not score high on trait anger. The consequences are likely to be far more negative for those who are prone to experience anger frequently and intensely. Tafrate, Kassinove, and Dundin (2002) conducted a descriptive study of adults aged 25–50. They compared the anger episodes of individuals with high trait anger (HTA) to those of people with low trait anger (LTA). High-anger adults reported a greater tendency toward irrational thinking and cognitive distortions, more verbal outbursts, and greater physical aggression associated with their anger episodes. HTA individuals also reported greater levels of depression, anxiety, and guilt following their anger than their low-anger peers. Finally, in this study, high-anger individuals reported that their anger resulted in more negative long-term outcomes. Fifty-three percent of the LTA group rated the long-term consequence of their anger as positive, versus only 27 percent of the HTA group. This suggests that the LTA adults were more likely to choose actions that solved conflicts in the long term.

Given the negative outcomes, the hurtful negative emotions, and the negative effects of verbal expression and physical aggression on social relations, one could hypothesize that the high-anger individuals in the above study met the criteria of a harmful dysfunction. In fact, based on their descriptive data, the authors proposed the following four criteria be considered in identifying a clinical-anger disorder: (a) significant angry affect as indicated by frequent, intense, and enduring episodes, (b) a clear pattern of outward expressiveness (e.g., negative verbal responses and periodic physical aggression), (c) regular damage to social or vocational relationships, and (d) anger episodes that are associated with subjective distress (e.g., followed by negative feelings or other negative consequences).

Dysfunctional Anger

Like all basic emotions that have adaptive value, anger can be dysfunctional at times. Anxiety becomes maladaptive when people experience it in response to stimuli that are nonthreatening, and spend considerable time and energy avoiding benign stimuli. Similarly, anger can be dysfunctional when one responds to nonthreatening stimuli as if one were threatened. Excessive anger results in the person's being in attack mode too frequently and aggressing against friendly or benign people. Below are some areas in which anger has been shown in the research literature to be dysfunctional and harmful. Although the following list is not exhaustive, it provides an overview of divergent areas and the potential for chronic anger experiences to be considered clinically problematic.

Anger Interferes With Judgment

Anger may interfere with a person's judgment and result in more competitive responses and poorer outcomes. Kassinove, Roth, Owens, and Fuller (2002) had high- and low-anger college students play the prisoner's-dilemma game. High-anger participants had more competitive, attack-style responses than their low-anger peers. A high-anger participant made even more attacks when he or she played against another high-anger person. The results also suggest that angry players require fewer trials before engaging in retaliation than do low-anger players.

Anger and Illness

Medical and social researchers have reported a relationship between anger and illness since the 1950s. Anger and hostility have consistently been identified as risk factors in hypertension (Spielberger, 1992) and coronary heart disease (see review by Suls & Bunde, 2005). Heart-related illness remains the leading cause of death in the United States (R. N. Anderson &

Smith, 2003) and other developed countries (World Health Organization, 2003).

Research on the relationship between anger and heart disease began with the observation that many individuals who suffered from heart disease shared characteristics such as poor self-control, time consciousness, competitiveness, aggressiveness, impatience, and hostility. They termed this cluster of characteristics the Type A behavior pattern (M. Friedman & Roseman, 1959). However, the relationship between Type A behavior and heart disease was not replicated in all studies (Dembroski, MacDougall, Costa, & Grandits, 1989; Diamond, 1982; Haynes, Feinleib, & Kannel, 1980). Focus shifted to the variables of anger and hostility as many studies (Dembroski, MacDougall, Costa, & Grandits 1989; Suarez & Williams, 1989) showed a link between anger–hostility and coronary artery disease. Anger and hostility were also implicated as risk factors in the development of hypertension (Diamond, 1982). Essential hypertension afflicts approximately 10–20% of adults in the United States (Diamond, 1982). Hypertension is also considered an independent risk factor for coronary heart disease.

Although anger is implicated as a risk factor in the development of hypertension, the research literature reveals some inconsistent findings. Some studies show that holding anger in results in greater cardiovascular reactivity (Holroyd & Gorkin, 1983; MacDougall, Dembroski, & Krantz, 1981), whereas others show that the outward expression of anger is associated with greater reactivity (Diamond, Schneiderman, Schwartz, Smith, Vorp, et al., 1984). In an attempt to reconcile these inconsistent findings, Engebretson, Matthews, and Scheier (1989) found that cardiovascular reactivity quickly declined in those subjects permitted to use their preferred mode of anger expression. The reactivity persisted in those subjects asked to engage in a nonpreferred mode of anger expression. Thus, having to express anger in an incongruent manner might account for anger's relationship with cardiovascular disease. Many studies have failed to account for the subject's preferred mode of anger expression. Also, the timing of the reactivity measurements varied across studies, making comparisons problematic.

Although anger and hostility have been proposed as emotional risk factors for both coronary heart disease and essential hypertension, different patterns may exist among individuals who suffer from the two disorders. According to Diamond (1982), hypertensives are chronically hostile, resentful, and anxious when provoked to anger. In contrast, coronary patients are more aggressive, more likely to act on their emotional arousal, and characteristically less ambivalent about expressing anger.

Williams, Paton, Siegler, Eigenbrodt, Nieto, et al. (2000) conducted a prospective study to assess whether trait anger could predict who developed coronary heart disease in a biracial population of almost 13,000 men and women around 55 years old. Anger significantly predicted heart disease as measured in normotensive subjects but not in hypertensive subjects. They concluded: "Anger proneness as a personality trait may place normotensive middle-aged men and women at a significant risk for coronary heart disease and death independent of established biological risk factors" (p. 2038).

Despite the importance of these studies on establishing anger's potential role in the development of disease, we believe that a major weakness has been the quality of the assessment instruments employed. Few investigators have explicitly provided definitions of *anger, hostility,* and *aggressive behavior.* In fact, Siegel (1986) included a footnote to her study on anger and illness by noting that *anger* and *hostility* were interchangeable terms. This lack of clarity has hampered efforts to prove the construct validity of these instruments and has created "the potential for miscommunication and confusion if it is incorrectly assumed that all hostility measures reflect the same psychological construct" (Barefoot, 1992, p. 13).

Anger often overlaps with other negative emotions. Suls and Bunde (2005) believe that it may be the overlap of all negative emotions that have an effect on heart disease. They noted that it is unclear if only negative affectivity leads to heart disease or if in fact any of the three major negative emotions can cause disease through a common or similar pathway. Regardless of the outcome of future research in this area, it is clear that anger plays a role in disease development. Clearly, medical illness and consequent premature death are harmful. Since anger has been related to increases in these, excessive anger can be considered harmful.

Anger and Death

The most harmful outcome is, of course, death. Although much research has associated anger with illness in general, few researchers have investigated the relationship of anger to fatal illness. One study matched hostile and non-hostile men who suffered from cardiovascular disease by using demographic measures and physical indicators such as blood pressure, cholesterol, smoking, and nonfatal heart attacks (Matthews, Gump, Harris, Haney, & Barefoot, 2004). They followed the men for 16 years. At follow-up, the hostile men were 1.61 times more likely to have died than the matched nonhostile men. The hostile men's death from cardiovascular disease was 5.06 times higher than the nonhostile comparison group.

Two other studies suggest that suppressed anger or anger-in may better predict death than outwardly expressed anger. In a study of elderly Catholic clergy with a mean age of 75, measures of anger-in and depression independently predicted mortality over an eight-year period (R. S. Wilson, Bienias, Mendes de Leon, Evans, & Bennett, 2003). A Michigan study predicted mortality in a representative community sample (Harburg, Julius, Kaciroti, Glieberman, & Schork, 2003). After controlling for seven demographic and health-risk factors, anger-in was found to interact with systolic blood pressure to predict death both by cardiovascular disease and by all causes. These studies suggest that anger may lead to the ultimate harm—death.

Anger and Involvement in the Criminal Justice System

Compared to LTA individuals, HTA people have more interactions with the criminal justice system. R. Tafrate and Kassinove (2002) reported criminal justice involvement in a sample of HTA and LTA community adults. Anger-prone individuals were more than twice as likely to have been arrested and three times more likely to have served time in prison. The most frequent crimes reported by HTA adults were fighting (brawling) and assault. One of us routinely consults with criminal justice agencies. Agencies such as prisons and probation departments are more concerned about offenders' anger than their anxiety or depressive symptoms. Anger is more of a treatment priority because it is more closely related to aggression against other offenders and staff and to overall chaos in a criminal justice institution, agency, or program.

Anger and Reduced Medication Compliance

Dodds and Dowd (1997) investigated the effect of anger, hostility, and psychological reactance on compliance with medical advice and treatment in 84 patients treated for documented heart attack. Although the three independent variables of anger, hostility, and psychological reactance were highly inter-correlated, only anger independently predicted noncompliance ($r = -.40$). The fact that higher anger predicted poorer compliance with medical treatment for a life-threatening illness again shows the harm anger can render.

Anger Expressions Interfere With Caring for Other

Expressed emotion (EE) represents the anger, criticism, hostility, and emotional overinvolvement of parents and caretakers of psychiatric patients (G. W. Brown & Rutter, 1966). Considerable research has identified that the degree of EE communicated to patients with severe psychiatric illnesses such as Schizophrenia, Bipolar Disorder, and Unipolar Major Depression predicts the relapse of these disorders and the need for rehospitalization (Hooley & Teasdale, 1989). Factor analysis of a measure of EE demonstrated that the items yielded three interrelated factors: lack of emotional support, intrusiveness–overcontrol, and irritability–anger (Gerlsma, van der Lubbe, & van Nieuwenhuisen, 1992). Anger at a family member who suffers from a serious psychiatric illness can lead to a lack of emotional support. The cognitions underlying anger, such as the demands that people not act as they do (Ellis & Tafrate, 1997), can lead to overcontrol and attempts to have the patient behave better. EE is self-defeating. Those high in EE are angry with a relative for displaying symptoms, and their anger results in a relapse of the symptoms about which they are angry. This harms the patient. EE is dysfunctional since it causes the opposite of what the person wants, which is a well relative. In this regard, EE may represent both the harmful and dysfunctional aspects of Wakefield's (1992a, 1992b) definition of pathology.

Anger Impedes Sexual Functioning

Hyposexual Desire Disorder (American Psychiatric Association, 2000) has been hypothesized to result from excessive anger and anxiety (H. S. Kaplan, 1984). More research exists to show the effects of anxiety than anger (J. G. Beck & Barlow, 1984). Several experimental studies have confirmed this (J. G. Beck & Bosman, 1995; Bosman & Beck, 1991). Although both emotions reduce sexual desire, in both studies anger reduced sexual desire more than did anxiety. Also, gender differences were reported. Women were much more likely than men to want to end a sexual encounter if either party were angry. As our colleague Janet Wolfe is so fond of saying, anger is not an aphrodisiac.

Anger and Dangerous Driving

Motor vehicle accidents account for considerable financial cost, physical injuries, and many deaths in our society. In 1997, automobile accidents accounted for $96.1 billion, more than 3 million injuries, and 42,643 deaths (National Highway Traffic Safety Administration Preliminary Report, 2005). Considerable concern has emerged recently about the role of angry drivers in auto accidents. The National Highway Safety Administration estimates the number of automobile crashes caused by angry, aggressive drivers to be substantial, based on the violations committed by the drivers involved in the collisions and the reports of law enforcement agencies. The American Automobile Association (Rathbone & Hickabee, 1999) surveyed more than 500 randomly selected jurisdictions in the 50 largest metropolitan areas in the United States in 1998. Thirty-nine percent of the jurisdictions surveyed reported that road rage was definitely a problem in their area and another 15% believe that it was a problem. In another study by the American Automobile Association, Mizel (1997) estimated that the rate of accidents caused by aggressive drivers increased 7% a year between 1990 and 1995. They also estimated that aggressive drivers killed approximately 200 people and injured 12,000 during this period.

In testimony before Congress on July 17, 1997, Dr. Martinez of the National Highway Traffic Safety Administration addressed the role of angry–aggressive drivers on U.S. highways. Dr. Martinez reported that automobile accidents had declined in the United States for 15 years but increased in 1992. The percentage of accidents resulting from alcohol use, involving trucks, or occurring at railway crossings have continued to decrease, so other variables must account for the recent increase in accidents. Dr. Martinez estimated that about one-third of crashes and two-thirds of the resulting deaths are attributable to angry–aggressive driving.

Although no one has directly correlated drivers' affective states at the time of motor accidents, considerable evidence suggests that anger leads to risky behaviors related to auto accidents and fatalities (Lynch, Deffenbacher, Oetting, & Yingling, 1995). J. L. Deffenbacher (2000) has identified a group of high-anger drivers and their similarities and differences from nonangry motorists. He surveyed people on the driving-anger scale (Lynch et al., 1995). Compared with their low-anger peers, high-anger drivers got angry about more situations. They became angrier when provoked. They became angry more frequently. Also, angry drivers traveled as many miles as low-anger motorists. Compared with low-anger drivers, high-anger motorists behaved more aggressively in many ways. These are listed in Table 13.1. Also, high-anger drivers were more likely than low-anger drivers to have taken risks that could increase the possibility of accidents (J. L. Deffenbacher, 1999). These risky behaviors also appear in Table 13.1. Not surprisingly, high-anger drivers reported having had three times as many automobile accidents as did low-anger drivers.

Filetti and Deffenbacher (2000) replicated the findings mentioned above, but several new findings emerged from self-report driving logs that were added to the outcome measures. High-anger drivers were approximately twice as likely to engage in high-risk behaviors as low-anger drivers. High-anger drivers were three to four times more likely to engage in aggressive behaviors than low-anger drivers. Over a three-month period, the high-anger drivers had significantly more tickets for moving violations, major or minor accidents, loss of concentration while driving, loss of control of the vehicle, and "close calls."

Table 13.1
Difference in Aggressive and Risky Behaviors Between High-Anger and Low-Anger Drivers[1]

High-anger drivers commit these aggressive behaviors significantly more than do low-anger drivers.	High-anger drivers commit these risky behaviors significantly more than do low-anger drivers.
1. They argue more with passengers.	1. They speed less than 20 miles over the limit.
2. They argue with other drivers.	2. They speed more than 20 miles over the limit.
3. They yell at other drivers.	3. They pass unsafely.
4. They make angry gestures and swore at other motorists.	4. They change lanes unsafely.
5. They flash their lights.	5. They tailgate.
6. They honk their horns at others.	6. They frequently switch lanes in traffic.
7. They cut off other drivers in anger.	7. They make illegal turns.
8. They hit or damage their own cars in anger.	8. They drive recklessly.
	9. They run stoplights or signs.
	10. They enter intersections when the light is turning red.

[1]These results were reported by Deffenbacher (2000).

Angry–aggressive driving can lead to serious injury and even death. In a Canadian study, Smart and Man (2002) reviewed newspaper reports of road rage from 1998 to 2000 and uncovered 59 reported cases. They found that 73% of road-rage incidents involved serious injury that required medical attention. An additional 7% caused death, and the drivers were charged with manslaughter. Smart and Man believe that the incidences of auto accidents involving serious injury or death are under-reported.

These results strongly suggest that angry driving is a harmful behavior, both to oneself, passengers, and other motorists. The good news is that angry driving does respond to psychological intervention (J. L. Deffenbacher, Filetti, Lynch, Dahlen, & Oetting, 2002).

Anger Interferes With Vocational Success

The phrase *going postal* is commonly used to describe anger that people experience on the job. This phrase comes from a few extreme incidents of postal employees' becoming violent on the job. Nonetheless, more commonplace experiences regarding anger in the workplace may be a considerable problem. Gibson and Barsade (1999) surveyed 1,000 adults and found that 25% were angry at work. Anger at work was associated with sapped energy and reports of lower productivity. Anger at work has also been linked to lower performance evaluations (Carroll, 2001). Although people in positions of less power (e.g., subordinate) were evaluated more negatively for their anger expressions than people in positions with more power (e.g., supervisory), both groups received overall negative evaluations for their anger expressions. Thus, anger at work could result in lower ratings and fewer raises and promotions. Although Kiewitz (2002) found that anger at work contributed to decreases in employees' organizational commitment and increases in turnover, anger did not necessarily mean that employees would engage in seriously deviant work behaviors. Anger at work resulting from job stress has also been related to changes in the hypothalamic–pituitary–adrenocortical system (Steptoe, Cropley, Griffith, & Kirschbaum, 2000). Thus, anger at work is directly linked to physiological stress.

Anger and Aggressiveness in a Larger Context

Regarding history and sociology, neither of us claims the level of expertise, breadth of knowledge, or precision of professional academics in those fields. Nonetheless, it is difficult not to make some parallel observations regarding the dysfunction of anger and aggressive strategies on a larger scale. The social psychologists Baumeister, Smart, and Boden (1996) concur with Seneca in the belief that anger, aggression, and hate usually fail to achieve their goals. Below are some comments that seem timely as of the writing of this book.

War

Military historians often see war functioning as an extension of negotiations. Clearly, the history of warfare shows that people go to war to confiscate others' valuable and productive lands and resources. Although wars often result in the aggressor's obtaining the coveted resources, war usually results in great loss to the aggressor (Keegan, 1993). For example, R. K. White (1990) believes that aggressors' losses have outnumbered victories since 1914. He analyzed 30 wars occurring between 1914 and 1990 and concluded that in 20 cases the outcomes were catastrophic for the aggressor. The most obvious examples are Germany in both World War I and World War II, and Japan in World War II. The victims totally vanquished the aggressors. In only five cases did the aggressor gain a clear benefit. These included Japan's invasion of Manchuria, the Soviet Union's incursion into Finland, China's conquest of Tibet, Israel's Suez War with Egypt, and Turkey's domination of part of Cyprus. In each case, the aggressor was larger or more powerful than the vanquished.

Five other wars resulted in ambiguous outcomes for the transgressors. Among these five examples, White (1990) included the United States' military actions from 1945 to 1975, most of which occurred in the third world and attempted to counter Soviet Communist expansion. Although we may judge these military activities now as successful in their objective, White concluded that they also created an image of American imperialism that cost the United States as much as was gained. Of course at the time of the writing of this book, it is still uncertain whether the most recent U.S. war, in Iraq, will ultimately produce a favorable long-term outcome.

White (1990) proposed four reasons that aggressors lose. First, aggressors are overconfident. For example, Hitler invaded Russia without giving his troops winter uniforms, believing that they would triumph quickly despite lessons from Napoleon's failed venture into Russia (Keegan, 1993). Second, aggressors fail to predict the strength of victims' resistance. Hitler believed that the bombing of London would weaken British resolve to fight. In fact, it strengthened their spirit and the German's lost the air battle of Britain (Keegan, 1993). Third, aggressors fail to consider interventions by third parties. The late-twentieth-century Serbian incursion into Kosovo failed to account for the involvement of Western powers that came to the aid of the ethnic Albanians. Fourth, aggressors lack realistic empathy for their victims and do not predict their responses. For example, in the American Revolution the British consistently predicted that the tactics of the well-trained regular British army would overwhelm the colonial forces (Keegan, 1995). The British failed to see how their tactics would unite the colonists and result in more-persistent fighting. These characteristics of nation–aggressors may also reflect the narcissism, high self-esteem, and lack of empathy that exist in individual aggressors. As technology provides more effective weapons, we can expect the cost of wars to escalate.

Terrorism

Terrorists rarely achieve their political gains through assassination or violence (Ford, 1983). From the assassination of the Archduke Ferdinand in Sarajevo to the most recent bus explosions in Israel, terrorists most often fail to accomplish their organizational goals and usually garner disdain for their cause among the public. The infamous September 11th attacks on the New York World Trade Center and the Pentagon may have produced fear in Americans. However, it united the country and failed to get American troops and cultural influence out of the Middle East, which was the terrorists' goal. There are some exceptions regarding the efficacy of terrorist tactics. South Africa's freedom fighters were considered terrorists and eventually won. The 2004 bombing of the Madrid trains influenced the elections and resulted in Spain's withdrawing its troops from Iraq. However, the long-term consequence of negative world opinion of terrorists may undermine their tactics. As of this writing the jury is still out.

Torture

The use of torture to coerce people to reveal information and help weed out enemies has often failed (Baumeister, 1997; Scary, 1985). The hate, anger, and aggression of the torturer elicit a host of false "truths" from the victim, who is trying just to stop the pain. "Information" extracted through torture is therefore useless.

Political Interrogations

Political interrogations that seek to intimidate people to reveal information not through inflicting physical pain but through embarrassing them socially also fail to extract truthful information or promote the interrogators' agenda. Consider the McCarthy hearings of the early 1950s, which endeavored to uncover Communists in the film industry. Most witnesses lied to the House Un-American Activities Committee and falsely accused their peers. McCarthy failed to gain political support, and he uncovered no Communist conspiracies.

Conclusions

In this chapter we have acknowledged that anger can be a healthy adaptive emotion. However, in excess, anger has a host of negative consequences that cause harm and disrupt a person's normal functioning. Thus, anger can be conceptualized as an emotional disorder like any other emotion. In the next two chapters we focus on specific criteria that would form the foundation for a formal anger-disorder diagnosis and the development of more-refined subtypes for disturbed anger.

14

Proposed Criteria for Anger Disorders

Whereof it is that anger is called Brevis Furor, a short madness,
because it differs not from madness but in time. Saving that herein it
is far worse, in that he who is possessed with madness is necessarily,
will he, nill he, subject to that fury: but this passion is entered into
wittingly and willingly. Madness is the evil of punishment, but anger is
the evil of sin also; madness as it were thrusts reason from its imperial
throne, but anger abuses reason by forcing it with all violence to be a
slave to passion. For Anger is a disease of the mind.
—John Downame, *A Treatise of Anger*

In the last chapter we presented a range of evidence that anger can be a
harmful dysfunction and worthy of inclusion in any diagnostic system.
Several scientific issues need resolution before the mental health community
recognizes anger as a clinical problem. Presently, Intermittent Explosive
Disorder (IED) represents aggressive behavior in the *DSM–IV–TR* (American
Psychiatric Association, 2000). Brief discussions of IED also appear in
chapters 4, 9, and 12. Is this disorder sufficient to describe most patients who
would present clinically with disturbed anger, and does it adequately describe
patients who present with disturbed aggression? Another issue is the lack of
consensus on how much anger is excessive before it is dysfunctional. No
consensus exists on what symptoms would constitute an anger syndrome.

In this chapter we will explore whether the IED criteria are sufficient for
our purposes and define when anger reaches a level of frequency, duration,
or intensity at which it could be considered dysfunctional. We will also
review some evidence to suggest what other symptoms would make up an
anger disorder and propose a basic criterion set of symptoms that contribute
to a syndrome of disturbed anger.

Is Intermittent Explosive Disorder
Sufficient to Represent Disturbed Anger?

As reviewed in chapter 12, our research has shown that most clinicians use
the *DSM–IV–TR* diagnostic category of Intermittent Explosive Disorder

(IED) when faced with an angry client. Because we believe that aggression is more common among those with problematic anger reactions, any inclusion of an anger disorder in the *DSM* would require the redefinition of the criteria for IED or the merging of IED with an anger disorder. Of course, another possibility is the elimination of the IED diagnosis altogether. Thus, a detailed discussion of this disorder is warranted. IED focuses on disturbed aggressive behavior, and is characterized by the following specific criteria.

1. Several discrete episodes of failure to resist aggressive impulses that result in assault or the destruction of property.
2. The degree of aggressiveness expressed is grossly out of proportion to any precipitating psychosocial stressor.
3. The aggressive disorder is not better accounted for by another disorder.

Coccaro (1992; Coccaro, Kavosi, Berman, & Lish, 1998) has criticized this definition on several conceptual grounds. The definition does not define what types of aggressive behavior are disturbed. He points out that some forms of aggression are socially sanctioned, and a definition must make that distinction. Also, the term *explosive* is not defined. Coccaro points out that most clinicians and researchers interpret this term to mean *impulsive.* The frequency of aggressive acts is not specified nor is the period over which the aggressive acts are committed. Is one aggressive act per day, week, or month sufficient for the diagnosis? Does this rate of aggressive acts need to persist for a month, six months, or a year before one is classified as disturbed? Coccaro also noted that the definition is too exclusive and fails to include verbal expression or aggression that does not sufficiently damage property. Thus, someone who loses their temper and yells a curse at another or who bangs on walls without making a hole in it would not be considered disturbed. Also, those with Axis II personality disorders, such as Borderline and Antisocial, would be excluded. It seems that excluding a patient from having an Axis I disorder based on the presence of an Axis II disorder defeats the purpose of the *DSM*'s multiaxial system.

We concur with Coccaro's criticism and would add that IED fails to mention emotion at all, let alone anger, as either an inclusionary or exclusionary criterion. Most people who engage in the behavior covered by IED would experience state anger at the time of the aggression. Also, trait anger would increase the probability that aggression would occur. It is unclear why the authors of the *DSM* focused more on aggression than anger. Did they believe anger was irrelevant for the aggressive behavior in IED? Perhaps the lack of anger as an exclusionary criterion allowed for both anger-driven aggression and nonaffective aggression to be considered when making the diagnosis. The presence of "explosive" aggression without affect seems unlikely, and the exclusion of anger from the description of the disorder ignores an important part of the experience. Of course it is possible that people with explosive aggression may have average not high trait anger and frequently act aggressively when they get angry. Thus, this disorder may reflect only difficulty controlling the desire to strike out when angry and not a disorder characterized by more-frequent anger episodes. However, a description of IED that does not address emotion is inadequate. We propose that anger drives the aggressive impulsive that IED patients fail to control. Surprisingly, studies of IED usually do not include measures of anger. However, several lines of evidence suggest that IED is an anger-expressive disorder.

First, using a cluster analysis of high-school boys, Furlong and Smith (1998) described a group similar to IED. However, anger was present and they behaved aggressively when angered. For this group, trait-anger levels were average, but aggression was high. This suggests that IED includes people who behave aggressively during episodes of state anger but that these episodes occur with only average frequency.

Coccaro's (2004) research on IED relies on recruiting participants by advertising in local newspapers to seek people whose anger has caused them problems. Although Coccaro fails to screen his research participants for anger, anger problems bring them to the lab. Those with IED would most likely either score high on trait anger or experience a state of anger when they behave aggressively, whether their trait anger is average or higher.

Some researchers, however, have included measures of anger when studying impulsive aggression. McElroy, Soutullo, Beckman, Taylor, and Keck (1998) showed that most patients with IED reported affect before their aggression and had resentment or hostile attitudes associated with anger. Barratt (1991) reported that impulsive aggression results from two separate processes: poor impulse control and anger–hostility. He found that the use of both variables predicted aggressive behavior better than either alone. This supports our contention that the impulsive aggression mentioned in IED is linked with anger.

As mentioned in chapter 6, our data suggest that angry ruminations and impulses to act aggressively are linked. People who often, but not always, aggress when angry report the phenomenon of losing control of their behavior. They also report failure to control their thoughts. Thus, rumination may increase the motivation to act. This increased desire to act may over time wear down and decrease resistance or inhibition because the rumination causes an extended need to resist aggression.

Coccaro has suggested that new research criteria for IED be developed and that future versions of the *DSM* rename the disorder Impulsive Aggression Disorder (IAD). He proposes the following criteria:

1a. The person displays verbal or physical aggression toward other people, animals, or property no less than twice weekly or an average of at least once a month; or
1b. The person commits at least three episodes of physical assault against people, or episodes involving destruction of property, over the course of one year; and
2. The person exhibits aggressive behavior grossly out of proportion to the provocation or any precipitating psychosocial stressors.

3. The aggressive behavior is impulsive and is not committed to achieve some tangible objective (e.g., money, power, intimidation).
4. The aggressive behavior either markedly distresses the individual or impairs his or her occupational or interpersonal functioning.
5. The aggression is not caused by mental disorders (e.g., major depression, ADHD, mania, psychosis) or by the direct physiological effect of a chemical substance.

Cocarro's criteria represent a great improvement over those in the *DSM-IV-TR*. We do not disagree with his criteria for IED, and we have seen many clients who meet these criteria. However, we believe these criteria are too exclusionary and leave out many people who experience dysfunctional anger.

An anger disorder would expand the criteria in two ways. First, Coccaro's reformulated IED identifies impulsive aggression and restricts the motive of the aggression by stating that it is not committed to achieve some tangible objective (e.g., money, power, intimidation). Second, the frequency of aggression may be too high, and many people with dysfunctional anger with or without aggression would fall below this standard and not be diagnosed as having IED.

The motivation exclusion reminded us of the distinction between impulsive, affect-driven aggression and premeditated, instrumental, nonaffective aggression discussed in chapter 4. Such clear distinctions between premeditated and affective or impulsive aggression have not stood up to research or clinical observations. Consider the following case.

Jack was referred to our anger-management group after an arrest for domestic violence. He met all of Cocarro's inclusionary criteria for IED. Jack and his wife, Jill, had recently separated, and he had gone to the home several times to discuss the details of the separation agreement under negotiation. When Jill asked for things that Jack felt were unreasonable, he exploded. He became angrier when his outbursts failed to gain her compliance. During the evaluation, Jack reported he hated not getting his way. He had a long history of verbally abusing romantic partners and family members during conflicts. He was conscious of his desire to intimidate his wife. He would ruminate for hours and sometimes days planning how he would yell and insult her before going to see her. On the Anger Disorder Scale profile (ADS; DiGiuseppe & Tafrate, 2004) Jack scored above the 97th percentile on the Verbal Expression, Rumination, Impulsivity, and Coercion subscales. Jack simultaneously experienced angry ruminations and a strong desire to yell and coerce. Treatment focused on teaching Jack the effect that his anger and coercive attitudes had on his interpersonal relationships, how to control his impulses to express himself in a verbally aversive manner, how to negotiate assertively, and how to lose negotiations gracefully.

Based on the motivation exclusion, Jack and most of the domestic-violence perpetrators would not meet the revised criteria for IED. This exclusion and the failure to have a diagnosis for people involved in such a major societal problem limits research into this area and affects treatment. Our research with the ADS suggests that intense anger and aggression frequently occur with the motive of coercing others. We can think of many cases in which the patient's aggression has a mixture of impulsivity and coercive goals. We suggest another category is needed to capture the complete picture.

The second problem with the revised IED criteria is the frequency of aggression. We see many clients who have frequent, intense, and dysfunctional anger, and yet their aggression is too infrequent to meet the IED diagnosis. Others express anger in a nonverbal, indirect manner that fails to destroy property but is still dysfunctional. Many of those with low-frequency aggression are not impulsive and are selective in their targets. Consider the following cases involving ethnic violence.

> Harris was a 20-year-old man who lived at home with his parents and younger twin brothers. Harris was a high school graduate, had never been in trouble, and had a responsible job. However, he felt diminished by the success of his twin brothers who were scholar–athletes. The twins had recently graduated from high school, and the local newspapers had run several articles on them for the number of college scholarships the boys had been offered based on their grades and athletics. One evening when the family was out to dinner, the restaurant owner came to their table and honored the twins and spoke about their success. The restaurant owner and his cuisine were Asian. Within a week, the police arrested Harris for instigating a fight with an Asian man on the street. While out on bail, Harris was arrested again for stealing the purse of an Asian woman on the street. He disposed of her purse behind a store a few blocks away without removing the contents. Harris revealed that he had attacked the Asians because of his anger at the restaurant owner who had made the big fuss about his twin brothers. He said that he had always taken a back seat to his brothers and he hated everyone who had acknowledged them and failed to pay attention to him.

This young man's aggressive behavior occurred too infrequently to meet Coccaro's revised IED criteria. Also, his behavior was not really impulsive. He attacked only people of a certain ethnicity because he perceived social rejection by one of its members. Harris's anger had been brewing for a long time. Our experience has included many seriously aggressive people whose case resembles that of Harris. They have low-frequency aggression. They have strong resentment and a desire to even the score. They experience an uncontrollable urge to aggress, but the selection of their target suggests that they have planned their aggression, and their loss of control is restricted to a very narrow range of stimuli. Some of the high school shooters we see on television are similar to Harris. Such individuals hurt others, destroy property, and sometimes even take their own lives, yet their anger and its resulting aggression do not meet the criteria for a mental disorder.

Another group of clients, missed by both the original and revised IED criteria, are those who are angry yet do not behave aggressively. Anger-in is not recognized at all. Sometimes people with anger-in display passive-aggressive behavior to seek revenge. Sometimes they use social alienation or resort to talking negatively about the person at whom they are angry. In the validation of the ADS (DiGiuseppe & Tafrate, 2004), we reported that both the Brooding (anger-in) and Relational Aggression subscales correlated significantly with having been terminated from employment, whereas no such associations emerged for verbal expression or physical aggression. No one is assaulted. No property is damaged. However, the anger of these nonaggressive individuals does interfere with their lives. Consider the case of Glen.

> Glen sought treatment for his anger after he had been arrested for the
> third time in a year for not leaving a store. This last arrest occurred after
> Glen had been standing in line at a bakery for some time. When it
> was his turn, the couple behind him jumped in front of Glen and placed
> their order with the baker. Glen was furious and whispered some hostile
> words in a barely audible voice. He then stood in front of the couple to
> prevent them from getting their order from the counter. This went
> on for more than ten minutes. The store manager told Glen that his
> order would be free if he would just relax and let the couple leave. Glen
> gave no ground. After several more minutes the couple and other cus-
> tomers left the store, and the manager called the police. His parents had
> seriously neglected Glen as a child. He thought no one respected him and
> that he had done nothing as a child to deserve such treatment. He
> thought he could not stand to be neglected or disrespected anymore.
> Glen lacked assertiveness skills and did not speak up when he felt
> annoyed or inconvenienced. All of Glen's arrests involved passive-
> aggressive behaviors taken to extremes after mild conflicts with others.

Glen's behavior resulted in a mild inconvenience for those who had conflicts with him. They resulted in small amounts of lost income for the stores where these events occurred. For Glen they were very costly.

Glen's aggressive behavior, while mild, still resulted in strong negative consequences. We can go even farther along this continuum: can anger also be dysfunctional if the person makes no attempt to express his anger outwardly? Consider the case of Raul.

> Raul had been married to Marge for 15 years. He had grown annoyed at
> many of Marge's habits over the years. He did not like the way she
> cleaned the house, did the dishes, shopped, or prepared meals. Raul
> found many things to criticize. Raul had high standards, as he would
> say. He liked things just so. He could not believe that people did not do

things the way he did them. However, he rarely revealed his dissatisfaction. Raul, a pediatrician, was equally unhappy with his partners at work. None of them did things quite as well as he did. Here, too, he kept his dissatisfaction to himself. Although Raul did not mention his dissatisfactions and disappointments to his wife or partners, he felt very hostile toward them. His thoughts focused on condemnation. As a result he withdrew and rarely spoke to the people he encountered on a daily basis. Instead he ruminated about how poorly they behaved. He rarely felt happy or satisfied. He spent his time thinking critical things of others and being disappointed in their actions. Raul's wife left him suddenly. She said that she had tried to resolve things with him but he was too distant. Although he had not told her, she was aware of his contempt for her by his grimaces and tone of voice. Her leaving devastated Raul. Now he had another reason to condemn her. It was at this point that Raul entered therapy.

A new diagnostic category that considers both anger and aggression would need to cover traditionally defined cases of IED plus people like Jack, Harris, Glen, and Raul. In the next section we will review when anger and aggression crosses the line to a disorder.

Characteristics of People With Disordered Anger

Clinicians need to identify people with anger disorders on an individual basis. The primary determining factor will be whether the individual's anger is dysfunctional and causes harm. This definition leaves much to the judgment of clinicians, who may differ concerning the dysfunctionality and harmfulness of anger. Also, such a definition fails to provide an operational definition of disturbed anger because one must wait for the consequences of an emotional reaction before defining it. In this section we discuss some logical decision-making criteria for disturbed anger, concerning the intensity, frequency, and duration of anger episodes. For this discussion we have drawn primarily from the data in several published sources. The first source is Kassinove, Tafrate, and Dundin's (2002) investigation of the experience of anger among high- and low-anger adult volunteers recruited through newspaper advertisements. The high-and low-anger groups scored in the upper and lower quartiles on Spielberger's (1988) trait-anger scale. The second source is DiGiuseppe & Tafrate's (2004) analysis of data from the standardization sample of the ADS.

Anger Intensity

Researchers and clinicians often ask people to rate their emotional intensity on a scale of 0 to 100. Zero represents "none" or the lowest possible emotional intensity, and 100 represents the strongest emotional intensity. Such ratings have been used as outcome measures in anger-research studies. Their validity has been established, and they correlate well and change accordingly with self-report scales (Hazaleus & Deffenbacher, 1986).

Tafrate et al. (2002) asked their high- and low-anger subjects to pick a recent experience of anger and make some ratings about that experience. The high-anger group had a mean intensity rating of 75.3 ($n = 51$) and a standard deviation of 16.9. The median rating was 80. The mean for the low-anger group was 58.6 ($n = 42$), and the standard deviation was 18.8. The median was 60. These differences between the groups were significant. However, two observations are noteworthy. First, the distribution of scores for the low-anger group normally reflected a bell-shaped curve. Very few people got very angry. The distribution of scores for the high-anger group was bimodal. Very few of them had scores below the mean. Most people scored around the mean and the mode, and a large number rated their intensity between 95 and 100. Second, considerable overlap of scores existed between the two groups. That is, some high-anger subjects got a score near the mean of the low-anger group and vice versa. This study fails to clearly distinguish high-anger subjects from low-anger subjects based on intensity ratings.

These researchers also asked their subjects to choose two additional anger experiences and rate their anger intensity for each. The averages of two anger episodes produced larger differences. The mean for the group with high trait anger (HTA) was 77 ($n = 49$), the standard deviation 16, and the median 75. The distribution was also bimodal. The mean for the group with low trait anger (LTA) was 43 ($n=37$), the standard deviation 22.8, and the median 45. The distributions between the two groups overlapped, and the mean and median for the LTA group were lower than the ratings based on one episode rating.

These results, if replicated by other researchers, suggest several characteristics concerning how people experience the intensity of anger. LTA people may experience anger as intensely as those with high trait anger for any individual episode or anger state. It would be inappropriate to diagnosis or evaluate peoples' anger as too intense because of one episode. The HTA person consistently experiences high intensity over many episodes. These findings are consistent with earlier research by J. L. Deffenbacher et al. (1996) and with Spielberger's (1972b) state–trait theory of emotions. Anger-intensity ratings in the 70s are high and represent the mean for HTA individuals.

Thus, those with problematic anger reactions are likely, but not certain, to have extreme scores on anger intensity. Also, some individuals who typically do not have anger-related problems will have intensity ratings close to those who experience more serious anger episodes. Overall anger intensity provides a good but not perfect measure of disturbed anger, and rating multiple episodes seems to produce a more accurate clinical picture.

Anger Episode Length

As noted in the previous chapter, the average length of an anger episode can provide a marker of a harmful dysfunction. Overall, data from the ADS standardization sample indicated that about 67% of individuals stay angry for several minutes to a few hours. Fifteen percent report their anger persists for several days. Only 2.5% have anger that lasts for a week or longer. The pattern of anger expression may relate to the episode length. Highly impulsive and coercive people tend to have short anger episodes. However, those who suppress or hold their anger in and experience high resentment and suspicion experience longer episodes. However, our research and clinical experience again suggest that the distribution of episode lengths for highly angry people is bimodal.

Anger Duration

Anger duration refers to the length of time that a person admits that anger has been a problem for them. The *DSM–IV–TR* (American Psychiatric Association, 2000) requires that a person experience clinical syndromes for six months or more before they can meet the criteria for some Axis I disorders. Our ADS (DiGiuseppe & Tafrate, 2004) includes three items that measure duration of problematic anger. Most people reported that anger had not been a problem, and a small group reported that anger had been a problem for several weeks to about a month. However, about 8% endorsed one or more of the items showing that anger had been a problem for six months or more. If other researchers replicate this finding, 8 percent of the population may potentially experience an Axis I anger disorder.

Anger Frequency

Spielberger's (1988) state–trait theory of anger predicts that HTA individuals will experience state anger more frequently than LTA people. J. L. Deffenbacher, Oetting, Lynch, and Morris (1996) confirmed this hypothesis. However, exactly how frequently do high-anger people experience anger? Tafrate et al. (2002) asked high- and low-anger adults how often they experienced states of anger. The choices were *once a day* to *rarely*. Eighty-six percent of the HTA group reported that they got angry *a few days a week* to *once a day* or more. Only 7.3% of the low-anger group reported this frequency. This suggests that most of those with an anger disorder will experience state anger several times a week or more.

Anger and Social-Conflict Frequency

Tafrate and Kassinove (2002) also asked their HTA and LTA groups how often their anger resulted in verbal conflicts with romantic partners. No one in the HTA group reported that they had a romantic relationship without verbal conflicts, while approximately 20% of the LTA group reported conflict-free romantic relationships. Forty-three percent of the high-anger group reported that they had had verbal conflicts in all their past romantic relationships. This compared with only 2% of the LTA group. As for physical conflicts, 71% of the LTA group reported never having had a physical confrontation with a romantic partner. However, 76% of the HTA group reported physical conflicts with one, some, most, or all of their romantic partners. Clearly, individuals who report higher levels of anger are more likely to intimidate and harm their romantic partners.

How often can one expect verbal arguing from highly angry individuals? Again, Tafrate and Kassinove (2002) report that 60% of the HTA group indicated verbal conflicts with romantic partners once a week or more. This compares with only 28% of the low-anger group. Also, 47% of the high-anger group reported verbal conflicts with friends once a month or more, versus only 5% for the LTA group. Clearly, high-anger adults argue quite frequently with their romantic partners; they also argue with friends much more than their low-anger peers. Concerning physical conflict, 36% of the HTA group reported physical confrontation with romantic partners once a year or more, compared with just 10% of the low-anger group. Thirty-four percent fought with friends over the last year compared with 7% of the low-anger group. Approximately a third of high-anger individuals will become involved in fights with their friends and a third will become involved in fights with lovers.

Anger and Aggression Frequency

As implied above, the frequency of the aggressive expression of anger could be another way to suggest the existence of psychopathology. Coccaro's (2004) integrated research criteria for IED requires at least three episodes of physical assault against people or three episodes involving destruction of property in a year. In our conceptualization, aggressive expressions of anger occurring at least once a month would place someone in a disturbed range. This is well within Coccaro's criteria for IED for physical aggression. To calculate these percentages we decided to set cutoff scores on the different aggression subscale scores on our ADS (DiGiuseppe & Tafrate, 2004). We chose the anchored Likert choices that indicated that the person reported engaging in the behavior once a week or more. We then multiplied this by the number of items in each subscale. This score gave us the cutting score at which individuals said that they performed either all of the behaviors on the subscale once a week or more or performed some behaviors more frequently and some less frequently but averaged once a week. We then looked at the number of people who scored above the cutoff in the standardization sample of more than 1,000 people from across the United States.

The number of people at or above this cutoff score was 9.3% on the Relational Aggression subscale. Thirteen percent scored at or above this cutoff on the Passive Aggression subscale and 5% scored at or above the cutoff on Physical Aggression toward objects or people. A different set of Likert choices was used for the Indirect Aggression subscale because we believed that secretly damaging others' property would occur rarely. The Likert choices ranged from the least frequent *never* (1), to a mid-level *several times in my life* (3), to the highest, *I have done this to most people at whom I have been angry* (5). The cutoff score was the point at which an individual indicated that he or she had performed all the indirect-aggression behaviors on the subscale an average of several times in his or her life. More than 10% of the sample indicated that, several times in their lives, when angry, they secretly destroyed another person's property or secretly tried to make the person fail.

These results from our ADS (DiGiuseppe & Tafrate, 2004) revealed that, depending on the type of aggressive behavior, 5–13% of the sample received a score above our cutoff. It is not surprising that the percentage of people who chose items in the disturbed range was highest for passive-aggression since this is the least risky type of aggression. These data, like the data presented on duration of anger as a problem, suggest that anger may be a clinical problem for about 10% of our nationwide sample. Clearly, we need a large epidemiological study to assess more accurately the base rate of anger disorders and related behaviors.

Symptoms in an Anger Syndrome

Based on the literature we have presented in the previous chapters and our clinical experience with angry clients, we created a list of symptoms for an anger disorder that we incorporated into two assessment devices. The first is the self-report ADS (DiGiuseppe & Tafrate, 2004), and the second is the Structured Interview for Anger Disorders (SIAD). Power and Dalgleish (1997) proposed that five domains best describe the aspects of emotional experiences and disorders. These domains include provocations, cognitions, motives, arousal, and behaviors. We incorporated Power and Dalgleish's five-domain model to organize both assessment instruments.

The ADS provides a total score, three higher order factor scores, and 18 subscales. The factor structure of the ADS is outlined in Table 14.1. Research with the ADS compared the standardization sample, containing more than 1,000 people, to several clinical groups. These groups included clients referred for anger treatment in New York City and Ottawa, a general psychotherapy outpatient sample in New York City, and men and women correctional inmates from Connecticut and Pennsylvania. All of the clinical groups had significantly higher scores than the standardization sample, with clients referred for anger problems scoring even higher than the general psychotherapy sample. The symptoms of anger represented in the ADS appeared more frequently in a clinically angry sample than in normal or general psychotherapy clients. This research not only confirmed the validity

Table 14.1
Anger Disorder Scale Higher Order
Factors and the Subsets Contributing
to Them

Reactivity/Expression Higher Order Factor
Scope of anger provocations
Physiological arousal
Duration of anger problems
Rumination
Impulsivity
Coercion
Verbal Expression
Anger-In Higher Order Factor
Hurt/social rejection
Episode length
Suspiciousness
Resentment
Tension reduction
Brooding
Vengeance Higher Order Factor
Revenge
Physical aggression
Relational aggression
Passive aggression
Indirect aggression

Reproduced with permission © 2004 Multi-
Health Systems, Inc.

of the ADS but also described the characteristics of angry clients. Detailed reliability and validity information for the ADS is provided in the technical manual (DiGiuseppe & Tafrate, 2004).

Structured interviews have been the gold standard in psychopathology research and require more time but provide a more valid assessment of psychopathology. They identify fewer false positives. That is, structured interviews diagnose fewer people as having a disorder when they do not. We developed the SIAD with A. G. Ahmed, a forensic psychiatrist at the University of Ottawa. The SIAD incorporates all the symptoms covered in the ADS and includes additional items that more broadly sampled elements of the provocations and cognitions domains. We included more items concerning the thought processes that patients experience during anger, more items describing episodes that triggered the patients' anger, and items describing the results of anger episodes. We administered the ADS and the

Table 14.2

Anger Symptoms by Domain That Appear in the Anger Disorders Scale and the Structured Interview for Anger Disorders and Whether or Not the Symptoms Occur More in Angry Patients than in a Normal Sample

Domain	Symptoms	Measured in ADS	Measured in SIAD	Discriminates Normals From Angry Clients
Provocations	Wide range of provocations	Yes	Yes	Yes—ADS; No SIAD
	Hurt and rejection	Yes	Yes	Yes—Both
	Listing of specific situations that trigger anger	No	Yes	No
	Problem duration more than six months	Yes	Yes	Yes—Both
Arousal	Long episodes of state anger	Yes	Yes	Yes—Both
	Intensity of anger	No	Yes	Yes
	Physiological arousal	Yes	Yes	Yes—Both
	Resentment	Yes	Yes	Yes—Both
	Suspicion	Yes	Yes	Yes—Both
	Rumination	Yes	Yes	Yes—Both
	Impulsivity	Yes	Yes	Yes—Both
Cognitions	Condemnation of the target	No	Yes	Yes
	Need for cathartic expression	No	Yes	Yes
	Being treated unfairly	No	Yes	No
	Target of anger should be punished	No	Yes	No
	Anger is justified	No	Yes	No
	Negative events should not occur	No	Yes	No
Motives	Revenge	Yes	Yes	Yes—Both
	Coercion	Yes	Yes	Yes—Both
	Tension reduction	Yes	Yes	ADS only for Sex offenders
Behaviors	Resolve conflict	No	Yes	No
	Anger is held in	Yes	Yes	Yes—Both
	Verbal expression	Yes	Yes	Yes—Both
	Physical aggression toward objects	No	Yes	Yes

(*continued*)

Table 14.2 (*continued*)

Domain	Symptoms	Measured in ADS	Measured in SIAD	Discriminates Normals From Angry Clients
	Physical aggression toward people	Yes	Yes	Yes—Both
	Indirect aggression	Yes	Yes	Yes—Both
	Passive aggression	Yes	Yes	Yes—Both
	Relational aggression	Yes	Yes	Yes—Both
Consequences	Others fear client's anger	No	Yes	Yes
	Lost friends	No	Yes	Yes
	Problems with extended family	No	Yes	Yes
	Problems with romantic partners	No	Yes	Yes
	Problems at work	No	Yes	Yes
	Conflicts with neighbors	No	Yes	Yes
	Used alcohol or drugs to cope	No	Yes	Yes
	Fearful of one's own anger	No	Yes	Yes
	Depression or guilt about getting angry	No	Yes	Yes

SIAD to more than 100 angry clients who failed to meet the diagnostic criteria for other *DSM–IV–TR* Axis I disorders and did not suffer from seizures or other central nervous system disorders. These angry patients were compared with a similar number of nonreferred individuals. These results identified the symptoms experienced more frequently by patients referred for anger problems (Fuller, Ahmed, & DiGiuseppe, 2005). Table 14.2 lists Power and Dalgleish's five domains of emotional experiences plus the consequences of the emotional experience, the individual symptoms within each domain included in the ADS and the SIAD, and whether the symptom distinguished angry patients from "normals."

People who have dysfunctional anger report many situations that trigger their anger. However, no specific triggers arouse anger more in the patient group than the comparison group. The one exception concerns hurt or social rejection. Angry patients appear more likely to get angered by social rejection than normal subjects. Angry patients reported that their anger had been a problem for six months or longer. This represents the symptom duration used in the *DSM–IV–TR* (American Psychiatric Association, 2000) for identification of most Axis I disorders. Those with clinical anger problems experience each episode of state anger for longer periods than others. For angry patients, anger episodes last for days, weeks, or months. Also, those with anger problems have reported experiencing more intense physiological reactions when angry. These reactions include experiencing muscle tension, trembling hands, stiffness, clenched fists, increased perspiration, and shallow or heavy breathing. As of yet we have not measured physiological responses in anger patients.

Angry clients assert that they have more frequent and intense resentful and suspicious thoughts. They usually believe that their anger is justified because they have been wronged. They attribute others' behaviors to hostile motives. They ruminate about the events about which they are angry to the extent that the ruminations interfere with work or recreational activities. The contents of their thoughts focus on the unfairness of events, condemnation of the person at whom they are angry, the need to punish the responsible party, the need for the cathartic expression of their anger, the importance of confronting the responsible party, and the belief that the event about which they are angry should not have occurred. When they do act on their anger, their phenomenology includes an overwhelming impulse to act and a loss of control.

Anger aroused four primary motives more in the angry sample than in the "normal" sample. Those in the angry sample want revenge for the wrong done to them. Although this desire is present in normal people when they experience anger, it is much stronger in the clinically angry group. Angry clients also want to change the behavior of the target of their anger. They want to coerce or force others to comply with their wishes or to behave as they think they should. Sometimes they wish to end the tension produced by their anger. Another motivation concerns resolution of conflict. However, when angered, "normal" people and angry clients reported this motivation equally.

Angry clients reported using a host of behavioral reactions more frequently than the normal subjects. Despite the increased aggression in angry patients, they also report that they will brood, do nothing, and hold their anger in more than did the normal subjects. Long periods of brooding may be punctuated by aggressive actions. Angry clients usually fail to use assertive responses to resolve conflicts. When they do act, they most often use verbal expression. This includes yelling, threatening others, sarcasm, cursing, insults, and nagging. They also bang furniture, walls, or doors; throw objects; or break things. Less often they strike or assault people. They do all these behaviors significantly more than those with more typical anger experiences. While these behaviors are the most dramatic, angry clients also engage in covert aggressive acts more than the normal subjects. They frequently destroy the property of those at whom they are angry. They passively fail to comply with implicit social contracts with the person at whom they are angry. They defame the people at whom they are angry and solicit others to take sides in their fight. Social alienation becomes a weapon.

They erect barriers to their target's success and attempt to have the people at whom they are angry fail at important endeavors. Once their anger episodes pass, angry patients often regret their anger. They experience depression or guilt about their anger experiences or expressions, or fear the recurrence of an anger episode significantly more than most people do. Most clients will experience many of the symptoms presented above. However, besides having their anger lead to dysfunctional outcomes, angry clients have reported at least one symptom from each domain. The events that provoke anger are the most variable aspect of anger symptoms and appear less important in identifying the syndrome.

Now that we have identified a cluster of symptoms that make up a dysfunctional anger syndrome, we will explore how these symptoms might converge to represent a distinct disorder.

Proposed Diagnostic Criteria for an Anger Regulation–Expression Disorder (ARED)

Acceptance of a disorder is a scientific and a political process. The possibility of adding a new disorder to the *DSM–V* appears unlikely. We believe that the best way to have anger acknowledged in the future versions of the *DSM* or International Classification of Diseases would be to include dysfunctional anger in an already existing disorder. The two closest disorders are Intermittent Explosive Disorder (IED) and Passive-Aggressive Personality Disorder (PAPD). PAPD appears in Appendix B and does not have full recognition. Also, many angry patients are far from passive, and their anger expression goes beyond that found in the behavior descriptions of PAPD.

The presence of aggressive behavior in those with anger problems seems to follow a continuum. Those with the lowest levels of anger appear to suppress their expressiveness and aggressive behavior. Those with subclinical levels score higher on anger-in and express some anger and aggression indirectly. At the next level, people express anger without directly confronting their target, instead using indirect strategies such as relational and passive aggressive strategies. At the highest levels of anger, people are likely to express themselves verbally in aversive ways and to engage in physically aggressive behaviors. Despite support for different clusters of angry patients (as discussed in more detail in the next chapter), cluster membership seems most related to intensity of anger experiences. Thus, one diagnostic category with several basic subtypes is a good starting point, given existing knowledge.

We propose that a new anger disorder, Anger Regulation–Expression Disorder (ARED), replace the existing IED. However, unlike IED, clients can meet the criteria in two ways. The first is through subjective anger experiences, and the second is through expressive patterns associated with anger experiences. Although there are two pathways to the disorder, they are both connected to anger experiences. Thus, patients can meet criteria by experiencing

Table 14.3
Diagnostic Criteria for Anger Regulation–Expression Disorder

A. Either (1) or (2)

    (1) Significant **angry affect** as indicated by frequent, intense, or enduring anger episodes that have persisted for at least six-months. Two or more of the following characteristics are present during or immediately following anger experiences:

        (a) Physical activation (e.g., increased heart rate, rapid breathing, muscle tension, stomach related symptoms, headaches)

        (b) Rumination that interferes with concentration, task performance, problem-solving, or decision-making

        (c) Cognitive distortions (e.g., biased attributions regarding the intentions of others; inflexible demanding view of others' unwanted behaviors, code of conduct, or typical inconveniences; low tolerance for discordant events; condemnation or global rating of others who engage in perceived transgressions)

        (d) Ineffective communication

        (e) Brooding or withdrawal

        (f) Subjective distress (e.g., awareness of negative consequences associated with anger episodes, anger experiences perceived as negative, additional negative feelings such as guilt, shame, or regret follow anger episodes)

    (2) A marked pattern of **aggressive/expressive behaviors** associated with anger episodes. Expressive patterns are out of proportion to the triggering event. However, anger experiences need not be frequent, of high intensity, or of long duration. At least one of the following expressive patterns is consistently related to anger experiences:

        Direct Aggression/Expression

        (a) Aversive verbalizations (e.g., yelling, screaming, arguing nosily, criticizing, using sarcasm, insulting)

        (b) Physical aggression toward people (e.g., pushing, shoving, hitting, kicking, throwing objects)

        (c) Destruction of property

        (d) Provocative bodily expression (negative gesticulation, menacing or threatening movements, physical obstruction of others)

        Indirect Aggression/Expression

        (e) Intentionally failing to meet obligations or live up to others' expectations

        (f) Covertly sabotaging (e.g., secretly destroying property, interfering with task completion, creating problems for others)

        (g) Disrupting or negatively influencing others' social network (e.g., spreading rumors, gossiping, defamation, excluding others from important activities)

B. There is evidence of regular damage to social or vocational relationships due to the anger episodes or expressive patterns.

C. The angry or expressive symptoms are not better accounted for by another mental disorder (e.g., Substance Use disorder, Bipolar Disorder, Schizophrenia, or a personality disorder) or medical condition.

Code based on type:
Anger Disorder, Predominately Subjective Type
Anger Disorder, Predominately Expressive Type
Anger Disorder, Combined Type

anger episodes that are intense, frequent, or enduring. The first criteria of ARED identify the disorder as one of emotion regulation. To meet the first criteria several characteristics that are typical of those with problematic anger reactions, which have already been identified through research, must be present (see Table 14.3: criteria A1). The second criteria are focused on expressive behaviors and aggressive reactions associated with anger episodes. However, episodes do not have to be of high intensity or duration. This part of the disorder is similar to IED and Coccaro's (2004) criteria for IAD. Both indirect and direct forms of expression are listed (Table 14.3: criteria A2).

Individuals meeting the criteria for the disorder, either through criteria A1 or A2, would also have to experience some type of dysfunctional outcomes associated with anger episodes such as damage to social or vocational relationships (Table 14.3: criteria B). Of course, the disorder would not be diagnosed if better accounted for by another existing disorder (Table 14.3: criteria C).

ARED would have three subtypes, much like Attention Deficit–Hyperactivity Disorder. Table 14.3 lists the proposed anger-diagnostic criteria for each subtype. In considering the number of potential subtypes for dysfunctional anger, we have chosen to err on the side of parsimony and combine categories unless empirical evidence or compelling logic suggests otherwise. The next chapter explores additional subtype categories.

The first subtype, Predominately Subjective Type represents a primarily angry group. The level of expression and aggression would be lower than for those in the Predominately Expressive Type or in Coccaro's (2004) criteria for IAD. Those patients with strong, persistent, and dysfunctional anger reactions but with moderate or low levels of expressive behaviors or aggression would meet this subtype. Also, patients who experienced anger and suppressed its expression could meet these criteria if their anger were high enough or dysfunctional enough.

The second subtype, Predominately Expressive Type, has similar criteria to IED and Coccaro's (2004) Impulsive Aggressive Disorder (IAD). We include this subtype because research in this area is new.

The third subtype, Combined Type, is for patients that meet the criteria for both the Subjective and Expressive subtypes. We suspect that most patients who would presently receive a diagnosis of IED or meet Coccaro's (2004) criteria for IAD would fall in this category.

Conclusions

Anger can be dysfunctional in several ways. First, it can be frequent and intense and be subjectively experienced as painful and disruptive. Anger does not necessarily have to be expressed to be problematic. Second, people can experience intense anger and routinely express it verbally or through aggressive behaviors. Another possibility is that people experience anger but only express it infrequently. Thus, an anger disorder could occur in which the person has either frequent anger experiences or anger episodes of average intensity and either holds anger in or engages in outward expression. Presently, angry clients most often receive the diagnosis of IED. The present description of IED represents only problems with the serious outward expression of anger and fails to distinguish between those people who get angry less frequently but behave aggressively when they do get angry, and those who have frequent anger and aggressive episodes.

Our proposal of ARED allows for finer discriminations. Patients who presently receive a diagnosis of IED could fit the Anger Disorder, Predominately Expressive Type, or the Anger Disorder, Combined Type. Also, patients whose anger expression is less physically destructive, not involving hitting or destroying property and limited to relational or passive-aggressive behavior, could receive the same two diagnoses. Those clients who have long durations of anger and who commit aggressive actions with premeditation and not impulsively, and thus do not qualify for IED, could also receive the diagnosis of Anger Disorder, Predominately Expressive Type. Those patients who do not typically express anger in aversive ways and who do not commit aggressive behaviors frequently enough to meet the present criteria for IED would meet the criteria for Anger Disorder, Predominately Subjective Type.

Our clinical experiences as well as those of colleagues we work with across different settings suggest that there is a great deal of variability among those with problematic anger reactions. Certainly the possibility exists that more refined and complex subtypes exist. This has certainly been the case with other emotion-based disorders such as depression and anxiety. Our proposal is meant as a starting point for future research. Thirteen variations within these three subtypes are presented and discussed in chapter 15.

15

Subtypes of Disturbed Anger

In the previous chapter we proposed a set of criteria for an Anger Regulation–Expression Disorder (ARED) with three subtypes. Is one diagnostic category sufficient to cover all cases of disturbed anger? Alternatively, perhaps one diagnostic category with several subtypes adequately explains disturbed anger. Perhaps adequate diagnosis requires several separate and distinct disorders to encompass the varieties of anger syndromes, as happens with mood and anxiety disorders. In this chapter we review the clinical, theoretical, and empirical literature on anger subtypes and present some of our recent research and conceptualizations regarding potential patterns of disordered anger.

Philosophical Contributions

The first description of anger subtypes appeared in Aristotle's *Nicomachean Ethics*. Aristotle described the quick-tempered person as one with a sudden onset of anger and a quick recovery. This description indicates a rapid rise in physiological arousal and a short episode length. Aristotle described this group as engaging in "blunt interchanges" or what we might call *negative verbal expression*. However, he did not discuss whether such people were physically aggressive. Aristotle's second subtype includes people who were sullen and brooding and suppressed their anger for long periods. He saw this group as unable to confront those at whom they were angry. Thousands of years ago, Aristotle described such people as teeming with resentment and taking pleasure in fantasies of retaliation. This classical text laid the foundation for much of the empirical research that we will discuss below.

Psychometrically Derived Subtypes

Spielberger's Subtypes

Building on Aristotle's descriptions, Spielberger (1988) categorized anger problems using factor analysis that focused on means of anger expression. He identified three anger subtypes: anger-out, anger-in, and anger-control, from the factor structure of his State–Trait Anger Expression Inventory (STAXI, Spielberger, 1988). Feindler found the same categories in her Children's Anger Response Checklist (Feindler, Adler, Brooks, & Bhurmitra, 1993). Individuals who score high on anger-in suppress their anger expression. Those who fit the anger-out subtype frequently engage in either verbal or physical expressions of anger. Anger–control refers to individuals who have strong anger experiences but are vigilant about controlling the expression of such feelings. Spielberger also made the distinction between state anger and trait anger. State anger refers to one's present, transient emotional experience of anger; experiencing such states frequently leads to trait anger. Spielberger's model for anger has strong empirical support, provides a useful model for clinical work and research, and represents the foundation for most other models. Few researchers have moved beyond this categorization scheme because of its simplicity and utility.

Cluster Analytic Solutions With Adolescents

Furlong and Smith (1998) used cluster analysis of the Multidimensional School Anger Inventory (MSAI) to detect anger subtypes among adolescent boys. They used only male participants because adolescent girls may express anger differently from boys. For example, girls express anger primarily through relational aggression (Crick & Bigbee, 1998). However, Furlong and Smith's anger measure did not include any subscales assessing relational aggression. Therefore, their anger subtypes reflect a male nosology, and different categories may exist for girls. The first three subtypes represent boys who portray maladaptive anger.

The Extreme Anger Subtype (Raging Rick)
This subtype scored high on anger experience, cynical attitudes, and destructive expression, and low on positive coping. Adolescents with this subtype scored highest on other measures of anger and demonstrated poor academic performance. They had high trait anger and anger-out. Their teachers described them as aggressive and distracted from their schoolwork. They were more likely to be in special education.

The Cynical Subtype (Bitter Bill)
This subtype scored one standard deviation above the mean on anger experience and cynicism. This group had moderate scores on destructive anger expression and positive coping. They were suspicious of others and tended to externalize blame for negative events. This group resembles Spielberger's anger-in type.

The Impulsive Subtype (Dynamite Don)
This subtype scored high on destructive expression, despite average scores on anger experience and cynicism. That is, they did not experience anger often or intensely. Their primary characteristic was poor impulse control. This subtype suggests that high anger is not the problem but expressive–aggressive reactivity while angry is.

The next three subtypes represent people who have nonclinical anger experiences.

The Prosocial Subtype (Social Sam)
Furlong and Smith characterized this group by average scores on most subtests but low scores on destructive expression. They did not experience anger often or intensely and were much less likely than average to respond with aggression when angry.

Low-Arousal and Low-Coping Subtype (Suppressive Sal)
Adolescents in this subtype scored low on anger experience and cynicism, and lower than the other adaptive anger types on positive coping. They rarely got angry, but when they did, they did not cope well.

Low-Arousal and Average-Coping Subtype (Tranquil Tom)
This subtype experienced low anger but had average scores on positive coping.

Clinically Derived Subtypes

Hecker & Lunde's Subtypes

Hecker and Lunde (1985) described six anger subtypes based on their clinical experiences with angry cardiac patients. They derived their model from Spielberger's anger-out and anger-in distinction. However, they further divided the anger-in category into inward expressed and suppressed types. Overall, they proposed a 3 × 2 factorial model (see Table 15.1). The first factor in their schema distinguished between anger problems that were undercontrolled, overcontrolled, or suppressed. Hecker and Lunde's second factor had two levels. Although they did not provide a label for this factor, each level of anger expression includes an impulsive–disorganized subtype contrasted with a deliberate–organized group.

Table 15.1
Hecker and Lunde's Model of Anger Disorders

Level of Organization	Mode of Anger Expression		
	Under Controlled	Over Controlled	Suppressed
Organized	Deliberate	Stable	Normal
Disorganized	Impulsive	Unstable	Psychotic

Source: Hecker, M. H. & Lunde, D.T. (1985). On the diagnosis and treatment of chronically hostile individuals. In M.A. Chesney & R.H. Rosenman (Eds.), *Anger and Hostility in Cardiovascular and Behavioral Disorders* (pp. 227–240). Washington, DC: Hemisphere Publishing.

John Douglas, the creator of the FBI's Behavioral Science Unit (Douglas & Olshaker, 1995, 1997, 1998) used a similar distinction that he called *organized versus disorganized behavior* to classify aggressive and violent offenders. Organized crimes have been committed by someone who acted deliberately and with premeditation. In disorganized crimes, the perpetrators acted spontaneously, failing to plan their aggression, and may not have intended to act violently. This distinction can help us understand anger disorders as well. We can characterize the two disorders at each level as organized or disorganized.

Hecker and Lunde's six subtypes are as follows:

Type 1. Undercontrolled Anger Expression
Undercontrolled, Impulsive   These individuals experience high anger and impulsive anger expression and aggressive behaviors. Since their anger outbursts involve little deliberation or planning, this category could include people who get involved in barroom brawls, those who drive recklessly after being passed by another driver, or those who have sudden verbal arguments triggered by another's words or actions.
Undercontrolled, Deliberate   People in this category experience high anger; however, they plan for later retaliation, thus they have better impulse control. This category could include those who plan attacks on others.

Type 2. Overcontrolled, Inward Expression of Anger
Overcontrolled, Stable   These individuals have strong inhibitions about expressing anger. Such individuals experience frequent and high-anger arousal yet fail to express it adaptively. They rarely engage in physical or verbal attack. They take a passive stance and harbor resentment. Nonetheless, their anger interferes with daily functioning. It is uncertain whether such individuals would engage in passive-aggressive sabotage. Examples of people in this category might include those who complain but take no action to resolve their problems.

Overcontrolled, Unstable These individuals also possess strong inhibitions about the outward expression of anger, yet they occasionally lose control during strong states of anger.

Type 3. Suppressed Anger

Suppressed, Normal This group suppresses many emotions, including anger, yet their reality testing is intact. People in this group do not consciously experience their anger, but their hostile attitude often emerges from their words and actions. They are usually shocked, surprised, or defensive when others suggest that they are angry, and they strongly deny their anger. They are prone to experience somatic complaints and frantically engage in behavioral activities that occupy their consciousness and distract their awareness of negative feelings.

Suppressed, Psychotic This group suppresses anger, but their affect is inappropriate because of distortions of reality. In addition to a lack of awareness of their anger, they have disorganized thinking, psychotic ideas of reference, paranoid suspicions, and loose associations. They view others as critical of them. A good example of people in this group would be patients with paranoid spectrum disorders.

Hecker and Lunde (1985) suggested that anger-in results from either of two psychological mechanisms, the overcontrol or failure to express anger or the suppression of anger. These two mechanisms are conceptually different and have significant implications for assessment and treatment. People with overcontrolled anger experience their anger and can identify the situations and cognitions that occur with it. Therefore, they can readily engage in assessment and treatment activities. Their anger is conscious and their choice not to express it is conscious. Hecker and Lunde suggested that those with suppressed anger lack awareness of their anger. Because people in such a subtype are unaware of their anger, they do not endorse angry items or report the experience of anger. Thus, such people would be difficult to assess and treat in clinical practice.

The description of overcontrolled or repressed anger has long appeared in the literature on violent criminal offenders. Magargee (1966) classified violent offenders as undercontrolled or overcontrolled. Overcontrolled violent offenders reported that they experienced either low levels of trait anger or no anger at all when they committed their violent offense. This research led to the Overcontrolled Hostility Scale on the MMPI and MMPI–2. Although there has been some research on this scale, studies have still failed to ascertain whether or not the overcontrolled group included those who experience anger and control its expression or only those who inhibited and blocked the experience and arousal of anger altogether (Blackburn, 1993; Davey, Day, & Howells, 2005).

Davey et al. (2005) have recently revived interest in suppressed anger. They report frequently encountering two types of overcontrolled violent offenders. The first group has a history of angry feelings and experiences and reports intense angry episodes that involve ruminating about perceived transgressions but has no history of violence or aggression. One dramatic provocation then results in a violent outburst and overwhelms their behavior controls. Those who know these offenders described them as mild-mannered and nonaggressive and were shocked by the violent outburst. Offenders in the second group have low-trait-anger scores and no history of aggression. However, when they experience some traumatic or dramatic provocation they erupt into violence. When interviewed about their violent offense they report no awareness of anger or aggressive motivations. These descriptions correspond to Hecker and Lunde's anger-in and suppressed-anger subtypes.

The construct of suppressed anger presents some difficulties, the first of which is a definitional problem. What Hecker and Lunde refer to as suppressed anger is actually repression. Repression is a psychological defense that prevents people from becoming aware of emotions that are unacceptable. Research does support that humans may repress emotions. In this research, some participants deny their emotional experiences on self-report measures, but physiological measures indicate the emotion is present. A literature search on the topic of *suppressed anger*, however, indicates that most researchers who publish in this area mean *anger-in* when they refer to *suppressed anger*. So, repressed anger is what Hecker and Lunde mean when they refer to suppressed anger. Repressed anger is, by definition, difficult to explore because researchers cannot use self-report measures since people are unaware of it. In anxiety disorders, and PTSD in particular, the role of repressed emotions (and memories) is hotly debated, although some researchers report evidence that some humans do repress anger (Burns, Evon, & Strain-Saloum, 1999). Certainly the existence of suppressed or repressed anger has not evoked much debate in the literature compared to what exists in the area of anxiety. Repressed anger is thought to be one risk factor for cardiovascular disease. However, there is no agreed-upon assessment method other than comparing polygraph records to self-reports of anger.

People who repress emotions may fail to experience the sensations of their emotions. LeDoux (1997) made the distinction between emotional memory and verbal memory. LeDoux suggested that people could be unaware or fail to remember the events or experiences of an emotion. However, the physiological arousal associated with the emotion remains intact and one still reacts physiologically to the emotional triggers or conditioned stimuli. This fact may account for Hecker and Lunde's report that anger repressors exude some hostile attitudes that others perceive, yet the repressors are surprised when others bring these reactions to their attention.

The process that accounts for such repressed fear has been well documented. Classical conditioning of fear can occur without the awareness of higher mental functioning (LeDoux, 1997). Fear can be classically conditioned and maintained once it has been learned, even after the higher mental functions are disabled (LeDoux, 1997). The classically conditioned fear response remains if the episodic memory is destroyed or failed to develop. Thus, people experience fear in the presence of the arousing stimuli regardless of whether or not they are aware of the connection between their fear and the eliciting stimulus. However, as we discussed in chapter 7, research has failed to show that classical conditioning plays a role in anger. If this is so, we require a mechanism other than classical conditioning to account for how people suppress anger. We remain skeptical that repressed anger is analogous to repressed fear.

It is possible that anger repressors experience their anger but deceive others because they believe that the expression, acknowledgment, or report of anger is either generally or situationally unacceptable or may implicate them in some crime or reveal their motives for aggressive behavior. Thus, their anger is experienced but not expressed for fear of retaliation or social censure.

Another possibility is that the experience of anger has become frightening and unacceptable and that some individuals immediately engage in cognitive strategies that turn their attention away from the experience, thereby reducing awareness. Research has appeared recently around the concept of experiential avoidance, which refers to active attempts to avoid experiencing painful emotions. Self-report assessment strategies have identified patients strong in this characteristic (Hayes, Strosahl, Wilson, Bissett, Pistorello, et al., 2004). It remains uncertain whether or not those who identify themselves as having experiential avoidance are in fact repressing their emotions since some awareness is necessary for them to identify themselves as avoiding the emotional experience. Perhaps true repression does exist but as of yet remains outside the grasp of scientific psychology. However, experiential avoidance has been a helpful construct for conceptualizing some patients with addictions (K. G. Wilson & Byrd, 2005), pain (Lackner & Quigley, 2005), PTSD (Orsillo & Batten, 2005), Borderline Personality Disorder (Chapman, Specht, & Cellucci, 2005), and trichotillomania (Begotka, Woods, & Wetterneck, 2004). No research has yet appeared on the experiential avoidance of anger specifically. It is possible that the exploration of this relationship may better explain the anger-in construct and the repression of anger experiences.

The primary question is whether or not overcontrolled (anger-in) and suppressed (repressed) anger subtypes warrant two diagnostic categories. Separate diagnostic categories would be justified if we could prove that these two groups of angry patients truly have different mechanisms that mediate their anger and if they respond differently to treatment interventions. Anger suppressors are not apt to participate in assessment or treatment activities. If such individuals consulted mental health professionals, their suppression would hamper assessment. This distinction has not yet received scientific support.

Eckhardt and J. L. Deffenbacher's Subtypes

Eckhardt and J. L. Deffenbacher (1995) proposed a two-dimensional scheme for classifying Axis I anger disorders. Their model is analogous to the existing classification of anxiety disorders. The first dimension considers the existence of anger problems across a range of situations and has two levels. At one level, specific stimuli or discrete situational domains trigger dysfunctional anger. This is labeled a Situational Anger Disorder. At the other level, dysfunctional anger is triggered across many situations, resulting in a Generalized Anger Disorder. This dimension reflects the distinction made in anxiety disorders with specific phobia and social anxiety representing the single-situational end of the continuum, and generalized anxiety disorder representing the generalized-triggers end of the continuum. Eckhardt and J. L. Deffenbacher's second factor considers whether anger arises with or without aggressive behavior. It should be noted that they include verbal expressiveness under the term aggression. The resulting four disorders include Situational Anger Disorder with Aggression, Situational Anger Disorder without Aggression, Generalized Anger Disorder with Aggression, and Generalized Anger Disorder without Aggression. This model has good clinical utility because it helps practitioners understand the scope of dysfunctional anger and the presence of aggressive–expressive behavior. This encourages treatment plans that focus on treating anger across multiple situations and reducing aggressive behavior.

Eckhardt and J. L. Deffenbacher (1995) also proposed that anger-out varies in the generalization of triggering stimuli. Some people express outward anger only in a limited context, such as when driving, while others express anger-out across a wide range of stimuli. This conceptualization receives some research support from Jacobson and Gottman's (1998) research on spouse abusers. One subtype of spouse abusers expressed aggression only at home and not outside the family. J. L. Deffenbacher's (J. L. Deffenbacher, Lynch, Fietti, Dahler, & Oetting, 2003) research on road rage showed that many people can yell and scream at other drivers but remain more circumspect in other environments.

Integrating the Various Conceptualizations

Although some overlap exists in the anger subtypes mentioned above, each system introduces unique dimensions for classifying anger problems. Table 15.2 presents these different subtype schemes. There is one column for each set of authors. Categories occupying the same rows share similar characteristics and may be equivalent. All the models of dysfunctional anger distinguish between the internalization of anger and the externalization of anger. Thus, any taxonomy of anger problems should include this dimension. However, the distinction between anger-in and anger-out may be too simplistic by itself and provides little information to guide interventions.

Table 15.2
Proposed Subtypes of Anger Disorders by Authors

Aristotle	Spielberger (1988)	Hecker & Lunde (1985)	Eckhardt & Deffenbacher (1996)	Furlong & Smith (1998)
Quick-tempered; Verbally Aggressive Hot-Tempered type; Wider range of anger triggers	Anger-out	Under-controlled, Impulsive	Generalized Anger Disorder with aggression Situational Anger Disorder with aggression	Extreme anger subtype Anger-in and Anger-out Impulsive subtype
		Under-controlled, Deliberate		
Sullen type	Anger-in	Overcontrolled, stable	Generalized Anger Disorder Without aggression Situational Anger Disorder Without aggression	Cynical subtype
		Overcontrolled, unstable Suppressed, normal reality testing Suppressed Psychotic		Low arousal & low coping subtype
	High Anger Control			Average arousal & low aggression subtype Low arousal & average coping subtype

As noted, Spielberger's idea of anger-out does not require that the person be impulsive. Furlong and Smith's (1998) impulsive subtype supports the dimension of the anger-out category but adds the additional characteristic of impulsivity to anger-out. Hecker and Lunde (1985) distinguished between impulsive and deliberate outward anger expression. They propose that some people deliberately think about perceived injustices and plan their revenge. Thus, some disagreement exists about whether anger-out needs to be impulsive. This returns us to the debate concerning affective versus instrumental aggression discussed in chapter 4. Clearly, deliberate, angry aggression occurs in clinical samples and needs to be represented in any diagnostic discussion.

Another question concerns whether anger-in and anger-out represent mutually exclusive means of anger expression or could be considered nonorthogonal yet distinct dimensions of anger expression. Furlong and Smith's (1998) clusters revealed a group of adolescents who scored high on all anger subtests including both anger-in and anger-out. Research with our Anger Disorders Scale (ADS; DiGiuseppe & Tafrate, 2004) showed a high correlation between the anger-in subscale and both the verbal expression and physical aggression subscales. In addition, Hecker and Lunde (1985) reported a group of people who maintained control over the outward expression of anger and held their anger in most of the time yet occasionally exploded with aggression. Thus, anger-in and anger-out seem highly correlated and may not represent mutually exclusive anger-expression categories. They could be considered non-orthogonal yet distinct dimensions of anger expression. Therefore, a useful anger taxonomy would include Furlong and Smith's extreme anger group. Individuals in this category display high anger-in and high verbal expression or physical aggression.

Combining the categories of all the above schemes of anger disorders would yield a multifactorial format for deriving anger disorders. The first dimension would be anger expression and would have four levels: (1) anger-in and anger-out combined, (2) anger-out, (3) overcontrolled anger-in, and (4) suppressed anger-in. The second factor would be organization and would have two levels: (1) impulsive–disorganized and (2) deliberate–organized. The third factor would be the scope of eliciting stimuli and could have at least two levels: (1) responses to general stimuli (generalized anger disorders), and (2) responses to specific stimuli (specific anger disorders). This $4 \times 2 \times 2$ matrix renders 16 different anger-disorder subtypes. However, such a model would generate an unwieldy and large system. Some cells in this matrix would be unlikely to occur in the real world of human disturbance, while others might provide distinctions that fail to lead to different treatments. The most important dimension of this matrix may be anger expression. What people do more directly determines the consequences and therefore the adaptiveness of their reaction. Despite the complexity of the models presented above, they include few dimensions of the anger experience. An empirical investigation of anger subtypes should include the measurement of more aspects of anger.

Cluster Analysis Using the Anger Disorders Scale (ADS)

We explored anger subtypes with our ADS. The 18 subscales are divided into 5 domains (see Table 15.3). As of this writing, we have administered the scale to 2,882 people. The normative sample included 1,649 individuals. An additional clinical sample of 1,233 cases included: angry drivers, general psychotherapy outpatients, psychotherapy outpatients seeking help for anger problems, people seeking court-mandated anger management, inmates from the Connecticut State Department of Correction, incarcerated sex offenders from the Connecticut State Department of Correction, and outpatients from the University of Ottawa Anger Clinic. To identify the subtypes of people with anger problems we submitted the T scores on all 18 ADS subscales to cluster analysis with Ward's method of clustering using squared euclidean distances. Cluster analysis groups people together because their profiles or patterns of scores are similar. The statistical procedure does this without considering the absolute values of their scores. Thus, two people may be assigned to the same cluster because their scores share the same pattern, yet one person may have scores in the average range and the other may have all their scores in the disturbed range.

Cluster analysis can identify a cluster only from the variables entered into the program. The fewer variables used in the cluster analysis, the fewer clusters emerge and the broader-based the clusters; the more variables entered, the narrower or more specific the clusters. We wanted clusters with more-specific information about the groups, so we entered all 18 subscales from the ADS. Cluster analyses were conducted on three separate samples from our data set, and a different number of clusters were obtained depending on the sample

Table 15.3
Subscales of the Anger Disorders Scale by Domains of Anger

Domain	Provocations	Arousal	Cognitions	Motives	Behaviors
	Scope of anger	Physiological	Suspicion	Tension reduction	Anger-in
	Provocations	Duration	Resentment	Coercion	Physical aggression
Subscales	Hurt/social rejection	Episode length	Rumination	Revenge	Verbal expression
			Impulsivity		Indirect aggression
					Passive aggression
					Relational aggression

used. We first used the entire sample. This provided interesting results on the types of clusters that exist when normal subjects and clinical cases were combined. However, this research strategy fails to answer the question concerning subtypes of disturbed angry patients. The large number of people from the normative sample who did not have anger problems produced many clusters with all average or below-average scores. This is the strategy used by Spielberger and by Furlong and Smith. They included both normal subjects and clinical samples in their analyses to determine anger subtypes. Because the majority of people do not have any disorder, including normal subjects in such an analysis will produce fewer clusters of disturbed individuals. Next, we used a clinically derived sample. We selected all research participants in the normative sample who scored in the clinical range and could be considered a clinical case. We included people who were from every one of our clinical samples, that is, all the psychotherapy outpatients, prison inmates, people mandated by the courts for anger treatment, those self-referred for anger treatment, and the patients at the Ottawa Anger Clinic. Again, these results provided some interesting information concerning how anger was experienced in clinical samples. However, many people in the clinical samples were not necessarily clinically angry. This was especially true of those in the general outpatient and prison samples. Although both of these groups scored higher on anger than the normative sample, many members of both samples did not have anger problems. Although they may have met the criteria for some disorder or criminal behavior, it was not anger. This is similar to the sample used by Hecker and Lunde. They included a clinical sample wherein some but not all the people had anger problems. Including a clinical sample with clients who were not angry provided information concerning how anger was experienced in people who presented with general mental health problems or were in criminal justice settings but for whom anger was not their central problem. Obviously, this data fails to address the issue of how many subtypes of an anger disorder exist.

The best strategy to discern what subtypes of anger disorders exist would be to perform a cluster analysis on people with high anger or high aggression. As noted in the previous chapter, the present edition of the *DSM* includes the category of Intermittent Explosive Disorder, which is defined by the presence of frequent aggression but does not mention anger. Including in the sample people who scored high on aggression without regard to anger allows us to confirm the possibility suggested by the *DSM–IV–TR* criteria that people could have high aggression without high trait anger. We were doubtful that people who met the criteria for Intermittent Explosive Disorder (IED) would fail to score high on other aspects of anger and questioned whether the *DSM* description of IED adequately reflects the symptoms of angry–aggressive people. The inclusion in the sample of a high-aggression group allowed us to test whether the present definition of IED is adequate and whether a group of patients exists with aggression and average or low trait anger. To be included in the sample a person had to score at the 90th percentile or higher on one of the following ADS scales: the ADS total score or any one of the three higher-order factor scores (i.e., Vengeance, Anger-In, or Verbal Expression/Reactivity). People who had difficulty only with high aggression but not with the experience of anger would have been selected by having a high score on Vengeance. (See Table 14.1 for a complete listing of ADS higher-order factor and subscale scores.) These selection criteria resulted in 998 participants. The use of a reverse Scree test on the output of the cluster analysis yielded a 13-cluster solution.

In the previous chapter, we suggested that the proposed ARED include three subtypes. The first would be a predominately expressive subtype that engages in frequent verbal expression or physical aggression, as suggested by Coccaro (2004; Coccaro, Kavoussi, Berman, & Lish, 1998). The second subtype would be a group who experiences frequent and intense dysfunctional anger and expresses either little anger or aggression or low levels of aggression. The third subtype, the combined type, would experience dysfunctional anger and meet the threshold of frequent verbal expression or physical aggression set by Coccaro (2004; Coccaro, Kavoussi, Berman, & Lish, 1998). Each of the 13 clusters appears to fall within one of these three broad categories and will be presented in that order.

For each of the clusters, we have presented a description of the group based on their ADS scores, information concerning what sample the cluster was likely to be drawn from, information on the gender distribution, and a graph displaying the ADS subscale scores. For most of the clusters, we have provided a prototype case study drawn from our experiences.

High Expression and Aggression Without High Anger

Our proposed ARED includes a subtype of patients who express anger verbally and/or behave aggressively yet do not experience strong, intense, or frequent anger. This group would best exemplify the present *DSM-IV* diagnosis of IED, Coccaro's Impulsive Aggression Disorder (IAD; Coccaro, 2004; Coccaro, Kavoussi, Berman, & Lish, 1998), and would match Furlong and Smith's (1998) impulsive subtype (Dynamite Don). Our criteria for this disorder do not require that behavior appear impulsive. However, for one of the four clusters that emerged in this group, impulsivity was high. Also, the *DSM-IV-TR*'s IED and Coccaro's IAD focus on physical aggression that is dramatic and impulsive. Three of the four clusters that emerged in our analysis involve passive and indirect forms of aggression that have not been included in other subtypes.

Cluster 1. Average Anger and Passive Aggression

On the ADS Anger Scale, cluster 1 produced a profile with a distinctive spike, a T score of 73 on the *Passive Aggression* subscale. All of the other T scores fell within the range of 48 to 59, except for *Relational Aggression*, which reached a

T score of 60. The next highest subscale scores were for *Revenge* (T = 59) and *Suspicion* (T = 59). The *Impulsivity* (T = 49) and *Physiological Arousal* (T = 49) subscale scores were the lowest. This group can be characterized as having average trait anger. Their *Total Anger* T score average was 59.

An examination of the data indicates that people in this group were included in the clinical sample because they had received a score above the cutoff on their ADS *Higher-Order Vengeance Factor* scores. Participants in this group did not appear to get angry often, nor did they stay angry for a long time, and they did not identify themselves as having an anger problem. However, when they became angry they were totally non-cooperative with the target of their anger. Perhaps the relatively high scores on *Revenge* fueled their *Passive Aggressive* behavior. This group was comprised of 60 percent women ages 18 to 60, with an average age of 31. Figure 15.1 displays the profiles of ADS subscale scores for this cluster.

> An example of this profile is Herb, a 40-year old man who was a trader and collector of antiques. Herb had never married and was unusually close with and financially dependent on his parents. His parents were very wealthy and supported Herb, buying him a condominium, paying his credit charges when he was over-extended, and sending him on vacations. Herb said he appreciated his parents and would do little to annoy them. Herb came for anger treatment after an event in a local

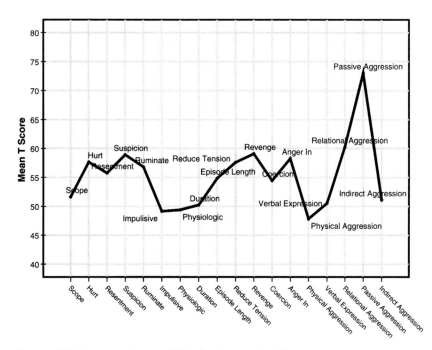

Figure 15.1. Average-Anger and Passive-Aggression Cluster

store when another customer cut in front of him in line. Herb became furious and blocked access to the store counter and refused to move until the offending line-jumper apologized. He remained there for 15 minutes and had to be removed by the police. After arriving in treatment, Herb reported that he had previously had a similar incident when he attempted to get off the elevator in his apartment building. A woman tried to enter the elevator before Herb got off and had bumped into him. Herb just stood there and blocked the entrance to the elevator until other residents called the building manager. Herb reported that he neither saw himself as having an anger problem nor as a person who often got angry. But when he did get angry at people, he would become very non-cooperative and refuse to move or communicate with them. At one point, he became angry with his parents and refused to speak to them for a month.

Herb seriously lacked assertiveness skills. Thus, his treatment was focused on developing new ways of expressing his feelings when he felt transgressed upon. Once he became more confident that he could express his feelings and desires, he became more willing to address the anger with his parents.

Cluster 2. Vengeful, Indirect Aggression

Cluster 2 represents a group of patients who have average trait anger but have a strong motive for revenge that they tend to accomplish through non-confrontational yet aggressive means. An examination of the data indicates that the patients in this cluster met the inclusion criteria by scoring above the cutoff on the ADS *Higher-Order Vengeance Factor* score. The mean ADS *Total Score* for this group was 58. Their highest mean ADS subscale score was on *Revenge* (T = 64), and their next highest score was *Indirect Aggression* (T = 63), followed by *Relational* and *Physical Aggression* (T = 60). Their other scores ranged from 52 to 59.

Indirect Aggression measures the secret destruction of property or hidden attempts to destroy the target of one's anger socially, emotionally, or professionally. Based on these scores, people in this group could be characterized as having moderate levels of trait anger. They do not see their anger as a problem nor do they ruminate or have the hostile attitudes typically associated with anger-in. When people in this cluster do experience anger, they have a strong desire for retaliation. They achieve this retaliation through indirect albeit aggressive means rather than face-to-face confrontation. However, their tendency to seek vengeance with physical aggression is still about one standard deviation above the mean. Figure 15.2 displays the profiles of ADS subscale scores for this cluster.

Rob, a 35-year-old Caucasian man, provides a prototypical example for this cluster. Rob did not see himself as an angry man. He reported that

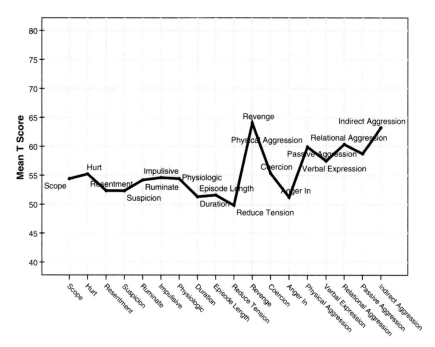

Figure 15.2. The Vengeful, Indirect Aggression Cluster

he rarely got angry, but when others triggered his anger, he needed to show them that they could not take advantage of him and get away with it. Rob had a strong belief in the Biblical proverb, "an eye for an eye." He came to our anger group after he was arrested for domestic violence. Although he did not physically assault or verbally attack his girlfriend Cindy, she had called the police and said that she had felt unsafe and believed that Rob would hurt her. The couple had been living together for about two years when Rob discovered that Cindy had been e-mailing other men. Although the e-mails demonstrated some flirtation between Cindy and these men, Rob had no evidence that Cindy had actually met with them. Rob felt that she had cheated on him and resolved that she would pay for the betrayal. He did not confront her, but instead managed to infect her computer with several viruses that permanently disabled the machine. Rob also contacted the IRS and secretly informed them that Cindy reported only a small fraction of her earnings from her cash-based business. Rob also removed the starter from her car late one night while she was sleeping, dismantling the vehicle and making her late for work that morning. Cindy noticed that Rob expressed little empathy for her when she experienced these crises, and she accused Rob of knowing something about the chain of events.

Rob said nothing but packed his bags and left the house. At this point Cindy called the police and worried for her safety, believing that Rob would do more to hurt her. Rob's attorney then suggested that Rob join the anger management group.

As Rob told his story, he seemed proud of his stealth attacks against Cindy. He gloated that there was no way that she or the district attorney could prove that he did any of these things. He commented, "The slut got what she deserved." Our self-report measures and interviews confirmed that Rob did not get angry often. However, a similar string of misfortunes befell Rob's supervisor after they had had a disagreement on the job six months earlier. Treatment with Rob focused on the nature of the pleasure he received from revenge and the long-term effects that revenge had on his life.

Cluster 3. Poly-Aggressive, Impulsive, Average Anger

As with Furlong and Smith's "Dynamite Don," or impulsive-aggressive type, this cluster had high aggression levels, but average levels on other aspects of anger. Unlike the previous cluster, this group's aggression is more physical and relational in nature. Figure 15.3 displays the profile for this cluster. This profile has an extreme spike on the ADS *Physical Aggression* subscale (T = 79) along with similar spikes in *Relational Aggression* (T = 76) and *Indirect Aggression* (T = 73). The next highest score on the ADS subscale is for *Impulsivity* (T = 70). The subscales of *Revenge, Passive Aggression,* and *Coercion* were also just above the 90th percentile (T = 65). While other scores, such as *Verbal Expression* were high as well, many others fell within the average range, especially the scores usually associated with trait anger and anger-in. The average T score for the ADS *Total Anger* was 67.

People in this cluster have an average frequency of anger episodes and little of the resentment and suspicion associated with anger. However, when they do become angry they impulsively aggress toward others, socially disparage and alienate them, and secretly try to hurt them. They have a moderately high desire for revenge and feel that they cannot control their desire to attack. Men accounted for 62% of this cluster. Participants in this cluster were more likely to come from the standardization sample and the angry-driver sample. As with the second cluster, this group was less likely to seek out or appear for mental health services. This cluster clearly matches Furlong and Smith's (1998) impulsive subtype and typifies the *DSM–IV–TR* diagnosis of Intermittent Explosive Disorder and Coccaro's Impulsive Aggression Disorder (IAD; Coccaro, Kavoussi, Berman, & Lish, 1998; Coccaro, 2004). This cluster supports the inclusion of disorders or subtypes that experience impulsive aggression when they become angry.

The case of Dan adequately represents this cluster. Dan was arrested one afternoon driving to his bartender job on the parkway. A car cut him off

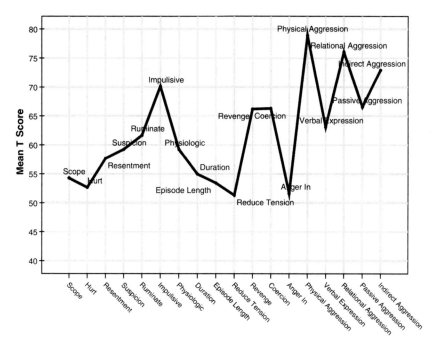

Figure 15.3. The Poly-Aggressive, Impulsive, Average-Anger Cluster

and Dan was incensed. He could not let this guy get away with such driving. Therefore, he sped up, caught up to the other car, rolled down his window, and threw his bottle of iced tea at the other car's windshield. The other car swerved off the road. However, the other driver caught up to Dan, got his license plate number, and filed a complaint with the police. Dan's scores on several anger tests showed that he had overall moderate levels of anger but high scores on aggression and anger-out measures.

Dan, like many people in this group, thinks that he must react when others transgress against him. This thought, rather than frequent episodes of anger, appears to lead to the aggressive behavior.

Cluster 4. Enduring, Controlling, and Nagging Anger

This profile has three striking areas of elevation. The first and highest score was on the ADS D*uration of Anger Problems* subscale (T = 72), followed by the *Coercion* (T = 68) and the *Verbal/Expression* (T = 67) subscales. The profile for this group appears in Figure 15.4. The mean scores on these scales suggest that the group experiences anger problems at least six months or more; that they primarily express their anger through yelling, screaming

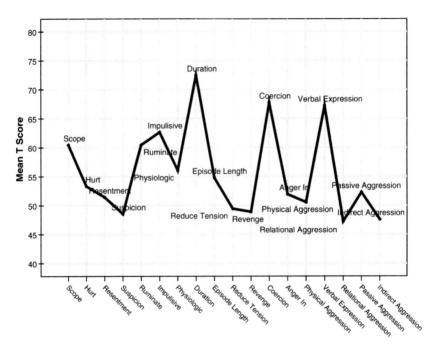

Figure 15.4. The Enduring, Controlling, and Nagging Anger Cluster

sarcasm, or by banging objects; and that they use their anger to coerce or intimidate others into compliance. The mean ADS *Total Anger* score was in the moderate range (T = 60). The next-highest scores in descending order were *Impulsivity* (T = 63), *Rumination* (T = 60), and *Scope of Provocations* (T = 61). All the other subscales had scores ranging from 47 to 56. Thus, the majority of the anger experiences for this group were within the normal range. The present *DSM-IV-TR* criteria for diagnosis of Intermittent Explosive Disorder limits the type of aggression displayed to "serious assaultive acts or destruction of property" (American Psychiatric Association, 2000, p 612). Thus, patients in this cluster would fail to qualify for the *DSM* diagnosis of IED. However, Coccaro's (2004; Coccaro, Kavoussi, Berman, & Lish, 1998) proposed criteria for an Impulsive Aggressive Disorder allows individuals to receive this diagnosis if their aggression is limited to verbal expressions. This cluster clearly meets Coccaro's criteria. People in this cluster appear to have low levels of most characteristics that we would consider as part of trait anger. However, when they do get angry, they express themselves in a loud, dramatic, and offensive style. The degree of impulsivity for members of this group might disqualify them from Coccaro's Impulsive Aggressive Disorder, since high impulsivity is not a characteristic. But the fact that this group scores so high on the ADS *Coercion* subscale suggests that they have an instrumental goal in their anger expression. Remember that the distinction between impulsive/affective aggression and instrumental aggression discussed in chapter 4 has failed to gain empirical support, and the inclusion of the impulsivity criterion is not necessary for one to have average anger and high expressiveness.

Sixty percent of this group was men. This group was significantly more likely to have been recruited from the general outpatient samples. We believe this profile is common among those who seek mental health services for relationship or marital problems.

> Susan had been married to Tom for 20 years, and she had experienced intermittent anger episodes with him for most of that time. Susan just could not understand why Tom could not do things the way she wanted them done. When Tom agreed to do a chore, she would follow him around, give advice, and criticize him. She also had difficulty compromising. When a decision had to be made, she would become and remain angry with Tom until he agreed to do it her way. Susan's anger was always a reaction to her not getting her way. She admitted that she expected others to give in to her because she was usually right. Her decisions were best for the family. Tom saw it differently. The overall relationship pattern was one in which she would have a tantrum and argue until he gave in. She used her anger to coerce him and others into letting her have her way. Susan's anger episodes were sandwiched between periods of truly loving and affectionate times. She loved Tom immensely and did not want to leave him. She just wanted him to do things her way. Susan was shocked when Tom left her for another woman. She called him incessantly, demanding that he come back. Her anger did not stop until he charged her with harassment and petitioned the court for an order of protection.

Higher Anger With Lower Levels of Expression and Aggression: *Classic Anger-In Profiles*

This group corresponds to the predominately subjective type of our proposed ARED mentioned in the previous chapter. It includes patients who experience frequent, intense, and dysfunctional anger but either hold their anger in or express their anger less frequently than in the criteria set by Coccaro (2004; Coccaro, Kavoussi, Berman, & Lish, 1998) for an Impulsive Aggression Disorder. The clusters within this type are characterized as anger-in subtypes from the classification systems of Spielberger (1988), Hecker and Lunde (1985), Eckhardt and J. L. Deffenbacher (1995), and Furlong and Smith (1998).

Cluster 5. Subclinical, Enduring Anger With Behavior Control

Individuals in this cluster have a longstanding experience of anger problems, yet they do not have any daily episodes that lead to aggressive outbursts. Their highest ADS subscale score occurred on the *Duration* subscale (T = 66). This indicates that they believe they have had problems with anger for six months or longer. Their other subscale scores are just below the T score cutoff of 64 that represents the 90th percentile. They were included in this clinical sample because they had a T score of 64 or above on either the ADS Total Score or one of the Higher Order Factor scores. However, an inspection of the data indicates that most of these patients just barely made it into the clinical sample. Their mean scores on the *Revenge, Resentment, Suspicion,* and *Rumination* subscales were all just below the 90th percentile, with T scores hovering around 63. No significant or subclinical elevations existed on any of the aggression scales. This group was 54% women with an average age of 32.3.

This group represents people with a low level of consistent subclinical anger characterized by rumination, resentment, suspicion, and a desire for retribution. Despite their failure to strike out at others, they perceive that their anger impairs their life functioning. This group is unlike any other proposed anger subtype. Individuals in this cluster are likely to come from general outpatient samples where people have other comorbid clinical problems, yet their anger is a persistent part of their personality profile. Figure 15.5 presents the profile of ADS subscale scores for this group.

> A case example from this profile is Ted, a 59-year-old executive who came to therapy because of the longstanding resentment at his wife. Ted was still very much in love with his wife after 30 years of marriage. Despite his affection, he became bitter about some of her characteristics and behaviors. His wife was critical at times, did not get along with Ted's mother or brother, and followed some restrictive routines that limited their recreation. Whenever his wife would commit any of these behaviors, Ted would bitterly ruminate for several days, and sometimes even up to a week. He had some arguments with her but he never yelled, cursed, or displayed physical aggression. Ted's resentment toward his wife never reached the level where he fought with her or wanted to leave. However, it regularly infringed on his marriage, and his rumination about how she should change interfered with his work. At times, Ted lost hope that she would ever change, and his anger led to sadness that he would have a less-than-fulfilling marriage.

Ted sought therapy after a recent bout of anger. He ruminated and pouted for two weeks about how unfair it was that his wife would not try a new restaurant. In therapy, we helped Ted focus on what he loved about his wife and accept her human foibles. He learned to evaluate her rigid and critical moments as indications of her humanness and not crimes against him.

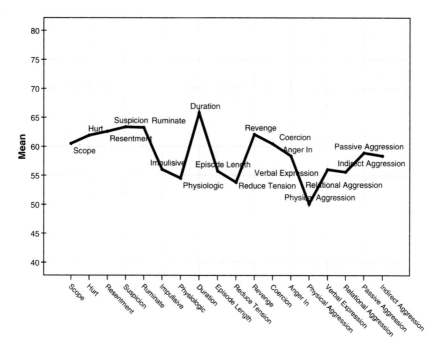

Figure 15.5. Subclinical, Enduring Anger with Behavior Control

Cluster 6. Ruminating, High Arousal, Enduring Anger-In

The profile for this anger cluster appears in Figure 15.6. This group is characterized by a dramatic spike on the ADS *Rumination* subscale (T = 75) and by somewhat lower peaks on the *Physiological Arousal* subscale (T = 72), the *Duration of Anger Problems* subscale (T = 71), and, of course, the *Anger-In* subscale (T = 66). Moderate elevations also occurred on the *Hurt, Scope of Provocations, Resentment* and *Suspicion* subscales. The ADS *Total Score* was higher than the previous anger-in cluster, with a mean T score of 70. The lowest scores were obtained on the *Physical* and *Relational Aggression* subscales. This group constituted 9.3% of the research sample. Women made up 47% of this cluster. People in this group were significantly more likely to have been recruited from the general outpatient sample and were unlikely to have been recruited from the criminal justice settings or the anger clinic.

People in this cluster most likely have their anger triggered by social rejection, social disappointments, or failures to receive attention from others. They have moderate levels of resentment and suspiciousness. Their anger appears to be fueled by their excessive rumination. They hold their anger in and fail to express it. This cluster represents the classic example of anger-in as suggested in all previous anger taxonomies.

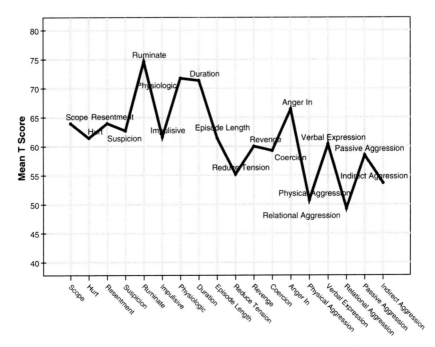

Figure 15.6. The Ruminating, High-Arousal, Enduring, Anger-In Cluster

The case of Sharon provides an example of this cluster. She came to our anger-treatment group because of conflict with her family. At 29 years of age, she continued to live with her parents, her younger sister, and the sister's child. Sharon had adopted the caretaking role in order to "keep the family together." She planned all the holidays, vacations, and social engagements for everyone. She did the shopping, managed the money, paid the bills, and planned everyone's life. As a result, Sharon had no time for her own life. She had no hobbies and no romantic attachments, which was just fine with her family. On occasion, Sharon thought that she needed to get on with her life. She would mildly suggest that her parents or her sister take more responsibility for family issues, but they would not, and Sharon would become intensely angry with them. Her thoughts continually focused on her family members' failure to meet their responsibilities. Sharon's anger would last more than a month, during which time her mind was filled with ruminations about how they had to change and take responsibility. She reported being miserable during these episodes. While Sharon could not believe that they left everything for her to do, she never expressed her anger. Although she thought about the situation frequently, she did not seek revenge. Rather, she just thought that her family members had to do the right thing.

Therapy helped Sharon accept that they would not change if she did everything for them. She reduced her sense of responsibility and eventually accepted that her family would continue to depend on her if she let them. When she accepted this, her anger lifted and within two months she started dating.

Cluster 7. Low-Intensity Hostile Attitudes, and Anger-In

A graph of this third anger-in cluster appears in Figure 15.7. This group has the lowest mean ADS *Total Score* (T = 60) of any cluster. Inspection of the data indicates that the majority of people in this cluster met the criteria for being included in the clinical sample by scoring above the cutoff on the ADS *Higher-Order Anger-In Factor* score. This profile is characterized by its high *Anger-In* (T = 63), *Resentment* (T = 63) and *Suspicion* (T = 63) subscale scores. This cluster differs from cluster 6 in several important ways. Cluster 6 has much higher scores on *Rumination, Physiological Arousal,* and *Duration of Anger as a Problem* subscales. Clearly, this is a much less angry group than the others. But generally, clients with anger-in only experience less intense anger than those with more outward expressive problems. Women comprised 64% of this group, and they were most likely to have been recruited from the general patient sample. Surprisingly, this cluster accounted for 40%

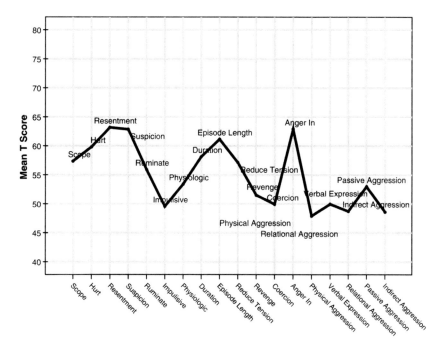

Figure 15.7. The Low-Intensity, Hostile Attitudes, Anger-In Cluster

of our sample of incarcerated sex offenders, all of whom were men. This finding calls out for replication with a larger sample of sex offenders in the hope that a profile for this group can be identified and lead to an effective treatment.

> The case of Peter provides an example of this cluster. Peter had worked for the same law firm for 15 years. At age 41, he thought that he should have been promoted to partner by now. He had worked for this firm since graduating law school and had shown great loyalty. Unfortunately, Peter had seen some "faster-track" younger lawyers make partner, and he was very bitter. He believed he was just as good a lawyer, if not better, than the people who had made partner. He resented the firm and especially the partner to whom he reported. When other lawyers were assigned interesting cases, he thought that the managing partner had purposely slighted him. Each day when he came to work he would feel agitated. At times, he thought about ways to get even. He would go for coffee, make personal phone calls, or straighten his desk—anything but work billable hours, thus allowing those lousy partners to make money off his good work. His superiors noticed Peter's negative attitude. He was given six months to find another job or be terminated.

High Anger With Expressive–Aggressive Behavior

The next group of clusters corresponds to the combined type proposed in chapter 14. Individuals in this group experience both high levels of anger and expressive or aggressive behaviors. Six clusters fit this subtype.

Cluster 8. Nonconfrontational-Vengeance

The profile of this cluster, which appears in Figure 15.8, has a striking appearance because of the high scores on the *Indirect Aggression* (T = 80), *Revenge* (T = 78), and *Passive Aggression* (T = 75) subscales. This group's preference for indirect means of anger expression contrasts with their average, and therefore relatively low, scores on *Physical Aggression* (T = 54) and *Relational Aggression* (T = 57) subscales. This group has a moderately high score on V*erbal Expression* (T = 64). People in this group scored very high on the ADS *Total Score* (T = 78). More than 62% of this group were men. They were significantly more likely to come from the court-mandated treatment group, correctional facilities, and the Ottawa anger clinic, which receives many forensic cases. This group is significantly less likely to be drawn from the standardization sample.

Individuals with this profile express their anger indirectly. They will attempt secretly to damage the property of those at whom they are angry.

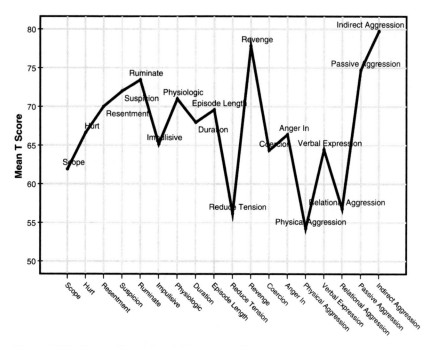

Figure 15.8. Nonconfrontational-Vengeance Cluster

They will also use covert techniques to have the person fail occupationally or financially. They will fail to comply with any activities or responsibilities that they and their anger target share. People in this group have strong desires for revenge, are suspicious of the motives of others, and expect hostility. They feel resentful about the circumstances of their life. When angered, they stay aroused for several days.

The low scores on the *Physical Aggression* and *Relational Aggression* subscales and the preponderance of participants drawn from correctional and forensic settings suggest that people in this group do not want others to see their anger expression. It would be interesting to know if this pattern of anger expression evolved before or after their involvement with the legal system. Our clinical experience with people in this group suggests that both possibilities exist. For those who have established this pattern after their legal involvement, their failure to engage in even relational aggression shows their commitment to secrecy. The existence of this profile also suggests that when societal constraints against aggression are imposed by the legal system, some people remain very angry, have strong desires for revenge, and will seek retribution in covert activities. The moderately high verbal scores in this group are due to the arguments and venting that occur when they confront the target of their anger alone. People in this cluster may appear compliant with orders of protection or probationary requirements but will verbally confront those at whom they are angry and attempt to achieve revenge through subtle passive aggression and covert means.

We have observed that those who developed this angry profile before or without legal involvement are intelligent, have great impulse control, exhibit obsessive personality characteristics, and have good planning abilities. They will plot revenge strategies to achieve their goals secretly. They will also insult and bate the target of their anger in private.

> Paula and Frankie had been married for 10 years and had two children. When Paula filed for divorce, Frankie was furious. He could not accept that she was ruining his family. He swore that he would get even with her for this and she would curse the day she filed for divorce. He thought about revenge daily. He knew that she would cheat him out of seeing the kids and his fair share of their money. As a respected civil servant, Frankie could not appear angry in public; he would hurt Paula in other ways. He "forgot" to pay the oil bill and laughed when she called in the middle of a cold night without heat. He sent all child-support checks late and wrote the wrong amount on the check. He found every way possible not to cooperate with her. When the oil was drained out of Paula's car and cable to the house was cut, Frankie denied responsibility for these acts and expressed concern for her safety. However, the smile on his face seemed to express pleasure at her misfortune. Paula reported that when she spoke to Frankie alone he was vile and nasty. However, in front of others he was mannerly and polite.

Cluster 9. Social-Vengeance

This cluster gets its name from the extremely high mean score on the *Relational Aggression* subscale (T = 93). The next two highest subscales include the *Revenge* (T = 75) and *Passive Aggression* (T = 75) subscales. Given that anger is not expressed physically or through direct verbal confrontation, people in this cluster would not traditionally be considered aggressive and would thus fail to meet the criteria for IED or IAD. Moderately high scores also occurred on the *Suspicion* and *Rumination* subscales. This profile appears in Figure 15.9. Two-thirds of this sample was comprised of men. This cluster more frequently occurred in the New York clinical-anger sample and among the general psychotherapy outpatients. The total score for this group (T = 75) was significantly higher than for eight other clusters.

People with this profile are likely to alienate socially those at whom they are angry. They will make disparaging comments about the target of their anger and will force people to take sides. Those in this cluster will fail to cooperate with the target of their anger and have strong desires for revenge. They will ruminate considerably about perceived transgressions against them and will be suspicious of others.

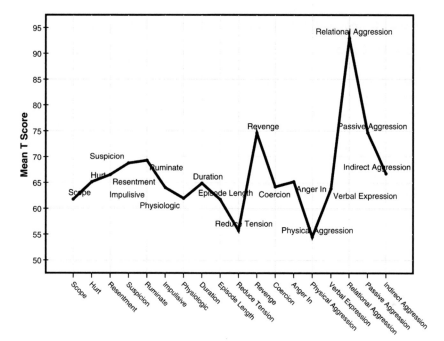

Figure 15.9. The Social-Vengeance Cluster

Vinny and Sal ran Two Brothers' Pizza Place for 15 years. Then the business hit hard times, and Vinny wanted to sell and go into a different line of work. Sal blamed Vinny and condemned him for breaking up the family business. He resented Vinny's new job and apparent success. Sal was also very suspicious of Vinny's financial situation. He thought that Vinny must have planned to leave when it was good for him and bad for Sal. Sal also thought that the pizza place must have failed because Vinny cheated over the years by skimming money for himself. He wanted nothing more than to see his brother fail. Thus, he thought of ways to sabotage his brother's life. In every conversation, he managed to defame Vinny, disparage his success, and blame him for the closing of Two Brothers' Pizza. To Sal, Vinny was dead. Everyone in the family had to choose between being friends with Vinny or with Sal. If a cousin or an uncle talked to Vinny, he was considered a traitor. The brothers could not visit their parents together. Vinny went to see their parents on Christmas Eve, and Sal on Christmas Day, so they never had to confront each other. No christening or wedding in the family could be held without planning how to appease Sal. This hostility lasted until after their father died and Sal refused to speak to anyone in the family because they allowed Vinny to come to the wake.

Cluster 10. Impulsive, High-Arousal, Confrontational Aggression

Figure 15.10 presents a profile showing high impulsivity and explosive verbal behavior. People in this group would probably meet the criteria for IED based on these two dimensions. Although somewhat similar to the profile presented for cluster 4, this group is much angrier and scores higher in other areas as well. The highest scores were on *Impulsivity* (T = 78) and *Verbal Expression* (T = 75) subscales. *Physical Aggression* was also high (T = 67). This group had average or relatively low scores on all other behavior domain subscales (*Relational Aggression, Passive Aggression,* and *Indirect Aggression*), indicating that they do not typically engage in covert expressions of anger. In addition, people in this group do not appear to express anger in order to seek revenge or to achieve coercive power or intimidation over others. Absent from the *DSM* and Coccaro's description of this subtype are their high scores on *Rumination* (T = 71) and *Physiological Arousal* (T = 71) subscales. People in this group lack cognitive control over their thoughts and experience intense state anger when confronting others. In addition, this group displayed relatively brief episodes of anger compared with other groups. Their *Episode Length* subscale score (T = 52) was significantly lower than for nine of the other subtypes.

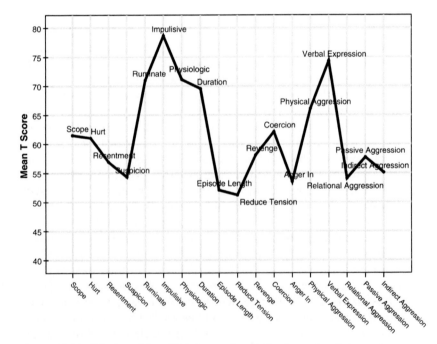

Figure 15.10. The Impulsive, High-Arousal, and Confrontational Aggression Cluster

Men comprised 51% of this sample, so no gender differences exist here. This probably surprises most people and challenges the stereotype that only men are impulsively expressive or aggressive. In addition, individuals in this cluster were evenly distributed across the entire sample used in this analysis.

People in this cluster typically experience uncontrollable desires to confront others both verbally and physically. They are unlikely to hold their anger in and will act on their anger when they experience it. They are unlikely to express anger covertly or indirectly, and they have no apparent motive for their anger expressions or aggressive behaviors. They also experience ruminative thoughts and high physiological arousal when angry. Compared with other clusters, their episodes are relatively short, lasting at most a few hours.

Kevin, a 23-year-old Caucasian man, was arrested for assaulting a neighbor. The neighbor had started an argument with Kevin's brother when the family dog wandered into the neighbor's yard. Kevin had a long history of assaults, starting when he was in middle school. He was known to have a "hot temper" and easily exploded when people insulted him or failed to show him respect. Kevin's father and grandfather had physically abused members of the family when he was a child. Kevin reported that he would sometimes stand between his father and mother or father and younger brother in order to protect them. Despite this history of abuse, Kevin expressed little resentment or suspicion and had no desire for revenge. Once a fight was over, Kevin could be friendly with the person. He seemed to hold no grudges. Nor did Kevin use anger to control or intimidate others. He had had good relationships with romantic partners and no history of violence against his present or previous lovers. As an adult, when Kevin perceived an insult or slight transgression, he could not stop thinking about it until he confronted his transgressor, which he always sought to do. He would "lose control" and experience an uncontrollable desire to scream, yell, insult, and assault the person who slighted him. When his therapists initiated aggression-replacement training, Kevin responded, "I cannot think of any way to handle these conflicts. I guess I have become my father."

Cluster 11. Verbal/Expressive, Passive, but Not Relational Aggression

Clinically we have encountered people in this cluster in couples counseling, and we have called it the dysphoric-mate profile. A graph of this profile appears in Figure 15.11. Cluster 11 had the second-highest ADS *Total Anger* score (T = 83). This was significantly higher than in the 12 other clusters. The profile of this group is similar to Cluster 10. The two highest ADS subscale

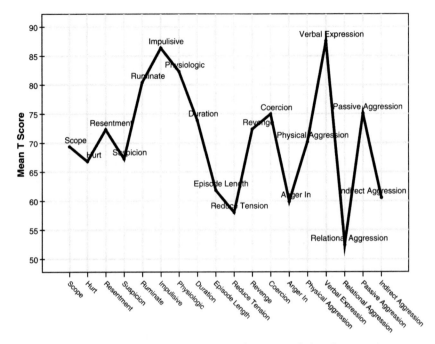

Figure 15.11. The Verbal/Expressive, Passive, but Not Relational Aggression Cluster

scores were for *Impulsivity* (T = 87) and *Verbal Expression* (T = 88). The group also had less-intense but still clinically high scores on *Physical Aggression* (T = 70). Like Cluster 10, Cluster 11 has relatively high elevations on the *Rumination* (T = 81) and *Physiological Arousal* (T = 83) subscales. Like Cluster 10, Cluster 11 had relatively low scores on two of the three non-confrontational aggression styles, *Relational Aggression* (T = 53) and *Indirect Aggression* (T = 61).

In addition to experiencing more intense anger, people in cluster 11 differed from those in cluster 10 in two important ways.

First, this group had much higher scores on *Passive Aggression* (T = 76). The combination of higher verbal expression, high passive aggression, and low indirect or relational aggression is expected by those angry with their romantic partner. Those in couple's therapy usually experience constant arguments, so the high score on verbal expression is expected. Dysfunctional, dissatisfied couples also would be expected to fail to cooperate with their partners, thus, the high score on the *Passive Aggression* subscale. People angry with their mate are unlikely to use relational aggression against their partner if they are still living together. People in dysfunctional, dissatisfied relationships still maintain joint friendships and family relationships. Also, indirect aggression appears unlikely in dysphoric couples since the angry person would be destroying his or her own property.

The second way in which individuals in this cluster differed from those in cluster 10 is that they scored higher on two of the motive-domain sub-scales, *Revenge* (T = 73) and *Coercion* (T = 75). Unlike those in cluster 10, who also had impulsive, verbal expression and physical aggression, the dysphoric couples experience strong revenge and a desire to control their partner to have things their way. This cluster accounted for 4.4% of the total research sample. It consisted of 53% women, so both genders were almost equally represented. Individuals in this cluster were most likely to come from one of the clinical samples and seemed to be most prevalent in the Ottawa anger clinic sample.

People in this cluster experience intense anger along with an un-controllable urge to strike out against those at whom they are angry. They frequently yell, curse, argue, and insult those who trigger their anger. However, they will less often escalate their arguments into pushing, shoving, and other forms of physical aggression. They are unlikely to attempt to alienate socially or disparage those at whom they are angry or secretly to destroy property. When angered, they often fail to cooperate with people. Besides losing behavioral control, people in this group also lose cognitive control. Their rumination greatly interferes with their recreational, occu-pational, and housekeeping activities. Revenge over past transgressions and a strong desire to coerce others to comply with their own wishes motivates the negative behavior in this group.

Wilma and Fred had been married for 10 tumultuous years and had attended couples counseling for 8 of those years. Wilma's anger dominated the therapy sessions and their marriage. When Fred behaved in a way she disliked, she would ruminate about the event. Sometimes she would explode in rage over trivial circumstances. Rumination, impulsive acts, and extreme physiological arousal were the hallmarks of her outbursts. Sometimes Wilma would be passive aggressive toward Fred. She would not speak to him or cooperate in any household chores. For example, she cooked for one and refused to make his side of the bed. When she exploded, Wilma would insult Fred's physique, in-telligence, family line, and personality and throw things at walls and doors. This was often followed by more physical attacks at Fred, such as pushing, shoving, or slapping him. On several occasions, she threw pots at him. Wilma's aggression had two goals: to punish Fred for his stupid behavior and to change him into the man she wanted him to be. Wilma resented Fred for taking a job that involved their leaving their home-town. She would rarely let others know she was upset with Fred. More often than not, she would say positive things about Fred to those outside the family.

Cluster 12. Total-War, High Arousal, Low-Anger-In

Of all the clusters we have discussed so far, cluster 12 has the highest scores on the *Physical Aggression* subscale (T = 98). The profile for cluster 12, which appears in Figure 15.12, shares many elements with clusters 10 and 11. People in this group have high scores on the *Impulsivity* (T = 79) and *Physiological Arousal* (T = 83) subscales. They also had significant elevations on the *Rumination* subscale (T = 69); but lower scores are noted on *Anger-In* (T = 57) and the *Suspicion* and *Resentment* subscales, which are usually associated with such brooding. The Total-War cluster differs from clusters 10 and 11 most in the behavior-domain subscales. For cluster 12, all the aggression subscales were significantly high. Besides the *Physical Aggression* subscale mentioned above, this group had high scores on the *Verbal Expression* (T = 71), *Relational Aggression* (T = 87), *Passive Aggression* (T = 73), and *Indirect Aggression* (T = 84) subscales. All three clusters have high verbal expression scores, but cluster 12 had the lowest verbal expression score of the three. As with cluster 11, and unlike cluster 10, people in the Total-War cluster had significantly high scores on the *Revenge* (T = 72) and *Coercion* (T = 70) subscles. People in this cluster were significantly more likely to come from the New York angry-outpatient sample, from the court-mandated treatment sample, and from

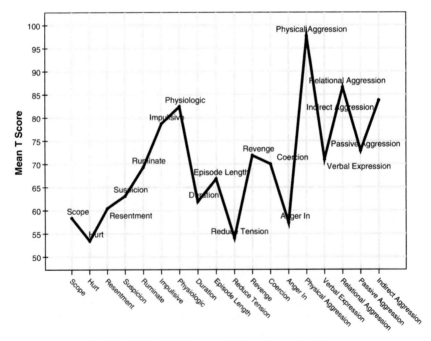

Figure 15.12. The Total-War, High-Arousal, Low Anger-In Cluster

among correctional inmates. They would rarely be encountered in a general outpatient population.

People in the Total-War cluster are extremely likely to use physical aggression when angered. When angry, they experience a strong, uncontrollable desire to strike out along with intense physiological arousal. They also ruminate intensely, and this cognitive dyscontrol seriously interferes with their activities. They have a strong desire to seek revenge on those who transgress against them and a desire to coerce others into doing things their way. They use all types of aggressive behaviors to get revenge or to control others (e.g., physical aggression, verbal confrontation, social alienation, passive aggression, and secret covert aggression).

Cluster 13. Extreme Anger and Aggression

The profile of Cluster 13, which appears in Figure 15.13, is similar to Furlong and Smith's group who scored high on anger-in and anger-out. Participants in this group had the highest ADS *Total Score* and the highest *Higher-Order Factor* scores of any other group. Patients in this cluster had T scores greater than 95 on the ADS subscales of *Impulsivity, Physical Aggression, Relational Aggression,* and *Physiological Arousal.* The *Revenge* score (T = 94) was almost as high. The other aggression subscale scores were also very high: *Passive Aggression* (T = 89), and *Indirect Aggression* (T = 88). Overall, people in this group scored in the clinical range on 17 of the 18 subscales. Although they would meet the criteria for both the *DSM*'s IED category and Coccaro's research criteria, this profile shows high elevations on *Vengeance, Physical Aggression,* and *Verbal Expression,* with significant but relatively lower elevations on *Anger-In.* People in this cluster were significantly more likely to come from the New York angry-outpatient sample, from the court-mandated treatment sample, from among correctional inmates, and from the Ottawa anger clinic. Men comprised 74% of this cluster. People in this group would rarely be encountered in a general outpatient population.

> Sonny had a successful father. At 24 years old, Sonny had failed to achieve the fame and respect that his father received from others, let alone the financial remuneration. Sonny had done poorly at school and had not been offered a place in the family business, which he thought he deserved. Sonny's father reported that he had always given his son the best of everything and had bailed him out of every problem. Although Sonny's father paid his rent, car payments, and debts and provided a large weekly allowance, he would not have Sonny join the business. Thus, Sonny was extremely resentful. His resentment toward his father was always on his mind. His anger about it was always just under the surface. Trivial remarks or the facial expressions of acquaintances or strangers would evoke assaults from Sonny. He would experience a flash

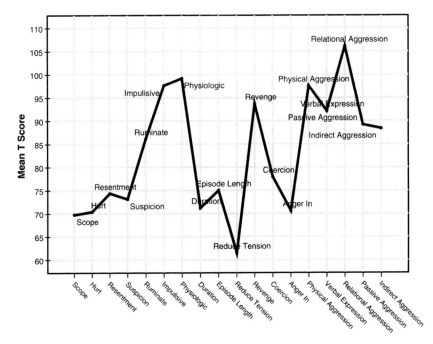

Figure 15.13. The Extreme Anger and Aggression Cluster

of physiological arousal and an uncontrollable urge to strike out at his perceived transgressor. Once, while walking down a city street, Sonny hit a street vendor in the face because he looked at Sonny's girlfriend disrespectfully. Anyone who disagreed with Sonny in public was "on his list" and he would plot ways to hurt them and get revenge. Getting even was an all-or-nothing thing for Sonny. He was not happy unless he ruined a person's face, career, or reputation. He would use any and all means to accomplish these goals.

Conclusions

This cluster analysis represents the most inclusive attempt to discover anger subtypes. It included measures of a wide range of anger constructs in a large sample representing diverse clinical cases. Several conclusions can be drawn from these results. The most obvious is that the measures employed matter. Previous research into anger subtypes could not have generated the clusters found here because their measures failed to assess the constructs that characterized some of our clusters. For example, no other study has reported anything resembling the social vengeance cluster because those studies failed to include a measure of relational aggression.

Also, the subject pool that was sampled matters. Cluster membership differed significantly by sample. Some clusters were more likely to be drawn from one sample or another. Had any of the samples included in this analysis been left out, it might have weakened the power to detect some clusters. We have often thought that the varying views of anger presented by researchers and clinicians occurred because they encountered angry people from a variety of settings. Nonetheless, our sample is missing two groups that may yet reveal additional profiles of anger subtypes not encountered here. One area of omission was a sample of patients presenting for medical treatment with cardiovascular disease. Some evidence suggests that hostile attitudes are a risk factor for cardiovascular disease, while other studies suggest it is not the attitude but holding anger in that leads to cardiovascular disease (see Gallagher, Yarnell, Sweetman, Elwood, & Stanfeld, 1999). The inclusion of angry cardiovascular patients could yield an additional subtype. Second, a rich clinical literature has appeared on anger in combat veterans. The inclusion of such a group may reveal other patterns of dysfunctional anger. Finally, while several criminal-justice related groups were included, we did not have large samples of specific offender types. The inclusion of spouse abusers, drug dealers, gang members, and a larger group of sex offenders might potentially yield additional subtypes related to offending patterns.

We also found some differences among the clusters in age and gender distribution. More men than women occurred in the Poly-Aggressive, Impulsive Average-Anger, Nonconfrontational, Vengeance, Social Vengeance, and Extreme Anger and Aggression clusters. In most of these clusters, revenge seems to be the strongest motive of anger. More women than men appeared in the Low-Intensity Hostile Attitudes, Anger-In and the Average-Anger, Passive-Aggressive clusters. On the remainder of the clusters men and women were equally represented.

In age, clients in the Vengeful Indirect Aggression, Poly Aggressive Impulsive Average-Anger, and Total War clusters were significantly younger than those in the other clusters. People in the three Anger-In clusters and the Enduring Controlling Nagging cluster were significantly older than those in the other clusters. Thus, with age comes either Anger-In or Verbal/Expressive anger. Future research needs to sample across these variables to ensure that all types of anger groups will be uncovered.

The overall level of anger also matters. We used a liberal cutoff score, selecting participants in the top 10% on one of the ADS Total or Higher-Order Factor scores. Some researchers would have selected a more stringent cutoff, perhaps using a T score of 70 (or the 95th percentile). If we had selected a cutoff score representing the top 5% or 2.5% of participants on each scale, the anger-in subtypes would have dropped out of the results. Although we agree that people with anger-in face a real clinical problem, their anger may be sufficiently low to exclude them from diagnosis. Those with anger-in only may have more comorbid disorders such as major depressive or dysthymic disorders that may prevail over an anger diagnosis.

Higher cutoff scores would also have eliminated the expression–aggression with moderate anger clusters. Those with higher expression–aggression scores were usually angry.

Research comparing the identification of clinical cases for any type of disorder has found that classifying people as having a disorder by structured interview usually identifies a smaller group of people as clinically disturbed than if they were to be selected by self-report inventories. Thus, the development of an accepted ARED disorder might not include patients such as those in our first two clusters, who had aggression with average anger, and most clients with anger-in only. Overall, anger was lowest in the aggression–average anger and anger-in clusters. This has implications for Coccaro's (2004; Coccaro, Kavoussi, Berman, & Lish, 1998) diagnosis of impulsive aggression and our ARED, predominately expressive subtype. Our impression is that his patients with IAD actually have high levels of anger and aggression and would fit into our ARED combined category. Those participants who received only high scores on the *Physical Aggression* or *Verbal Expression* subscales did not score as high on them as those participants in the extreme anger and aggression clusters such as cluster 12 and 13.

As noted earlier, the idea of suppressed anger has been around since Aristotle. It is no surprise that our cluster analysis confirmed an anger-in subtype as suggested by the work of Spielberger (1988), Hecker and Lunde (1985), Eckhardt and J. L.Deffenbacher (1995), and Furlong and Smith (1998). However, high scores on the brooding or Anger-In subscale more often occurred with hurtful aggression. In fact, the Anger-In subscale was higher in cluster 13 than any of the anger-in clusters. This result confirms our belief that when people hold their anger in, the desire to express anger leads to other forms of expression. Also, clusters with high *Anger-In* scores occurred with high *Passive Aggressive* subscale scores. Again, this has not been reported before because other anger measures have failed to measure passive-aggressive behaviors. Thus, people who hold their anger in may not be so innocent, and they get revenge through a failure to cooperate. In addition, our cluster analysis of the ADS scores for all the participants in our pool and the cluster analysis for all clinical cases, whether or not they scored high on anger, suggested that clusters with high *Anger-In* scores have high scores on the *Indirect Aggression* subscale. Again, this is not such an innocent group as one may think by its description. Thus, anger-in may occur alone, with hurtful physical aggression, verbal expression, or with more indirect or passive-aggressive behaviors.

Part VI

Intervention

16

A Review of the Anger
Treatment-Outcome Literature
What We Know Works

Recent trends in American health care have emphasized provider account-ability. For most of the history of mental health services individual providers used whatever interventions they deemed appropriate. As more third-party payers, such as governments and insurance companies, entered the scene there has been a greater call for accountability and treatment guidelines so that payers can ensure that they are paying for the most effective treatment. In addition to standardizing the general practice trends in the field, panels of experts review the empirical and clinical literature to generate guidelines and determine what interventions should be considered the best practice for a specific problem. For example, the National Guideline Clearinghouse (NGC) is a database of evidence-based clinical-practice guidelines initiated by the Agency for Healthcare Research and Quality (AHRQ) of the U.S. Department of Health and Human Services. Various professional groups can submit peer-reviewed treatment guidelines to the NGC. The American Psychiatric Association has published treatment guidelines developed by expert consensus committees for the treatment of PTSD, suicidal behavior, Obsessive-Compulsive Disorder, bipolar disorders, and other conditions, and that are available on the association's Web site. Several managed-care organizations distribute practice guidelines to their own panels of therapists. Although attempts have been made to provide treatment guidelines for numerous disorders, no agency or organization has yet proposed or endorsed a set of treatment guidelines for anger.

Another attempt to ensure accountability has been the identification of empirically supported treatments (EST; Task Force on the Promotion and

Dissemination of Psychological Procedures, 1995). The idea behind ESTs is to provide practitioners, consumers, and payers with conclusions from reviews of the scientific research on what interventions have proven effective for which specific problems. Relatively recent reviews have been published for both the treatment of adults (Roth & Fongay, 2005) and children and adolescents (Fongay, Target, Cottrell, Phillips, & Kurtz, 2002). The trend toward ESTs has been controversial in the psychotherapy field. Some professionals support the establishment of ESTs, whereas others believe that they represent an infringement on their professional judgment. We take the position that treatment guidelines and ESTs help clinicians, because most of them do not have the time to keep up with the information explosion and the newest scientific studies in all areas. Critics of this reliance on scientific evidence to guide treatment raise some important points. First, all treatments have not been scientifically tested. An effective treatment may have eluded researchers. Second, research studies often include participants who are less disturbed and have fewer comorbid disorders than people one encounters in real-world clinical practice. Therefore, other interventions may be needed to help guide the treatment for clinical populations. Some clinicians have used this reasoning to continue to use interventions that have no empirical or scientific support. Kazdin (2000) has noted that although there is merit to their arguments, it is more prudent to start treatment with an EST, evaluate it, and switch to other interventions after the EST has failed. In terms of identifying ESTs for anger, most treatment modalities have not been evaluated. Practitioners must choose between using unsupported interventions or starting with the most efficacious before using untested methods.

Limitations of the Anger Literature

Compared to other common emotional problems such as anxiety and depression, substantially less outcome research exists on the efficacy of anger treatments. This is not surprising given the dearth of information on diagnosis and conceptualization discussed in the previous section. Even though the scientific study of anger treatment has lagged behind that of other disorders, anger-management programs have become increasingly popular. Anger-management groups and self-help classes are routinely found in school settings, community mental health centers, and correctional facilities, and have been incorporated into alternative-sentencing programs for criminal offenders. Because of this proliferation of anger programs, there is a growing concern that many "real-world programs" are not based on empirically supported interventions and may have little or no therapeutic or lasting effect on clients (Koerner, 1999). Questions remain about whether or not anger treatment works and what interventions are most likely to be effective.

In addition to the relative paucity of studies, several important methodological issues have been neglected in the therapy-effectiveness research that have resulted in an incomplete understanding of the effectiveness of treatments for those with problematic anger reactions. We propose that one critical issue in conducting anger treatment-outcome research is the selection of appropriate outcome measures that tap the clinical dimensions of dysfunctional anger. Given the potentially wide range of anger dimensions that clients might experience and the lack of an anger diagnostic category, there is little consensus concerning which standardized assessment measures should be used to select research subjects and evaluate their progress. The type of dependent measure used in research can account for a significant amount of variance in outcomes. An analysis of treatment outcomes by different types of dependent variables may provide information regarding which treatments are more effective for a given aspect of anger or for a given type of angry client. So far no researchers have tested a priori if one intervention is more or less effective for a particular type of angry client. For example, we have no data to suggest that one type of intervention will be more effective with people who experience primarily anger-in than with those who impulsively express their anger outwardly. Nor have researchers presented data to determine if one or another intervention affects different dimensions of anger with all or a set of angry clients. For example, no studies have tested a priori if some interventions have a greater impact on the experience of anger, the physiological arousal, or clients' verbal or aggressive behavior. In many ways, our understanding of anger treatment is still quite limited.

Approximately 50 published research studies have appeared that test some kind of anger intervention with adults (DiGiuseppe & Tafrate, 2003). Another 40 published research studies have tested anger interventions with children or adolescents (Sukhodolsky, Kassinove, & Gorman, 2004). This clearly represents a small outcome literature to guide the practice of mental health professionals treating such a common clinical problem. Nonetheless, several recent meta-analytic reviews have provided useful summaries of the adult and child anger treatment-outcome literature.

Meta-Analysis

Meta-analysis is a method of reviewing a body of empirical research studies by calculating the degree of change that occurred in each study for each dependent measure. A statistical procedure is used to calculate the difference between the posttest mean of the experimental treatment group and the posttest mean of its control group. This difference is converted to a common statistic known as an effect size by dividing it by the standard deviation of both groups. Also, one can calculate the change that occurred in the group who received treatment by calculating the difference between the mean at post-treatment with the mean of the same group before they started treatment (pre-test) and again dividing by the combined standard deviation. The most common statistic used for this is Cohen's (1977) *d* statistic. The formula to calculate *d* appears below:

$$d = \frac{ex - cx}{sd_{pooled}}$$

In the equation, *d* equals the mean of the experimental group minus the mean of the control group divided by the pooled standard deviation. In studies without a control group, the equation calculates the difference between the means of subjects at pretest and posttest divided by the pooled standard deviation. The *d* statistic is interpreted as a standard deviation. A *d* of +1.00 means that, following treatment, the mean for the experimental treatment group was one standard deviation higher than the mean for the control group. This indicates that the experimental group improved (positive *d*'s indicate improvement while negative *d*'s indicate the superiority of the control condition). A *d* of −.50 would mean that the mean for the experimental treatment group was one half of a standard deviation below the mean for the control group. In the area of treatment outcome research, an effect size of .2 is considered small, .5 moderate, and those of .8 or greater are considered large (Cohen, 1977).

Since studies differ on the number and types of dependent measures they use, it is common in meta-analysis to average all the effect sizes for different dependent measures across each treatment to get one effect size per treatment or to average the effect sizes across the same type of dependent measures so you would get one effect size per study per type of measure. This second averaging technique would yield, for example, one effect size per treatment for all self-report measures of anger even though the studies may have included two or three self-report measures. In addition, all studies are coded for characteristics that the researcher believes will influence the effect size (*d*). For example, the researchers may code for whether the study used individual or group therapy, whether the participants were college students, prison inmates, or therapy outpatients, or whether or not the practitioners followed a treatment manual. Statistical analyses can then be carried out to test the effect of these coded variables on the effect sizes to determine which variables correlated with larger or smaller effect sizes.

Meta-Analytic Reviews of Anger Treatments

There have been several meta-analyses on anger treatments. Tafrate (1995) identified 17 published studies of anger treatments and found empirical support for cognitive, relaxation-based, skills-training, and multicomponent interventions. The outcome measures in the studies were restricted to subjective reports of anger intensity and frequency and physiological measures. Several methodological limitations existed in this pool of studies to limit the conclusions that could be drawn for clinical practice. Most of the studies relied on undergraduate student subjects and had short treatment lengths, and few studies used individual therapy sessions.

A second meta-analysis examined the same sample of studies but included a wider range of outcome measures (Edmondson & Conger, 1996). Although these authors noted that varied treatment approaches had different effects on different types of anger measures, the small number of studies did not allow for statistical examination of the differences between effect sizes. Overall, Edmondson and Conger's (1996) review reached similar conclusions and found support for the same four classes of treatments identified in the earlier review.

R. Beck and Fernandez (1998) expanded the database on anger treatment-outcome studies by including studies of schoolchildren and adolescents, unpublished doctoral dissertations, and studies that utilized single-group or pre- to post-test designs. Although their sample included 50 studies, they restricted their meta-analysis to interventions that combined cognitive and behavioral components in their treatment. Thus, single-modality treatments and some non–cognitive behavioral treatments were excluded from this review. This exclusion prevented one from addressing the issue of whether single-modality treatments can be effective or whether including multiple-treatment modules increases treatment effectiveness over single-modality treatments. Although R. Beck and Fernandez (1998) increased the sample of anger studies, we criticize their review on several grounds. Combining effect sizes from studies that focused on both children and adults may have masked differences in treatments used with different age groups. Also, pooling or analyzing the data for studies using both between-group research designs and within-group designs seems unjustified to us (DiGiuseppe & Tafrate, 2003). The difference between how much a treatment changes compared to its control group (the between-group d), and how much it changes versus its pre-test (the within-group d) are two different mathematical questions. The between-group d and the within-group d represent different measures. Our analysis found that for anger studies the within-group d statistics are higher than the between-group d statistics. Thus, combining them gives an inaccurate picture. In addition, in contrast to the reviews by Tafrate (1995) and Edmondson and Conger (1996), R. Beck and Fernandez (1998) averaged across multiple dependent measures to yield one effect size per treatment. Given the finding by Edmondson and Conger (1996), that the type of dependent measure accounts for a significant amount of the variance in outcome, it is not surprising that R. Beck and Fernandez (1998) found insignificant heterogeneity among their sample of effect size values and thus did not further examine the effects of moderator variables. Nevertheless, R. Beck and Fernandez concluded that cognitive behavioral interventions have utility in anger management and produced moderate improvements.

In regard to the children and adolescent outcome literature, Sukho-dolsky et al. (2004) concluded that cognitive behavioral interventions for anger-related problems were moderately effective and, in that respect, similar to the effects of interventions for other types of psychological problems. Active interventions around skill development seemed to be more effective than those that were focused on education and internal feelings.

We (DiGiuseppe and Tafrate, 2003) attempted to provide a clinically relevant and comprehensive meta-analytic review of the adult anger-treatment literature to add to our knowledge by improving upon previous reviews. First, we greatly increased the sample of studies that focused on adults by widening the search for more published studies, unpublished doctoral dissertations, and uncontrolled pre- to post-test investigations. We included studies that treated anger with more modalities. Second, the larger database allowed for an empirical analysis of the effects of methodological issues, study attributes, and subject characteristics. The Q statistic was used to expose the influence of moderator variables. Third, effect sizes (d) were averaged or aggregated according to the type of outcome measure used for each intervention. This allowed for an empirical examination of the effects of different treatments on various anger measures. Fourth, separate analyses were performed for studies using "between" and those using "within" designs. Finally, the persistence of treatment effects was examined through analysis of follow-up data. Based on the results of our most recent meta-analytic review and Sukhodolsky et al.'s (2004) review of the child-treatment studies, some conclusions can be drawn about effective anger treatments.

Findings Regarding Anger Treatments

Remember that there are relatively few anger treatment-outcome studies, and any conclusions should be considered tentative. Nonetheless, the existing literature can be helpful in guiding clinical practice and future research. We hope our results will assist practitioners in choosing the most effective interventions for their angry clients and help researchers pinpoint those areas that have not been adequately explored.

First, optimism is justified. Successful treatments for anger exist with adults, adolescents, and children. Researchers have applied these treatments to college students selected for high anger, angry men who volunteered, outpatients, spouse abusers, prison inmates, special-education populations, and people with medical problems, such as hypertension or medical risk factors like Type A behavior. Our present knowledge suggests that anger treatments are equally successful for all age groups and all types of populations. Anger treatments appear equally effective for men and women.

However, this enthusiasm needs to be tempered by one limitation of the outcome research. Most studies used volunteer participants. Many practitioners treat angry clients whom courts, employers ("Get help or you are fired!"), or spouses ("Get help or I am leaving you") have coerced into treatment. The research participants used to date may not be representative of many clients who actually present for treatment. This could mean that clients in many settings arrive with less awareness of the costs of their anger and have less of a desire to change than did the volunteers. This point seems to be especially true for some extreme groups such as violent offenders (Howells, 2004; Novaco, 1997). We will return to this point in the next chapter.

Second, the average amount of change per treatment is of a moderate to large magnitude. The average effect size per treatment for the between-group studies in our most recent study was .71, and the upward range of effect sizes for Cohen's d statistic for various anger interventions was 1.16. This means that people receiving anger treatment will change about one standard deviation more than those people in the control condition. Anger treatment is superior to doing nothing. The average effect size per treatment for the within-group studies was .99, and the upward range of effect sizes for Cohen's d statistic across various interventions was 1.55. Again, clinicians might expect those people receiving anger treatment to improve about one standard deviation over time. Unfortunately, the upward range of the effect sizes (d) for anger interventions is less than the upward range of effect sizes reported in meta-analytic reviews of treatments for anxiety and depression. The upward range of the effect sizes in treatment studies of depression is a little greater than 3.00, and for anxiety, more than 2.00. As Norcross and Kobayashi (1999) lamented, we cannot treat anger as successfully as we do other emotional problems. We need new creative interventions.

Third, treatment effects appear to last. We analyzed the effect sizes of all the anger outcome studies that included follow-up measurements (DiGiuseppe & Tafrate, 2003). Most studies held the gains accomplished at post-tests, and some even showed improvement at follow-up. Studies that maintained their effectiveness at follow-up used treatments that incorporated multiple interventions. Arnold Lazarus's (1989) notion that multimodal treatment produces the most enduring change appears to apply to anger.

Fourth, change occurs across different types of dependent measures not only self-reports of anger. Researchers have reported large magnitudes of change on physiological measures, self- and other-reports of positive and assertive behaviors, and self-ratings and significant others' ratings of aggressive behavior. This last finding may be the most important. Spouses and other family members should see changes from our interventions.

Sukhodolsky et al. (2004) reported little change on measures completed by the peers of children and adolescents. Two interpretations of these results are possible. Perhaps peers represent the most valid measure of behavior, and people really do not change. But this seems unlikely since parents, teachers, and unbiased observers all report large changes in these studies.

Perhaps peers stigmatize angry people and retain their stereotypes despite changes made in therapy.

Fifth, symptom and treatment-modality matching has not been supported. Clinicians often try to match an intervention to the client's primary symptoms. This comes from the generally accepted notion that the treatment modalities will affect their corresponding outcome measures.

Sixth, 80% of all published and unpublished research studies employed group therapy. We would speculate that most practitioners treating anger problems who work in correctional facilities, substance-abuse programs, hospitals, residential centers, and schools regularly employ a group format. Our meta-analytic review indicated that the group-treatment format had significantly lower effect sizes than individual treatment on measures of aggression (DiGiuseppe & Tafrate, 2003). Group and individual anger interventions are equally effective on measures of anger self-reports, assertion, and physical symptoms related to anger.

Seventh, studies that use treatment manuals and integrity checks to ensure that therapists follow the manual produced higher effect sizes than ones that did not use manuals or integrity checks. This finding, again, occurred only for measures of aggression. If one wants to reduce aggressive behavior, the use treatment manuals and monitoring of the practitioners may be important considerations.

Finally, most of the empirical literature tested behavioral, cognitive, or cognitive behavioral therapies. Two studies evaluated mindfulness meditation, which could be considered a Buddhist intervention. One study included Yalom's (1985) process-oriented or experiential group therapy. The most widely supported anger treatments included: (a) relaxation training, (b) cognitive restructuring as proposed by A. T. Beck (1999), Ellis (1962, 2003), D'Zurilla and Nezu (1999), Seligman (1975), and self-instructional training (Novaco, 1975), (c) rehearsal of new positive behaviors to resolve conflict such as assertiveness training and aggression-replacement training, and (d) multi-model treatments that include cognitive and behavioral interventions such as J. L. Deffenbacher's (1999) anger-management training. Exposure-based interventions (discussed in chapter 7), that is, teaching a new emotional response to the eliciting stimuli, received some support in our analysis.

We found no psychodynamic, family-systems, Gestalt, or client-centered research studies upon which to draw. Adherents of other theoretical orientations have not empirically corroborated the effectiveness of their treatments on anger. Our first reaction to this, as cognitive behavioral therapists, was enthusiastic rejoicing. However, realizing that so many theoretical orientations are absent from the empirical outcome-research literature makes this a shallow victory.

The lack of research results supporting different types of interventions could be taken to mean that these therapies are not efficacious. But it actually means that they have not yet been tested. This fact has limited what we know of anger. Prochaska and DiClemente (1988) have noted that treatments may have differential effectiveness based on a client's stage of change (see discussion in chapter 17). Because we believe that most angry clients arrive for therapy in the precontemplative or contemplative stages of change, and because the effectively proven therapies all tested action-stage interventions with volunteer participants, there is a strong possibility that there are therapies that are more effective in the real world. The anger literature would be enriched by outcome studies of other interventions. If cognitive behavioral interventions fail with a particular client, practitioners have little empirical evidence to help them choose the next intervention.

Clearly, if one uses the criteria of empirically supported treatments in clinical psychology to establish practice guidelines for the treatment of anger, a range of cognitive-behavioral interventions, such as assertiveness training, cognitive restructuring, problem solving, self-instructional training, and complex combinations such as anger-management training, would form the foundation of an evidence-based approach. We recommend that clinicians first evaluate a client's awareness of the costs associated with anger episodes and his or her motivation for change. If a client presents with poor motivation for change, the best clinical strategy to pursue would be interventions designed to help the client move from the precontemplative toward the action stage of change. To accomplish the goal of increasing motivation, the strategies suggested in chapter 18 might be the most useful once the client has achieved some level of awareness of the cost of his or her anger. Practitioners would be advised first to use interventions from the list of those that have some degree of empirical support. If these fail, they can then try untested interventions.

17

Roadblocks to Successful
Treatment of Angry Clients

The Problem of the Therapeutic Alliance

Practitioners frequently complain that angry clients resist treatment. Perhaps angry clients enter psychotherapy reluctantly not because of some subconscious resistance but because they simply do not see change as desirable. The major premise of this chapter is that many angry clients are often unmotivated to change because employers, spouses, the criminal justice system, parents, or schools typically coerce them into treatment. The existing psychotherapy theories fail to address anger disorders adequately because they were designed for self-referred patients who desire change. The following chapter focuses on the problem of motivating angry clients to participate in treatment.

Clients often initially respond with shock and disbelief to the suggestion that they change their anger. For example:

- A man referred for therapy because of spouse abuse responded with surprise to the suggestion that he change his anger. He readily admitted that he had never considered feeling anything but angry because he did not know what emotion he might experience instead.
- In a family therapy session, a therapist failed to convince a father to give up his anger and to stop yelling at his children. The father confronted the therapist for trying to change his anger and argued that anger was necessary for a parent. Without anger, he said, he would not succeed in disciplining his children. Anger was a cue to the child that his or her behavior needed to be amended in some way. He presumed that not experiencing anger would be ignoring his parental responsibility.

- A young adult with a history of ongoing interactions with the criminal justice system responded to the suggestion that his anger was contributing to his problems by expressing the idea that his anger was necessary to survive in his tough neighborhood.
- During a marriage counseling case, a wife refused to discuss changing her level of anger toward her husband. Giving up her anger, she said, would mean that she accepted or condoned his inappropriate behavior.
- A court-referred adolescent boy who frequently fought with his peers resisted all attempts to help control his anger. He believed that failure to express his anger would result in others' failing to respect him.
- The president of a small corporation sought consultation because of continued conflict with his staff. According to him, his "incompetent staff had failed to reach their sales quota." He defended his anger with reports of its success at controlling sales personnel and secretaries. Surrendering anger, he confided, would be abandoning his only management tool.
- A business executive expressed concern that eliminating her anger when she interacted with her family after work would prevent her from expressing the anger she had built up during the day. She said that not having an outlet for regularly releasing her anger would result in more explosive outbursts.
- A married man concluded that his therapist's attempts to change his anger meant that the therapist did not believe that the man's wife mistreated him. The man persisted in attempts to convince the therapist that his wife's behavior was inappropriate and needed changing.
- A 14-year-old boy diagnosed as having an Attention Deficit Hyperactivity Disorder was rebellious toward his special-education teacher. He refused all attempts to control his anger in class because he believed the teacher was wrong to call the students "dummies" and to read the newspaper rather than teach.

Spouses, courts, teachers and other school officials, employee-assistance programs, and other agencies or individuals often instigate the referral for treatment of angry individuals. When such angry people come to therapy, they do not want treatment. They want supervision. They seek to learn how to change the target of their anger. Typically, they want the target (spouse, employees, students, etc.) to comply with their own demands, and they have low frustration tolerance for the individuality of these targets. As a result, therapists often have difficulty forming a therapeutic alliance with angry clients (DiGiuseppe, 1991; Ellis, 1977).

In psychotherapy supervision, one often finds therapists working to change their clients' anger, while the clients are working to change the person at whom they are angry. The clients fail to agree to change their anger because they do not even recognize that it is problematic. They typically believe that they are justified and that it is appropriate to feel anger, or they may not believe that any other emotional reaction is appropriate to the event. Practitioners and clients clash because they disagree on the goal and target of intervention. The practitioner desires to change the angry emotionality, whereas the patient desires revenge against, condemnation of, or change in the transgressor. It is not surprising that therapists treating angry clients, regardless of age, fail to develop a therapeutic alliance with them.

Research Findings on the Therapeutic Alliance

The therapeutic alliance in adult psychotherapy has received considerable attention from researchers, and many things about it have been learned. Horvath and Luborsky (1993) concluded that the following principles are strongly supported by research:

1. The alliance is a trans-theoretical construct. Research results concerning the alliance are the same across all therapy orientations.
2. The alliance is established by the third or fourth session.
3. Once established, the alliance can be ruptured.
4. The alliance is one of the best predictors of therapy outcomes.
5. For adults, agreement on the tasks best predicts outcomes.
6. The clients' ratings of the alliance are a better predictor of the therapy outcome (compared with therapists' or observers' ratings).
7. The alliance is not related to the type or severity of psychopathology.
8. The therapeutic alliance is not related to any particular psychotherapeutic technique.

Although considerable research exists on the therapeutic alliance in psychotherapy, none of this research appears to focus on angry clients (see reviews by Horvath & Luborsky, 1993; and Horvath & Symonds, 1991). It is important for research and theory to explore the nature of the therapeutic alliance with angry clients and propose why the problem of formulating a therapeutic alliance might exist for this emotional disorder more than for others.

The concept of a therapeutic alliance involves more than the therapeutic relationship. Bordin (1979) proposed that a successful therapeutic alliance includes three elements: (1) agreement between the therapist and client on the goals of therapy, (2) agreement on the tasks of therapy, and (3) the bond—a warm, accepting, trusting relationship. This last aspect of the alliance—the bond—is what most psychotherapy theories call the therapeutic relationship. A successful alliance, however, is more than the therapeutic bond.

In terms of developing the three areas of the alliance, different strategies may work for depressed, anxious, and angry patients. As already noted, agreeing on a treatment goal is often a difficult roadblock to overcome.

Once patients gain insight that their anger is not working for them and the goal of anger reduction is established, the alliance is easier to achieve. Angry patients are often quite willing to engage in a variety of methods or therapeutic tasks to achieve their goals. We have rarely found resistance in this area of alliance development. Of course, it is useful to carefully explain the rationale for engaging in the chosen treatment activities, such as thought monitoring or exposure practice, and to ensure that what is expected is fully understood before proceeding.

The willingness of angry patients to quickly embrace active change strategies differs in some respects from that of depressed and anxious patients. For example, adults with anger problems (when not comorbid with depression) generally possess a greater overall level of energy than do depressed adults. They are rarely helpless or mired in nonaction. Rather, they desire and are willing to take active steps to deal with problems and may become frustrated (or angry) with psychotherapists who take too long to prescribe a concrete plan of action. Compared to patients with anxiety disorders, angry patients show a greater willingness to engage in exposure activities, imagery, simulations, and real-life practice. The tendency to avoid the emotionally charged stimulus, which often makes cognitive behavioral treatments for anxiety slow, is not typically problematic for angry patients. They jump right in. Additional discussions related to the use of exposure-based techniques for angry patients can be found in Brondolo, DiGiuseppe, and Tafrate (1997), Grodnitzky and Tafrate (2000), Kassinove and Tafrate (2002), and Tafrate and Kassinove (1998).

In terms of the relationship bond, angry patients who have agreed on the goal of treatment often do establish a positive connection and productive working relationship with the practitioner. Nevertheless, issues related to external coercion and characteristics of the treatment setting require careful attention. Certain environments, such as high schools, where an adolescent may be mandated for treatment as a condition of remaining in school, or correctional institutions, pose serious alliance-related challenges. Since custody and security are the main missions of prisons, treatment issues are often considered to be low priorities. Offender–clients are likely to be distrustful of anyone who is viewed as part of the staff. Even when a positive relationship and bond are established, custody issues may interfere with treatment. For example, sessions may be interrupted or cancelled over security concerns (e.g., head counts may be mandatory and unannounced). Or offender–clients might be moved from one institution to another with little notice or consideration given to their relationship with a particular practitioner. Thus, the relationship will be influenced to some degree by the setting in which the treatment is delivered.

Attitudes Likely to Interfere With Treatment

DiGiuseppe (1991) and Ellis (1977; Ellis & Tafrate, 1997) suggested some attitudes that are commonly found among angry persons, which may hinder the development of the therapeutic alliance. The perception of being transgressed upon by another person or group of people is a central focus for angry adults. This fact contrasts with the perceptions of depressed and anxious patients. Anxious patients tend to overestimate danger from a variety of sources (e.g., internal sensations, loss of control, specific stimuli such as dirt, bugs, one's own unpleasant thoughts, evaluative situations), and depressed patients focus on self-denigration, helplessness, and pessimism regarding the future. Angry patients, in contrast, tend to focus on the unwanted behavior of others. These beliefs can prevent clients from agreeing with the therapist that the goal is to change their own anger. An angry client's attitudes might include the following.

Appropriateness of Strong Anger

Angry clients may not experience their emotions as deviant because they cling to emotional scripts that sanction their anger, possibly because the person may not have been socialized to react with alternative emotions. That is, their culture, family, or peer group may not have modeled alternative emotional reactions, or they may have actually sanctioned high levels of anger. In such situations the person may fail to evaluate his or her angry reactions as deviant.

Misinterpretations and Distortions

Aspects of anger-engendering triggers are often distorted, seen in an unrealistic manner, or exaggerated. The tendency to make negative attributions, for example, has been well documented in angry and aggressive children and adolescents, who typically show deficits in interpreting the intentions of others (K. A. Dodge & Coie, 1987) and often misinterpret ambiguous or benign interactions as hostile (K. A. Dodge, Price, Bachorowski, & Newman, 1990). Anger-prone adults seem to possess a similar negative bias when they interpret ambiguous and potentially provocative situations. Adults who are high in trait anger report more distortions and exaggerations in their own thinking during anger episodes than do less-angry adults (Tafrate, Kassinove, & Dundin, 2002). Thus, patients with anger problems may be predisposed to misinterpret practitioners' verbal statements. Cognitive therapists are especially prone to become the targets of distorted thinking and patient anger because they may directly challenge the accuracy of a patient's thinking.

Lack of Emotional Responsibility and Other-Blame

Angry people often fail to take responsibility for their emotions; they assign responsibility for their emotions to external events. It is common to hear angry clients report, "He (she or it) made me angry." Since the cause of their anger is perceived to lie outside of them, angry people are unlikely to try to change the emotion. Since someone else is thought to be responsible for their anger by behaving badly, the people who caused the anger are perceived as needing change. Even if the angry client perceives his or her emotion as deviant (i.e., excessive and personally harmful), he or she may not take steps to manage the emotion if he or she believes that the responsibility for the emotion is externally controlled.

Other-Condemnation

Anger is usually accompanied by the belief that the target of one's anger is a totally worthless human being. The angry person does not differentiate the person from the person's acts. In turn, since the transgressor responsible for one's anger is a worthless, condemnable individual, she or he deserves one's wrath and must pay for the transgression. The worthless individual is perceived to be a deserving target of the anger outburst, or at least of contempt. Obviously, this belief works against changing the anger.

Self-Righteousness

Angry patients usually report believing that they have been wronged or treated unfairly. The transgressors are portrayed as morally wrong, whereas the patients see themselves as the aggrieved parties. Angry clients are rarely willing to examine their own role in an interpersonal conflict and rigidly adhere to the correctness of their behavior and the folly or immorality of their enemies. Self-righteousness leads angry people to believe that justice and God are on their side.

Cathartic Expression

Many angry clients maintain the belief that people must "release" their anger. Our culture (e.g., teachers, TV and radio commentators, psychodynamic psychotherapists) promotes a "hydraulic" model of anger. This includes the notion that anger must be dissipated or it will build up and the person will explode! Clients believe that holding their anger in will eventually lead to greater anger outbursts and psychosomatic illness and that anger expression is healthy and necessary. Again, such a belief mitigates against attempts to change the anger.

Rigidly Held, Demand-Based Assumptions

The most common anger-related belief is that persons who are viewed as the source of anger "should" or "ought to" have acted differently, as they could have if they "really wanted to" (Kassinove, Tafrate, & Dundin, 2002). Thus, the trigger is conceived to be a person who could have controlled his or her behavior but simply didn't. Patients engaged in demand-based thinking elevate their personal wishes to dictates or rigid rules that are then imposed on others. Demand-based assumptions frequently have a moral tone. Thus, angry patients typically see themselves as having been treated unfairly. And, therapists' efforts to challenge their demand-based assumptions are sometimes seen as confusing. For example:

THERAPIST: Why must your boss treat you with respect?
STEVE: Because that's the way you are supposed to treat people.
THERAPIST: I agree, it would be "nice" and even "preferred." But, why "*must*" people always treat others with respect?
STEVE: So, you are saying it is OK for my boss to treat me like crap?

In this example, the therapist's efforts to challenge the abstract assumption that people must always treat others with respect is quickly seen by the patient as the therapist's taking the wrong side of a moral argument. Such straightforward challenging will often backfire with angry patients.

Short-Term Reinforcement

Angry patients are often temporarily reinforced for their temper tantrums by the compliance of significant others. Of course, these rewards are offset by the negative consequences of using coercive processes in interpersonal relationships. Although significant others often do comply (at least initially), they may remain resentful, bitter, and distant. The angry patients, however, seem unaware of the negative effect the anger has on their interpersonal relationships. This belief is similar to A. T. Beck's (1976) cognitive error of selective abstraction. Angry patients selectively abstract the positive reactions to their anger outbursts and ignore the negative consequences. Attending to the short-term reinforcement of one's behavior and ignoring the long-term negative consequences of the behavior is a common human foible.

Reactance and Perceived Lack of Empathy by Others

Patients often perceive practitioner's attempts to change their anger as indicating that the practitioner does not believe that the transgressor is responsible for the problem. Possibly the practitioner does not agree that the patient was aggrieved. Even worse, perhaps the practitioner fails to see the transgressor as wrong (Walen, DiGiuseppe, & Dryden, 1992). Patients may experience practitioners' attempts to change their anger as efforts to invalidate their experience of being wronged and dispel their moral outrage against the offender, or as the therapist's refusal to acknowledge and accept their moral standard.

Models of Change

Models are needed to suggest how clinicians can motivate clients to change and avoid the resistance discussed above. Prochaska and DiClemente (1988) have investigated the process of change both inside and outside psychotherapy. They identified five stages of attitudes people have about change. In the *precontemplative stage* people are not even thinking about changing. In the *contemplative stage* people are evaluating the pros and cons of changing but have not yet decided to change. During the *readiness–preparation stage* people have decided to change and are preparing to take some action. During the *action stage* people actually implement active change strategies. Finally, in the *maintenance stage* the person attempts to continue and strengthen changes that have already been made (Prochaska, DiClemente, & Norcross, 1992).

Most consumers of psychotherapy arrive for treatment in the contemplative, readiness, or action stages. They are thinking that they "might" change and so wish to explore that possibility, or they have already decided to change. In contrast, using Prochaska and DiClemente's scheme, most angry clients seem to arrive in the precontemplative or contemplative stages for changing their anger, and in the action stage for changing others. They want to change others who, they believe, make them angry. We would predict that research using Prochaska and DiClemente's Stages of Change scale would provide evidence for the hypothesis that angry clients have not decided to change their anger when they arrive for therapy. Prochaska and DiClemente suggest that clients in the precontemplative or contemplative stages of change may not respond to active, directive, therapeutic procedures. Instead, they suggest that therapists should focus on self-awareness.

To help the angry client focus on the goal of changing his or her destructive anger, it may first be necessary to acknowledge and validate the frustration and disappointment at the hands of "the enemy." Even then, however, changing the anger may not become a goal for patients until they gain self-awareness and reach two insights. First, they must understand that their present emotion (i.e., anger) is dysfunctional over time, even though it may temporarily lead to satisfaction. Second, they must imagine an alternative emotional reaction that is socially and personally acceptable to them. Such insights are usually reached quite readily by anxious or depressed self-referred clients, often even before they arrive for treatment. Angry clients, regrettably, usually do not have such insights.

We propose that a primary task in formulating a therapeutic alliance with angry clients is to move them from the precontemplative stage of change toward the action stage. However, to agree on the goal of changing one's anger, it must be agreed that the anger is dysfunctional and that there is an alternative emotional reaction to replace the anger.

Prochaska and his group have done considerable research observing how people change. They studied people who were not in treatment or self-help groups for many months to see what variables changed as they moved from the precontemplative to the action stage. Two major findings of this research program are noteworthy. First, when people do not wish to change, they view the benefits of the problem behavior as greater than the cost. They also view the costs of any new replacement behaviors as greater than the benefits. At the action stage the situation is reversed (see Table 17.1). The costs of the problem behavior are seen as greater than the benefits. The new behaviors' benefits are evaluated as greater than their costs. Ellis (1962) calls this type of analysis a *hedonic calculus*. People appear to make some type of ratings about the desirability of behaviors and their alternative options. Given this fact, it is not surprising that social problem solving (Chang, D'Zurilla, & Sanna, 2004; D'Zurilla & Nezu, 1999) is one of the most successful cognitive behavior therapies. It involves evaluating the consequences of one's reactions and the generation of alternative responses. Social problem solving is among the empirically supported interventions for anger.

People usually do not advance directly from the precontemplative to the action stage of change. Over the course of many months they may start in the precontemplative stage and move to the contemplative for a while, and then return to the precontemplative stage. They may do this several times before arriving at the action stage. This means that most self-referred clients have experienced considerable self-exploration and have developed insights into themselves and their behavior. Coerced clients will not have these

Table 17.1
The Costs and Benefits of Behaviors in the Precontemplative and Action Stages of Change

Precontemplative Stage	Action Stage
The Costs of change are greater than the costs of remaining the same.	The Costs of change are less than the costs of remaining the same.
The Costs of remaining the same are less than the costs of change.	The Costs of remaining the same are greater than the costs of change.
The benefits of change are less than the benefits of remaining the same.	The benefits of change are greater than the benefits of remaining the same.
The benefits of remaining the same are greater than the benefits of change.	The benefits of remaining the same are less than the benefits of change.

insights and may need some time in therapy to develop them. The first steps in treatment will aim to develop these insights. In addition, we have found it helpful to review the clients' motivation for change on an ongoing basis throughout the treatment process.

Culture, Language, and Anger

To establish a therapeutic alliance, clients must agree to learn an alternative reaction to replace their dysfunctional anger. We propose that language often prevents clients from accomplishing this step. People have had difficulties describing the differences between different forms of anger for centuries, as shown in this quote from Seneca.

> The other categories (of anger), of which the Greeks, using a multi-plicity of terms, establish for the different kinds of anger, I will pass over. Since we have no distinctive words for them: and yet we call men bitter and harsh, and just as often choleric, rabid, clamorous, captious, and fierce. All of which designate different types of anger. (Basore, 1958, p. 117)

As discussed in detail in chapter 3, the script theory of emotions (Abelson, 1981; deSousa, 1980; Fehr & Russell, 1984; Hochschild, 1983; Sabini & Silver, 1982; Tomkins, 1979) is helpful in understanding clients' reluctance to change. According to this theory, emotional experiences and expressions result from a socially derived scheme concerning a group of subevents. Accordingly, emotional scripts consist of schemes that include the eliciting stimuli, the evaluations and beliefs about those events, cultu-rally sanctioned emotional experiences, and the social expression and be-havioral displays associated with the emotions.

Since emotional scripts evolve in a culture across time, cultures may contain many or few scripts of each emotion prototype. That is, there can be few or many variations of anger, guilt, sadness, and so on. Sadly, cultures and subcultures can fail to contain a script or schema for an adaptive form of anger. The emotional script concept appears helpful in understanding maladaptive anger reactions and in the treatment of anger disorders. Based on this perspective, it is hypothesized that the American culture possesses too few scripts concerning the prototype of anger. As a result, people often respond with an anger script that is inappropriate because of its frequency, intensity, or duration and because of the maladaptive interpersonal and intrapersonal effects it produces.

Kemper (1978, 1991; Kemper & Collins, 1990) suggests that emotions need to be understood through the social structure in which the individual resides, and he believes that power and status are important influences on emotional scripts. Scripts that include the suppression of anger in relationships with superiors, or those in power, may be particularly problematic. For example, Hochschild (1979) studied flight attendants, a group who must suppress any annoyance, anger, or irritation at passengers' aversive and obnoxious behaviors to ensure their future business. Flight attendants reported feeling emotionally "numb" and experience considerable emotional problems. Hochschild generalizes from these results to suggest that any individual in an occupational or social role that includes strong rules to suppress anger will experience difficulties similar to flight attendants. Some immigrants, members of minority groups, and women often have rules that encourage the suppression of emotional expression when they interact with those perceived as having higher status, and, as a result, they will experience detrimental, suppressed anger. Such persons lack an adaptive script to react to negative actions from those perceived as having higher status.

Culture, Families, and Emotional Scripts

Cultural considerations are important in helping clients reach the goal of changing their anger. The development of nondisturbed and functional alternative emotional scripts such as annoyance or "nondisturbed anger" may depend on the availability of such scripts in the clients' (and therapists') culture and family. Over the years, one of the authors has had considerable worldwide experience training therapists in Rational–Emotive Behavior Therapy. Based on observations the author made during these training sessions, it became clear that therapists from different cultures have varying degrees of difficulty understanding Ellis's (1977; Ellis & Tafrate, 1997) notion that there are both disturbed and nondisturbed types of anger. People from English-speaking countries have some difficulty understanding the difference between disturbed anger and nondisturbed annoyance. It is not that the English language does not have alternative words for anger-type emotions. The term *anger* is used indiscriminately in English to describe a variety of internal experiences. One can use the word *anger* to reflect a range of similar but unique emotions from the mildest level of infrequent irritation to persistent homicidal rage.

Therapists from Spanish-speaking countries, on the other hand, seem to grasp Ellis's distinction easily. They report that their language has words similar to English to express disturbed variations of anger such as *rabio* and *furioso*. These words are used more precisely in Spanish. Israeli therapists seem to have the greatest difficulty attempting to apply Ellis's distinction in their language. They claimed that there was one commonly used word for what we call *anger* that was translated literally as *I am nervous at you*. Not surprisingly, they reported difficulty helping clients accept the goal of changing their anger and had few culturally accepted alternative scripts available to replace clinically dysfunctional anger.

These examples are similar to the distinction in Russian reported by Kassinove and Sukhodolsky (1995) between *gnev* and *zlost*. *Gnev* is generally seen as mature and appropriate anger that requires no psychotherapeutic intervention. *Zlost*, on the other hand, is an immature and inappropriate experience that requires intervention if it is frequently experienced. Of note, in Russian these are moderately intense emotions that are different both from annoyance and rage.

Emotion words actually reflect different scripts whose distinctions the person has learned through socialization. The greater the number of words used in common conversation to describe alternative scripts to similar events, the more these alternative scripts will be found in the culture. It follows that cultures, subcultures, or linguistic groups whose languages do not have many commonly used words to represent alternative emotional reactions to the same situation will have fewer emotional scripts. The crucial question is whether the vocabulary words that distinguish between emotions in a culture or a language group may influence the availability of scripts that people in that group have to experience their emotions. We think not. People may experience emotions for which their language does not have an identifier. However, the use or experience of alternative emotional scripts is influenced by the frequency with which such distinctions are made in the language. The fewer alternative emotional scripts that can be accessed by common words, the more difficulty people in that group will have experiencing that emotion. Simply stated, the lack of a variety of acceptable, socially sanctioned emotional scripts leads to inflexibility of emotional reactions to anger triggers. This hypothesis can be tested by crosscultural research that attends to the emotional scripts and the vocabulary used to express them in various cultures.

Cultural scripts for anger may differ by gender. Many researchers propose gender-specific patterns of anger expression and inhibition (e.g., Tavris, 1989, 1992). Biological arguments suggest that subhuman primate males are more aggressive, as are human males (Lorenz, 1966). Another view suggests that men and women are equally capable of anger expression, but our male-dominated society inhibits female anger expression. However, Averill's (1983) data showed that men and women experience and express anger at a similar frequency, with similar intensity, and for similar reasons. Nevertheless, one gender difference did emerge. When angry, women reported crying significantly more often than did men. Averill's finding of few gender differences between men and women has been supported by several other investigations using Russian and English students (Kassinove, Sukhodolsky, Tsytsarev, & Soloyova, 1997) and high- and low-anger adults (Tafrate, Kassinove, & Dundin, 2002). Other studies do report gender differences in the expression of anger. For example, Suter, Byrne, Byrne, Howells, and Day (2002) found higher rates of anger experiences and expressions among female inmates. Clearly, research on anger and gender differences has produced mixed results.

Cultures and their languages may vary greatly in the distinctions they make between affective states. Therapists need to be aware of how the emotional scripts for anger (or any other emotion) are valued in a patient's culture or subculture and what alternative scripts are available within that culture. If the patient's cultural, subculture, or family group has no alternative script for a functional emotional response, the therapist will have to attempt to build a scheme for him or her. Practitioners, of course, should be sensitive to what the client's subculture considers acceptable alternative scripts.

Clinical experience suggests that families (and subcultures) have idiosyncratic scripts that differ from those of their larger culture. In addition, we often find that families with anger problems have few emotional scripts, and family members fail to make distinctions between the various reactions they *could* have to events. Perhaps because only one script has been modeled, clients behave rigidly, implementing the same emotional reaction. This lack of flexibility results in dysfunctional family interactions. The failure to have an emotional script for a type of adaptive, nondisturbed anger will likely lead to a failure to want to change one's anger. This will translate into a failure to agree on a therapeutic goal of changing one's anger.

Conclusions

Those individuals with problematic anger reactions who have little awareness regarding the costs of their anger episodes are likely to respond negatively to attempts to change their reactions. This will of course be a significant issue in certain settings such as criminal justice–related programs. With resistant clients, a variety of attitudes interfere with treatment. Thus, two insights form the foundation of successful treatment: the insight that anger is not working, and the availability of an alternative emotional response. Many clients with problematic anger reactions will need time to develop such insights and motivation for change. Thus, we recommend several strategies that prepare clients to actively engage in treatment. These strategies are the focus of the next chapter.

18

Preparing Clients for Anger Treatment

This chapter will cover strategies that can be used to help motivate angry clients to change. The proposed model encompasses a variety of components that may be useful in the early stages of anger treatment. These include: successful client engagement, working with client ambivalence about changing angry reactions, increasing client awareness of the negative outcomes associated with anger episodes, and identifying more constructive ways to experience and express anger.

Building an Alliance

As noted in the previous chapter, the first obstacle that therapists usually encounter is the clients' belief that their anger is justified because they have been wronged. Frequently clients' anger is out of proportion to the actual transgression that occurred. Often, they have participated in a *ménage à deux*, in which both they and their anger target have acted poorly. Employing cognitive or behavioral interventions before acknowledging the transgression to the client is an easy mistake for practitioners. Most angry clients believe they have been purposely and voluntarily treated unfairly and they deserve (or demand) to be heard. Patients often experience therapeutic attempts to change their anger as invalidating their moral outrage against the perceived transgressor or suggesting that the therapist disagrees with their moral standard. Many clients respond to attempts to change their anger with the accusation that the practitioner has taken the side of the significant other at whom the anger is directed.

To help clients reach the goal of changing their anger, it is first necessary to acknowledge and validate their frustration and disappointment at the hands of their enemy. Validation by the therapist that a negative event or transgression has occurred to the client helps them move on to evaluate the adaptiveness of their anger.

> A couple sought help for their arguments about the husband's 21-year-old daughter from a previous marriage, who lived with them. The daughter had dated a drug user who stole from the couple's house to support his habit. The father felt hurt but forgave the daughter. The wife felt angry with the daughter for allowing their family home to be violated. She was also angry with her husband for forgiving the daughter. The therapist's first intervention was to evaluate and challenge the wife's dysfunctional anger. However, this resulted in more anger. The wife believed that attempts to change her anger meant that the therapist and the husband believed that the daughter had done no wrong and that the wife had not been harmed. The therapist then switched to acknowledge the wife's hurt and validate her sense of vulnerability and betrayal by the daughter before implementing other anger-reduction strategies. Agreeing that one goal of therapy would be to discuss how to prevent the daughter from putting the family at risk helped the alliance and allowed the wife to examine whether her anger toward her husband actually accomplished her goal.

> In another example, a family was referred by the school because of their high school senior's truancy and poor grades. The father would yell and scream when he discovered his son's misbehaviors. When the family arrived for therapy, the mother identified the problem as the father's yelling. His behavior upset the family, and she believed it also motivated the son's misbehavior. The mother blocked any attempt by the father to focus on the son's misbehavior and defended the boy. The father responded by raising his voice and appeared obviously angry. The therapist focused on the father's anger and started to teach the father anger-management strategies. The father listened and commented that the therapist must think that his son's behavior is okay and that the father should not be angry. The father did not go to any more sessions.

The following strategies are presented as a menu of options that practitioners can choose from depending on the client's level of motivation. These strategies can be used individually or sequentially over the first few treatment sessions. In addition, several of these techniques can be adapted for group-treatment formats and become the focus of initial group meetings designed to build motivation.

Start With Empathy

Most psychotherapists acknowledge the importance of empathy in the therapeutic process. However, anger often fails to generate empathy or support. People often fail to experience empathy for people who are angry (Palfai & Hart, 1997). This may also apply to practitioners who treat angry clients.

> Consider the following case study of Sal, a 38-year-old Italian immigrant who entered mandated treatment after he threw a kitchen table at his wife. The table bounced off his wife and hit his 4-year-old daughter, breaking her arm. We asked Sal to recount the events that led up to this anger episode so as to understand his anger triggers. Sal, who owned a construction company, came home from work one hot summer day. His wife had dinner waiting for him as she usually had. After dinner, Sal smoked a cigarette as usual. As he smoked, the cigarette ash grew longer; his wife cleaned up as usual and attended to the young child. The cigarette ash bent under its own weight. Sal looked at the ash, then his wife, and then the ash. She usually brought him an ashtray when he smoked. Before she did so that night, the ash broke under its weight and fell in Sal's plate. This event triggered his anger and aggression.

As good cognitive behavior therapists, we asked Sal what thoughts entered his mind as he got angry. He looked up and said, "Doc, if I have to get things myself, why the fuck did I get married?" As you think about this case, imagine yourself experiencing empathy toward Sal. Angry clients frequently engage in verbally or physically abusive behavior, or they think globally condemning thoughts about their victims. These acts, which are so out of proportion to the incidents that trigger them, fail to evoke empathy.

We propose that it is typical for practitioners to experience less empathy toward angry clients than toward clients with other emotional problems. While observing conversations between therapists and angry clients, we noticed an interaction we call the *retaliation to transgression ratio accusation*. After the angry client reveals an anger episode that includes hostile retaliation toward the instigator that appears more offensive than the initiator's original transgression, the therapist responds to the client's story by indicating the excessiveness of the retaliation. In Sal's case, a therapist might say, "But did your wife really deserve to have a table thrown at her because she didn't get an ashtray?"

Notice that the therapist's remark failed to acknowledge Sal's perceived injustice. From his perspective, there had for years been a tacit agreement regarding each partner's role. Because his wife transgressed against Sal first, he perceived the retaliation as justified. As a result, Sal demonstrated no desire to change his anger and felt no remorse for the vengeful act. Since angry clients often perceive their retaliation as justified, they tend to perceive a therapist's failure to acknowledge the transgression as invalidating their experience. This lack of motivation unnerves the practitioners, who point out to the client that the revenge was out of proportion to the initiator's act. Therapists often use this imbalance of transgressions as a reason for the desirability of change. Clients feel invalidated by such arguments. They experienced a transgression, and the therapist failed to acknowledge it. Therefore, the clients repeatedly reiterate their stories, emphasizing the details of the other persons' transgressions. The clients feel unheard and attempt to convince the therapist that they were transgressed upon. Correspondingly, therapists continue to voice their shock over the clients' inappropriate actions in hopes of convincing the clients to surrender their anger. This interaction usually ends with the clients' feeling angry with the practitioner and, depending on the setting, may result in a failure to return for further treatment. Angry clients who do not experience empathy from their practitioners will not move on until they believe someone acknowledges their experience of a transgression.

Avoid the retaliation-to-transgression-ratio debate by first acknowledging the perceived transgression the client has experienced, even if you find it difficult. Clients such as Sal challenge our ability to empathize. Arnold Lazarus (1989) has often said that a good therapist is an authentic chameleon. You do not have to deeply experience empathy. You need only understand what the client perceived as the transgression and say so. Letting the client know that you can see the situation through his or her eyes does not in any way sanction the poor behavior. It only lets the client know that you can see his or her view.

A practical way to empathize with clients and begin to create awareness of the costs associated with anger episodes is to use a motivational interviewing style as outlined by W. Miller and Rollnick (2002). A forceful "change message" from the therapist often results in a strengthening of the client's arguments that anger is necessary, proper, and valid, given the circumstances. At least initially, indirect and client-centered methods appear to be more effective. The goal in this approach is to subtly increase awareness of the negative costs of anger while not increasing patient resistance. Once a commitment to change exists then an active–directive style, as well as a variety of change strategies will usually be acceptable to angry patients. Using motivational interviewing with angry patients involves the same principles as originally developed and applied to patients with substance-abuse problems (W. Miller & Rollnick, 2002). The initial sessions involve using reflective statements and open-ended questions to encourage clients to verbalize some of the negative aspects of their anger. By eliciting and differentially reinforcing verbalizations related to the problematic aspects of anger, clients' commitment to change is strengthened (e.g., "Sal, it seems that you are pretty frustrated about your wife deciding to change the way things have been done for years. Also, you have concerns about the effects of your anger reactions on your daughter.") This is done in a nonjudgmental way, allowing the therapist to empathize with the patient's perceptions of being mistreated. The therapist's role is simply to highlight the costs that the client indicates are associated with anger episodes. Costs may be further amplified through the use of open-ended questions designed to elicit patient statements regarding problematic aspects of their anger experiences (e.g., "Sal, how do you think this whole situation will affect your relationship with your daughter?"). W. Miller and Rollnick (2002) have identified four client verbalization themes believed to be predictive of behavioral change. These have been termed *self-motivational* or *change-talk statements* and include problem recognition, expression of concern, intention to change, and optimism. Increasing statements about problem recognition is the goal of the initial meetings. Evidence for the connection between client-commitment language and behavioral outcomes is presented and reviewed by Amrhein, Miller, Yahne, Palmer, and Fulcher (2003). Once clients begin to make the argument for change they will be more receptive to learning cognitive and behavioral skills.

Assess the Client's Goals and Align Treatment Accordingly

The therapist needs to clearly assess whether angry clients have as their goal a change in their anger. This is a simple matter of overt verbal agreement between patient and therapist. Failure to closely attend to the issue of agreement on therapeutic goals will surely lead to a rupture in the alliance. Although clients may not see changing their anger reactions as a legitimate treatment goal, they may find other outcomes more acceptable. For example, one client wanted to be more successful in his business relationships. As long as emotional control was emphasized in the context of being more effective on the job, he was quite willing to consider new behaviors. We have also found that many parents' goals include to be more effective with their children, to create healthier parent–child interactions, and to reduce household chaos. As discussed above, the suggestion that a parent needs to better control his or her anger may be met with resistance. On the other hand, showing empathy regarding a challenging family situation and focusing on the goal of the parent, to create a less chaotic environment, will often be a more productive starting point.

Secure Agreement on the Goal and Task of Exploring

If the client does not wish to change the anger, and the practitioner believes that anger is a problem, the therapist may seek an agreement with the client that they spend some time reviewing the functionality and adaptiveness of the client's anger. At the very least, this will put the matter of the anger on the table and will provide an opportunity for the therapist and client to collaboratively examine the role of anger in the client's life.

Explore the Consequences of the Clients' Anger

There are several strategies that focus directly on the costs of anger.

Reviewing Individual Episodes of Anger

One method of increasing awareness of the consequences of anger is to review with clients the components of their anger experiences. Kassinove and Tafrate (2002) have proposed a simple but formal model that provides a framework for connecting specific anger events to consequences (Figure 18.1).

They have also translated their anger-episode model into an Anger Episode Record (Figure 18.2). By monitoring and reporting individual episodes of anger, both the patient and practitioner can specifically target key features of anger that are problematic. Thus, treatment can be tailored to a patient's symptom patterns. Examining multiple episodes over time allows practitioners to better understand typical functioning.

Depending on client motivation, the model and tool can be applied in several ways. The first uses the model as a structure for having a conversation about a recent and significant anger episode. The model guides practitioner questions, and the overall tone of the session is conversational, allowing the client freedom to expand on each area. The motivational interviewing style can be incorporated by selectively reflecting back to the client the more negative aspects of anger reactions. We have found this strategy to be useful for developing awareness and strengthening the therapeutic relationship, while not engendering resistance. Of course, when using this approach, it is important to stay focused on a single anger episode, to be

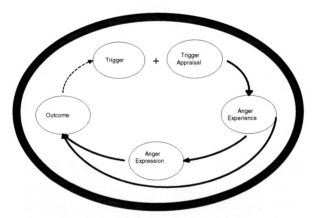

Figure 18.1. Anger Episode Model (Adapted from Kassinove & Tafrate, 2002, used by permission of Impact Publishers, Inc.). This model provides a framework for connecting specific anger events to consequences.

Anger Episode Record
Triggers + Appraisals -> Experiences -> Expressive Patterns -> Outcomes

Directions. Fill out one record for each episode of anger that you experience. Provide information in each box.

Triggers

[Describe the event(s) you were angry about]

The date of this episode was:

The target of my anger was:

The situation surrounding my anger was:

+

Appraisals

[Place a check next to each thought that you had]

___ *Demandingness* (e.g. I thought the other person should have acted differently)

___ *Other rating* (e.g. I thought the other person was "bad," "worthless," or, an "asshole," "#@*%&," etc.)

___ *Low frustration tolerance* (e.g. I thought I could not handle or deal with this situation)

___ *Awfulizing* (e.g. At the time, I thought this was one of the worst things that could be happening)

___ *Self-rating* (e.g. Deep down I thought I was less important or worthwhile)

___ *Distortion* (e.g. My thinking got distorted and exaggerated due to my anger in this situation)

___ *Unfairness* (e.g. I thought the other person acted unfairly)

___ *Revenge* (e.g. I thought that this person deserves to suffer or be punished)

->

Experiences

How intense was your anger in this situation?

0				100
none	mild	moderate	strong	extreme

How long did your anger last? ___ minutes ___ hours ___ days

What physical sensations did you experience? *(Place a check next to each physical sensation you experienced)*

___ Muscle tension
___ Rapid heart rate
___ Headache
___ Upset stomach
___ Flushing
___ Trembling

___ Fluttering in stomach
___ Nausea
___ Rapid breathing
___ Tingling sensations
___ Feelings of unreality
___ Dizziness

___ Sweating
___ Indigestion
___ Diarrhea
___ Positive energy
___ Fatigue

->

Figure 18.2. Anger Episode Record (Adapted from Kassinove & Tafrate, 2002, used by permission of Impact Publishers, Inc.).

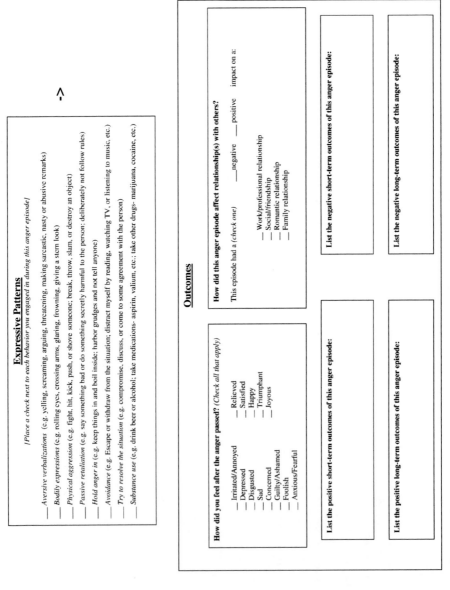

Expressive Patterns

[Place a check next to each behavior you engaged in during this anger episode]

___ *Aversive verbalizations* (e.g. yelling, screaming, arguing, threatening, making sarcastic, nasty or abusive remarks)

___ *Bodily expressions* (e.g. rolling eyes, crossing arms, glaring, frowning, giving a stern look)

___ *Physical aggression* (e.g. fight, hit, kick, push, or shove someone; break, throw, slam, or destroy an object)

___ *Passive retaliation* (e.g. say something bad or do something secretly harmful to the person; deliberately not follow rules)

___ *Hold anger in* (e.g. keep things in and boil inside; harbor grudges and not tell anyone)

___ *Avoidance* (e.g. Escape or withdraw from the situation; distract myself by reading, watching TV, or listening to music, etc.)

___ *Try to resolve the situation* (e.g. compromise, discuss, or come to some agreement with the person)

___ *Substance use* (e.g. drink beer or alcohol; take medications- aspirin, valium, etc.; take other drugs- marijuana, cocaine, etc.)

∧

Outcomes

How did you feel after the anger passed? *(Check all that apply)*

___ Irritated/Annoyed   ___ Relieved
___ Depressed   ___ Satisfied
___ Disgusted   ___ Happy
___ Sad   ___ Triumphant
___ Concerned   ___ Joyous
___ Guilty/Ashamed
___ Foolish
___ Anxious/Fearful

How did this anger episode affect relationship(s) with others?

This episode had a *(check one)*   ___ negative   ___ positive   impact on a:

___ Work/professional relationship
___ Social/friendship
___ Romantic relationship
___ Family relationship

List the positive short-term outcomes of this anger episode:

List the negative short-term outcomes of this anger episode:

List the positive long-term outcomes of this anger episode:

List the negative long-term outcomes of this anger episode:

Figure 18.2. *continued*

342

concrete and specific, and to avoid theoretical discussions about anger in general. To completely review the components of a single anger episode can take anywhere from 5 to 20 minutes or more.

The second strategy is to ask the client, at the beginning of the meeting or in the waiting room prior to a session, to complete a single record for the most significant anger experience that occurred since the last meeting. The practitioner then reviews the record and looks for opportunities to point out the costs related to the anger episode. The third strategy is to use the Anger Episode Record as an ongoing self-monitoring tool, as is typical in cognitive behavioral therapy interventions. Used in this manner, the records can provide an indicator of treatment progress. The number of episodes reported early in treatment can serve as a baseline from which improvement can be measured. Other dimensions of anger can also serve as indicators of progress, depending on the areas that the practitioner wishes to target. These might include average intensity of anger episodes, duration, and/or the number of episodes containing aversive verbalizations or aggressive behaviors.

Socratic Dialogue and Disputing Anger-Entrenching Beliefs

Therapists can lead clients, by Socratic dialogue, through an analysis of the consequences of anger. Exploring the consequences of a client's anger usually involves challenging some of the beliefs mentioned in the previous chapter.

Emotional Responsibility

Angry clients are quick to blame the transgressor who elicited their reaction for their anger. Teaching clients that *they* are responsible for their anger is much easier after the therapist has acknowledged that the transgressor has done some wrong. Two important issues arise in challenging emotional responsibility. The first is, "Does your anger get you what you want?" Many clients are so stuck on the issues of moral blame of the transgressor that they fail to focus on the practical aspects of their reactions. If the transgressor does not and will not change, which is often true, then how will the client cope with the situation, and how does the anger help in problem solving? The useful clinical strategy here is to repeatedly acknowledge the transgressor's behavior, acknowledge the client's emotion, and then ask how he or she is solving the problem and how the anger will help reach the goal.

> A middle-level manager was referred by a friend because of persistent anger at his company and supervisors after he was passed over for promotion. The man reported that he deserved the promotion more than the person who received it but was passed over because his immediate supervisor personally liked the successful candidate. During the ensuing two years, the client had openly berated his superiors, the upper management, and the company. Most of his peers avoided contact with

him because of his continual angry tirades. For the first four sessions, the client attempted to convince the therapist of how he was mistreated and the guilt of those who were involved or who failed to appreciate his work. The therapist responded, "All right, so you were treated unfairly, and you are unappreciated. How are you coming to live with these facts? How has your anger and your ranting and raving helped you cope with the situation?" Further conversation resulted in the client's admitting that his behavior had alienated his peers, compromised the quality of his work, prevented him from considering a job change, and prevented him from doing good work to impress other managers in the organization. Although he had "gotten even" by reducing his productivity, he hurt himself because others in his industry perceived him as an angry person who they wished to neither promote nor employ. A continued focus on the consequences helped develop these insights and an alliance to change his anger.

It Is Healthy to Express Anger

All scientists who have studied the issue agree that catharsis is ineffective (Bushman, 1998). However, it remains difficult to dislodge the notion that cathartic expression of anger is healthy and desirable. This is a particularly difficult belief to challenge socratically. Clients may not have sufficient information about the long-term effects of anger expression to allow their experiences to lead them to the correct conclusions. Instead, we have found it better to use more didactic teaching to challenge this belief. Clients who believe in cathartic expression are correct in their belief that holding one's anger in results in illness. However, this definitely does not mean that the opposite, the outward expression of anger, results in psychological or physical health! Research has demonstrated that the outward expression of anger also leads to physical illness (Chesney, 1985; Diamond, 1982; Diamond, Schneiderman, Schwartz, Smith, Vorp, & Pasin, 1989; Spielberger, 1992). Thus, one can become physically ill whether one holds anger in or expresses it outwardly.

Similarly, psychological adjustment is not accomplished by inwardly harboring anger. The internal rumination that angry people experience can consume their lives. However, the outward expression of anger leads not to psychological health but to more anger. This is often difficult for angry clients to see because people often feel better (immediately and temporarily) after they unload their anger on someone. One may feel better after an anger outburst because one stops ruminating and because the muscles may actually relax after the long period of preparing to "tell that person off." Thus, there is a moment of relaxation similar to what one might feel in deep muscle relaxation when tense muscles are released. Unfortunately, this emotional improvement is short lived. Cathartic expression results in an increase in the probability that the person will respond to a similar situation with anger (Tavris, 1989). Thus, the belief that catharsis is a corrective experience that reduces the buildup of anger is false. Instead, catharsis leads to temporary relief and increases the chances that one will become angry in the future. I usually remind clients of the old joke, "How do you get to Carnegie Hall?" Answer: "Practice, practice, practice." "How do you become a really angry person?" "Practice, practice, practice."

Angry clients appear stuck in a conundrum. Do they hold their anger in or let it out? "Neither," most of us would argue. They would best find a way to control, eliminate, or dissipate the anger and work toward experiencing another emotion. Spielberger (1992) uses the metaphor of a pressure cooker. To deal with the build-up of steam, one can wait until the cooker explodes, or one can periodically reduce the pressure by siphoning off some of the steam. However, a better solution would be to just lower the flame.

Anger Is an Effective Way to Control Others

As noted in the previous chapter, clients are likely to focus on the immediate consequences of their anger rather than the longer-term social consequences. Thus, a client might focus on the outcome of anger ventilation, such as succeeding in getting someone to comply with the client's rules, but ignore the fact that venting seriously damaged the relationship. Frequently, clients lack empathy about how their anger affects others. Thus, it is helpful for them to recount how they feel when others are angry with them and use this to imagine how their significant others feel when the client gets angry. It is important to make the distinction between short-term and long-term consequences. Clients can usually convince the therapist that the short-term consequences are in their favor. Since immediate reinforcement is more effective than delayed reinforcement, it is not surprising that clients have difficulty focusing on longer-term effects. It is important to ask about the outcome of previous anger outbursts on social relationships and about social relationships wherein the client does not express anger, and have the client explain why things turned out as they did. Clients usually answer by saying that they do not express anger to those in a higher social position (for fear of consequences) or to people who would not tolerate the anger expression. This information can be used to make the case that people do not like anger.

Empathetic role taking is a successful strategy to help angry clients become aware of the social–relationship consequences of their anger. We ask the clients how they have reacted to those who have expressed anger at them. Most clients relate well to this exercise and report disliking and distancing themselves from the angry persons in their life.

- The corporate president mentioned above reported that numerous bosses had expressed anger at him while he was moving up the corporate ladder. He reported that he always responded with an attempt at revenge through passive-aggressive behavior. He did only what they asked and nothing more. When asked if sales personnel and secretaries were likely to do the same to him, he got the point and agreed to change his anger.

- The angry father was asked who in his life had behaved angrily toward him. He recalled how his father had yelled and hit him. He thought that his father was successful at demanding obedience. But he then went on to describe how he hated his father and had avoided contact with him since reaching adulthood. The hard question was whether or not he sought the same relationship with his children when they became adults. After contemplating the fact that generations can easily repeat the cycle, he was eager to learn if there were better ways to discipline his children than yelling in anger.

Using Feedback From Standardized Assessment Instruments

Another way to increase awareness and to enhance motivation is to provide feedback on standardized tests. Several instruments are available that specifically address anger, such as the State–Trait Anger Expression Inventory (STAXI–2; Spielberger, 1999) and the Novaco Anger Scale (NAS; Novaco, 1994). As noted previously, we prefer the Anger Disorders Scale (ADS; DiGiuseppe & Tafrate, 2004) because it measures the greatest range of clinically relevant anger dimensions. The ADS subscales are listed in Table 14.1 in the previous section.

In terms of providing feedback, we again recommend the motivational interviewing style (W. Miller & Rollnick, 2002). Since the ADS provides information on 22 different scores, practitioners can choose to highlight those scores that show the highest elevations and which are areas of concern. In addition, low scores can also be noted as areas of relative strength. Scores are usually presented in terms of percentiles, and the dimensions being measured are explained in easy-to-understand language. Here is an example: "Carmine, your score on the Verbal Expression Scale was at the 99th percentile. This means that when you get angry you are likely to express yourself by saying negative things to others, yelling, arguing, or making nasty comments. Your score in this area was higher than 99% of men your age."

Although clients will have a variety of reactions to hearing how their scores compare to a standardization group, these are usually limited to a few themes:

- *Agreement.* "Yeah that's exactly right! I always get myself in trouble with my mouth."
- *Surprise.* "Really! I did not think I was that high."
- *Minimizing.* "I look around and other people in my neighborhood act the same way that I do."

- *Justifying.* "I need to be tough in my neighborhood. So I have to say shit to people."
- *Disagreement.* "That score can't be right. There must be something wrong with your test."
- *Indifference.* "Whatever. I don't believe in tests."
- *Confusion.* "Is 99% good?"

Practitioners follow the initial reaction with reflective statements and open-ended questions. These are designed to get the client to verbalize his or her concerns related to anger. The one exception might be confusion, in which the role of the practitioner is to explain the score in a way that is likely to be understood. The following is a brief sample of dialogue following agreement:

THERAPIST: So this is really on target for you.
CLIENT: Yeah, I'm always getting myself in trouble and saying stupid stuff.
T: Sounds like this has created problems for you.
C: Oh yeah. Big time.
T: Tell me about the last time you got yourself in trouble when you were angry.

Of course the discussion would continue. The score is simply used as a platform to launch a discussion of what the client sees as problematic. Below is a brief sample of dialogue if disagreement is expressed:

THERAPIST: "So, this score doesn't make sense for you."
CLIENT: "No. I do not think that my anger is worse than 99% of the population."
T: "So, it is really hard to see it presented like that."
C: "Yeah. It makes it sound like I am out of control."
T: "Seeing yourself compared to others like this is really uncomfortable."
C: "Yeah, others have told me that my anger is a problem. But I'm not sure that I am as bad as your test says."
T: "What have others said about your anger?"

In this example, the conversation can now be steered toward an exploration of how the client's anger reactions have affected his or her social relationships. Again, the score is used as a catalyst to create problem recognition statements that will be followed-up by the practitioner. Other initial responses can be handled in the same manner. It is not unusual for clients to agree with some scores and not others. When using this approach it is important for the practitioner not to be too forceful in attempting to have the client accept all the feedback. Rather, it is done in the spirit of providing the information for the client to consider. They are free to reject it. However, most people are grateful for the information even if it is uncomfortable to hear. A demonstration DVD showing such assessment feedback can be found in Kassinove and Tafrate (2006).

Explore Different Types of Anger Scripts

Once clients agree that it is in their best interest to reduce or eliminate their anger, they can still be thwarted because they may not know what to replace it with. As discussed in the previous chapter, they may have a limited number of alternative scripts that they consider socially appropriate. Helping clients generate alternative scripts is similar to generating alternative solutions in the problem-solving model of adjustment (Spivack, Platt, & Shure, 1976). New scripts can often be developed by having the client recall the successful, but nonangry reactions of others whom they respect and to generate a model for an alternative script. Clients from very dysfunctional families may have few such models.

Most patients and therapists consider anger as varying along one quantitative continuum. In contrast, rational–emotive theory maintains that emotions differ not only on a quantitative continuum. It posits that adaptive and maladaptive variants of each emotion exist and differ qualitatively as well. Of these, only physiological arousal is a quantitative dimension.

To accept one's anger as a target for mental health intervention requires recognizing at least two different anger-related emotional scripts. The first, which we will call *adaptive non-disturbed anger* (or what Ellis [1977; Ellis & Tafrate, 1997] calls annoyance), would have several components. Cognitively, it would acknowledge that the person was aggrieved and that the transgressor's action was perceived as wrong. It would include an experiential negative affect along a continuum from mild to moderate. It could lead to clear assertive communications by the aggrieved party, communicating his or her feelings and desires. It could lead to other adaptive behaviors that would avoid victimization in the future. If no adaptive behavior were readily available in the person's repertoire, this emotion might initiate problem-solving activities to consider and evaluate new responses. Also, this state would not lead to the unnecessary disruption of the person's functioning. Such an emotion may have moderate, although not excessive, affective arousal.

The second anger script, which we will call *dysfunctional* or *clinical anger,* would lead to a much more unpleasant phenomenological experience. It would include a more intense, hostile, and attacking form of social expression, which might cause additional long-term problems. It might interfere with problem solving and could restrict consideration of more adaptive behavior that would avoid victimization in the future. Finally, it would lead to disturbed affect and rumination that greatly interfered with the individual's functioning. Some support for the view that people can distinguish between disturbed clinical anger and nonclinical functional annoyance comes from Averill (1982, 1983). His data suggests that people view anger as a more intense emotional experience than annoyance. They also view anger as a more serious or inappropriate emotional reaction.

The rational–emotive theory of emotions is similar to the script theories of emotions mentioned above. Discussion of the script idea with angry clients usually results in several themes. First, they typically defend their anger script and report that attacking their transgressor is necessary lest they be overwhelmed by them. Second, they often insist that expressing anger avoids the negative health consequences that accompany anger suppression.

However, some people may perceive using Ellis's term *annoyance* for an adaptive type of anger to be invalid. Imagine an African American, angry at racist behavior, a Jew angered about the denial or trivialization of the Holocaust, a war refugee angered by the destruction of his or her village and the extermination of his or her family, or a rape victim angry at her attacker. Asking them to change their anger to annoyance, a mild emotion, diminishes the event about which they are angry. Nonetheless, their anger may lead to their committing destructive, hateful, and equally prejudiced behaviors. Suggesting to such people that they replace their anger with annoyance may appear invalidating. But if anger at such perpetrators is dysfunctional, with what emotion should people replace their anger?

Models do exist for adaptive reactions to real harm and injustice. Consider Martin Luther King Jr. Most people would find his reaction to racism to be adaptive. Yet his emotional reaction to racism was strong. We doubt that he would have reported feeling a mild affect like annoyance. His emotion elicited a behavioral response that was planned, orderly, personally risky, and consuming. What do we call such an emotion? King's emotion was experienced intensely. His determination was evident to his peers, enemies, and bystanders. He recognized a problem and planned a long-term strategy to overcome it. However, I doubt his physiological arousal was always high. Such high and sustained sympathetic arousal would have been exhausting.

Nelson Mandela's reaction to apartheid provides another great model of adaptive anger. A South African psychologist, Ray Lafera, who studied with us, reported on his personal interactions with Mandela. Like King, Mandela acknowledged the problem. He had a strong emotional reaction. However, he was focused on the long-term solution to both ending apartheid and rebuilding his country. He communicated this response to those around him. Again his physiological arousal did not appear to be in a constant high state. Lafera hypothesized that the key aspect that led to Mandela's adaptive emotional reaction was his focus on the future acknowledgment of reality. He mentioned to Lafera that the past was over. Only by acknowledging it and focusing on the future could the problems of his country be resolved. He also acknowledged that white South Africans were part of his country and that any solution had to include them.

The adaptive anger to personal and social injustice experienced by King and Mandela have the following characteristics. First, the phenomenological experience was strongly felt. Second, although the experience included disgust at the actions of others, there was hope that things could be different.

Third, the emotion was expressed socially as a confident, dedicated commitment to overcoming the problem. Fourth, the behavioral predispositions elicited by the emotion included reflective planning rather than impulsive reactions. The behaviors were persistent and involved courage and a willingness to expend time and resources to overcome the problem along with the willingness to be exposed to personal risks. The physiological sympathetic arousal in such an emotion is probably moderate. As sympathetic arousal rises, people have changes in their attentional focus. At low levels of sympathetic arousal, people do not focus enough attention on a problem to resolve it. People are easily distracted and their attention wanders. Goldfried and Davison (1994) referred to this phenomenon of extreme relaxation and performance as *relaxed incompetence.* As sympathetic arousal increases, the degree of attention to the eliciting stimuli increases. At moderate levels of arousal one attends sufficiently to the problem to resolve it. As arousal increases to high levels, people narrow their attention to such a degree that they focus on the problem so narrowly that they cannot generate solutions. For this reason, we believe that these strongly felt adaptive anger reactions include moderate emotional arousal. Of course this is the well-known Yerkes–Dodson Law (Yerkes & Dodson, 1908).

In addition to the characteristics of emotions suggested by Izard (1989), we would hypothesize some cognitive components to this emotion. First, this emotion includes a sense of disgust and a strong negative evaluation of the eliciting stimuli. Second, there is an acknowledgment that, despite the strong negative evaluation, the problem exists. Reality is acknowledged and not denied. Third, the person maintains a future orientation. They think about how the problem can be resolved and what the world would be like without the problem. As Martin Luther King Jr. said, "I have a dream." Fourth, acknowledgment of reality, future orientation, and moderate sympathetic arousal promote a problem-solving focus. People with this emotional reaction think of alternative ways to solve their problems or achieve their dreams. Fifth, people hold their enemies responsible for their unjust actions, yet they experience forgiveness. People with this emotion do not think of revenge or personal condemnation of their enemies. They appear to recognize that retribution produces a vanquished, yet bitter, foe. If the vanquished are not part of the peace, they hold their resentment until they have the strength to retaliate. Thus, the cycle of violence continues.

This last aspect of the cognitive elements of an adaptive angry response to injustice may be the hardest to describe. It is helpful to contrast the results of a forgiving attitude from the consequences of a vengeful one. History provides some models that make this clear. Consider again Mandela's reaction to apartheid. He instituted the Peace and Reconciliation Council to uncover the tragedies of apartheid and hold the offenders responsible for their actions. However, forgiveness was a major focus of this project. The goal was to promote healing. One could have easily imagined the Black population of South Africa engaging in revenge killings of Whites.

This occurred in other African countries, such as when White Rhodesia evolved into Botswana. In another example, toward the end of the American Civil War many Union politicians desired to severely punish the Confederate states and their leaders. President Lincoln favored a policy of forgiveness for secession. Lincoln was shot, and the vengeful politicians won the day. The resulting policy of Reconstruction of the South produced animosity that still exists in American society (McPherson, 1988, 1996). Consider also the Allied response to conquered Germany after World War I. Historians view the Treaty of Versailles as extremely punitive. The resentment that followed sowed the seeds for the next great war (Keegan, 1993). The Allies learned their lesson from World War I; the Marshal Plan attempted to rebuild vanquished Germany, and a similar policy infused economic growth into Japan (Keegan, 1993). Both these defeated countries have remained allies with nations that defeated them more than 50 years later. The historical record verifies the futility of revenge.

But what do we call this emotional reaction? We often ask this question in professional training workshops on anger. Most of the audience has no idea, and they are the professionals that people turn to for help with anger problems. Some respond with the term *righteous indignation*. This is a good word but too big for most of our clients. Most people have no word for such an affective response to real injustice. We suggest the word *commitment*. This word identifies the energizing aspect of the emotion and its focus on problem resolution. However, the reader may have more appropriate words. It is most important that the concept of the reaction is shared with clients and that their words are used in therapy.

The reader or your clients might respond that we have proposed mythic and heroic figures for models reacting to injustice. Many normal everyday people may believe that they are incapable of such reactions. They are not King, Mandela, Lincoln, or Gandhi, but average people. How can they be expected to react in such a heroic manner? But the alternative is to experience consuming hatred, seek revenge, and perpetuate a cycle of violence. We propose all of us need role models for forgiveness in everyday life. They are out there.

One of us recently interviewed a man whose son was murdered. His initial reaction was anger, hatred, and a desire for vengeance. However, over the period of a year, after spending time with others who had suffered similar losses, he came to the conclusion that he could not continue to live with extreme anger and bitterness. He began the process of communicating with his son's killer in prison and eventually visited. He began to understand the circumstances in the offender's life that influenced his decision to kill. Over a period of years, he repeatedly reached out to help the incarcerated individual. Eventually, he spoke at his parole hearing and was instrumental in securing the release of the man who had taken his son's life. Outside of prison they formed a friendship. When asked why he had pursued this path, he replied that "forgiveness was the only way [he] could find to move forward." He also stated that forgiveness benefited him more than the other man. For more information about this case, readers are referred to http://www.willsworld.com/~mvfhr/rev.htm, or to a DVD interview on the process of forgiveness in Kassinove and Tafrate (2006).

In essence, it seems that our culture has limited scripts for anger. American cultural scripts usually incorporate an instinctual link between anger and aggression, and they (wrongly) stress the importance of the cathartic release of anger. We propose that anger treatment will be more effective when researchers and clinical practitioners investigate the common scripts that people hold concerning anger, how these scripts relate to adaptive behavior, and how scripts relate to labeling anger as a problem.

One practical strategy that therapists might consider is to suggest models from the general culture or from the literature, folklore, or films of a client's culture or extended family. A model that shares some features with the client is best. Research has demonstrated that shared characteristics between the observer and the model increases the effectiveness of modeling interventions. A model that appears too different or behaves too well may not be viewed as someone with whom the client can identify. I like to think that all cultures and all families have some adaptive and pathological models for anger. However, the pathological models are more salient. They get our attention and leave an impression. Those people who handle anger-provoking situations adaptively are much less salient or memorable, and we fail to notice them. Thus, the disturbed family members may have the most influence on development.

After a model is chosen for an alternative script, it is important to review the consequences of the model's behavior following the script. Next, the client is asked to imagine reacting in the same manner as the model and to envision the consequences of his or her actions. In this way clients can provide information about how they believe the script may or may not be socially or personally acceptable to them. This process is repeated until the client accepts an alternative emotional script.

A male adolescent, Guido, was referred by his father because he was continually angry and fought with peers at least once a day. Guido was quite proud of his anger. He believed it was functional, despite several lost friendships and expulsions from four parochial high schools. The therapists easily convinced Guido that his anger was dysfunctional, given that his father almost always learned of the fights from the school authorities and punished him severely. However, Guido could not conceptualize any socially acceptable alternative. Fortunately, Guido was enamored with the *Godfather* movies. The therapist pointed out how Guido's behavior was similar to the behavior of Sonny Corleone. Like the character in the film, Guido got intensely angry, expressed his anger in a histrionic manner, and impulsively attacked his instigators. The therapist asked, "What happened to Sonny?" The client reported that because Sonny's enemies knew how he typically acted, they were able to provoke his anger and then ambush and kill him! "Well, you're just like Sonny! How long before the same thing happens to you?" the therapist responded. After examining how the client's and film character's behavior were similar, the therapist suggested that other models were available. Guido imagined himself reacting like the other son, Michael Corleone, who eventually became the new don. The senior don gave Michael some good advice. He said, "Never hate your enemies. It clouds your judgment." This character rarely reacted impulsively but thought through his reactions and never let others know what he felt. Guido identified with the character and was now able to conceptualize an alternative reaction. Therapy was highly successful after this intervention.

Of course, the value of using a gangster as a model for an adolescent boy may be questioned. After all, Michael Corleone was a violent man who eventually killed all his enemies! However, it is important that the client respects the model. We focused on prosocial aspects of the model's behavior—remaining calm and not letting others know what you are thinking until you decide how best to respond. We also downplayed the negative aspects of the model's behavior. Guido could always decide to avoid retaliation once he calmly thought through the situation.

In the case discussed above, we asked Guido how the character Michael Corleone would respond to an ongoing anger-provoking situation that Guido was facing. Then we asked if he could react the same way and if he thought the character's reaction was appropriate. Once Guido agreed that he could accept the new model, we had established an alternative script. With some clients, the behavior of three or four persons will have to be reviewed before an acceptable model is found.

> Jamil was an inner-city Black adolescent referred by the school psychologist because of his frequent conflicts with authority figures. School authorities were considering placing him in an out-of-district school for disruptive children. Jamil reported that his anger was justified since he believed that the white staff members at his school were racists. He was quite convincing, reporting situations in which the teachers used racial slurs and derogatory remarks about Jamil and other black students. Jamil's angry outbursts usually resulted in the teachers' and administrators' perceiving him to be violent and out-of-control. The therapist told Jamil that his anger and violent reactions gave the racist teachers an excuse to place him in a special school. His anger was, in fact, making it easy for them to ensure that Jamil did not get a high-quality education. Jamil agreed that his reactions were self-destructive. However, he reported that anger was the only reaction available to him. Any other reaction would fail to acknowledge the injustice committed by the transgressors.

The therapist asked Jamil if he knew of any persons or characters he thought responded to prejudice in a more productive, successful manner, that is, without losing control and acting impulsively to play into the hands of the tormentor. Jamil discussed several people and eventually reported a scene from the movie *Malcolm X*. In this scene, one of Malcolm's friends was seriously injured by the police for no reason. Malcolm led an orderly military march of the Black Muslims to the police station. All the Muslims stood at attention outside the police station while Malcolm confronted the police desk sergeant. Jamil said that Malcolm's behavior was intense but controlled. He did not act or speak in any manner that would give the police an excuse to retaliate violently. Jamil called this reaction *controlled anger*. The person experiencing it is reacting to a real injustice. It is a strong but not destructive emotion. The person can think clearly about the best course of action. Jamil decided he would use this scene from the film to model his own behavior. He rehearsed how Malcolm X might respond to his teachers' racist comments. He practiced responding directly, in a controlled voice, pointing out the insult that had been made without yelling or resorting to verbal abuse. Once Jamil agreed that his anger was disruptive and had discovered a socially acceptable script, we focused on how he could begin to respond with the new script. A therapeutic alliance to change his anger had been made.

The Motivational Syllogism

Once the therapist and client have successfully accomplished these steps, the therapist can continue with treatment of the clients' anger using any strategy that is mutually agreed upon. These strategies and steps constitute what we call the motivational syllogism. The first premise is: "My present anger is dysfunctional." The second premise is: "There is an alternative script that is more functional." The third premise is: "I can control which reaction I have to the activating event." The conclusion is: "I need to examine ways in which I can change my emotional reaction." We recommend reviewing the motivational syllogism at several points in therapy: the beginning of each therapy session, when the client reports a new anger episode or anger-provoking event, when the therapist introduces a new therapeutic task, and whenever the therapist switches therapeutic tasks. In this way the client is reminded of what was agreed upon earlier in therapy. These reviews strengthen the therapeutic alliance by reconfirming the agreement on the goals and tasks of therapy and thereby allow further interventions to proceed. Even the most well-researched and effective intervention is destined to fail if the client does not use it because she or he does not believe it is desirable to eliminate the anger. We believe interventions such as these, which are designed at increasing the motivation for change, hold great promise for helping angry clients.

Conclusions

The biggest mistake that we see practitioners make in treating anger is moving too quickly into active changes strategies. Without adequately preparing clients for treatment, initial attempts to change anger will often be met with resistance or, worse yet, anger at the therapist. A variety of strategies can be used in the preparatory phase of treatment. A good starting point almost always involves the deliberate use of empathy.

Throughout this chapter we have emphasized the motivational interviewing approach for those who have not decided to change their anger. This approach can be easily integrated into reviews of individual episodes of anger using the anger-episode model. The motivational interviewing style can also be used to provide feedback on standardized tests of anger. In using either of these strategies, the goal is to get the client to provide the arguments for change. Finally, practitioners may have to help clients conceptualize alternative emotional reactions to struggle and adversity that are different from typical angry reactions. This often involves the exploration of different scripts and role models.

19

A Comprehensive Treatment
Model for Anger Disorders

This chapter describes what we consider to be an ideal general approach for treating anger. We employed two strategies to devise this comprehensive approach. In chapter 16, we reviewed the anger treatment-outcome literature to uncover treatments with empirical support. However, our meta-analysis (DiGiuseppe & Tafrate, 2003) revealed that anger interventions are not as successful as are treatments for other disorders, namely anxiety and mood disorders. Based on the research reported in chapter 16, relaxation training, cognitive restructuring, problem solving, exposure to anger-eliciting stimuli, and learning new adaptive responses to stimuli are strategies with emerging empirical support. Throughout this book we reviewed the scientific research on anger and uncovered characteristics about the emotion that may important in treatment but have not yet been incorporated in treatment outcome research. Part of our comprehensive treatment model is based on these empirically identified characteristics of anger. Thus, we now address several anger-related issues to be considered when devising effective intervention programs.

Characteristics of Anger

Distinguishing Healthy From Problematic Anger Reactions

Anger is one of the most frequent of human emotions (Scherer & Wallbott, 1994). It is unlikely that we can achieve interventions that totally eliminate anger, despite Seneca's recommendation (Basore, 1958). Without the experience of anger or a closely related emotion, we could fail to recognize problems and take corrective action. Psychotherapy has traditionally relied on the dimensions of frequency, intensity, and duration for guidance in determining whether anger (or other emotions) is healthy or disturbed. Nevertheless, quantitative dimensions may sometimes fail to discriminate adaptive from maladaptive anger. Someone who is the victim of a frequent or enduring moral transgression may experience intense or frequent anger yet respond adaptively. Some theorists (Tangney, Hill-Barlow, Wagner, Marschall, Borenstein, et al., 1996) have suggested that the goals of anger discriminate best between adaptive and disturbed anger. Revenge or tension reduction will lead to maladaptive anger. The desire to correct a problem will likely lead to adaptive anger.

It is unclear how this qualitative characteristic correlates with frequency, intensity, and duration. Constructive goals refer to maintaining a friendship, maintaining or asserting authority, causing a change in the anger instigator's behavior, or resolving the problem. Malevolent goals refer to getting revenge or hurting the anger instigator. Selfish or fractious goals refer to getting the anger instigator to comply with one's wishes or letting off steam to feel better. Bowlby (1973) employs the phrase "anger of hope" for constructive anger and the phrase "anger of despair" for malevolent goals. People with secure emotional attachment styles, as defined by Bowlby, seem to have constructive goals, and therefore have more functional anger. People with anxious–ambiguous attachment style have a dysfunctional anger derived from malevolent goals, avoid active confrontation, and ruminate on hostile thoughts (Mikulincer, 1998). Such qualitative aspects of anger may provide more information concerning disturbance and clearer therapeutic goals. As noted earlier, angry clients see themselves as the victims of injustice. They will often reject the goal of totally eliminating their anger. Teaching angry clients the distinction between adaptive anger reactions and destructive anger may be a first step in change.

Motivation for Change

People feel little desire to change or control their anger. The only emotion people wish to change less is joy (Scherer & Wallbott, 1994). This feature of anger poses the greatest problem for practitioners. We often say that angry clients do not come for therapy; they come for supervision. They have tried and failed to change their bosses, coworkers, or mates. They come to us for advice on how to change their transgressors. Angry clients often have difficulty forming a therapeutic alliance because the therapist and client fail to agree on the goals of therapy. Therapists want to change their clients' anger, and clients want to change their instigators or get revenge.

As noted in chapter 17, most angry clients are in the precontemplative or contemplative stages of change. Unfortunately, the most frequently researched interventions (cognitive and behavioral interventions) are designed to target those in the action stage of change. Perhaps this explains why anger treatments fail to attain the magnitude of effect sizes seen in treatments for anxiety and depression. Anger-treatment researchers can learn much from studying other behaviors people are reluctant to change, such as addictions. As discussed in the previous chapter, we have found that W. Miller and Rollnick's (2002) motivational-interviewing model works well with angry clients. Initial sessions of anger treatment might focus on helping angry clients understand the destructive nature of their anger, explore ambivalence, and construct alternative emotions and behaviors. To date, no empirical outcome studies have appeared that use motivational interventions for anger.

Empathy

No one likes to hug a porcupine. People usually fail to elicit empathy from others when they express anger (Palfai & Hart, 1997). This suggests that since psychotherapists are people, they may often fail to experience empathy for angry clients. As mentioned in chapter 18, the deliberate use of empathy—trying to understand how the client is viewing the situation is often a productive starting point.

Approach and Impulsivity

Anger produces a stronger tendency to approach rather than avoid triggering events than do all emotions except joy (Scherer & Wallbott, 1994). This tendency to approach "anger triggers" often results in angry clients' engaging in self-defeating and destructive behaviors. Clients often need impulse-control strategies in anger treatment to prevent such destructive actions.

Close Interpersonal Relationships

People target most of their anger episodes at others they know well, like, or love. Anger occurs at home more often than at other places (Kassinove, Sukhodolsky, Tsytsarev, & Soloyova, 1997). Rarely do people become angry with strangers. Practitioners are more likely to confront anger in family-related problems more than in individual ones. However, the family- and marital-therapy literature fails to address anger. In preparing this chapter, we consulted the tables of contents and indexes of several influential marital- and family-therapy texts. Anger never appeared in the table of contents. Only 2 of the 20 books mentioned anger in the index. These entries reflected passing references to anger and not major discussions. Despite the ubiquity of anger in family-therapy sessions, we do not have a family systems literature to draw on for treatment implications. Robins and Novaco (1999) were the first authors to approach anger from a systemic perspective. Perhaps we should also employ a systems approach in the treatment of anger. This would mean including significant others in our assessment and at some point conducting conjoint-therapy sessions.

Damaged Interpersonal Relationships

People perceive anger as negatively affecting their interpersonal relationships more than any other emotion (Scherer & Wallbott, 1994). Succinctly put, anger damages interpersonal relationships. Angry clients are often embroiled in conflicts, and systemic analysis is required to understand the damage they have done in order to plan how to rebuild their social networks. Overcoming one's anger problems will not automatically rebuild the relationships damaged by anger. Perhaps angry people need to recognize and prepare to make restitution and rebuild their damaged relationships, the same way substance abusers in 12-step programs are recommended to do.

Like-Minded Peers

Those with problematic anger reactions often associate with others who share their acceptance of anger and its expression (Robins and Novaco, 1999). This may result in a peer environment that reinforces anger (and also aggression). Such a situation will likely support the angry person's belief that his or her anger is not a problem and will decrease the motivation for change. Successful treatment may involve helping the client become aware of the influence of their peer group and consider a change.

Self-Esteem

The clinical literature on anger reveals the popularity of the idea that low self-esteem is central to anger experiences. The connection between anger and self-esteem is also discussed in detail in chapter 8. Practitioners often target low self-esteem when attempting to treat anger. Baumeister, Smart, and Boden (1996) and our own search have failed to find any empirical evidence to support this idea. Anger does seem to follow perceived threats to high, unstable self-esteem (Baumeister, Smart, & Boden, 1996). High, unstable self-esteem refers to extremely positive self-evaluations that persist or rebound despite feedback from reality that they do not warrant such grandiosity. People experience anger and aggression against others when they believe they are better than others. Of course, high self-esteem does not always lead to anger and aggression. (Bushman & Baumeister, 1998). Anger also includes a greater experience of power or potency than the eliciting threat (Scherer & Wallbott, 1994). Most theorists believe that anger is associated with cognitions involving positive self-efficacy.

Only a few anger outcome studies included measures of self-esteem (DiGiuseppe & Tafrate, 2003). Even when large improvements in anger reduction are documented, measurements of self-esteem remained unchanged. The hypothesized connection between self-esteem and anger has remained unfounded, and successful anger treatments fail to change self-esteem. Perhaps the role of low self-esteem as a mediator of anger and a target of intervention should be abandoned until research supports any proposed mediating influence. However, high, unstable self-esteem should be addressed in treatment.

Forgiveness

Anger is a moral emotion. Angry episodes are often triggered by violations of moral codes and involve the perception of injustice or a grievance against oneself (Tedeschi & Nesler, 1993), and/or the perceptions of another's blameworthiness (Clore & Ortony, 1991; Clore, Ortnoy, Dienes, & Fujity, 1993). The cognitive component of anger often includes condemning others. Most mental health professionals have ignored this dimension of anger treatment. Forgiveness appears crucial to the treatment of anger because so much anger arises from condemning those who have trespassed against us.

A literature independent of psychotherapy has evolved on forgiveness (Enright, 2001). This literature was not included in our meta-analytic review because these studies do not include anger among their dependent measures. Rather, they assess changes on forgiveness (Enright & Fitzgibbons, 2000). Recent research supports the idea that forgiveness can be achieved in psychotherapy.

Proposed Ideal Treatment Components

The anger research literature and the results of our own and others' research reviews direct us to a comprehensive menu or package of anger treatments. We recommend the following components in an ideal treatment package for all types of anger disorders. Our recommendations are similar to Kassinove and Tafrate's (2002) stages of the treatment process.

Cultivate the Therapeutic Alliance

Anger does not stimulate empathy. Therefore, therapists need to validate angry clients' sense of transgression. Lack of practitioner empathy will negatively affect attaining agreement on the goals of therapy. Thus, we recommend that practitioners maintain a strong spirit of empathy during all sessions.

Address Motivation for Change

As mentioned above, people do not wish to change anger. An important aspect of the therapeutic alliance is agreement on the goals of therapy. Angry clients need to focus on the distinctions between functional and dysfunctional anger and become aware of the negative consequences for them of their dysfunctional anger. Conflict on the goals of treatment appears more likely to occur with angry clients than those with other affective excesses. Self-monitoring procedures and feedback from standardized tests will help angry clients realize how frequently they get angry and how often they reap the destructive consequences of anger.

Manage Physiological Arousal

Anger often causes immediate and high physiological arousal. Lowering the bodily tension before focusing on other aspects of the treatment will help the client attend to the interventions.

Foster Cognitive Change

Cognitive processes that increase perceptions of threat are targets of change. Cognitions concerning blame, unfairness, demandingness, resentment, and suspiciousness operate in anger experiences. Changing these cognitions will lead to emotional and behavioral change.

Implement Behavior Change

Angry clients often have deficient repertoires of behaviors and substantial automaticity for over-learned reactions. Learning and practicing new responses will introduce new reactions. We recommend that therapists employ some type of exposure interventions such as exposure to imaginal scenes of anger triggers or role-played anger triggers. These will help the person learn new, calmer responses to the eliciting stimuli. Angry clients can benefit from rehearsing new behaviors such as assertive responses to social conflict. A more in-depth discussion of the rationale for integrating exposure into treatment is presented in chapter 7.

Teach Relapse Prevention

Given the automaticity of anger, low motivation for change, the likelihood that anger-triggering events will prevail, the tendency to see one's anger as justified, and the impossibility of totally avoiding anger, we perceive the possibility of a relapse as high. Anger problems share many characteristics with substance abuse. Therefore, we believe that angry clients can benefit substantially from relapse-prevention training by learning how to react to lapses in their anger-control skills and prepare for future high-risk situations.

Additional Components for a Comprehensive Treatment

Forgiveness

Clients who present with a rigid focus on past injustices or attaining revenge may fail to make progress with the ideal treatment package. Their ruminations about past transgressions and desires for revenge will interfere with achieving a therapeutic alliance since their goal of staying focused on the past or obtaining revenge differs from the therapist's goal of anger reduction. The incorporation of forgiveness interventions that target the desire for revenge and the thoughts of condemnation of others will augment the treatment plan. Practitioners may wish to add forgiveness interventions to the cognitive component of anger treatment. Several successful outcome studies have appeared teaching forgiveness, and these interventions could be added to anger-control treatments.

Systemic Interventions

Clients who present with marital and/or family violence or conflict experience their anger in a family or systems context. Since people often aim their anger at significant others, we will often want to consider the social system or context in which the anger occurs. Such considerations may include having significant others provide assessment data on the client's anger or having significant others involved in some sessions.

Catalyzing Restitution and Reintegration

The embedded systemic effects of anger on interpersonal relationships may be stalled because family members may remain distant or estranged from the angry person. Angry clients may have destroyed interpersonal relationships and may have self-selected anger-supporting environments. Rebuilding relationships through positive caring will go a long way to encouraging systemic change.

Providing Environmental Supports

Angry clients may have created a support group that reinforces their anger. Clients who belong to social groups that encourage or support their anger may benefit from environmental change. Becoming aware of the social support for anger and attempting to avoid such groups may help further reduce anger.

Formatting the Therapy

If you wish to influence anger-driven aggression, structured and goal-directed treatments appear best. Practitioners may develop and use treatment manuals that ensure a structured treatment plan for each session and stick to the plan. Individual treatment formats may be preferred to group formats. If group treatment is employed, the therapist must pay careful attention to group members who may reinforce each other's antisocial or anger-provoking attitudes or behaviors.

There are several things missing from this chapter. The first is any discussion of psychopharmacological treatments for anger. We considered reviewing the literature in this area but decided against it because of space limitations and the disorganization of the field. Many different types of drugs have been used to treat people with anger problems, but most of these have been researched as interventions for aggression (Citrome, Nolan, & Volavka, 2004). These drugs include the selective serotonin reuptake inhibitors (SSRIs), which are widely used for depression and anxiety disorders. SSRIs have been tested to treat anger in patients with comorbid depression (Fava, Alpert, Nierenberg, Ghaemi, O'Sullivan, et al., 1996) or with Intermittent Explosive Disorder and personality disorders (Coccaro & Kavoussi, 1997). Also used are the mood stabilizers, which are actually anticonvulsive medications, and atypical antipsychotic medications. No one seems to know why these drugs work when they do. Presently, no drugs have been developed exclusively for anger problems. The SSRIs have been identified as affecting serotonin. Perhaps the SSRIs work for anxiety, depression, and anger because all three emotional problems rely on rumination, and the SSRIs may decrease rumination. Also, increases in serotonin have been shown to inhibit aggression. However, it is uncertain whether this helps clients' anger since research in this area measures aggression and rarely includes measures of anger. The primary neurotransmitter involved in the human RAGE system in the brain is Substance P. As of yet, no psychopharmacological agent has been developed that influences Substance P. As of this point, we appear to be a long way away from targeted and effective psychopharmacological treatments for anger.

As mentioned in chapter 15, several theorists developing anger taxonomies have now included the category of repressed anger, another area that has previously been neglected. As of now, we are uncertain which interventions may be most effective for repressed anger. Some emotional-awareness interventions would appear necessary, but so far we have no evidence as to what type of intervention would be most helpful here.

Conclusions

Presently many people in North America and possibly Australia and the United Kingdom receive anger treatment after some involvement with the criminal justice system. These interventions are often referred to as anger-management classes. These interventions rely heavily on a psycho-educational model and teach clients management skills in large groups with little opportunity for feedback on skill performance and individualized treatment. As we mentioned in chapter 16, research on anger interventions has been sparse. However, we know of almost no research on the effectiveness of anger-management classes, which are presently delivered to most people in anger treatment.

The idea of anger classes is acceptable to many people with anger problems because individuals mandated to take such classes come with such low motivation, and the application of the term *therapy* (absent from the course title) to their treatment somehow implies that they have a problem. We find that even in the small therapy groups that we run, clients refer to the meetings as classes. It appears that consumers are loath to admit that their anger problems require psychological treatments.

This focus on anger-management classes, the lack of an official anger diagnosis, and the fact that the majority of anger-treatment studies use high-anger college students as participants has led to a limited view of psychological treatments for anger problems. We have attempted to offer a preliminary list of interventions that will help practitioners develop individual treatment plans for their clients. However, we have avoided a treatment-manual approach and instead have offered a menu. The choices to be drawn from this menu should be based on adequate psychological assessments and case conceptualizations for individual clients. Each client will have several factors that have caused and maintained his or her anger. A treatment plan based on an understanding of these will most likely help the individual client. We like to echo the words of Arnold Lazarus, who thought that treatment was most effective when it included interventions from a wide range of modalities. We hope we have offered the reader at least the beginning of such a list.

20

Epilogue

Anger is certainly a common and universal human experience. Although our scientific knowledge concerning anger has lagged behind that of other emotional disorders, anger is nonetheless a common emotional excess that practitioners encounter in a wide range of treatment settings. For many individuals, difficulties with anger experiences have contributed to significant loss and suffering. We believe that the time has come to conceptualize anger as a legitimate clinical problem.

Perhaps a logical first step in improving our understanding of anger would be a greater emphasis on descriptive investigations of the phenomenon. This might include epidemiological investigations concerning the range of anger experiences, as well as baseline data regarding the characteristics of anger episodes such as intensity, frequency, duration, physical activation patterns, expressive patterns, and outcomes connected with anger. Another important area would be a greater understanding of those people who are effective in using anger to change their environment or improve their relationships. We are reminded of Abraham Maslow's idea of "growth tips statistics"—the study of people who function well. With the greater emphasis on positive psychology in this century perhaps we will see investigations of how people use anger arousal wisely. From this we may better learn what to teach our dysfunctionally angry clients. Epidemiological research on this topic was begun by Gates (1926), Meltzer (1933), Averill (1982) and more recently Kassinove, Sukhodolsky, Tsytsarev, and Soloyova (1997).

On the opposite side, descriptive research on anger has rarely been conducted on clinical samples. A greater understanding of how anger manifests itself in different diagnostic and clinical groups would also add to our current knowledge, as would greater attention to cultural differences in the experience and expression of anger. A clearer conceptualization of the distinction between everyday anger experiences and anger that may be regarded as a clinical problem is still necessary. Also, it is important to know the number and type of comorbid disorders in those with disturbed anger. Studies that assess the whole range of psychopathology in those who come for help with anger problems would increase our understanding of the range of disturbances typically found among angry patients.

In spite of what seems to be an obvious connection, the role of anger in aggressive behaviors is still poorly understood. Basic questions remain regarding distinctions between instrumental and reactive forms of aggression, and whether emotion can really be taken out of the equation. Even if anger has a significant function in most forms of aggression, where exactly in the chain of events does anger fit in? This question may be more than academic, as professionals across different settings struggle with the importance of anger in criminal offenses. Can anger-control skills reduce certain acts of aggression, such as intimate partner violence, and should such skills be incorporated into rehabilitation or prevention programs? Also, as hypothesized more than 2,000 years ago, by the Roman stoic philosopher Seneca, anger may be a contributing factor in larger scale conflicts and atrocities. Surprisingly, the study of anger experiences in those involved in such acts of violence has remained almost completely unexplored by social psychologists and sociologists.

Recognition of anger in our present diagnostic system is probably the single most important issue likely to influence growth in this area. Diagnostic criteria would allow for further research and refinements in conceptualization. In addition, diagnostic inclusion would foster greater attention to the topic in behavioral science textbooks and graduate training programs.

While emerging empirical support for several interventions exists, it seems unlikely that clinical breakthroughs can occur without greater understanding of anger experiences and some type of common conceptualization. The development of treatments would certainly be enhanced by epidemiological investigations and some preliminary agreement of what disordered anger looks like. Whereas a number of promising interventions have been identified, a wide range of potentially useful strategies have not yet been investigated. At this stage, lack of empirical support does not mean lack of effectiveness, just that more research attention is required. Most, if not all, anger treatment studies evaluate the efficacy of cognitive behavioral interventions. We find it interesting that very few studies exist from other theoretical orientations. Clearly there is a need to expand the number of treatment options that can be used to treat dysfunctional anger, and we encourage others from different perspectives to do research in this area.

Very little is known about the origins of anger. How does this emotion develop in infants, children, and adolescents? What learning and family-systems factors contribute to the development of dysfunctional anger? How do we learn it and from whom? Answers to such questions could lead to prevention programs.

We hope that this book helps address some of the important history of anger research and the current challenges practitioners and researchers face. Our primary purpose is to spark scientific inquiry and debate about anger disorders, and we invite readers to participate in this mission. We certainly hope that as our knowledge increases, much that has been written in this volume will change over the years.

References

Abelson, R. (1981). The psychological status of script concepts. *American Psychologist, 36,* 715–729.

Abraham, K. (1927). *Selected papers on psychoanalysis* (D. Bryan & A. Strachey, Trans.). Honolulu, HI: Hogarth Press.

Agnew, R. (1992) An empirical test of general strain theory. *Criminology, 30*(4), 475–499.

Ahmed, A.G., DiGiuseppe, R. A., McDermut, W., & Zimmerman, M. (2005). *Axis I comorbidity in outpatients with angry symptoms.* Paper presented at the symposium The Clinical Face of Anger: Clinical Presentation, Comorbidity and Treatment, Annual Convention for the Association for Behavior and Cognitive Therapies, Washington, DC.

Akiskal, H. S. (1991). Subaffective disorders: Dysthymic, cyclothymic, and bipolar II disorders in the "borderline" realm. *Psychiatric Clinics of North America, 4,* 25–46.

Alberti, R. E., & Emmons, M. L. (2001). *Your perfect right.* Atascadero, CA: Impact.

Alschuler, C. F., & Alschuler, A. S. (1984). Developing healthy responses to anger: The counselor's role. *Journal of Counseling and Development, 63,* 26–29.

American Psychiatric Association (1980). *Diagnostic and statistical manual of mental disorders* (3rd ed.). Washington, DC: American Psychiatric Association.

American Psychiatric Association (1987). *Diagnostic and statistical manual of mental disorders* (3rd ed., rev.). Washington, DC: American Psychiatric Association.

American Psychiatric Association (1994). *Diagnostic and statistical manual of mental disorders* (4th ed.). Washington, DC: American Psychiatric Association.

American Psychiatric Association (2000). *Diagnostic and statistical manual of mental disorders* (4th ed., text revision). Washington, DC: American Psychiatric Association.

Amrhein, P. C., Miller, W. R., Yahne, C. E., Palmer, M., & Fulcher, L. (2003). Client commitment language during motivational interviewing predicts drug use outcomes. *Journal of Consulting and Clinical Psychology, 71,* 862–878.

Anastasia, G. (1991). *Blood and honor: Inside the Scarfo mob—the Mafia's most violent family.* New York: Morrow.

Anderson, C. A., & Bushman, B. J. (2002). Human aggression. *Annual Review of Psychology, 53*(1), 2002, 27–51.

Anderson, E. (1994, May). The code of the streets. *Atlantic Monthly, 273* (5), 81–94.

Anderson, K., Cooper, H., & Okamura, L. (1997). Individual differences and attitudes toward rape: A meta-analytic review. *Personal and Social Psychology Bulletin, 23*(3), 295–315.

Anderson, R. N., & Smith, B. L. (2003). *Deaths: Leading cause for 2001. National vital statistics reports 52*(9). Washington, DC: Centers for Disease Control.

Apter, A., Bleich, A., Plutchik, R., Mendelsohn, S., & Tyano, S. (1988). Suicidal behavior, depression and conduct disorder in hospitalized adolescents. *Journal of the American Academy of Child and Adolescent Psychiatry, 27*, 696–699.

Aristotle. (1943). Nicomachean ethics. In L. R. Loomis (Ed.), *On man in the universe: Metaphysics, parts of animals, ethics, politics, poetics* (pp. 85–245). New York: W. L. Black.

Aristotle. (1963). *Rhetoric,* edited and with a commentary by Edward Meredith Cope. New York: Arno Press.

Atkinson, C., & Polivy, J. (1976). Effects of delay, attack and retaliation on state depression and anxiety. *Journal of Abnormal Psychology, 85*(6), 570–576.

Ausberger, D. (1986). An existential approach to anger-management training. *Journal of Psychology and Christianity, 5*, 25–29.

Averill, J. R. (1975). A semantic atlas of emotional concepts. *JSAS Catalog of Selected Documents in Psychology, 5*, 330. (Ms. No. 421).

Averill, J. R. (1979). Anger. In W. Howe & R. Dienstlier (Eds.), *Nebraska symposium on motivation* (Vol. 26, pp. 1–80). Lincoln, NE: University of Nebraska Press.

Averill, J. R. (1980). A constructivist view of emotion. In R. Plutchik & H. Kellerman (Eds.), *Theories of emotion* (Vol. 1, pp. 305–340). San Diego, CA: Academic Press.

Averill, J. R. (1982). *Anger and aggression: An essay on emotion.* New York: Springer-Verlag.

Averill, J. R. (1983). Studies on anger and aggression: Implications for theories on emotion. *American Psychologist, 38*, 1145–1160.

Averill, J. R. (1993). Illusions of anger. In R. B. Felson & J. T. Tedeschi (Eds.). *Aggression and violence: A social interactionists perspective.* Washington, DC: American Psychological Association.

Awalt, R. M., & Reilly, P. M. (1997). The angry patient: An intervention for managing anger in substance abuse treatment. *Journal of Psychoactive Drugs, 29*, 353–358.

Ax, A. (1953). The physiological differentiation between fear and anger in humans. *Psychosomatic Medicine, 15*, 433–432.

Babcock, J. C., Costa, D., Green, C. E., & Eckhardt, C. I. (2004). What situations induce intimate partner violence? A reliability and validity study of the Proximal Antecedents to Violent Episodes (PAVE) scale. *Journal of Family Psychology, 18*(3), 433–442.

Babcock, J. C., Green, C. E., & Robie, C. (2004). Does batterers' treatment work? A meta-analytic review of domestic violence treatment. *Clinical Psychology Review, 23*, 1023–1053.

Bandura, A. (1973). *Aggression: A social learning analysis.* Englewood Cliffs, NJ: Prentice-Hall.

Bandura, A. (1977). Self-efficacy: Toward a unifying theory of behavior change. *Psychological Review, 84,* 191–215.

Barefoot, J. (1992). Developments in the measurement of hostility. In H. Friedman (Ed.), *Hostility, coping, and health* (pp. 13–31). Washington, DC: American Psychological Association.

Barkley, R. A. (1996). Attention-deficit/hyperactivity disorder. In E. J. Mash & R. A. Barkley (Eds.), *Child psychopathology* (pp. 63–112). New York: Guilford.

Barkow, J., Cosmides, L., & Toobey, J. (1992). *The adapted mind: Evolutionary psychology and the generation of culture.* New York: Oxford University Press.

Barlow, D. H. (1988). *Anxiety and its disorders: The nature and treatment of anxiety and panic.* New York: Guilford Press.

Barlow, D. H. (1991). Disorders of emotion. *Psychological Inquiry, 2*(1), 58–71.

Barlow, D. H., Rapee, R. M., & Brown, T. A. (1992). Behavioral treatment of generalized anxiety disorder. *Behavior Therapy, 23*(4), 551–570.

Barratt, E. S. (1991). Measuring and predicting aggression within the context of a personality theory. *Journal of Neuropsychiatry and Clinical Neurosciences, 3*(2), S35–S39.

Barrett, C., & DiGiuseppe, R. A. (2001). *Does high or low self-esteem induce anger? A state induction experiment with foster care adolescents.* Poster session presented at the 35th annual convention of the Association for the Advancement of Behavior Therapy, Philadelphia, PA.

Bartlett, S. J. (2005). *The pathology of man: A study of human evil.* Springfield, IL: Charles C. Thomas.

Basore, J. W. (1958). *Seneca: Moral essays. Vol. 1.* Cambridge, MA: Harvard University Press.

Baumeister, R. F., Bratslavsky, E., Muraven, M., & Tice, D. (1998). Ego depletion: Is the active self a limited resource? *Journal of Personality & Social Psychology, 74*(5), 1252–1265.

Baumeister, R. F., Bushman, B. J., & Campbell, W. K. (2000). Self-esteem, narcissism, and aggression: Does violence result from low self-esteem or from threatened egotism? *Current Directions in Psychological Science, 9*(1), 26–29.

Baumeister, R. F., Smart, L., & Boden, J. (1996). Relation of threatened egotism to violence and aggression: The dark side of high self-esteem. *Psychological Review, 103,* 5–33.

Baumeister, R. F. (1997). *Evil: Inside human cruelty and violence.* New York: W. H. Freeman.

Baumeister, R. F. (2003). Ego depletion and self-control failure: A resource model of self-control. *Alcoholism: Clinical and Experimental Research, 27*(2), 281–284.

Baumeister, R. F., & Boden, J. M. (1998). Aggression and the self: High self-esteem, low self-control, and ego threat. In R. G. Geen & E. Donnerstein (Eds.). *Human aggression: Theories, research, and implications for social policy.* New York: Academic Press.

Baumeister, R. F., Catanese, K. R., & Wallace, H. M. (2002). Conquest by force: A narcissistic reactance theory of rape and sexual conquest. *Review of General Psychology, 6*(1), 92–135.

Beck, A. T. (1967). *Depression: Causes and treatment.* Philadelphia, PA: University of Pennsylvania Press.

Beck, A. T. (1976). *Cognitive therapy and the emotional disorders.* New York: International Universities Press.

Beck, A. T. (1987). *Beck Depression Inventory: Manual.* San Antonio, TX: The Psychological Corporation.

Beck, A. T. (1996). *Beck Depression Inventory 2: Manual.* San Antonio, TX: The Psychological Corporation.

Beck, A. T. (1999). *Prisoners of hate: The cognitive basis of anger, hostility, and violence.* New York: Harper Collins.

Beck, A. T., & Emery, G. (1985). *Anxiety disorders and phobia: A cognitive perspective.* New York: Basic Books.

Beck, A. T., Freeman, A., Pretzer, J., Davis, D. D., Fleming, B., Ottaviani, R., et al. (1990). *Cognitive therapy of personality disorders.* New York: Guilford Press.

Beck, A. T., & Hurvich, M. S. (1959). Psychological correlates of depression, I. Frequency of "masochistic" dream content in a private practice sample. *Psychosomatic Medicine, 21,* 50–55.

Beck, J. G., & Barlow, D. H. (1984). Current conceptualizations of sexual desire: A review and alternative perspective. *Clinical Psychology Review, 4,* 363–378.

Beck, J. G., & Bosman, A. W. (1995). Gender differences in sexual desire: The effects of anger and anxiety. *Archives of Sexual Behavior, 24*(6), 595–612.

Beck, R., & Fernandez, E. (1998). Cognitive-behavioral self-regulation of the frequency, duration, and intensity of anger. *Journal of Psychopathology and Behavior Assessment, 20*(3), 217–229.

Begotka, A. M., Woods, D. W., Wetterneck, C. T. (2004). The relationship between experiential avoidance and the severity of trichotillomania in a nonreferred sample. *Journal of Behavior Therapy and Experimental Psychiatry, 35*(1), 17–24.

Berg-Cross, L. (1993). A practitioner's guide to the psychological and psychopharmacological relationship between anxiety and depression. *Psychotherapy in Private Practice, 12*(3), 59–71.

Berkowitz, L. (1962). *Aggression: A social psychological analysis.* New York: McGraw-Hill.

Berkowitz, L. (1983). Aversively stimulated aggression: Some parallels and differences in research with animals and humans. *American Psychologist, 38*(11), 1135–1144.

Berkowitz, L. (1990). On the formation and regulation of anger and aggression: A cognitive-neoassociationistic analysis. *American Psychologist, 45*(4), 494–503.

Berkowitz, L. (1993). Towards a general theory of anger and emotional aggression: Implications of the cognitive-neoassociationistic perspective for the analysis of anger and other emotions. In R. W. Wyer & T. K. Srull (Eds.), *Perspectives on anger and emotion* (Vol. 5, pp. 1–46). Hillsdale, NJ: Lawrence Erlbaum.

Berkowitz, L. (2003). Affect, aggression and antisocial behavior. In R. J. Davidson, K. R. Scherer, H. H. Goldsmith (Eds.). *Handbook of affective sciences* (pp. 804–823). New York: Oxford University Press.

Berkowitz, L., & Harmon-Jones, E. (2004). Toward an understanding of the determinants of anger. *Emotion, 4*(2), 107–130.

Berman, M., E., Fallon, A. E., & Coccaro, E. F. (1998). The relationship between personality psychopathology and aggressive behavior in research volunteer. *Journal of Abnormal Psychology, 107,* 651–658.

Biaggio, M. K., & Goodwin, W. H. (1987). Relation of depression to anger and hostility constructs. *Psychological Reports, 61,* 87–90.

Bibring, E. (1953). Mechanisms of depression. In P. Greenacre (Ed.), *The affective disorders* (pp.13–48). New York: International Universities Press.

Bies, R. J., & Tripp, T. M. (2001). A passion for justice: The rationality and morality of revenge. In R. Cropanzano (Ed.), *Justice in the workplace: From theory to practice, Vol. 2. Series in applied psychology* (pp. 197–208). Mahwah, NJ: Erlbaum.

Bifulco, A. T., Brown, G. W., & Harris, T. O. (1987). Childhood loss of parent, lack of adequate parental care and adult depression: A replication. *Journal of Affective Disorders, 2*(2), 115–128.

Bing, L. (1991). *Do or die.* New York: Harper Collins.

Blackburn, R. (1993). *The psychology of criminal conduct: Theory, research, and practice.* New York: Wiley & Sons.

Blackburn, I. M., Lyketsos, G., & Tsiantis, J. (1979). The temporal relationship between hostility and depressed mood. *British Journal of Social and Clinical Psychology, 18,* 227–235.

Blashfield, R. K., Sprock, J., & Fuller, A. K. (1990). Suggested guidelines for including or excluding categories in the DSM-IV. *Comprehensive Psychiatry, 31*(1), 15–19.

Blatt, S. J., Cornell, C. E., & Eshkol, E. (1993). Personality style, differential vulnerability, and clinical course in immunological and cardiovascular disease. *Clinical Psychology Review, 13,* 421–450.

Bordin, E. S. (1979). The generalizability of the psychoanalytic concept of the working alliance. *Psychotherapy: Theory, Research, and Practice, 16,* 252–260.

Born, L., & Steiner, M. (1999). Irritability: The forgotten dimension of female-specific mood disorder. *Archives of Women's Mental Health, 2,* 153–167.

Bornstein, R. F., Greenberg, R. P., Leone, D. R., & Galley, D. J. (1990). Defense mechanism correlates of orality. *Journal of the American Academy of Psychoanalysis, 18,* 654–666.

Bowlby, J. (1961). Childhood mourning and its implications for psychiatry. *American Journal of Psychiatry, 118,* 67–93.

Bowlby, J. (1973). *Attachment and loss.* New York: Basic Books.

Bosman, A. W., & Beck, J. G. (1991). Covariation of sexual desire and arousal: The effects of anger and anxiety. *Archives of Sexual Behavior, 20,* 47–60.

Bromberg, P. M. (1986). The mirror and the mask: On narcissism and psychoanalytic growth. In A. P. Morrison (Ed.), *Essential papers on narcissism.* New York: New York University Press.

Brondolo, E., DiGiuseppe, R., & Tafrate, R. C. (1997). Exposure-based treatment for anger problems: Focus on the feeling. *Cognitive & Behavioral Practice, 4*(1), 75–98.

Bronstein, P. M. (1988). Socially mediated learning in male Betta splendens: III. Rapid acquisition. *Aggressive-Behavior, 14*(6), 415–424.

Brooks, J. S., Whiteman, M. M., & Finch, S. (1992). Childhood aggression, adolescent delinquency and drug use: A longitudinal study. *Journal of Genetic Psychology, 153*(4), 369–383.

Brown, G. W., & Rutter, M. (1966). The measurement of family activities and relationships: A method study. *Human Relations, 19,* 241–263.

Brown, N. W. (1998). *The destructive narcissistic pattern.* Westport: Praeger.

Brown, S. A., Christiansen, B. A., & Goldman, M. S. (1987). The Alcohol Expectancy Questionnnaire: An instrument for the assessment of adolescent and adult alcohol expectancies. *Journal of Studies on Alcohol, 48*(5), 483–491.

Brownmiller, S. (1975). *Against our wills: Men, women, and rape.* New York: Simon & Schuster.

Buck, R. (1988). *Human motivation and emotion* (2nd ed.). New York: John Wiley and Sons.

Buie, D. H., & Adler, G. (1973). The misuses of confrontation in the psychotherapy of borderline cases. In G. Adler & P. G. Myerson (Eds.), *Confrontation in Psychotherapy* (pp. 123–146). New York: Science House.

Burns, J. W., Evon, D. A., & Strain-Saloum, C. (1999). Repressed anger and patterns of cardiovascular, self-report and behavioral response: effects of harassment. *Journal of Psychosomatic Research, 47*(6), 569–581.

Bushman, B. J. (2004). The effects of expressing aggression. Paper presented at the Anger and Aggression Conference, University of Arkansas, [CITY].

Bushman, B. J., & Baumeister, R. (1998). Threatened egotism, narcissism self-esteem, and direct and misplaced aggression: Does self-love or self-hate lead to violence? *Journal of Personality and Social Psychology, 75*(1) 219–229.

Bushman, B. J., & Anderson, C. A. (2001). Is it time to pull the plug on hostile versus instrumental aggression dichotomy? *Psychological Review, 108*(1), 273–279.

Bushman, B. J., & Baumeister, R. F. (1998). Threatened egotism, narcissism, self-esteem, and direct and misplaced aggression: Does self-love or self-hate lead to violence. *Journal of Personality and Social Psychology, 75*(1), 219–229.

Bushman, B. J., Baumeister, R. F., & Stack, A. D. (1999). Catharsis, aggression, and persuasive influence: Self-fulfilling or self-defeating prophecies? *Journal of Personality and Social Psychology, 76*(3), 367–376.

Buss, A. H. (1961). *The psychology of aggression.* New York: Wiley.

Buss, A. H., & Durkee, A. (1957). An inventory for assessing different kinds of hostility. *Journal of Consulting Psychology, 21,* 343–349.

Buss, A. H., & Perry, M. (1992). The aggression questionnaire. *Journal of Personality and Social Psychology, 63*(3), 452–459.

Butow, P. N., Hiller, J. E., Price, M. A., Thackway, S. V. Kricker, A., & Tennant, C. C. (2000). Epidemiological evidence for a relationship between life events, coping style, and personality factors in the development of breast cancer. *Journal of Psychosomatic Research, 49,* 169–181.

Byrne, M., & Carr, A. (2000). Depression and power in marriage. *Journal of Family Therapy, 22,* 408–427.

Cairns, R. B., Peterson, G., & Neckerman, H. J. (1988). Suicidal behavior in aggressive adolescents. *Journal of Clinical Child Psychology, 17,* 298–309.

Cannella, C., Fuller, J. R., & DiGiuseppe, R. A. (2005). *Can anger be a disorder distinct from depression?* Manuscript submitted for publication.

Caplan, N. (1970). The new ghetto man: A review of recent empirical studies. *Journal of Social Issues, 26,* 59–73.

Caprara, G. V., Cinanni, V., D'Impario, G., Passerini, S., Renzi, P., & Travaglia, G. (1985). Indicators of impulsive aggression: Present status of research on the irritability and emotional susceptibility scales. *Personality and Individual Differences, 6*(6), 665–674.

Carlson, N. R. (2003). *Physiology of behavior* (8th ed.). Boston: Allyn and Bacon.

Carmony, T. M., & DiGiuseppe, R. A. (2003). Cognitive induction of anger and depression: The role of power, attribution, and gender. *Journal of Rational, Emotive, and Cognitive Behavior Therapies, 21*(2), 105–118.

Carraher, S. M., & Michael, K. W. (1999). An examination of the dimensionality of the Vengeance Scale in an entrepreneurial multinational organization. *Psychological Reports, 85*(2), 687–688.

Carroll, C. E. (2001). Anger at work: The influence of contextual and intrapersonal factors on the evaluation of the expression of anger in a work context. *Dissertation Abstracts International, Section B. The Sciences & Engineering, 61*(10-B), 5605.

Cattell, R. (1975). *The 16 personality factor questionnaire.* Champagne, IL: Institute for Personality and Ability Testing.

Cattell, R., Cattell, A. K., & Cattell, H.E.P. (1994). *The 16 personality factor questionnaire* (5th ed.). Champagne, IL: Institute for Personality and Ability Testing.

Cavanaugh, M. M., & Gelles, R. J. (2005). The utility of male domestic violence offender typologies. *Journal of Interpersonal violence, 20,* 155–166.

Chang, E. C., D'Zurilla, T. J., & Sanna, L. J. (Eds.) (2004). *Social problem solving.* Washington, DC: American Psychological Association.

Chapman, A. L., Specht, M., & Cellucci, T. (2005). Borderline personality disorder and deliberate self-harm: Does experiential avoidance play a role? *Suicide and Life-Threatening Behavior, 35*(4), 388–399.

Chase, K. A. (1999). Categorizing partner violent men within the reactive-proactive typology model: A categorization system development and evaluation project (proactive aggressors, reactive aggressors, domestic violence). *Dissertation Abstracts International, Section B. The Sciences and Engineering, 60*(6-B), 2935.

Chemtob, C. M., Novaco, R. W., Hamada, R. S., & Gross, D. M. (1997). Cognitive-behavioral treatment for severe anger in posttraumatic stress disorder. *Journal of Consulting and Clinical Psychology, 65,* 184–189.

Chemtob, C. M., Novaco, R. W., Hamada, R. S., Gross, D. M., & Smith, G. (1997). Anger regulation deficits in combat related posttraumatic stress disorder. *Journal of Traumatic Stress, 10,* 17–26.

Chesney, M. A. (1985). Anger and hostility: Future implications for behavioral medicine. In M. A. Chesney & R. H. Rosenman (Eds.), *Anger and hostility in behavioral disorders.* Washington, DC: Hemisphere.

Choquet, M., & Menke, H. (1989). Suicidal thoughts during early adolescents: Prevalence, associated troubles and help seeking behavior. *Acta Psychiatrica Scandinavia, 81,* 170–177.

Christensen, M. J., Brayden, R. M., Dietrich, M. S., McLoughlin, F. J., Sherrod, K. B., & Altemeier, W. A. (1994). The prospective assessment of self-concept in neglectful and physically abuse low-income mothers. *Child Abuse and Neglect, 18,* 225–232.

Citrome, L., Nolan, K. A., & Volavka, J. (2004). Science-based treatment of aggression and agitation. In D. H. Fishbein (Ed.). *The science, treatment, and prevention of antisocial behaviors: Evidence-based practice* (pp. 11–1 to 11–32). Kingston, NJ: Civic Research Institute.

Cleckley, H. (1976). *The mask of sanity* (5th ed.). St. Louis, MO: Mosby.

Clore, G. L., & Centerbar, D. B. (2004). Analyzing anger: How to make people mad. *Emotion, 4*(2), 139–144.

Clore, G. L., & Ortony, A. (1991). What more is there to emotional concepts than prototypes? *Journal of Personality and Social Psychology, 60,* 48–50.

Clore, G. L., Ortony, A., Dienes, B., & Frujity, F. (1993). Where does anger dwell? In R. W. Wyer & T. K. Srull (Eds.), *Perspectives on anger and emotion* (Vol. 5, pp.1–46). Hillsdale, NJ: Lawrence Erlbaum.

Cloward, R. A., & Ohlins, L. E. (1960). *Delinquency and opportunity: A theory of delinquent gangs.* Glencoe, IL: Free Press.

Coccaro, E. F. (1992). Impulsive aggression and central serotonergic systems functioning in humans: An example of a dimensional brain-behavior relationship. *International Clinical Psychopharmacology, 7*, 3–12.

Coccaro, E. F. (2004). Intermittent explosive disorder and impulsive aggression: The time for serious study is now. *Current Psychiatry Reports, 6*, 1–2.

Coccaro, E. F., Harvey, P. D., Kupsaw-Lawrence, E., Herbert, J., & Bernstein, D. P. (1991). Development of neuropharmacologically based behavioral assessment of impulsive aggressive behavior. *Journal of Neuropsychiatry and Clinical Neurosciences, 3*(2), 544–551.

Coccaro, E. F., & Kavoussi, R. J. (1997). Fluoxetine and impulsive aggressive behavior in personality-disordered subjects. *Archives of General Psychiatry, 54*(12), 1081–1088.

Coccaro, E. F., Kavoussi, R. J., Berman, M., & Lish, J. (1998). Intermittent explosive disorder revised: Development, reliability, and validity of criteria. *Comprehensive Psychiatry, 39*(6), 368–376.

Cochrane, N. (1975). The role of aggression in the pathogenesis of depressive illness. *British Journal of Medical Psychology, 48*, 113–130.

Coid, J. W. (1993). An affective syndrome in psychopaths with borderline personality disorder? *British Journal of Psychiatry, 162*, 641–650.

Colder, C. R., & Stice, E. (1998). A longitudinal study of the interactive effects of impulsivity and anger on adolescent problem behavior. *Journal of Youth and Adolescence, 27*, 255–274.

Cohen, J. (1977). *Statistical power analysis for the behavior sciences* (Rev. ed.). New York: Academic Press.

Connor, D. E. (2002). *Aggression and antisocial behavior in children and adolescents: Research and treatment.* New York: Guilford.

Conoley, J., Impara, J., & Murphy, L. (Eds.). (1995). The twelfth mental measurements yearbook. Lincoln, NE: Buros Institute of Mental Measurements.

Cooper, A. M. (1986). Narcissism. In A. P. Morrison (Ed.), *Essential papers on narcissism.* New York: New York University Press.

Costa, P., & McCrae, R. (1994). The stability of personality: Observation and evaluations. *Current directions in psychological science, 3*(6), 173–175.

Cowdry, R. W., & Gardner, D. L. (1988). Pharmacotherapy of borderline personality disorder: alprazolam, carbamazepine, trifluoperazine and tranylcypromine. *Archives of General Psychiatry, 45*, 111–119.

Cramerus, M. (1990). Adolescent anger. *Bulletin of the Menninger Clinic, 54*(4), 512–523.

Creer, T. L., Hitzing, E. W., Schaeffer, R. W. (1966). Classical conditioning of reflexive fighting. *Psychonomic Science, 4*(3), 89–90.

Crick, N. R., & Bigbee, M. A. (1998). Relational and overt forms of peer victimization: A multi-informant approach. *Journal of Consulting and Clinical Psychology, 66*(2), 337–347.

Crick, N. R., & Dodge, K. A. (1994). A review and reformulation of social information-processing mechanisms in children's social adjustment. *Psychological Bulletin, 115* (1), 74–101.

Crosby, F. (1976). A model of egoistic relative deprivation. *Psychological Review, 83*, 85–113.

Cullari, S. (1994). Levels of anger in psychiatric inpatients and normal subjects. *Psychological Reports, 75*, 1163–1168.

Dalrup, R. J., Beutler, L. E., Engle, D., & Greenberg, L. S. (1988). *Focused expressive psychotherapy.* New York: Guilford.

Damasio, A. R. (1994). *Descartes' error: Emotions, reason and the human brain.* New York: Grosset/Putnam Books.

Danesh, H. B. (1977). Anger and fear. *American Journal of Psychiatry, 134,* 1109–1112.

Darcangelo, S. M. (1997). Psychological and personality correlates of the Massachusetts Treatment Centre classification system for rapists. *Dissertation Abstracts International, Section B. The Sciences and Engineering, 58*(4-B), 2115.

Darwin, C. (1965). *The expression of emotion in man and animals* (K. Lorenz, Ed.). Chicago: University of Chicago Press. (Original work published in 1872)

Date, A. L., & Ronan, G. F. (2000). An examination of attitudes and behaviors presumed to mediate partner abuse. *Journal of Interpersonal Violence, 15,* 1140–1155.

Davey, L., Day, A., & Howells, K. (2005) Anger, over-control, and serious violent offending. *Aggression and Violent Behavior, 10*(5), 624–635.

Davidson, K., Stuhr, J., & Chambers, L. (2000). Constructive anger as a stress buffer. In K. D. Craig & K. S. Dobson (Eds.), *Stress, vulnerability and reactivity.* Thousand Oaks, CA: Sage.

Davidson, R. J., Scherer, K. R., & Goldsmith, H. H. (Eds.). (2003). *Handbook of affective sciences.* New York: Oxford University Press.

Davies, J. C. (1962). Toward a theory of revolution. *American Sociological Review, 27,* 5–19.

Davison, G. C., Navarre, S. G., & Vogel, R. S. (1995). The articulated thoughts in simulated situations paradigm: A think-aloud approach to cognitive assessment. *Current Direction in Psychological Sciences, 4,* 29–33.

Deffenbacher, J. (1993). General anger: Characteristics and clinical implications. *Psicolgia Conductual, 1*(1), 49–67.

Deffenbacher, J. (1994). Anger reduction: Issues, assessment, and intervention strategies. In A. W. Siegman & T. W. Smith (Eds.), *Anger, hostility and the heart* (pp. 239–269). Hillsdale, NJ: Erlbaum.

Deffenbacher, J. (1997). *Styles of anger expression and related consequences.* Unpublished manuscript, Colorado State University.

Deffenbacher, J. (1999). Cognitive-behavioral conceptualization and treatment of anger. *Journal of Clinical Psychology, 55*(3), 295–309.

Deffenbacher, J. (2000, August). *Characteristics of individuals high in driving anger: Prevention and intervention.* Paper presented at the 108th annual convention of the American Psychological Association, Washington, DC.

Deffenbacher, J., Oetting, E., Lynch, R., & Morris, C. (1996). The expression of emotion and its consequences. *Behaviour Research and Therapy, 34*(7), 575–590.

Deffenbacher, J., Oetting, E., Thwaites, G., Lynch, R., Baker, D., Stark, R., et al. (1996). State trait anger theory and the utility of the trait anger scale. *Journal of Counseling Psychology, 43*(2), 131–148.

Deffenbacher, J. L. & Deffenbacher, D. M. (2003). Where is the anger in introductory and abnormal psychology texts? *Teaching of Psychology, 30,* 65–67.

Deffenbacher, J. L., Filetti, L. B., Lynch, R. S., Dahlen, E. R., Oetting, E. R. (2002). Cognitive behavioral treatment of high anger drivers. *Behaviour Research and Therapy, 40*(8), 895–910.

Deffenbacher, J. L., Filetti, L. B., Richards, T. L., Lynch, R. S., & Oetting, E. R. (2003). Characteristics of two groups of angry drivers. *Journal of Counseling Psychology, 50*(2), 123–132.

Deffenbacher, J. L., & McKay, M. (2000). *Overcoming situational and general anger: Client manual.* Oakland, CA: New Harbinger.

Deffenbacher, J. L., Petrilli, R. T., Lynch, R. S., Oetting, E. R., & Swaim, R. C. (2003). The Driver's Angry Thoughts Questionnaire: A measure of angry cognitions when driving. *Cognitive Therapy & Research, 27*(4), 383–402.

Dembroski, T., MacDougall, J., Costa, P., & Grandits G. (1989). Components of hostility and predictors of sudden death and myocardial infarction in the Multiple Risk Factor Intervention Model. *Psychosomatic Medicine, 51*(5), 514–522.

De Quervain, D. J., Fischbacher, U. Treyer, V., Schellhammer, M., Schnyder, U., Buck, A., & Fehr, E. (2004). The neural basis of altruistic punishment. *Science, 305*(5688), 1254–1258.

De Rivera, J. (1977). *A structural theory of the emotions.* New York: International Universities Press. DeSousa, R. (1980). The rationality of emotions. In A. O. Rorty (Ed.), *Explaining emotions* (pp. 127–152). Berkeley, CA: University of California Press.

Diamond, E. (1982). The role of anger and hostility in essential hypertension and coronary heart disease. *Psychological Bulletin, 92,* 410–433.

Diamond, E. L., Schneiderman, N., Schwartz, D., Smith, J. C., Vorp, R., & Pasin, R. D. (1984). Harassment, hostility, and Type A as determinants of cardiovascular reactivity during competition. *Journal of Behavioral Medicine, 7,* 171–189.

Diener, E., Emmons, R. A., Larsen, R. J., & Griffin, S. (1985). *Journal of Personality Assessment, 49*(1), 71–75.

DiGiuseppe, R. (1991). *What do I do with my anger?* New York: Institute for Rational Emotive Therapy. [Speech.]

DiGiuseppe, R. (1995). Developing the therapeutic alliance with angry clients. In H. Kassinove (Ed.), *Anger disorders: Definition, diagnosis, and treatments* (pp. 131–149). Washington, DC: Taylor & Francis.

DiGiuseppe, R., Eckhardt, C., Tafrate, R. C., & Robin, M. (1994). The diagnosis and treatment of anger in a cross-cultural context. *Journal of Social Distress and the Homeless, 3*(3), 229–261.

DiGiuseppe, R., Leaf, R., Exner, T. M., & Robin, M. W. (1988, September) *The development of a measure of irrational/rational thinking.* Paper presented at the World Congress on Behavior Therapy, Edinburgh, Scotland.

DiGiuseppe, R., Szeszko, P., Robin, M., & Primavera, L. (1995). Cluster analysis of narcissistic personality disorders on the MCMI–II. *Journal of Personality Disorders, 9*(4) 304–317.

DiGiuseppe, R., & Tafrate, R. C. (2003). Anger treatment for adults: A meta-analytic review. *Clinical Psychology: Science and Practice, 10,* 70–84.

DiGiuseppe, R., & Tafrate, R. C. (2004). *Anger Disorders Scale: Manual.* Toronto, Ontario: Canada: Multi Health Systems.

DiGiuseppe, R., Tafrate, R. C., & Eckhardt, C. (1994). Critical issues in the treatment of anger. *Cognitive and Behavioral Practice, 1*(1), 111–132.

DiGiuseppe, R., & Froh, J. J. (2002). What cognitions predict state anger? *Journal of Rational-Emotive and Cognitive-Behavior Therapy, 20,* 133–150.

Dimberg, U. (1986). Facial expressions as excitatory and inhibitory stimuli for conditioned autonomic responses. *Biological-Psychology, 22*(1), 37–57.

Dimberg, U., & Oehman, A. (1983). The effects of directional facial cues on electrodermal conditioning to facial stimuli. *Psychophysiology, 20*(2), 160–167.

Dishion, T. J., McCord, J., & Poulin, F. (1999). When interventions harm: Peer groups and behavior problems. *American Psychologists, 54*(9), 755–764.

Dobson, K. S. (1985). The relationship between anxiety and depression. *Clinical Psychology Review, 5,* 307–324.

Dodds, J. A., & Dowd, E. T. (1997, November). *Anger, hostility, and psychological reactance: Implications for intervention and medical adherence in the coronary patient.* Paper presented at the annual convention of the Association for Advancement of Behavior Therapy, Miami, FL.

Dodes, L. (1990). Addiction, helplessness, and narcissistic rage. *Psychoanalytic Quarterly, 59,* 398–419.

Dodge, K. A. (1985). Facets of social interactions and the assessment of social competence in children. In B. Schneider, K. Rubin, & J. Ledingham (Eds.), *Children's peer relationships: Issues in assessment and intervention* (pp. 3–27). New York: Springer-Verlag.

Dodge, K. A., & Coie, J. D. (1987). Social-information-processing factors in reactive and proactive aggression in children's peer groups. *Journal of Personality & Social Psychology, 53*(6), 1146–1158.

Dodge, K. A., Price, J. M., Bachorowski, J., & Newman, J. P. (1990). Hostile attributional biases in severely aggressive adolescents. *Journal of Abnormal Psychology, 99*(4), 385–392.

Dollard, J., Doob, L., Miller, N., Mowrer, O., & Sears, R. (1939). *Frustration and aggression.* New Haven, CT: Yale University Press.

Douglas, J., & Olshakher, M. (1995). *Mind hunter: Inside the FBI's elite serial killer unit.* New York: Scribner.

Douglas, J., & Olshakher, M. (1997). *Journey into darkness.* New York: Scribner.

Douglas, J., & Olshakher, M. (1998). *Obsession.* New York: Scribner.

Duckitt, John. (1994). The reliability and factorial validity of a multidimensional measure of psychological symptomatology in South Africa. *South African Journal of Psychology, 24*(4), 194–200.

Duckro, P. N., Chibnall, J. T., & Tomazic, T. J. (1995). Anger, depression, and disability: A path analysis of relationships in a sample of chronic posttraumatic headache patients. *Headache, 35*(1), 7–9.

Dunham, P. J., & Carr, A. (1976). Pain-elicited aggression in the squirrel monkey: An implicit avoidance contingency. *Animal Learning and Behavior, 4*(1-A), 89–95.

Dunkley, D. M., Blankstein, K. R., & Flett, G. L. (1995). Self-criticism and dependency in relation to anger. *Psychological Reports, 76,* 1342.

Dutton, D. G. (1995). Intimate abusiveness. *Clinical Psychology: Science and Practice, 2,* 207–224.

Dutton, D. G. (1998). The abusive personality: Violence and control in intimate relationships. New York: Guilford Press.

D'Zurilla, T. J., & Nezu, A. (1999). *Problem solving therapy: A social competence approach to clinical intervention.* New York: Springer.

Eckhardt, C., Barbour, K., & Davison, G. C. (1998). Articulated thoughts of maritally violent and nonviolent men during anger arousal. *Journal of Consulting and Clinical Psychology, 66,* 259–269.

Eckhardt, C., & Deffenbacher, J. (1995). Diagnosis of anger disorders. In H. Kassinove (Ed.), *Anger disorders: Definition, diagnosis and treatment* (pp. 27–47). Philadelphia, PA: Taylor & Francis.

Eckhardt, C., Jamison, R. T., & Watts, K. (2002). Anger experience and expression among male dating violence perpetrators during anger arousal. *Journal of Interpersonal Violence, 17,* 1102–1114.

Eckhardt, C., & Kassinove, H. (1998). Articulated distortions and cognitive deficiencies in maritally violent men. *Journal of Cognitive Psychotherapy: An International Quarterly, 12,* 231–249.

Edmondson, C., & Conger, J. (1996). A review of treatment efficacy for individuals with anger problems: Conceptual, assessment, and methodological issues. *Clinical Psychology Review, 16*(3), 251–275.

Eells, T. D., Fridhandler, B., & Horowitz, M. J. (1995). Self-schemas and spousal bereavement: Comparing quantitative and clinical evidence. *Psychotherapy: Theory, Research, Practice, Training, 32*(2), 270–282.

Eibel-Eibesfeldt, I. (1970). *Ethology: The biology of behavior.* New York: Holt, Rhinehart & Winston.

Eidelson, R. J., & Eidelson, J. I. (2003). Dangerous ideas: Five beliefs that propel groups toward conflict. *American Psychologist, 58*(3), 182–192.

Ekman, P. (1974). Universal facial expression of emotions. In R. LeVine (Ed.), *Culture and personality: Contemporary reading* (pp. 8–15). Chicago: Aldine.

Ekman, P. (1984). Expression and the nature of emotion. In K. Scherer & P. Ekman (Eds.), *Approaches to emotions* (pp. 319–344). Hillsdale, NJ: Lawrence Erlbaum.

Ekman, P. (1992). Are there basic emotions? *Psychological Review, 99,* 550–553.

Ekman, P. (1994). All emotions are basic. In P. Ekman & R. Davidson (Eds.), *The nature of Emotions: Fundamental questions* (pp. 15–19). New York: Oxford University Press.

Ekman, P., & Davidson, R. (Eds.) (1994). *The nature of emotions: Fundamental questions.* New York: Oxford University Press.

Elkin, I., Shea, M. T., Watkins, J., Imber, S., Stotsky, S. M., Collins, S. F., et al. (1989). National Institute of Mental Health Treatment of Depression Collaborative Research Program: General effectiveness. *Archives of General Psychiatry, 46*(11), 971–982.

Ellis, A. (1962). *Reason and emotion in psychotherapy.* New York: Citadel Press.

Ellis, A. (1977). *How to live with and without anger.* New York: Reader's Digest Press.

Ellis, A. (2003). *Overcoming resistance* (2nd ed.). New York: Springer.

Ellis, A., & Dryden, W. (1988). *The practice of rational emotive therapy.* New York: Springer.

Ellis, A., & Tafrate, R. (1997). *How to control your anger before it controls you.* Secaucus, NJ: Birch Lane Press.

Else, L. T., Wonderlich, S. A., Beatty, W. W., Christie, D. W. (1993). Personality characteristics of men who physically abuse women. *Hospital and Community Psychiatry, (44)*4, 54–58.

Endler, N., & Hunt, J. (1968). S-R inventories of hostility and comparisons of the proportions of variance from persons, responses, and situations for hostility and anxiousness. *Journal of Personality and Social Psychology, 9*(4), 309–315.

Engebretson, T., Matthews, K., & Scheier, M. (1989). Relations between anger expression and cardiovascular reactivity: Reconciling inconsistent findings through a matching hypothesis. *Journal of Personality and Social Psychology, 57*(3), 513–521.

Enright, R. D. (2001). *Forgiveness is a choice*. Washington, DC: American Psychiatric Association.

Enright, R. D., & Fitzgibbons, R. P. (2000). *Helping clients forgive: An empirical guide for resolving anger and restoring hope*. Washington, DC: American Psychological Association.

Erwin, B. A., Heimberg, R. G., Schneier, F. R., & Liebowitz, M. R. (2003). Anger experience and expression in social anxiety disorder: Pre-treatment profile and predictors of attrition and response to cognitive behavioral treatment cognitive-behavioral treatment. *Behavior Therapy 34*(3), 331–350.

Everson, S. A., Kaplan, G. A., Goldberg, D. E., Lakka, T. A., & Sivenius, J. S. (1999). Anger expression and incident stroke. Prospective evidence from the Kuopio Ischemic Heart Study. *Stroke, 30, 523–528*.

Farber, E. W., & Burge-Calloway, K. (1998). Differences in anger, hostility, and interpersonal aggressiveness in Type A and Type B adolescents. *Journal of Clinical Psychology, 54, 945–952*.

Farris, H. E., Gideon, B. E., & Ulrich, R. E. (1970). Classical conditioning of aggression: A developmental study. *Psychological Record, 20*(1), 63–67.

Fava, G. A., Kellnar, R., & Lisansky, J. (1986). Hostility and recovery from melancholia. *Journal of Nervous and Mental Diseases, 174, 414–417*.

Fava, G. A., Kellnar, R., Muanari, F., Pavan, L., & Pesarin, Fl. (1982). Losses, hostility, and depression. *Journal of Nervous and Mental Diseases, 170, 474–478*.

Fava, M., Alpert, J. E., Nierenberg, A. A., Ghaemi, N., O'Sullivan, R., Tedlow, J., et al. (1996). Fluoxetine treatment of anger attacks: a replication study. *Annals of Clinical Psychiatry, 8, 7–10*.

Fava, M., Rosenbaum, J., Pava, J., McCarthy, M. K., Steingard, R., & Bless, E. (1993). Anger attacks in unipolar depression. Part I: Clinical correlates and response to fluoxetine treatment. *American Journal of Psychiatry, 150, 1158–1163*.

Fehr, B., & Russell, J. (1984). Concepts of emotions viewed from a prototype perspective. *Journal of Experimental Psychology: General, 113, 464–486*.

Feindler, E. (1995). Ideal treatment package for children and adolescents with anger disorders. In H. Kassinove (Ed.). *Anger disorders: definition, diagnosis and treatment*. Philadelphia, PA: Taylor & Francis.

Feindler, E., Adler, N., Brooks, D., Bhurmitra, E. (1993). The Children's Anger Response Checklist. In L. VandeCreek, S. Knapp, et. al. (Eds). *Innovations in clinical practice: A source book* (Vol. 12). Sarasota, FL: Professional Resource Press.

Felson, R. B., & Tedeschi, J. T. (1993). A social interactionist apprroach to violence: Cross-cultural applications. *Violence and Victims, 8*(3), 295–310.

Fenichel, O. (1945). *The psychoanalytic theory of neurosis*. New York: Norton.

Ferster, C. B. (1973). A functional analysis of depression. *American Psychologists, 28*, 857–870.

Feshbach, S. (1964). The function of aggression and the regulation of aggressive drive. *Psychological Review, 71, 257–272*.

Feshbach, S. (1986). Reconceptualizations of anger: Some research perspectives. *Journal of Social and Clinical Psychology, 4*(2), 123–132.

Fiester, S., Ellison, J., Docherty, J., & Shea, T. (1990). Comorbidity of personality disorders: Two for the price of three. *New Directions for Mental Health Services, 47*, 103–114.

Filetti, L., & Deffenbacher, J. (2000, August). *Characteristics of high and low angry drivers.* Paper presented at the 108th annual convention of the American Psychological Association, Washington, DC.

Fine, M. A., Overholser, J. C., & Berkoff, K. (1992). Diagnostic validity of the passive-aggressive personality disorder: Suggestions for reform. *American Journal of Psychotherapy, 46,* 470–484.

Fine, S. (1973). Family therapy and a behavioral approach to childhood obsessive-compulsive neurosis. *Archives of General Psychiatry, 28,* 695–697.

Fish, E. W., DeBold, J. F., & Miczek, K. A. (2002). Aggressive behavior as a reinforcer in mice: Activation by allopregnanolone. *Psychopharmacology, 163,* 459–466.

Fishbein, D., Jaffe, J., Snyder, F., Haertzen, C., Hickey, P. (1993) Drug users' self-reports of behaviors and affective states under the influence of alcohol. *International Journal of the Addictions, 28*(14), 1565–1585.

Fives, C. (2003). *Anger and aggression.* Unpublished doctoral dissertation, St. John's University, Jamaica, NY.

Foa, E. B., & Kozak, M. J. (1986). Emotional processing of fear: Exposure to correct information. *Psychological Bulletin, 99,* 20–35.

Foa, E. B., Riggs, D., Massie, E., & Yarczower, M. (1995). The impact of fear activation and anger on the efficacy of exposure treatment for posttraumatic stress disorder. *Behavior Therapy, 26*(3), 487–499.

Foa, E. B., & Rothbaum, B. O. (1998). *Treating the trauma of rape: Cognitive-behavioral therapy for PTSD.* New York: Guilford Press.

Folger, R. (1997). Reformulating the preconditions of resentment: A referent cognitions model. In J. C. Masters & W. P. Smith (Eds.), *Social comparison, social justice, and relative deprivation: Theoretical and policy perspectives* (pp. 183–213). Hillsdale, NJ: Lawrence Earlbaum.

Folger, R., & Baron, R. (1996). Violence and hostility at work: A model of reactions to perceived injustice. In G. R. Van den Bos & E. Bulatao (Eds.), *Violence on the job: Identifying risks and developing solutions* (pp. 51–85). Washington, DC: American Psychological Association.

Folger, R., Robinson, S. L., Dietz, J., McLean-Parks, J., & Baron, R. A. (1998, August). *When colleagues become violent: Employee threats and assaults as a function of societal violence and organizational injustice.* Academy of Management Best Paper paper Proceedings of the 58th Annual Meeting of the Academy of Management, San Diego, CA.

Fongay, P., Target, M., Cottrell, D., Phillips, J., & Kurtz, Z. (2002). *What works for whom: A critical review of treatments for children and adolescents.* New York: Guilford Press.

Ford, F. L. (1983). *Political murder: From tyrannicide to terrorism.* Cambridge, MA: Harvard University Press.

Forrest, M. S., & Hokanson, J. E. (1975). Depression and autonomic arousal reduction accompanying self-punitive behavior. *Journal of Abnormal Psychology, 84,* 346–357.

Freud, A. (1946). *The ego and the mechanisms of defense.* New York: International Universities Press.

Freud, S. (1963). Mourning and melancholia. In J. Strachey (Ed. and Trans.), *The standard edition of the complete psychological works of Sigmund Freud* (Vol. 14, pp. 243–258). London: Hogarth Press. (Original work published 1917)

Freud, S. (1920). *A general introduction to psychoanalysis* (G. S. Hall, Trans.). New York: Boni and Liveright.

Friedman, A. S. (1970). Hostility factors and clinical improvement in depressed patients. *Archives of General Psychiatry, 23,* 534–537.

Friedman, M., & Roseman, R. H. (1959). Association of a specific overt behavior with increases in blood cholesterol, blood clotting time, incidence of arcus senilus and clinical coronary disease. *Journal of the American Medical Association, 2169,* 1286–1296.

Friedman, T. L. (2000). *The lexus and the olive tree.* New York, NY: Anchor Books.

Frijda, N. H. (1986). *The emotions.* England: Cambridge University Press.

Fritzon, K. (2001). An examination of the relationship between distance travelled and motivational aspects of firesetting behavior. *Journal of Environmental Psychology, 21*(1), 45–60.

Fuller, J. R., Ahmed, A. G., & DiGiuseppe, R. (2005). *Anger symptoms assessed by structured interview in outpatients from an anger clinic and a community sample.* Manuscript submitted for publication.

Furlong, M. J., & Smith, D. C. (1998). Raging Rick to tranquil Tom: An empirically based, multidimensional anger topology for adolescent males. *Psychology in the Schools, 35*(3), 229–245.

Galen, C. (1963). *On the passions and errors of the soul.* Columbus, OH: Ohio University Press.

Gallagher, E. J., Yarnell, W. G., Sweetman, P. M., Elwood, P. C., Stanfeld, S. A. (1999). Anger and incident heart disease in the Caerphilly study, *Psychosomatic Medicine, 61*(4), 446–453.

Garbarino, J. (1999). *Lost boys: Why our sons turn violent and how we can save them.* New York: Free Press.

Gardner, W., Lidz, C., Mulvey, E., & Shaw, E. (1996). A comparison of actuarial methods for identifying repetitively violent patients with mental illnesses. *Law and Human Behavior, 20*(1), 35–48.

Garfinkel, B., Froese, A., & Hood, J. (1982). Suicide attempts in children and adolescents. *American Journal of Psychiatry, 139,* 1257–1261.

Gates, G. S. (1926). An observational study of anger. *Journal of Experimental Psychology, 9,* 325–331.

Gay, P. (1988). *Freud: A life for our times.* New York: Norton.

Gaylin, W. (1989). *The rage within: Anger in modern life.* New York: Penguin Books.

Geen, R. G. (2001). *Human aggression* (2nd ed.). New York: Open University Press.

Geen, R. G., & Donnerstein, E. (1998). *Human aggression: Theories, research, and implications for social policy.* San Diego, CA: Academic Press.

Gellen, M., Hoffman, R., Jones, M., & Stone, M. (1984). Abused and non-abused women: MMPI profile differences. *Personnel and Guidance Journal, 62*(10), 601–604.

Gerard, D. I., & Kornetsky, C. (1955). Adolescent opiate addiction: A study of control and addicted subjects. *Psychiatric Quarterly, 28,* 367–380.

Gerard, J. W. (1933/1996). *A hymn of hate: A review of "My battle" by Adolph Hitler.* New York: New York Times Book Review, October 6, 1996.

Gergen, K. (1985). The social constructionist movement in modern psychology. *American Psychologist, 40*(3), 266–275.

Gerlsma, C., van der Lubbe, P. M., & van Nieuwenhuisen, C. (1992). Factor analysis of the levels of expressed emotion scale: A questionnaire intended to measure a perceived expressed emotion. *British Journal of Psychiatry, 160,* 386–389.

Gibson, D. C., & Barsade, S. C. (1999). *The experience of anger at work.* Paper presented at the annual meeting of the Academy of Management, Chicago.

Gilbert, H. L. (2000). The experience of being an obsessive-compulsive male. *Dissertation Abstracts International, Section B. The Sciences and Engineering, 61*(1-B), 529.

Gilbert, P. & Allan, S. (1998). The role of defeat and entrapment in depression: An exploration of an evolutionary view. *Psychological Medicine, 28,* 585–598.

Gilligan, J. (1996). *Violence: Reflections on a national epidemic.* New York: Vintage.

Gispert, M., Davis, M. C., Marsh, L., & Wheeler, K. (1987). Predictive factors in repeated suicide attempts by adolescents. *Hospital and Community Psychiatry, 38,* 390–509.

Glare, P. G. W. (Ed.) (1982). *Oxford Latin Dictionary.* New York: Oxford University Press.

Gloor, P., Olivier, A., & Quesney, L. F. (1982). The role of the limbic system in experiential phenomena of temporal lobe epilepsy. *Annals of Neurology, 12,* 129–144.

Goldberg, D. (1972). *The detection of psychiatric illness by questionnaire: A technique for the identification and assessment of non-psychotic psychiatric illness.* Oxford, UK: Oxford University Press.

Goldberg, E. (1981). Depression and suicidal ideation in the young adult. *American Journal of Psychiatry, 138,* 35–40.

Goldberg, S. C., Schulz, S. C., Schulz, P. M., Resnick, R. J., Hamer, R. M., & Friedel, R. O. (1986). Borderline and schizotypal personality disorders treated with low-dose thiothixene vs. placebo. *Archives of General Psychiatry, 43,* 680–686.

Goldfried, M. R., & Davison, G. C. (1994). *Clinical behavior therapy* (Expanded Ed.). New York: Wiley & Sons.

Goldstein, D., & Rosenbaum, A. (1985). An evaluation of the self-esteem of maritally violent men. *Family Relations: Journal of Applied Family and Child Studies, 34*(3), 425–428.

Gondolf, E. (1985). *Men who batter.* Holmes Beach, FL: Learning.

Goshtasbpour, F. (2001). A meta-analytic review of the components of adult anger management treatments. *Dissertation Abstracts International, Section B. The Sciences and Engineering, 62*(1-B), 548.

Gotlib, I. H., & Meyer, J. P. (1986). Factor analysis of the Multiple Affect Adjective Checklist: A separation of positive and negative affect. *Journal of Personality and Social Psychology, 50*(6), 1161–1165.

Gottesfried, M. R., & Hirschi, T. (1990). *A general theory of crime.* Stanford, CA: Stanford University.

Gottman, J. M., Jacobson, N. S., Rushe, R. H., Short, J. W. Babcock, J., La Taillade, J. J., et al. (1995). The relationship between heart rate reactivity, emotionally aggressive behavior, and general violence in batterers. *Journal of Family Psychology, 9,* 227–248.

Gould, S. J. (1987). Hat racks and theories. *Natural History, 96*(3), 12–16.

Graham, J. R. (1993). *MMPI-2: Assessing personality and psychopathology* (2nd ed.). New York: Oxford University Press.

Green, R. W. (1998). *The Explosive Child.* New York: Harper Collins.

Greenberg, L. S., & Safran, J. (1987). *Emotion in psychotherapy.* New York: Guilford Press.

Greenblatt, R. L., & Davis, W. E. (1992). Accuracy of MCMI classification of angry and psychotic Black and White patients. *Journal of Clinical Psychology, 48,* 59–63.

Grinker, R. R., Werble, B., & Drye, R. C. (1968). *The borderline syndrome.* New York: Basic Books.

Grodnitzsky, G., & Tafrate, R. C. (2000). Imaginal exposure for anger reduction in adult outpatients: A pilot study. *Journal of Behavior Therapy and Experimental Psychiatry, 31,* 259–279.

Grossman, D. (1995). *On killing: The psychological cost of learning to kill in war and society.* Boston: Little, Brown.

Groth, A. N. (1979). *Men who rape: The Psychology of the offender.* New York: Plenum Press.

Groth, A. N., & Burgess, A. W. (1977). Rape: A sexual deviation. *American Journal of Orthopsychiatry, 47*(3), 400–406.

Groth, A. N., Burgess, A. W., & Holmstrom, L. L. (1977). Rape: Power, anger, and sexuality. *American Journal of Psychiatry, 134*(11), 1239–1243.

Grover, S. M., & Thomas, S. T. (1993). Substance use and anger in mid-life women. *Issues in Mental Health Nursing, 14,* 19–29.

Gunderson, J. G. (1987). Interfaces between psychoanalytic and empirical studies of borderline personality. In J. S. Grotstein, M. F. Solomon, & J. A. Lang (Eds.), *The borderline patient: Emerging concepts in diagnosis, psychodynamics, and treatment* (Vol. 1, pp. 37–60). Hillsdale: Analytic Press.

Gunderson, J. G., & Zanarini, M. C. (1989). Pathogenesis of borderline personality. In A. Tasman, R. E. Hales, & A. J. Fraces (Eds.), *Review of psychiatry* (Vol. 8, pp. 25–48). Washington, DC: American Psychiatric Press.

Guntrip, H. (1969). *Schizoid phenomena, object-relations and the self.* New York: International Universities Press.

Hall, G. S. (1899). A study of anger. *American Journal of Psychology, 10,* 516–591.

Hallowell, E. M., & Ratey, J. J. (1994). *Driven to distraction.* New York: Pantheon.

Haney, T. L., Maynard, K. E., Houseworth, S. J., Scherwitz, L. W., Williams R. B., & Barefoot, J. G. (1996). Interpersonal hostility assessment techniques: Description and validation against the criterion of coronary artery disease. *Journal of Personality Assessment, 66,* 386–401.

Harburg, E. Julius, M., Kaciroti, N., Glieberman, L., & Schork, M. A. (2003). Expressive/suppressive anger-coping responses, gender, and types of mortality: A 17-year follow-up. *Psychosomatic Medicine, 65*(4), 588–597.

Hare, R., & Hart, S. (1993). Psychopathology, mental disorder, and crime. In S. Hodgins (Ed.), *Mental disorder and crime* (pp. 104–115). Thousand Oaks, California: Sage.

Harmon-Jones, E., & Sigelman, J. (2001). State anger and prefrontal brain activity: Evidence that insult-related left prefrontal activation is associated with anger and aggression. *Journal of Personality and Social Psychology, 80*(5), 797–803.

Harris T., Brown, G., & Bifulco, A. (1986). Loss of parenthood in childhood and adult psychiatric disorder: The role of lack of adequate parental care. *Psychological Medicine, 16*(3), 641–659.

Hart, P. L., & Joubert, C. E. (1996). Narcissism and hostility. *Psychological Reports, 79,* 161–162.

Hart, S. D., Dutton, D. G., & Newlove, T. (1993). The prevalence of personality disorders among wife abusers. *Journal of Personality Disorders, 7,* 329–341.

Harter, S., & Whitesell, N. R. (1988). Developmental changes in children's understanding of single, multiple and blended emotional concepts. In C. Saarni &

P. Harris (Eds.), *Children's understanding of emotions* (pp. 81–116). New York: Cambridge University Press.

Hartup, W. W. (1974). Aggression in childhood: Developmental perspectives. *American Psychologist, 29,* 336–341.

Hawton, K., Cole, D., O'Grady, J., & Osborn, M. (1982). Motivational aspects of deliberate self-poisoning in adolescents. *British Journal of Psychiatry, 142,* 286–291.

Hayes, S. C., & Gifford, E. V. (1997). The trouble with language: Experiential avoidance, rules, and the nature of verbal events. *Psychological Science, 8*(3), 170–173.

Hayes, S. C., Strosahl, K., Wilson, K. G., Bissett, R., T., Pistorello, J., Toarmino, D., et al. (2004). Measuring experiential avoidance: A preliminary test of a working model. *Psychological Record, 54*(4), 553–578.

Haynes, S., Feinleib, M., Kannel, W. (1980). The relationship of psychosocial factors to coronary heart disease in the Framingham study: III. Eight-year incidence of coronary heart disease. *American Journal of Epidemiology, 111*(1), 37–58.

Hazaleus, S. L., & Deffenbacher, J. L. (1986). Relaxation and cognitive treatments of anger. *Journal of Consulting and Clinical Psychology, 54,* 222–226.

Hecker, M. H., & Lunde, D. T. (1985). On the diagnosis and treatment of chronically hostile individuals. In M. A. Chesney & R. H. Rosenman (Eds.), *Anger and Hostility in Cardiovascular and Behavioral Disorders* (pp. 227–240). Washington, DC: Hemisphere.

Henrique, J. B., & Davidson, R. J. (2000). Decreased responsiveness to regard in depression. *Cognition and Emotion, 14,* 711–724.

Henrique, J. B., Glowacki, J. M., & Davidson, R. J. (1994). Rewards fail to alter response bias in depression. *Journal of Abnormal Psychology, 103,* 460–466.

Hilbrand, M., & Hirt, M. (1987). The borderline syndrome: An empirically developed prototype. *Journal of Personality Disorder, 1,* 299–306.

Hoberman, H. M., & Garfinkle, B. D. (1988). Completed suicide in youth. *Canadian Journal of Psychiatry, 33*(6), 494–504.

Hochschild, A. R. (1979). Emotion work, feeling rules and social structure. *American Journal of Sociology, 85,* 551–575.

Hochschild, A. R. (1983). *The managed heart: Commercialization of human feelings.* Berkeley: University of California Press.

Hoffmann, R. M. (1995). Silent rage: Passive-aggressive behavior in organizations. *Dissertation Abstracts International, Section B. The Sciences and Engineering, 56*(2-B), 1138.

Holbrook, M. I. (1997). Anger management training in prison inmates. *Psychological Reports, 81*(2), 623–626.

Hollander, E. (1999). Managing aggressive behavior in patients with obsessive-compulsive disorder and borderline personality disorder. *Journal of Clinical Psychiatry Monograph Series, 17,* 28–31.

Hollis, K. L., Cadieux, E. L., Colbert, M. M. (1995). The biological function of Pavlovian conditioning: A mechanism for mating success in the blue gourami (Trichogaster trichopterus). *Journal of Comparative Psychology, 103*(2), 115–121.

Holroyd, K., & Gorkin, L. (1983). Young adults at risk for hypertension: Effects of family history and anger management in determining responses to interpersonal conflict. *Journal of Psychosomatic Research, 27*(2), 131–138.

Holtzworth-Monroe, A., & Stuart, G. L. (1994). Typologies of male batterers: Three subtypes and the differences among them. *Psychological Bulletin, 116,* 476–497.

Hooley, J. M., & Teasdale, J. D. (1989). Predictors of relapse in unipolar depressives: Expressed emotion, marital distress, and perceived criticism. *Journal of Abnormal Psychology, 98*(3), 229–235.

Horowitz, M. J. (1997). Cognitive psychodynamics: The clinical use of states, person schemas, and defensive control process theories. In D. J. Stein (Ed.). *Cognitive science and the unconscious* (pp. 189–205). Washington, DC: American Psychiatric Association.

Horvath, A. O., & Luborsky, L. (1993) The role of the therapeutic alliance in psychotherapy. *Journal of Consulting and Clinical Psychology, 61*(4), 561–573.

Horvath, A. O., & Symonds, B. D. (1991). Relation between working alliance and outcome in psychotherapy: A meta-analysis. *Journal of Consulting and Clinical Psychology, 38*, 139–149.

Howells, K. (2004). Anger and its links to violent offending. *Psychiatry, Psychology, & Law, 11*, 189–196.

Hudson, S. M., & Ward, T. (1997). Intimacy, loneliness, and attachment style in sexual offenders. *Journal of Interpersonal Violence, 12*(3), 323–339.

Hughes, L. (1996). Trait anger compared to general impulsiveness as predictors of interpersonal violence while incarcerated. *Dissertation Abstracts International, Section B. The Sciences and Engineering, 57*(6-B), 4030.

Hunter, R., & Macalpine, I. (1963). *Three hundred years of psychiatry.* London: Oxford University Press.

Huprich, S. K. (2000). Describing depressive personality analogues and dysthymics on the NEO-Personality Inventory–Revised. *Journal of Clinical Psychology, 56*, 1521–1534.

Hyer, L., Brandsma, J., & Shealy, L. (1995). Experiential mood therapy with the MCMI–III. In P. D. Retzlaff (Ed.), *Tactical psychotherapy of the personality disorders: An MCMI–III-based approach.* Boston: Allyn & Bacon.

Izard, C. E. (1971). *The face of emotion.* East Norwalk, CT: Appleton Century Crofts.

Izard, C. E. (1977). *Human Emotions.* New York: Plenum.

Izard, C. E. (1991). *The psychology of emotions.* New York: Plenum.

Jackson, S. W. (1986). *Melancholia and depression: From Hippocratic times to modern times.* New Haven: Yale University Press.

Jacobson, N. S., & Gottman, J. M. (1998). *When men batter women: New insights into ending abusive relationships.* New York: Simon & Schuster.

Jakes, I. (1996). *Theoretical approaches to obsessive-compulsive disorder.* Cambridge: Cambridge University Press.

James, W. (1890). *The principles of psychology.* New York: H. Holt.

Jankowski, M. (1991). *Islands in the street: Gangs and American urban society.* Berkeley: University of California Press.

Johnson-Laird, P. N., & Oats, K. (1989). The language of emotions: An analysis of a semantic field. *Cognition and Emotion, 3*(2), 81–123.

Johnston, V., Rogers, B., & Searight, H. (1991). The relationship between overt hostility, covert hostility and depression. *Journal of Social Behavior and Personality, 6*, 85–92.

Jonas, J. M., & Pope, H. G. (1992). Axis I comorbidity of borderline personality disorder: Clinical implications. In J. F. Clarkin, E. Marziali, & H. Munroe-Blum (Eds.), *Borderline personality disorder: Clinical and empirical perspectives* (pp. 149–160). New York: Guilford.

Kadiangandu, J. K., Mullet, E., & Vinsonneau, G. (2001). Forgivingness: A Congo-France comparison. *Journal of Cross Cultural Psychology, 32*(4), 504–511.

Kalogjera, I. J., Jacobson, G. R., Hoffman, G. K., Hoffman, P., Raffe, I. H., White, H. C., et al. (1998). The narcissistic couple. In J. Carlson & L. Sperry (Eds.), *The disordered couple*. Bristol: Brunner/Mazel.

Kanin, E. J. (1994). False rape allegations. *Archives of Sexual Behavior, 23*(1), 81–92.

Kantor, M. (1993). *Distancing: A guide to avoidance and avoidant personality disorder.* Westport: Praeger.

Kaplan, H. L., & Sadock, B. J. (1993). *Pocket handbook of emergency psychiatric medicine.* Baltimore: Williams & Wilkins.

Kaplan, H. S. (1984). *The evaluation of sexual disorders.* New York: Bruner/Masel.

Kaslow, F. (1983). Passive-aggressiveness: An intrapsychic, interpersonal and transactional dynamic in the family system. In R. D. Parsons & R. J. Wicks (Eds.), *Passive-aggressiveness: Theory and practice.* New York: Brunner/Mazel.

Kassinove, H., Roth, D., Owens, S. G., & Fuller, J. R. (2002). Effects of trait anger and anger expression style on competitive attack responses in a wartime prisoner's dilemma game. *Aggressive Behavior, 28*(2), 117–125.

Kassinove, H., & Sukhodolsky, D. G. (1995). Anger disorders: Basic science and practice issues. In H. Kassinove (Ed.), *Anger disorders: Definition, diagnosis and treatment* (pp. 1–26). Washington, DC: Taylor & Francis.

Kassinove, H., Sukhodolsky, D., Tsytsarev, S., & Soloyova, S. (1997). Self-reported anger episodes in Russia and America. *Journal of Behavior and Personality, 12*(2), 301–324.

Kassinove, H., & Tafrate, R. C. (2002). *Anger management.* Atascadero, CA: Impact Publishers.

Kassinove, H., & Tafrate, R. C. (2006). *Anger management video program: An instructional guide for practitioners.* Atascadero, CA: Impact Publishers.

Kassinove, H., Tafrate, R. C., & Dundin, L. (2002). Anger episodes in high and low trait anger community adults. *Journal of Clinical Psychology, 58,* 1573–1590.

Kazdin, A. E. (2000). *Psychotherapy for children and adolescents: Directions for research and practice.* New York: Oxford University Press.

Keegan, J. (1976). *The face of battle.* New York: Penguin Books.

Keegan, J. (1993). *A history of warfare.* New York: Knopf.

Kellerman, A. L., & Mercy, J. A. (1992). Men, women, and murder: gender-specific differences in rates of fatal violence and victimization. *Journal of Trauma, 33*(1), 1–5.

Kellerman, H., & Burry, A. (1989). *Psychopathology and the differential diagnosis: Diagnostic primer* (Vol. 2). New York: Columbia University Press.

Kellner, R., Hernandez, J., & Pathak, D. (1992). Self-rated inhibited anger, somatization and depression. *Psychotherapy and Psychosomatics, 57,* 102–107.

Kemp, S., & Strongman, K. T. (1995). Anger theory and management: A historical analysis. *American Journal of Psychology, 108*(3), 397–409.

Kemper, T. D. (1978). *A social interaction theory of emotions.* New York: Wiley.

Kemper, T. D. (1987). How many emotions are there? Wedding social and autonomic components. *American Journal of Sociology, 93*(2) 263–289.

Kemper, T. D. (1991). An introduction to the sociology of emotions. In K. T. Strongman (Ed.), *International review of studies of emotion* (pp. 301–349). New York: Wiley.

Kemper, T. D., & Collins, R. (1990). Dimensions of microinteractions. *American Journal of Sociology, 96,* 32–98.

Kendell, R. E. (1970). Relationship between aggression and depression: Epidemiological implications of a hypothesis. *Archives of General Psychiatry, 22,* 308–318.

Kennedy, H. G. (1992). Anger and Irritability. *British Journal of Psychiatry, 161,* 145–153.

Kernberg, O. F. (1975). *Borderline conditions and pathological narcissism.* New York: Jason Aronson.

Kernberg, O. F. (1977). The structural diagnosis of borderline personality organization. In P. Hartocollis (Ed.), *Borderline personality disorders* (pp. 87–121). New York: International Universities Press.

Kernberg, O. F. (1979). Psychoanalytic psychotherapy with borderline adolescents. *Adolescent Psychiatry, 7,* 294–321.

Kernberg, O. F. (1990). *Borderline conditions and pathological narcissism.* New York: Jason Aronson.

Kernberg, O. F. (1986). Factors in the psychoanalytic treatment of narcissistic personalities. In A. P. Morrison (Ed.), *Essential papers on narcissism.* New York: New York University Press.

Kernis, M. H., Cornell, D. P., Sun, C. R., Berry, A., & Harlow, T. (1993). The roles of stability and level of self-esteem in psychological functioning. In R. Baumeister (Ed.). *Self-esteem: The puzzle of low self-regard* (pp. 167–182). New York: Plenum.

Kernis, M. H., Granneman, B. D., & Barclay, L. C. (1989). Stability and level of self-esteem as predictors of anger arousal and hostility. *Journal of Personality and Social Psychology, 65,* 1190–1204.

Khantzian, E. J. (1985). The self-medication hypothesis of addictive disorders: Focus on heroin and cocaine dependence. *American Journal of Psychiatry, 142,* 1259–1264.

Kiewitz, C. (2002). The work anger model (WAM!): An inquiry into the role of anger at work. *Dissertation Abstracts International, Section A. Humanities & Social Sciences, 63*(5-A), 1904.

Kinner, S. (2003). Psychopathy as an adaptation: Implications for society and social policy. In R. W. Bloom & N. Dess (Eds.). *Evolutionary psychology and violence: A primer for policymakers and public policy advocates* (pp. 57–81). Westport, CT: Praeger/Greenwood.

Kirschner, D. (1992). Understanding adoptees who kill: Dissociation, patricide, and the psychodynamics of adoption. *International Journal of Offender Therapy and Comparative Criminology, 36*(4), 323–333.

Klein, R., Orleans, J., & Soule, C. (1991). The Axis II group: Treating severely characterologically disturbed patients. *International Journal of Group Psychotherapy, 41*(1), 97–115.

Kliewer, D. (1986). A life-cycle approach to anger management training. *Journal of Psychology and Christianity, 5*(4), 30–39.

Knight, R. A., & Prentky, R. A. (1987). The developmental antecedents and adult adaptations of rapist subtypes. *Criminal Justice and Behavior, 14*(4), 403–426.

Knight, R. A., & Prentky, R. A. (1990). Classifying sexual offenders: The development and corroboration of taxonomic models. In W. L. Masshall, D. R. Laws, & H. E. Barbaree (Eds.), *Handbook of sexual assault: Issues, theories, and treatment of the offender* (pp. 23–52). New York: Plenum Press.

Knutson, B. (2004). Sweet Revenge? *Science, 305*(8), 1246–1247.

Kochanska, G. (2001). Emotional development in children with different attachment histories: The first three years. *Child Development, 72*(2), 474–490.

Kohut, H. (1978). Thoughts on narcissism and narcissistic rage. In P. H. Ornstein (Ed.). *The search for the self* (Vol. 2, pp. 615–658). New York: International Universities Press.

Kohut, H., & Wolf, E. S. (1978). The disorders of the self and their treatment. *International Journal of Psychoanalysis, 59,* 413–425.

Konecni, V. (1975). The mediation of aggressive behavior: Arousal level versus anger and cognitive labeling. *Journal of Personality and Social Psychology, 32*(4), 706–712.

Konner, M. (1982). *The tangled wing: Biological constraints on the human spirit.* New York: Holt, Rinehart, & Winston.

Kraeplin, E. (1899). *Clinical Psychiatry: A textbook for students and physicians* (6th ed., Vols. 1–2). Leipzig: Verlag von Johann Ambrosius Barth.

Kramar, M. (1977). Obsessive neurosis. *Psihijatrija-Danas, 9*(2-sup-3), 279–286.

Krokowski, M., Volvaka, J., & Brizer, D. (1986). Psychopathology and violence: A review of the literature. *Comprehensive Psychiatry, 27,* 131–148.

Kroll, J. (1988). *The challenge of the borderline patient.* New York: Norton.

Kroll, J. (1993). *PTSD/borderlines in therapy.* New York: W. W. Norton.

Krueger, A. B., & Maleckova, J. (2002). Education, poverty, political violence and terrorism: Is there a causal connection? *National Bureau of Economic Research, Working Paper 9074, http://www.nber.org/papers/w9074.*

Krueger, A. B., & Maleckova, J. (2003, June 6). Seeking the roots of terrorism. *The Chronicle of Higher Education, Section B, The Chronicle Review,* B10-B11.

Lachmund, E., DiGiuseppe, R., & Fuller, J. R. (2005). Clinicians' diagnosis of a case with anger problems. *Journal of Psychiatric Research, 39*(4), 439–447.

Lackner, J. M., & Quigley, B. M. (2005). Pain catastrophizing mediates the relationship between worry and pain suffering in patients with irritable bowel syndrome. *Behaviour Research and Therapy, 43*(7), 943–957.

Lane, R. D., Reiman, E. M., Ahern, G. L., Schwartz, G. E., & Davidson, R. J. (1997). Neuroanatomical correlates of happiness, sadness, and disgust. *American Journal of Psychiatry, 154,* 926–933.

Larsen, R. J., & Diener, E. (1987). Affect intensity as an individual difference characteristic: A review. *Journal of Research in Personality, 27,* 1–39.

Lazarus, A. A. (1989). *The practice of multimodal therapy: Systematic, comprehensive, and effective psychotherapy.* Baltimore, MD: The Johns Hopkins University Press.

Lazarus, R. S. (1991). *Emotion and adaptation.* London: Oxford University Press.

Leaf, R., DiGiuseppe, R., Ellis, A., Mass, R., Backex, W., Wolfe, J., et al. (1990). Healthy correlates of MCMI personality disorder scales 4, 5, 6, and 7. *Journal of Personality Disorders, 4*(3), 312–328.

Leaf, R., Ellis, A., DiGiuseppe, R., Mass, R., & Alington, D. (1991). Rationality, self-regard and the "healthiness" of personality disorders. *Journal of Rational-Emotive and Cognitive-Behavior Therapy, 9*(1), 3–38.

Leahy, R. L., & Holland, S. J. (2000). *Treatment plans and interventions for depression and anxiety disorders.* New York: Guilford Press.

LeDoux, J. E. (1996). *The emotional brain: The mysterious underpinnings of emotional life.* New York: Simon and Schuster.

LeDoux, J. E. (2002). *Synaptic self: How the brain becomes who we are.* New York: Viking.

Lee, D. J., Mendes de Leon, C. F., & Markides, K. S. (1988). The relationship between hostility, smoking and alcohol consumption in Mexican American. *International Journal of Addictions, 23,* 887–896.

Lehnert, K. L., Overholser, J. C., & Spirito, A. (1994). Internalized and externalized anger in adolescent suicide attempters. *Journal of Adolescent Research, 9*(1), 105–119.

Leibsohn, M., Oetting, E., & Deffenbacher, J. (1994). Effects of trait anger on alcohol consumption. *Journal of Childhood and Adolescent Substance Abuse, 3*(3), 17–32.

Leigh, Barbara C. (1989). Attitudes and expectancies as predictors of drinking habits: A comparison of three scales. *Journal of Studies on Alcohol, 50*(5), 432–440.

Leone, N. F. (1982). Response of borderline patients to loxapine and chlorpromazine. *Journal of Clinical Psychiatry, 43*, 148–150.

Levin, J., & McDevitt, J. (1993). *Hate crimes: The rising tide of bigotry and bloodshed.* New York: Plenum.

Levit, D. B. (1991). Gender differences in ego defenses in adolescence. *Journal of Personality and Social Psychology, 61*, 992–999.

Levy, T. M., & Orlans, M. (1999). Attachment disorder as an antecedent to violence and antisocial patterns in children. *Handbook of attachment interventions* (pp. 1–26). San Diego: Academic Press.

Lewis, M. (1993a). The development of anger and rage. In R. A. Glick & S. P. Roose (Eds.),*Rage, power, and aggression: The role of affect in motivation, development, and adaptation* (Vol. 2., pp. 148–168). New Haven: Yale University Press.

Lewis, M. (1993b). The emergence of human emotions. In M. Lewis & J. M. Haviland (Eds.), *Handbook of emotions* (pp. 223–235). New York: Guilford Press.

Lewis, M., Sullivan, M. W., Ramsay, D. S, & Alessandri, S. M. (1992). Individual differences in anger and sad expressions during extinction: Antecedents and consequences. *Infant Behavior and Development, 15*(4), 443–452.

Li, C., Wellen, D., Turchiano, T., Anderson, T., Jones, D., & DiGiuseppe, R. (1996). *A meta-analysis of behavioral and cognitive therapies for children and adolescent with externalized disorders.* Paper presented at the 30th annual convention of the Association for the Advancement of Behavior Therapy, New York.

Linehan, M. (1993a). *Cognitive behavioral treatment of borderline personality disorder.* New York: Guilford Press.

Linehan, M. (1993b). Problems of self and borderline personality disorder: A dialectical behavior analysis. In Z. Segal and S. Blatt (Eds.), *The self in emotional distress: Cognitive and psychodynamic perspectives* (pp. 301–333). New York: Guilford Press.

Linehan, M., Heard. H. L., & Armstrong, H. E. (1993). Naturalistic follow-up of a behavioral treatment for chronically parasuicidal borderline patients. *Archives of General Psychology, 50*, 971–974.

Linehan, M., Tutek, D., & Heard, H. L. (1992, November 20). *Interpersonal and social treatment outcomes for borderline personality disorder.* Paper presented at the Annual Meeting of the Association for the Advancement of Behavior Therapy, Boston, MA.

Lionells, M. (1984). Aggression as a hysterical mechanism. *Contemporary Psychoanalysis, 20*, 633–643.

Littrell, J. (1998). Is the reexperience of painful emotion therapeutic? *Clinical Psychology Review, 18*(1), 71–102.

Lively, W., Reiffer, L. I., Sheldon, A. E., & West, M. (1987). Prototypical ratings of the DSM–III criteria of personality disorders. *Journal of Nervous and Mental Diseases, 175*, 395–401.

Lively, W. J., Schroeder, M. L., Jackson, D. N., & Jang, K. L. (1994). Categorical distinctions in the study of personality disorder: Implications for classification. *Journal of Abnormal Psychology, 103*, 6–17.

Loeber, R., & Strouthamer-Loeber, M. (1998). Development of juvenile aggression and violence. *American Psychologists, 53*(2), 242–259.

Loge, D. V., Staton, R. D., & Beatty, W. W. (1990). Performance of children with ADHD on tests sensitive to frontal lobe dysfunction. *Journal of the American Academy of Child and Adolescent Psychiatry, 29*(4), 540–545.

Lohr, J. M., Hamberger, L. K., & Bonge, D. (1988). The relationship of factorially validated measures of anger-proneness and irrational beliefs. *Motivation and Emotion, 12,* 171–183.

Long, D. E. (1990). *The anatomy of terrorism.* New York: Free Press.

Long, W., & Brecke, P. (2003). *War and reconciliation: Reason and emotion in conflict resolution.* Cambridge: MIT Press.

Lorenz, K. (1966). *On aggression.* New York: Harcourt, Brace & World.

Lynch, R. S., Deffenbacher, J., Oetting, E. R., & Yingling, D. A. (1995 August). *Driving as a health risk factor.* Paper present at the 103rd Annual Convention of the American Psychological Association, New York.

Lyon, D. O., & Ozolins, D. (1970). Pavlovian conditioning of shock-elicited aggression: A discrimination procedure. *Journal of the Experimental Analysis of Behavior, 13*(3), 325–331.

Mabel, S. (1994). Empirical determination of anger provoking characteristics. *Journal of Social and Clinical Psychology, 13*(2), 174–188.

MacDonald, J. (1975). *Armed robbery: Offenders and their victims.* Springfield, IL: Charles C. Thomas.MacDougall, J., Dembroski, T., & Krantz, D. (1981). Effects of types of challenge on pressor and heart rate responses in Type A and B women. *Psychophysiology, 18*(1), 1–9.

MacKinnon, N. J., & Keating, L. J. (1989). The structure of emotions: Canada–United States comparisons. *Social Psychology Quarterly, 52*(1), 70–83.

Maiuro, R. D., Cahn, T., & Vitaliano, P. (1986). Assertiveness deficits and hostility in domestically violent men. *Violence and Victims,1*(4), 279–289.

Maiuro, R. D., Cahn, T., Vitaliano, P., Wagner, B., & Zegree, J. B. (1988). Anger, hostility, and depression in domestically violent versus generally assaultive men and nonviolent control subjects. *Journal of Consulting and Clinical Psychology, 56*(1), 17–23.

Maiuro, R. D., O'Sullivan, M., Michael, M., & Vitaliano, P. (1989). Anger, hostility, and depression in assaultive versus suicide-attempting males. *Journal of Clinical Psychology, 45,* 531–541.

Malan, D. H. (1979). *Individual psychotherapy and the science of psychodynamics.* London: Butterworths.

Malta, L. S., Blanchard, E. B., & Freidenberg, B. M. (2005). Psychiatric and behavioral problems in aggressive drivers. *behavior Research and Therapy, 43*(11), 1467–1484.

Maltsberger, J. T. (1993). Dreams and suicide. *Suicide & Life-Threatening Behavior, 23*(1), 55–62.

Marchetti, S. (2006). *The cognitions related to anger expression.* Unpublished doctoral dissertation, St. John's University, New York.

Margolin, G., & Wampold, B. (1981). Sequential analysis of conflict and accord in distressed and nondistressed marital partners. *Journal of Consulting and Clinical Psychology, 49*(4), 554–567.

Marlatt, G. A., & Gordon, J. R. (Eds.). (1985). *Relapse prevention: Maintenance strategies in the treatment of addictive behaviors.* New York: Guilford Press.

Mash, E., & Barkley, R. (Eds.). (1996). *Child psychopathology* (2nd ed.). New York: Guilford Press.

Masters, J. C., Burish, T. G., Hollon, S., & Rimm, D. (1987). *Behavior therapy: Techniques and empirical finding* (3rd ed.). New York: Harcourt, Brace, Jovanovich.

Masterson, J. F., & Rinsley, D. B. (1975). The borderline syndrome: The role of the mother in the genesis and psychic structure of the borderline personality. *International Journal of Psycho-Analysis, 56*(2), 163–177.

Matthews, K. A., Gump, B. B., Harris, K. F., Haney, T. L., & Barefoot, J. C. (2004). Hostile behaviors predict cardiovascular mortality among men enrolled in Multiple Risk Factor Intervention Trial. *Circulation, 109*(1), 66–70.

Mattson, A. J., & Levin, H. S. (1990). Frontal lobe dysfunction following head injury. *Journal of Nervous and Mental Disease, 178*, 282–291.

McCann, J. T., & Biaggio, M. K. (1989). Narcissistic personality features and self-reported anger. *Psychological Reports, 64*, 55–58.

McCrae, R. R., & Costa, P. T. (1986). Clinical assessment can benefit from recent advances in personality psychology. *American Psychologist, 41*, 710–721.

McCrae, R. R., & Costa, P. T. (1987). Validation of a five-factor model of personality across instruments and observers. *Journal of Personality and Social Psychology, 52*, 81–90.

McCullough, M. E., Bellah, C. G., Kilpatrick, S. D., & Johnson, J. L. (2001). Vengefulness: Relationships with forgiveness, rumination, well-being, and the Big Five. *Personality and Social Psychology Bulletin, 27*(5), 601–610.

McCullough, M. E., & Hoty, W. T. (2002). Transgression-related motivational dispositions: Personality substrates of forgiveness and their links to the Big Five. *Personality and Social Psychology Bulletin. 28*(11), 1556–1573.

McCullough, M. E., Pargament, K. I., & Thoresen, C. E. (2000). *Forgiveness: Theory, research, and practice.* New York: Guilford.

McDermut, W., Zimmerman, M. & Cheiminski, I. (2003). The construct validity of depressive personality disorder. *Journal of Abnormal Psychology, 112*(1), 49–60.

McDowell, L., & Newell, C. (1987). *Measuring health: A guide to rating scales.* New York: Oxford University Press.

McElroy, S., Soutullo, C., Beckman, D., Taylor, R., & Keck, P. (1998). Intermittent explosive disorder: A report of 27 cases. *Journal of Clinical Psychiatry, 59*(4), 203–210.

McGough, J., & Curry, J. (1992). Utility of the SCL–90 with depressed and conduct disordered adolescent inpatients. *Journal of Personality Assessment, 59*(3), 552–563.

McMurran, M., Egan, V., Richardson, C., Street, H., Ahmadi, S., & Cooper, G. (2000). Referrals for anger and aggression in forensic psychology outpatient services. *Journal of Forensic Psychiatry, 11*, 206–213.

McPherson, J. (1988). *Battle cry of freedom: The Civil War era.* New York: Oxford University Press.

McPherson, J. (1996). *Drawn with the sword: Reflections on the American Civil War.* New York: Oxford University Press.

McVey, M. E. (2000). Exposure and response prevention versus rational self-statements in the treatment of angry men. *Dissertation Abstracts International, Section A. Humanities and Social Sciences, 61*(6-A), 2197.

Megargee, E. I. (1966). Undercontrolled and overcontrolled personality types in extreme antisocial aggression. *Psychological Monographs, 80*(611), 1–29.

Megargee, E. I. (1970). Undercontrolled and overcontrolled personality types in extreme antisocial aggression. In E. Megargee & J. Hokanson (Eds.), *The dynamics of aggression* (pp. 108–120). New York: Harper & Row.

Meissner, W. W. (1978). *The paranoid process.* New York: Jason Aronson.

Meltzer, H. (1933). Students' adjustments in anger. *Journal of Social Psychology, 4,* 285–309.

Merton, R. K. (1957). Social structure and anomie. In R. K. Merton (Ed.). *Social theory and social structure* (Rev. ed.). Glenco, IL: Free Press.

Mikulincer, M. (1998). Adult attachment style and individual differences in functional versus dysfunctional anger. *Journal of Personality and Social Psychology, 74*(2), 215–524.

Millar, D. G. (1983). Hostile emotion and obsessional neurosis. *Psychological Medicine, 13,* 813–819.

Miller, R. J., Zadolinnyi, K., & Hafner, R. J. (1993). Profiles and predictors of assaultiveness for different psychiatric ward patients. *Journal of Psychiatry, 150,* 1368–1373.

Miller, W., & Rollnick, S. (2002). *Motivational interviewing: Preparing people for change* (2nd ed.). New York: Guilford Press.

Millon, T. (1983). *Millon Clinical Multiaxial Inventory manual* (3rd ed.). Minneapolis: National Computer Systems.

Millon, T. (1987). On the genesis and prevalence of borderline personality disorder: A social learning thesis. *Journal of Personality Disorders, 1,* 354–372.

Millon, T. (1992). The borderline construct: Introductory notes on its history, theory, and empirical grounding. In J. F. Clarkin, E. Marziali, & H. Munroe-Blum (Eds.), *Borderline personality disorder: Clinical and empirical perspectives* (pp. 3–23). New York: Guilford.

Millon, T. (1993a). *The Millon adolescent clinical inventory.* Minneapolis, MN: National Computer Systems.

Millon, T. (1993b). Negativistic (passive-aggressive) personality disorder. *Journal of Personality Disorders, 7,* 78–85.

Millon, T. (1994). *Millon clinical multiaxial inventory–III.* Minneapolis, MN: National Computer Systems.

Millon, T., Davis, R., & Millon, C. (1997). *Millon clinical multiaxial inventory–III manual* (3rd ed.). Minneapolis, MN: National Computer Systems.

Mizel, L. (1997). *Aggressive Driving.* Washington, DC: The AAA Foundation for Traffic Safety.

Mohr, D. C., Sohham-Solomon, V., Engle, D., & Beutler, L. E. (1991). The expression of anger in psychotherapy for depression: Its role and measurement. *Psychotherapy Research, 1*(2), 124–134.

Mongrain, M., & Zuroff, D. C. (1989). Cognitive vulnerability to depressed affect in dependent and self-critical college women. *Journal of Personality Disorders, 3,* 240–251.

Mook, J., Van Der Ploeg, H., & Kleijn, W. C. (1990). Anxiety, anger and depression: Relationship at the trait level. *Anxiety Research, 3,* 17–31.

Moore, B. E., & Fine, B. D. (1990). *Psychoanalytic terms and concepts.* New Haven: American Psychoanalytic Association and Yale University Press.

Moore, T. W., & Paolillo, J. G. (1984). Depression: Influence of hopelessness, locus of control and length of treatment. *Psychological Reports, 54,* 875–881.

Moreno, J. K., Selby, M. J., Furhiman, A., & Laver, G. D. (1994). Hostility in depression. *Psychological Reports, 75,* 1391–1401.

Morphy, R. (1980). An inner view of obsessional neurosis. *Gestalt Journal, 3,* 120–136.

Moyer, K. (1976). *The biology of aggression.* London: Harper and Row.

Muraven, M., & Baumeister, R. F. (2000). Self -control and depletion of limited resource: Does self-control resemble a muscle? *Psychological Bulletin, 126*(2), 247–259.

Muraven, M., Baumeister, R. F., & Tice, D. M. (1999). Longitudinal improvement of self-regulation through: Building self-control strength through exercise. *Journal of Social Psychology, 139*(4), 446–457.

Muraven, M., Tice, D. M., & Baumeister, R. F. (1998). Self-control as a limited resource: Regulatory depletion patterns. *Journal of Personality and Social Psychology, 74*(3), 774–789.

Murphy, F. C., Nimmo-Smith, I., & Lawrence, A. D. (2003). Functional neuroanatomy of emotions: A meta-analysis. *Cognitive, Affective, and Behavioral Neuroscience, 3*(3), 207–233.

Myers, K., McCauley, E., Calderon, R., Mitchell, J., Burke, P., & Schloredt, K. (1991). Risks for suicidality in major depressive disorder. *Journal of the American Academy of Child and Adolescent Psychiatry, 30,* 86–94.

Myers, K., McCauley, E., Calderon, R., & Treder, R. (1991). The three-year longitudinal course of suicidality and predictive factors. *Journal of the American Academy of Child and Adolescent Psychiatry, 30,* 804–810.

Nason, J. D. (1985). The psychotherapy of rage. *Contemporary Psychoanalysis, 21,* 167–191.

Nathan, P., & Ward, T. (2002). Female sex offenders: Clinical and demographic features. *Journal of Sexual Aggression, 8* (1), 5–21.

National Center for Health Statistics. (1991). *Vital statistics of the United States: Vol. 2. Mortality.* Washington, DC: U.S. Government Printing Office.

Nauth, L. L. (1995). Power and control in the male antisocial personality. *Journal of Rational-Emotive & Cognitive-Behavior Therapy, 13,* 215–224.

Nesbitt, R., & Cohen, D. (1996). *Culture of honor: The Psychology of violence in the South.* Boulder, CO: Westview Press.

Noel, P. S. (1980). *Effective anger versus cathartic anger in the treatment of depression.* Ann Arbor, MI: University Microfilms.

Norcross, J., & Kobayashi, M. (1999). Treating anger in psychotherapy: Introduction and cases. *Journal of Clinical Psychology, 55*(3), 275–282.

Norlander, B., & Eckhardt, C. (2005). Anger, hostility, and male perpetrators of intimate partner violence: A meta- analytic review. *Clinical Psychology Review, 25,* 119–152.

Novaco, R. W. (1975). *Anger control.* Lexington, MA: Lexington.

Novaco, R. W. (1976). The function and regulation of the arousal of anger. *American Journal of Psychiatry, 133,* 1124–1128.

Novaco, R. W. (1985). Anger and its therapeutic regulation. In M. A. Chesney & R. H. Roseman (Eds.), *Anger and hostility in cardiovascular and behavior disorders* (pp. 203–226). Washington, DC: Hemisphere.

Novaco, R. W. (1993). Clinicians ought to view anger contextually. *Behavior Change, 10*(4), 208–218.

Novaco, R. W. (1994). Anger as a risk factor for violence among the mentally disturbed. In J. Monahan & H. J. Steadman (Eds.), *Violence and mental disorders* (pp. 21–59). Chicago: University of Chicago Press.

Novaco, R. W. (1997). Remediating anger and aggression with violent offenders. *Legal and Criminological Psychology, 2*, 77–88.

Novaco, R. W. (2003). *Novaco Anger Scale and Provocation Inventory.* Los Angles, CA: Western Psychological Services.

Oats, R., & Forrest, D. (1985). Self-esteem and early background of abusive mothers. *Child Abuse and Neglect, 9*, 89–93.

Oehman, A., & Dimberg, U. (1978). Facial expressions as conditioned stimuli for electrodermal responses: A case of "preparedness"? *Journal of Personality and Social Psychology, 36*(11), 1251–1258.

O'Leary, K. D. (1995, November 10). *Personal communication.* Lecture on Domestic Violence, St. John's University, [CITY].

O'Leary, K. D., Barling, J., Arias, I., Rosenbaum, A., Malone, T., & Tyre, A. (1989). Prevalence and stability of physical aggression between spouses: A longitudinal analysis. *Journal of Consulting and Clinical Psychology, 57*(2), 263–268.

O'Leary, K. D., Curely, A., Rosenbaum, A., & Clarke, C. (1985). Assertion training for abused wives: A potentially hazardous treatment. *Journal of Marital & Family Therapy, 11*(2), 319–322.

Olweus, D. (1994). *Bullying at school: Long-term outcomes for the victims and an effective school-based intervention program.* In R. Huesman (Ed.), *Aggressive behavior: Current perspectives* (pp. 97–130). New York: Plenum.

Orsillo, S. M., & Batten, S. V. (2005). Acceptance and commitment therapy in the treatment of posttraumatic stress disorder. *Behavior Modification, 29*(1), 95–129.

Ortony, A., Clore, G., & Foss, M. (1987). The referential structure of the affective lexicon. *Cognitive Science, 11*, 341–364.

Palfai, T. P., & Hart, K. E. (1997). Anger coping styles and perceived social support. *Journal of Social Psychology, 137*, 405–411.

Panksepp, J. (1998). *Affective neuroscience: The foundation of human and animal emotions.* New York: Oxford University Press.

Papps, B. E., & O'Carroll, R. E. (1998). Extremes of self-esteem and narcissism and the experience and expression of anger and expression. *Aggressive Behavior, 24*, 421–438.

Peele, S. (1989). *Diseasing of America: Addiction treatment out of control.* Lexington, MA: Lexington Books.

Perls, F. S. (1969). *Gestalt therapy verbatim.* New York: Bantam.

Petersen, J. R., (1999). *The century of sex.* New York: Grove Press.

Pettigrew, T. F. (2003). Peoples under threat: Americans, Arabs, and Israelis. *Peace and Conflict: Journal of Peace Psychology, 9*(1), 69–90.

Pfeffer, C. R. (1986). Risk factors associated with youth suicide. *Psychiatric Annals, 18*, 652–656.

Pfeffer, C. R., Pluchik, R., & Mirzruchi, M. S. (1983). Suicidal and assaultive behavior in children: Classification, measurement, and intercorrelations. *American Journal of Psychiatry, 140*(2), 154–157.

Pfeffer, C. R., Zuckerman, S., Pluchick, R., & Mirzruchi, M. S. (1984). Suicidal behavior in normal schoolchildren: A comparison with child psychiatric inpatients. *Journal of the American Academy of Child Psychiatry, 23*, 416–423.

Pilowsky, I., & Spence, N. D. (1975). Hostility and depressive illness. *Archives of General Psychiatry, 32,* 1154–1159.

Pincus, J. H. (2001). *Base instincts: What makes killers kill.* New York: Norton.

Pinker, S. (1997). *How the mind works.* New York: Basic Books.

Pinker, S. (2002). *The blank slate:* New York: Basic Books.

Plutarch. (2004). *Moralia, VI. On the control of anger.* (E. N. O'Neil, Ed., & W. C. Helmbold, Trans.). Cambridge, MA: Harvard University Press.

Plutchik, R. (2003). *Emotions and life: Perspectives from psychology, biology, and evolution.* Washington, DC: American Psychological Association.

Polivy, J. (1981). On the induction of emotion in the laboratory: Discrete moods or multiple affect states? *Journal of Personality and Social Psychology, 41,* 803–817.

Portegal, M. (1979). The reinforcing value of several types of aggressive behavior: A Review. *Aggressive Behavior, 5,* 353–373.

Potter-Effron, P. S., & Potter-Effron, R. T. (1991). Anger as a treatment concern with alcoholics and affected family members. *Alcoholism Treatment Quarterly, 8,* 31–47.

Power, M. J., & Dalgleish, T. (1997). *Cognition and emotion: From order to disorder.* Hove: Psychology Press.

Powers, H. P. (1972). Psychotherapy for hysterical individuals. *Social Casework, 53,* 435–440.

Prins, H. (1995). Classification of fire-setters. *British Journal of Psychiatry, 166*(6), 821.

Prochaska, J., & DiClemente, C. (1988). *The transtheoretical approach to therapy.* Chicago: Dorsey Press.

Prochaska, J., DiClemente, C., & Norcross, J. (1992). In search of how people change: Application to addictive behaviors. *American Psychologist, 47*(9), 1102–1115.

Project MATCH Research Group (1997). Project MATCH secondary a priori hypotheses. *Addiction, 92,* 1671–1698.

Proulx, J., McKibben, A., & Lusignan, R. (1996). Relationships between affective components and sexual behaviors in sexual aggressors. *Sexual Abuse: Journal of Research and Treatment, 8*(4), 279–289.

Raine, A. (1993). *The psychopathology of crime: Criminal behavior as a clinical disorder.* San Diego: Academic Press.

Raskin, R., & Hall, C. S. (1981). The narcissistic personality inventory: Alternate form reliability and further evidence of construct validity. *Journal of Personality Assessment, 45*(2), 159–162.

Rathbone, D. B., & Hickabee, J. C. (1999). *Controlling road rage: A literature review and pilot study.* Washington, DC: AAA Foundation for Traffic Safety.

Reich, J. (1992). Measurement of DSM–III and DSM–III–R borderline personality disorder. In J. F. Clarkin, E. Marziali, & H. Munroe-Blum (Eds.), *Borderline personality disorder: Clinical and empirical perspectives* (pp.116–148). New York: Guilford.

Reilly, P. M., & Shropshire, M. S. (2000). Anger management group treatment for cocaine dependence: Preliminary outcomes. *American journal of Drug and Alcohol Abuse, 26*(2), 161–177.

Reiss, A. J., & Roth, J. A. (Eds.). (1993). *Understanding and preventing violence.* Washington, DC: National Academy Press.

Renouf, A. G., & Harter, S. (1990). Low self-worth and anger as components of depressive experiences in young adolescents. *Development and Psychopathology, 2,* 293–310.

Renzetti, C. (1992). *Violent betrayal: Partner abuse in lesbian relationships.* Newbury Park, CA: Sage.

Rhodewalt, F., & Morf, C. C. (1995). Self and interpersonal correlates of the Narcissistic Personality Inventory: A review and new findings. *Journal of Research in Personality, 29,* 1–23.

Rickles, N. (1971). The angry-woman syndrome. *Archives of General Psychiatry, 24,* 91–94.

Robins, S., & Novaco, R. (1999). A systems conceptualization and treatment of anger. *Journal of Clinical Psychology, 55,* 325–337.

Rose, A. J., & Asher, S. R. (1999). Children's goals and strategies in response to conflicts within a friendship. *Developmental Psychology, 35*(1), 69–79.

Roseman, I. J. (1984). Cognitive determinants of emotions: A structural theory. In R. Shaver (Ed.), *Review of personality and social psychology* (Vol. 5, pp.11–36). Beverly Hills, CA: Sage.

Roth, A., & Fongay, P. (2005). *What works for whom: A critical review of psychotherapy research* (2nd ed.). New York: Guilford Press.

Rothenberg, A. (1971). On anger. *American Journal of Psychiatry, 128,* 86–92.

Rubenstein, C. S., Altemus, M., Pigott, T. A., & Hess, A. (1995). Symptom overlap between OCD and bulimia nervosa. *Journal of Anxiety Disorders, 9,* 1–9.

Rubin, J. (1986). The emotion of anger: Some conceptual and theoretical issues. *Professional Psychology Research and Practice, 12*(2), 115–124.

Russell, J. A. (1983). Pancultural aspects of the human conceptual organization of emotions. *Journal of Personality and Social Psychology, 45,* 1281–1288.

Russell, J. A., & Fehr, B. (1994). Fuzzy concepts in a hierarchy: Varieties of anger. *Journal of Personality and Social Psychology, 67,* 186–205.

Russell, J. A., & Mehrabian, A. (1974). Distinguishing anger and anxiety in terms of emotional response factors. *Journal of Consulting and Clinical Psychology, 42,* 79–83.

Sabini, J., & Silver, M. (1982). *Mortalities of everyday life.* Oxford, England: Oxford University Press.

Salzinger, K. (1995). A behavior-analytic view of anger and aggression. In H. Kassinove (Ed.), *Anger disorders: Definition, diagnosis, and treatment* (pp. 69–79). Philadelphia, PA: Taylor & Francis.

Sampson, R. J., & Laub, J. H. (1993). *Crime in the making: Pathways and turning points through life.* Cambridge, MA: Harvard University Press.

Sanderlin, T. K. (2001). Anger-management counseling with the antisocial personality. *Annals of the American Psychotherapy Association, 4,* 9–11.

Scarry, E. (1985). *The body in pain: Making and unmaking of the world.* New York: Oxford University Press.

Scherer, K. R. (1984). Emotions as a multi-component process: A model with some cross-cultural data. In R. Shaver (Ed.), *Review of personality and social psychology* (Vol. 5, pp.11–36). Beverly Hills, CA: Sage.

Scherer, K. R. (Ed.) (1988). *Facets of emotions.* Hillsdale, NJ: Erlbaum.

Scherer, K. R. (1993). Neuroscience projections to current debates in emotion psychology. *Cognition and Emotion, 7(1),* 1–41.

Scherer, K. R., & Wallbott, H. G. (1994). Evidence for the universality and cultural variation of differential emotional response patterns. *Journal of Personality and Social Psychology. 67*(1), 55–65.

Scherer, K. R., Wallbott, H. G., & Summerfield, A. (Eds.). (1986). *Experiencing emotion: A cross-cultural study.* Cambridge, UK: Cambridge University Press.

Schimmel, S. (1979) Anger and its control in Graeco-Roman and modern psychology. *Psychiatry: Journal for the Study of Interpersonal Processes, 42*(4), 320–337.

Schless, A. P., Mendels, J., Kipperman, A., & Cochrane, C. (1974). Depression and hostility. *Journal of Nervous and Mental Diseases, 159,* 91–100.

Schoenfeld, C. (1988). Blacks and violent crime: A psychoanalytic-oriented analysis. *Journal of Psychiatry and the Law, 16,* 269–301.

Schulz, P. M., Schulz, S. C., Hamer, R., Resnick, R. J., & Friedel, R. O. (1985). The impact of borderline and schizo-personality disorders on patients and their families. *Community Psychiatry, 36,* 879–881.

Scully, D. (1990). Four theories of rape in American society: A state-level analysis. *Contemporary Sociology, 1990, 19*(5), 664–666.

Scully, D., & Marolla, J. (1985). "Riding the bull at Gilley's": Convicted rapists describe the rewards of rape. *Social Problems, 32*(3), 251–263.

Seligman, M. (1975). *Helplessness: On depression, development and death.* San Francisco, CA: W. H. Freeman.

Seward, J. P. (1945). Aggressive behavior in the rat, I. General characteristics: age and sex differences. *Journal of Comparative Psychology, 38,* 175–197.

Shader, R. I. (2003). Assessment and treatment of suicide risk. In Richard I. Shader. (Ed), *Manual of psychiatric therapeutics* (3rd ed., pp. 229–239). Philadelphia, PA: Lippincott Williams & Wilkins.

Shapiro, D. (1999). *Neurotic styles.* New York: Basic Books.

Sharkin, B. (1988). The measurement and treatment of client anger in counseling. *Journal of Counseling and Development, 66*(8), 361–365.

Shaver, P., Schwartz, J., Kirson, D., & O'Connor, C. (1987). Emotion knowledge: Further exploration of a prototype approach. *Journal of Personality & Social Psychology, 52*(6), 1061–1086.

Shearin, E. N., & Linehan, M. M. (1994). Dialectical behavior therapy for borderline personality disorder: Theoretical and empirical foundations. *Acta Psychiatrica Scandinavica, 89*(suppl. 379), 61–68.

Siegel, J. M. (1986). The multidimensional anger inventory. *Journal of Personality and Social Psychology, 51,* 191–200.

Sigler, R. (1989). *Domestic violence in context: An assessment of community attitudes.* Lindham, MD: Lexington Books.

Sinha, R., Lovallo, W., & Parsons O. (1992). Cardiovascular differentiation of emotions. *Psychosomatic Medicine, 54*(4), 422–435.

Slavik, S., Carlson, J., & Sperry, L. (1998). The passive-aggressive couple. In J. Carlson & L. Sperry (Eds.), *The disordered couple.* Bristol: Brunner/Mazel.

Smalley, R. L., & Stake, J. E. (1996). Evaluating sources of ego-threatening feedback: Self-esteem and narcissism effects. *Journal of Research in Personality, 30,* 483–495.

Smart, R. G., & Mann, R. E. (2002). Deaths and injuries from road rage: Cases in Canadian newspapers. *Canadian Medical Association Journal, 167*(7), 761–762.

Smith, C. A., & Ellsworth, P. C. (1987). Patterns of appraisal and emotions related to taking an exam. *Journal of Personality and Social Psychology, 52*(3), 475–488.

Smith, C. A., & Kirby, L. D. (2004). Appraisal as a pervasive determinant of anger. *Emotion, 4*(2), 133–138.

Smith, T. (1989). Assessment in rational-emotive therapy: Empirical access to the ABCD model. In M. E. Bernard & R. A. DiGiuseppe (Eds.), *Inside rational emotive therapy: A critical appraisal of the theory and therapy of Albert Ellis* (pp. 135–153). New York: Academic Press.

Snaith, R. P., Constantopoulos, A. A., Jardine, M. Y., & McGuffin, P. (1978). A clinical scale for the self-assessment of irritability. *British Journal of Psychiatry, 132,* 164–171.

Snaith, R. P., & Taylor, C. M. (1985). Irritability: Definition, assessment, and associated factors. *British Journal of Psychiatry, 147,* 127–136.

Snell, W. E., Gum, S., Shuck, R. L., Mosley, J., & Hite, J. (1995). The Clinical Anger Scale: Preliminary reliability and validity. *Journal of Clinical Psychology, 51*(2), 215–226.

Snyder, C. R., Crowson, J., Houston, B. K., Kurylo, M., & Poirier, J. (1997). Assessing hostile automatic thoughts: Development and validation of the HAT Scale. *Cognitive Therapy & Research, 21*(4), 477–492.

Sommers, J. A., Schell, T. L., & Vodanovich, S. J. (2002). Developing a measure of individual differences in organizational revenge. *Journal of Business & Psychology, 17*(2), pp. 207–222.

Sperry, L. (1995). *Handbook of diagnosis and treatment of the DSM–IV personality disorders.* New York: Brunner/Mazel.

Spielberger, C. D. (1972a). Anxiety as an emotional state. In C. D. Spielberger (Ed.), *Anxiety: Current trends in theory and research* (Vol. 1, pp. 24–49). New York: Academic Press.

Spielberger, C. D. (1972b). *Preliminary manual for the State–Trait Personality Inventory.* Tampa, FL: University of South Florida.

Spielberger, C. D. (1988). *Manual for the State–Trait Anger Expression Inventory.* Odessa, FL: Psychological Assessment Resources.

Spielberger, C. D. (1991). *State–Trait Anger Expression Inventory, professional manual.* Odessa: Psychological Assessment Resources.

Spielberger, C. D. (1992). *Anger/hostility, heart disease and cancer.* Invited address presented at the 100th annual convention of the American Psychological Association, Washington, DC.

Spielberger, C. D. (1995). *State–Trait Depression Scale.* Palo Alto, CA: Mind Garden Press.

Spielberger, C. D. (1999). *Manual for the State–Trait Anger Expression Inventory–2.* Odessa, FL: Psychological Assessment Resources.

Spielberger, C. D., Jacobs, G. A., Russell, S., & Crane, R. S. (1983). Assessment of anger: The state–trait anger scale. In J. N. Butcher & C. D. Spielberger (Eds.), *Advances in personality assessment* (pp. 112–134). Hillside, NJ: Erlbaum.

Spielberger, C. D., Johnson, E. H., Russell, S., Crane, R. S., Jacobs, G. A., & Worden, T. J. (1985). The experience and expression of anger: Construction and validation of an anger-expression scale. In M. A. Chesney & R. H. Rosenman (Eds.), *Anger and hostility in cardiovascular and behavioral disorders* (pp. 5–30). Washington, DC: Hemisphere.

Spirito, A., Overholser, J., & Stark, L. (1989). Common problems and coping strategies: Findings with adolescent suicidal attempters. *Journal of Abnormal Child Psychology, 17,* 213–221.

Spitzer, R. L., & Endicott, J. (1979). *Schedule of Affective Disorders and Schizophrenia* (SADS) (3rd ed.). New York: New York State Psychiatric Institute.

Spitzer, R. L., Endicott, J., & Gibbon, M. (1979). Crossing the border into borderline personality and borderline schizophrenia. *Archives of General Psychiatry, 36,* 17–24.

Spivack, G., Platt, J., & Shure, M. (1976). The social problem-solving approach to adjustment. San Francisco: Jossey-Bass.

Steptoe, A., Cropley, M., Griffith, J., & Kirschbaum, C. (2000). Job strain and anger expression predict early-morning elevations in salivary cortisol. *Psychosomatic Medicine, 62*(2), 286–292.

Sterling, S., & Edelmann, R. J. (1988). Reactions to anger and anxiety-provoking events: Psychopathic and nonpsychopathic groups compared. *Journal of Clinical Psychology, 44,* 96–100.

Sternberg, R. J. (2005). Understanding and combating hate. In R. Sternberg (Ed.), *The psychology of hate* (pp.37–49). Washington, DC: American Psychological Association.

Stevens, A., & Price, J. (1996). *Evolutionary psychiatry: A new beginning.* New York: Routledge.

Stolorow, R. D. (1984). Aggression in the psychoanalytic situation: An intersubjective viewpoint. *Contemporary Psychoanalysis, 20,* 643–651.

Stone, H. (1990). Personal reflections: Borderline personality disorder—contemporary issues in nosology, etiology, and treatment. *Psychiatric Annals, 20,* 8–10.

Stover, C. S. (2005). Domestic violence research: What have we learned and where do we go from here? *Journal of Interpersonal Vilence, 20*(4), 448–454.

Strachan, C. E., & Dutton, D. G. (1992). The role of power and gender in anger responses to sexual jealousy. *Journal of Applied Social Psychology, 22,* 1721–1740.

Straus, M., & Gelles, R. (1986). Societal change and change in family violence from 1975 to 1985 as revealed by two national surveys. *Journal of Marriage and the Family, 48*(3), 465–479.

Stuckless, N. (1998). The influence of anger, perceived injustice, revenge, and time on the quality of life of survivor–victims. *Dissertation Abstracts International, Section B. The Sciences and Engineering, 58*(7-B), 3971.

Stuckless, N., & Goranson, R. (1992). The vengeance scale: Development of a measure of attitudes toward revenge. *Journal of Social Behavior and Personality, 7,* 25–42.

Suarez, E. C., & Williams, R. B. (1989). Situational determinants of cardiovascular and emotional reactivity in high- and low-hostile men. *Psychosomatic Medicine, 51,* 404–479.

Suinn, R. M. (1990). *Anxiety management training: A behavior therapy.* New York: Plenum Press.

Sukhodolsky, D. G., Kassinove, H., & Gorman, B. S. (2004). Cognitive-behavioral therapy for anger in children and adolescents: A meta-analysis. *Aggression and Violent Behavior, 9,* 247–269.

Sullivan, H. S. (1953). *The interpersonal theory of psychiatry.* New York: W. W. Norton.

Suls, J., & Bunde, J. (2005). Anger, anxiety, and depression as risk factors for cardiovascular disease: The problem and implications of overlapping affective dispositions. *Psychological Bulletin, 131*(2), 260–300.

Swaim, R. C., & Deffenbacher, J. L. (1998). Cross-cultural aggressive anger expression and adolescent alcohol use. Poster presented at the annual convention of the American Psychological Association, San Francisco.

Swaim, R. C., Oetting, E. R., Edwards, R. W., & Beauvais, F. (1989). Links from emotional distress to adolescent drug use: A path model. *Journal of Consulting and Clinical Psychology, 57,* 227–231.

Swanson, D. W., Bohnert, P. J., & Smith, J. A. (1970). *The paranoid.* Boston: Little, Brown and Company.

Tafrate, R. C. (1995). Evaluation of treatment strategies for adult anger disorders. In H. Kassinove (Ed.), *Anger disorders: Definitions, diagnosis and treatment.* Washington, DC: Taylor and Francis.

Tafrate, R. C., & Kassinove, H. (1998). Anger control in men: Barb exposure with rational, irrational, and irrelevant self-statements. *Journal of Cognitive Psychotherapy, 12*(3), 187–211.

Tafrate, R. C., & Kassinove, K. (2002, August). Defining disruptive anger: The anger episode model. In R. DiGiuseppe (Chair), *Characteristics and types of disturbed anger: Implications for treatment.* Symposium conducted at the 110th annual convention of the American Psychological Association, Chicago.

Tangney, J. P., Hill-Barlow, D., Wagner, P. E., Marschall, D. E., Borenstein, J. K., Sanftner, J., et al. (1996). Assessing the individual differences in constructive versus destructive responses to anger across the life span. *Journal of Personality and Social Psychology, 70,* 780–796.

Task Force on the Promotion and Dissemination of Psychological Procedures. (1995). Training in the dissemination of empirically validated psychological treatments: Report and recommendations. *The Clinical Psychologist, 48,* 3–24.

Tavris, C. (1989). *Anger the misunderstood emotion* (2nd ed.). New York: Touchstone.

Tavris, C. (1992). *The mismeasure of woman.* New York: Simon & Schuster.

Tedeschi, J. T., & Nesler, M. S. (1993). Grievance, development and reaction. In R. B. Felson & J. T. Tedeschi (Eds.), *Aggression and violence: Social interactionist perspective.* Washington, DC: American Psychological Association.

Tedlow, J., Leslie, V., Keefe, B. R., Alpert, J., Nierenberg, A. A., Rosenbaum, J. F., et al. (1999). Axis I and Axis II disorder comorbidity in unipolar depression with anger attacks. *Journal of Affective Disorders, 52,* 217–223.

Terracciano, S. (2000). Effects of barb exposure and rational-statement rehearsal on anger and articulated thoughts in angry married men: Extinction or cognitive restructuring? *Dissertation Abstracts International, Section B. The Sciences and Engineering, 61*(6-B), 3294.

Thoits, P. A. (1985). Self-labeling process in mental illness: The role of emotional dissonance. *Journal of Sociology, 91* (2), 221–249.

Thoits, P. A. (1989). The sociology of emotions. *Annual Review of Sociology, 15,* 317–342.

Thompson, C. (1959). An introduction to minor maladjustments. In S. Arieti (Ed.), *American handbook of psychiatry.* New York: Basic Books.

Thoresen, C. E. (2000). Forgiveness and health: An unanswered question. In M. F. McCullough, K. I. Pargament, & C. E. Thoresen (Eds.), *Forgiveness: Theory, research, and practice* (pp. 254–280). New York: Guilford Press.

Thorpe, G., & Olsen, S. (1990). *Behavior therapy: Concepts, procedures, and applications.* Boston: Allyn and Bacon.

Tirrell, F. J., & Aldridge, R. G. (1983). Diagnostic classification of rape. *Corrective and Social Psychiatry and Journal of Behavior Technology, Methods and Therapy, 29*(2), 56–61.

Tivis, L., Parsons, O., & Nixon, S. (1998). Anger in an inpatient treatment sample of chronic alcoholics. *Alcoholism: Clinical and Experimental Research, 22*(4), 902–907.

Toch, H. (1969/1993). Good violence and bad violence: Self-presentations of aggressors through accounts and war stories. In Richard B. Felson and James Tedeschi (Eds.), *Aggression and violence: Social interactionist perspectives* (pp. 193–206). Washington, DC: American Psychological Association.

Tomkins, S. (1962). *Affect, imagery and consciousness: Volume 1. The positive affects.* England: Springer.

Tomkins, S. (1979). Script theory: Differential magnification of affect. In H. E. Howe & R. A. Dienstbier (Eds.), *Nebraska symposium of motivation 1978* (pp. 201–236). Lincoln: University of Nebraska Press.

Torestad, B. (1990). What is anger provoking? A psychological study of perceived causes of anger. *Aggressive Behavior, 16*(1), 9–26.

Tremblay, R. E. (2003). Why socialization fails: The case of chronic physical aggression. In B. B. Leahy, T. E. Moffitt, & A. Caspi (Eds.), *Causes of Conduct Disorders and Juvenile Delinquency* (pp. 182–223). New York: Guilford Press.

Trull, T. J., & McCrae, R. R. (1994). A five-factor perspective on the personality disorder research. In P. T. Costa & T. A. Widiger (Eds.), *Personality disorders and the five-factor model of personality* (pp. 59–72). Washington, DC: American Psychological Association.

Tryon, W. (2003, November). *Possible mechanism for why desensitizations and exposure-therapy work.* Poster presented at the annual convention of the Association for the Advancement of Behavior Therapy, Boston.

Tschannen, T. A., Duckro, P. N., Margolis, R. B., & Tomazic, T. J. (1992). The relationship of anger, depression and perceived disability among headache patients. *Headache, 32*(10), 501–503.

Turkat, I. D., Keane, S. P., & Thompson-Pope, S. K. (1990). Social-processing errors among paranoid personalities. *Journal of Psychopathology and Behavioral Assessment, 12,* 263–269.

Tweed, R. G., & Dutton, D. G. (1998). A comparison of impulsive and instrumental subgroups of batterers. *Violence and Victims, 13,* 217–230.

Ulrich, R., & Wolfe, M. (1969). Research and theory on aggression and violence. *Science Teacher. 1969, 36*(5), 24–28.

Vaughan, A. (1996, November). *Theories of anger.* Paper presented at the 30th annual convention of the Association for Advancement of Behavior Therapy, New York.

Vernon, W., & Ulrich, R. (1966). Classical conditioning of pain-elicited aggression. *Science, 152*(3722), 668–669.

Wade, W. C. (1987). *The fiery cross: The Ku Klux Klan in America.* New York: Touchstone/ Simon & Schuster.

Wadsworth, A. P., & Barker, H. R. (1976). A comparison of two treatments for depression: The antidepressive program versus traditional therapy. *Journal of Clinical Psychology, 32,* 445–449.

Wagar, J. M., & Rodway, M. R. (1995). An evaluation of a group-treatment approach for children who have witnessed wife abuse. *Journal of Family Violence, 10,* 295–306.

Wakefield, J. C. (1992a). The concept of mental disorder: On the boundary between biological facts and social values. *American Psychologist, 47*(3), 373–388.

Wakefield, J. C. (1992b). Disorder as harmful dysfunction: A conceptual critique of DSM–III–R's definition of mental disorder. *Psychological Review, 99*, 232–247.

Walen, S., DiGiuseppe, R., & Dryden, W. (1992). *The practitioner's guide to rational emotive therapy* (2nd ed.). New York: Oxford University Press.

Walfish, S., Massey, R., & Krone, A. (1990). Anxiety and anger among abusers of different substances. *Drug & Alcohol Dependence, 25*(3), 253–256.

Wallace, A., & Carson, M. (1973). Sharing and diversity in emotion terminology. *Ethos, 1*(1), 1–29.

Walley, J. C. (2002). Imaginal exposure and response prevention for anger and aggressive behavior. *Dissertation Abstracts International, Section B. The Sciences and Engineering, 63*(4-B), 2080.

Waltz, J. (1994). Borderline disorder. In M. Hersen, R. T. Ammerman, & L. A. Sisson (Eds.), *Handbook of aggressive and destructive behavior in psychiatric patients* (pp. 305–322). New York: Plenum Press.

Watson, D., & Clark, L. A. (1984). Negative affectivity: The disposition to experience aversive emotional states. *Psychological Bulletin, 96*, 465–490.

Watson, D., & Clark, L. A. (1992). On traits and temperament: General experiences and their relation to the five-factor model. *Journal of Personality, 60*(2), 441–476.

Watson, D., & Clark, L. A., & Tellegen, A. (1988). Development and validation of brief measures of positive and negative affects: The PANAS scales. *Journal of Personality and Social Psychology, 54*(6), 1063–1070.

Weissman, M., Fox, K., & Klerman, G. L. (1973). Hostility and depression associated with suicide attempts. *American Journal of Psychiatry, 130*, 450–455.

Weissman, M., Klerman, G. L., & Paykel, E. (1971). Clinical evaluation of hostility in depression. *American Journal of Psychiatry, 128*, 41–46.

Wellen, D. G. (1998). A meta-analysis of single-subject studies of therapies for children and adolescents with aggression. *Dissertation Abstracts International, Section B. The Sciences and Engineering, 59*(1-B), 0431.

White, R. K. (1990). Why aggressors lose. *Political Psychology, 11*(2), 227–242.

White, R. W. (1959). Motivation reconsidered: The concept of competence. *Psychological Review, 66*, 297–333.

Widiger, T. A., Miele, G. M., & Tilly, S. M. (1992). Alternative perspectives on the diagnosis of borderline personality disorder. In J. F. Clarkin, E. Marziali, & H. Munroe-Blum (Eds.), *Borderline personality disorder: Clinical and empirical perspectives* (pp. 89–115). New York: Guilford Press.

Wierzbicka, A. (1992a). Emotions, language and cultural scripts. In S. Kitatama & H. R. Markus (Eds.), *Emotion and culture* (pp.133–196). Washington, DC: American Psychological Association.

Wierzbicka, A. (1992b). *Semantics, culture, and cognition.* New York: Oxford University Press.

Williams, J. E., Paton, C. C., Siegler, I. C., Eigenbrodt, M. L., Nieto, F. J., & Tyroler, H. A. (2000). Anger proneness predicts coronary heart disease risk: Prospective analysis from the atherosclerosis risk in communities (ARIC) study. *Circulation, 101*, 2034–2039.

Wilson, J. Q., & Hernstein, R. J. (1986). *Crime and human nature.* New York: Simon & Schuster.

Wilson, K. G., & Byrd, M. R. (2005). ACT for Substance Abuse and Dependence. In S. C. Hayes, & K. D. Strosahl (Eds.), *A practical guide to acceptance and commitment therapy* (pp.153–184). New York: Springer Science.

Wilson, R. S., Bienias, J. L., Mendes de Leon, C. F., Evans, D. A., & Bennett, D. A. (2003). Negative affect and mortality in older persons. *American Journal of Epidemiology, 158*(9), 827–835.

Windholz, G. (1987). Pavlov's conceptualization of unconditional reflexes, or instincts, within the framework of the theory of higher nervous activity. *Pavlovian Journal of Biological Science, 22*(4), 123–131.

Wing, J. K., Cooper, J. E., & Sartorius, N. (1974). *The measurement and classification of psychiatric symptoms.* Cambridge: Cambridge University Press.

Withers, L., & Kaplan, D. (1987). Adolescents who attempt suicide: A retrospective clinical chart review of hospitalized patients. *Professional Psychology: Research and Practice, 18*(4), 391–393.

Witte, T., Callahan, K. L., & Perez-Lopez, M. (2002). Narcissism and anger: An exploration of underlying correlations. *Psychological Reports 90*(3), 871–875.

Wolpe, J. (1958). *Psychotherapy by reciprocal inhibition.* Stanford, CA: Stanford University Press.

World Health Organization. (2003). *World health report.* Geneva: World Health Organization.

Wurmser, L. (1984). The role of superego conflicts in substance abuse and its treatment. *International Journal of Psychoanalysis, 10,* 227–258.

Yalom, I. (1985). *The theory and practice of group psychotherapy* (3rd ed.). New York: Basic Books.

Yarvis, R. M. (1990). Axis I and axis II diagnostic parameters of homicide. *Bulletin of the American Academy of Psychiatry and Law, 18,* 249–269.

Yates, E., Barbaree, H. E., & Marshall, W. L. (1984). Anger and deviant sexual arousal. *Behavior Therapy, 15*(3), 287–294.

Yerkes, R. M., & Dodson, J. D. (1908). The relation of strength of stimulus to rapidity of habit formation. *Journal of Comparative Neurology of Psychology, 18,* 459–482.

Yesavage, J. A. (1983). Direct and indirect hostility and self-destructive behavior by hospitalized depressives. *Acta Psychiatrica Scandanavia, 68,* 345–350.

Zafiropoulou, M., & Pappa, E. (2002). The role of preparedness and social environment in developing social phobia. *The Journal of the Hellenic Psychological Society, 9*(3), 365–377.

Zanarini, M. C., Gunderson, J. G., Frankenburg, F. R., & Chauncey, D. L. (1989). The Revised Diagnostic Interview for Borderlines: Discriminating BPD from other Axis II disorders. *Journal of Personality Disorders, 3,* 10–18.

Zilboorg, G. (1996). Differential diagnostic types of suicide In J. T. Maltsberger & M. J. Goldblatt (Eds.), *Essential papers on suicide* (pp. 36–61). New York: New York University Press.

Zillman, D. (2003). Theory of affective dynamics: Emotions and moods, communication and emotion. In J. Bryant, D. Roskos-Ewoldsen, & J. Cantor (Eds.), *Essays in honor of Dolf Zillmann* (pp. 533–567). Mahwah, NJ: Lawrence Erlbaum.

Zimmerman, M. (2005). *The MIDAS Project at Rhode Island Hospital.* http://www.lifespan.org/services/mentalhealth/rih/MIDAS.

Index

Lightning Source UK Ltd.
Milton Keynes UK
28 February 2011

168251UK00007BB/3/P